For Michael Gibson,

warmest regards,

Christian Mo[r...]

NC,

Feb. '12

Theory in the "Post" Era

Theory in the "Post" Era

A Vocabulary for the 21st-Century Conceptual Commons

Edited by Alexandru Matei,
Christian Moraru, and
Andrei Terian

BLOOMSBURY ACADEMIC

NEW YORK · LONDON · OXFORD · NEW DELHI · SYDNEY

BLOOMSBURY ACADEMIC
Bloomsbury Publishing Inc
1385 Broadway, New York, NY 10018, USA
50 Bedford Square, London, WC1B 3DP, UK
29 Earlsfort Terrace, Dublin 2, Ireland

BLOOMSBURY, BLOOMSBURY ACADEMIC and the Diana logo
are trademarks of Bloomsbury Publishing Plc

First published in the United States of America 2022

Cover design by Eleanor Rose
Cover image: The cover painting, Joyeux Anniversaire to
Spring, is by Rebecca Darlington, a visual artist from New York, NY.
The artwork is 12x12″ with mixed media on panel. Her work can be found
online at www.rebeccadarlington.com and on Instagram at @darlingtonart
© Rebecca Darlington

A catalog record for this book is available from the Library of Congress.

ISBN: HB: 978-1-5013-5895-1
       ePDF: 978-1-5013-5897-5
       eBook: 978-1-5013-5896-8

Typeset by Integra Software Services Pvt. Ltd.
Printed and bound in the United States of America

To find out more about our authors and books visit www.bloomsbury.com
and sign up for our newsletters.

To Paul Cornea *(1923–2018), in memoriam*

Right now, this market's currency benefits, however, periphery commodities, that is, goods whose geocultural origin—and not their intrinsic value—renders them "peripheral." If such products are in high demand at present, that is because they lay bare, more clearly than the "center"'s own output, the tectonics of influences, the struggle for a literary recognition whose ideal no national frontier can rein in, and the circuitries of cultural capital.

—ADRIANA STAN, "THE RULE OF THE GAME"

[T]he birth of literary theory can never be a truly national affair ... [L]iterary theory only emerges as a result of connections between the national and the world.

—ȘTEFAN BAGHIU, "THE RELATIVE AUTONOMY OF LITERATURE"

CONTENTS

PART THREE   Critical Modes

PREFACE AND ACKNOWLEDGMENTS

This book does not mourn theory. Not by a long shot. Quite the contrary, our volume bears witness to theory's twenty-first-century renewed vitality. As a "world form" of sorts and collective effort of equally broad scope, the discipline is in fact, we think, doing better right now than in its High Theory heydays, although its revisionist, "post" mode of thriving can be confusing. Furthermore, not only is theory alive and well, but it is more present than ever across fields, domains of life, and geocultural boundaries. It has reenergized and brought into conversation areas as distinct, and sometimes as divergent, as formalism, environmentalism, digitality, and politics. Whether they are formally organized or not, its practitioners operate, even when they disagree, by largely shared lexicons, methods, knowledge, thematic preoccupations, and presuppositions. These are the discourse codes and professional lifeblood that afford theory expression and staying power while inherently pulling theorists into communities and weaving those groups into a steadily growing disciplinary body.

We submit that this body could and should work more democratically lest theory's new lease on life run out. For, in a fundamental sense, what makes this point in theory's history "post" is a whole spectrum of efforts of moving not only beyond inherited concepts and even beyond the human itself as traditional frameworks and pivots of theoretical reflection but also beyond the assumption that such notions and paradigms are monopolies and exclusive achievements of certain "geotheoretical" centers—of particular places and histories of intellectual endeavor, expertise, and authority. Theory's post time, then, is to us one of a twofold reset: conceptual, or *theoretical* properly speaking, and *metatheoretical*, or impacting what theory represents institutionally, how it is done inside its expanding world community, how this collective's many voices are heard, where they come from, and what disciplinary stories and counterstories they tell. This restart involves, in other words, a revision and a self-revision. For one thing, it pertains to substance, to theoretical "content," which we revisit by running culturally specific tests on some of the main posts marking it terminologically and by offering similarly grounded rationales for new concepts susceptible, we believe, to help us speak more fluently, with more attention to detail and cultural realities, the evolving language of theory during this transitional time. For another, we also take stock of that which contains theory itself, namely, community as container, production site, and engine of theoretical work.

It goes without saying—and yet this book's editors and contributors say it often, and deliberately so—theory needs community, and certainly not only the community of theorists, to flourish. But community needs theory as well because the need we are talking about is more than just "theoretical." The post vocabulary and related theoretical insights ironed out in *Theory in the "Post" Era* are more than an attempt to consolidate, refine, "localize," and sometimes critique the theory Esperanto of our commons. Today more than ever, that need is ontological, for, we propose, the theoretical is the existential prerequisite of the communal in communities big and small, "worlded" and less so, in the United States, Romania, and elsewhere in a world threatened by all kinds of anti-communal actions and reactions, from runaway globalization to exacerbated tribalism and tunnel-vision politics. It is as simple, and as complicated, as that. As we suggest, and as the post-millennial theorists gathered together in this volume show, in the new millennium, community will be *theorized*—more to the point, community will be *if* it will be responsibly theorized. Ours is only indirectly a book *about* community, but it is one that argues programmatically for the importance of "theorizing" and conceptual work at this moment in world history.

To make our case at all, we relied on wonderful colleagues, friends, and professionals. We want to thank first, at Bloomsbury, Editorial Director Haaris Naqvi, whose support and professional guidance have been one more time unparalleled. Senior Production Editor Rachel Walker and Editorial Assistants Amy Martin and Rachel Moore have been very effective and uniquely responsive. We would like to recognize our colleagues from marketing and production also.

To a significant degree, *Theory in the "Post" Era* is the result of a collaboration between University of North Carolina, Greensboro (UNCG), Lucian Blaga University of Sibiu, Romania (LBUS), and Transilvania University of Brașov, Romania (TUB). "The Conceptual Lab: A 'Post' Vocabulary for the Theory Commons," a UNCG-LBUS Critical Theory Institute symposium organized up in the Carpathians at Păltiniș, outside Sibiu between October 12 and 15, 2018, was the first step of the process leading to this book. Most of our book's chapters were presentations delivered and workshopped at this gathering. Laura Cernat's and Christian Moraru's essays have been written in English. The rest are translations, most of them by Laura Savu Walker. Teodora Dumitru's text has been translated by Daniela Falco and Ștefan Baghiu's by Anca Martin. Ovio Olaru has rendered into English Andrei Terian's contribution. Translator Andreea Teodorescu has also been involved at earlier stages of this project. All translations have been thoroughly revised by the editors. Beth Miller, our associate copyeditor, has done the general bibliography and the index as well.

Christian Moraru would like to recognize the following institutions, programs, and individuals who have provided funding, guidance, and other forms of assistance: UNCG's Class of 1949 Distinguished Professor in the Humanities Endowment; also at UNCG, Chancellor Franklin D. Gilliam, Jr., for his support of advanced research; the College of Arts and Sciences for travel grants awarded by Dean John Z. Kiss; UNCG's Atlantic World Research Network and its Director, Professor Christopher Hodgkins; UNCG's Office of Research and Economic Development and its Vice Chancellor, Dr. Terri L. Shelton, for a 2019 publication subsidy that has helped defray costs associated with the production of this volume; UNCG's International Programs Center, for recent travel awards, and the University's Walter Clinton Jackson Library staff; the UNCG English Department's Head, Professor Scott Romine, for his leadership in fostering an exigent culture of scholarly creativity among faculty. Gratefully acknowledged are also the support, kindness, and friendship of the following individuals: Henry Sussman, Brian McHale, Jeffrey Williams, Bertrand Westphal, Zahi Zalloua, Nicole Simek, Keith Cushman, Karen Kilcup, Stephen Yarbrough, Jean-Michel Rabaté, Corin Braga, Adrian Lăcătuş, and Radu Ţurcanu. Jeffrey R. Di Leo has been of great help also. Camelia's contribution has been invaluable once again.

Andrei Terian would like to convey his gratitude to Professor Sorin Radu, LBUS Rector. Alexandru Matei would like to thank colleagues from TUB's Department of Literature and Cultural Studies and, in particular, Professor Adrian Lăcătuş, Dean of TUB's Faculty of Letters.

Theory in the "Post" Era features only previously unpublished work. This book is dedicated to Paul Cornea, distinguished theorist and comparatist and teacher, at University of Bucharest, of some of this book's contributors. We also want to thank Bloomsbury's anonymous readers and Rebecca Darlington for allowing us to reproduce her painting *Joyeux Anniversaire to Spring* on the cover. We are also grateful to Thomas O. Beebee and Jean-Michel Rabaté for their permissions to reprint two brief excerpts from "What the World Thinks about Literature" (text included in *Futures of Comparative Literature: ACLA State of the Discipline Report*, edited by Ursula K. Heise, with Dudley Andrew, Alexander Beecroft, Jessica Berman, David Damrosch, Guillermina De Ferrari, César Domínguez, Barbara Harlow, and Eric Hayot [New York: Routledge, 2017, pp. 61–70]) and *Crimes of the Future: Theory and Its Global Reproduction* (New York: Bloomsbury, 2014, p. 37), respectively. The fragments are used as epigraphs: the former in the Introduction and the latter in Chapter 9.

The Editors

Introduction
Toward a "Post" Vocabulary—
A Lab Report

Alexandru Matei, Christian Moraru, and Andrei Terian

The next step in world literature should be the activation of a world literature theory and world literary criticism.
—THOMAS O. BEEBEE, "WHAT THE WORLD THINKS ABOUT LITERATURE"

Theory as world discourse formation or even world genre in its own right is in the third millennium, from India to Denmark and New Zealand to Romania, hardly a hypothesis anymore. It is a reality, and a paradoxical one to boot. Akin to the basic conundrum over which World Literature proponents have been losing sleep lately, the paradox—and its acknowledgment no less—is pivotal to what we hope to accomplish here. It inheres in the contradiction between modern theory as an international and inevitably internationalizing, world pursuit, on one hand, and, on the other, the sometimes culturally leveling and epistemologically standardizing thrust of this endeavor; between the internationalism of principle and the parochialism of practice; between theory's bedazzlingly variegated subject matter across cultures and theorists' tendency to articulate, deploy, retain in curricula, and otherwise fall back on terminologies, rhetorics, cognitive protocols, and concerns developed in or associated with just a handful of Western intellectual hubs; between, on one hand, recognizing that we have been living and working for some time now in what this book's editors call *theory commons* and, on the other hand, the risks we run if we are oblivious to the disregarded histories, multiple disparities, and other asymmetries and hegemonic reflexes still hindering our communal undertaking;[1] in sum, between the advantages and shortcomings of this communality—between joining the commons for the reward points of elite membership and doing it out of a dedication to theory as an ethic of nuance, to constantly attuning our language, tools, and foci to the world's wealth of shapes and noises.

It is over and against the backdrop of these contrasts, limitations, and biases that the chapters in *Theory in the "Post" Era* intervene in the cross-disciplinary remaking of theory for the age of mushrooming "posts." Roughly, these come under two categories. One comprises terms such as "postanalog," "postcritique," "posthumanism," "postcommunism," and the awkwardly sounding "post-postmodernism"; the other, items like "constructalism," "eastethics," "digicriticism," and "post-presentism," which, less known if known at all, bearing the "post" prefix or not, also participate in the "post" theoretical moment and logic. Mainstream or "exotic," familiar and idiosyncratic, overused and barely in use, these posts are both the driving force and the focus of this volume. Intrigued by their ongoing proliferation across fields and continents, we are committed to coming to grips with them and the post moment in theory overall in a deontological fashion, that is, in ways that do not compound the inconsistencies listed above and may in fact address some of them by bringing into the conversation a body of literary-cultural evidence, a tradition of critical-theoretical work, a theoretical language, and an understanding of theory history less present, if not in the actual making of theory over the world's times and spaces, then in the conventional accounts of this process. Thus, our collection is premised on the notion that literary and cultural theory, as well as theory largely, whose purview is no longer limited to the human sphere implied by "literature" and "culture," represent at this point in history more than ever before a world-scale, collective if politically lopsided venture. Further, we insist that post-1900 theory is, manifestly and to an unprecedented extent, a geosocial, loosely coordinated project incrementally carried out on and across the shifty planetary stage by way of exchanges, translations, frictions, venues, and routes that are transregional and frequently global in reach. We also argue, however, that such developments, itineraries, and sites could be pressed into service more effectively so as to challenge and over the long haul possibly reset the unbalanced interface of actual or putative centers and peripheries constituting what we see as the present world-system of theory production, consumption, and reproduction.[2] A major "post" missing from today's post-controversies is the one capturing the critical temporality of this potential, much-needed reset, this post-temporality, if you will, still to come, when doing theory *will* indeed come "after," and will happen in ways that do not merely echo, a few paradigm-setting intellectual events and traditions of theoretical reflection.

In this sense, our contributors make a point to theorize "from the margins" of this system. Taking up a central academic phenomenon of our world, they approach it from one of this world's geopolitical quarters that have been described as "peripheral" or "semi-peripheral." By the same token, the chapter authors extend a particular, at once eclectic and original, line of theoretical creativity and—quite programmatically—speak to it, theorize from it. And yet, far from pigeonholing or putting the Romanian critics and theorists reunited in *Theory in the "Post" Era* at a disadvantage, the location and timing of their intervention in specific debates refashioning theory in the twenty-first century afford them unique insights into what theory is in today's world, as well as into what it may or should be if our theory commons is to become effectively communal, drawing democratically from all manner of intellectual energies and letting all voices, "central" or less so, be heard. On this account, such theorizations do not reinforce the theorists' presumed "peripheral" status, nor do they buttress, directly or indirectly, the standard history of theory as a modern-era discipline.

Conspicuously narrow in scope, this history is a tale of Western origins, authority, and cultural compass. This story is, we contend, a "world-poor" narrative that finds itself at loggerheads with its own subject. It is by now well known that, as emphasized earlier, the mainstream biography of modern theory bespeaks deeper-seated ethnocentric habits responsible for reducing the history of theory to a Western affair at the expense of non-Western, indeed, non-European traditions of substantial theoretical work. It also goes without saying that the parochialism and narrowness of vision indicted below become significantly more serious offenses when the case is entered from a truly "worlded" and *longue durée* perspective that factors in, as critics like Revathi Krishnaswamy have, the "world literary knowledges" embedded, for example, in millennia of Asian theory.[3] But even when we limit the discussion, as we do here, to the Euro-American zone, the story ordinarily told still strikes one as exceedingly reductive. This story too is in urgent need of retelling, but the urgency is obvious especially for the last century and primarily for the recent decades, the period that concerns us here, when, much like other cultural and material interchanges, theory-making has gone verifiably global, in ways hitherto unmatched and in forms suggestive of widely shared generic parameters.

A subsystem of a cultural world-system roughly conceivable along the lines of Immanuel Wallerstein's model, the theory of the past one hundred years or so has been flaunting, in effect, its world-systemic makeup synchronically and diachronically, that is, in terms of what "doing theory" concretely is as well as in terms of how this disciplinary modus operandi has come to be what it is.[4] Not only does the practice of theory look to be—and, naturally, we speak with some approximation—largely one, on the whole coherent content- and structurewise across the humanities, inside and outside literary and cultural studies; not only do theorists, no matter their residence, mother tongue, ethnicity, immediate objective, or political allegiance, tend to turn routinely to a shared stock of references and buzzwords, methods and arguments, themes and vocabularies; and not only do these authors draw from the same knowledge repository, ply similar rhetorical tactics and styles, and otherwise give the impression of using, besides various schools and camps' lingos, a common language. But how theorists go about their work now—the very intellectual mechanics and institutional logistics of their activity—also enacts in the contemporary era modern theory's self-fashioning across time. In other words, today's theory performs its evolution, tells us something deeply revelatory about its own development: theory as a world genre is the outcome of a process itself world-historical. The theory that came about a century ago in the wake of the Saussurean-Formalist "linguistic turn" and has evolved on tracks both parallel to and intersecting those of Euroatlantic modernism has been a quintessentially cross-linguistic, cross-cultural, trans-, and intercontinental undertaking. The age of the "posts" and specifically the theory *labor* done in it, matters central to *Theory in "Post" Era*, bear out this fundamental truth more forcefully than any other moment in theory's history.

Remapping the Continent, or Can the "Peripheral" Speak?

Little wonder, then, that perhaps more than other humanist constituencies at present, those participating in theoretical work think, act, interact, influence each other, and on this ground belong in a theory commons—hence our book's subtitle. An incompletely and imperfectly structured, multiply asymmetric professional sodality and space, this is a transnational community unlikely to become an egalitarian utopia any time soon. In an important sense, it will always remain an aspiration, something to build rather than something to safely build on, already in place. But aspirational need not mean unrealistic as to what is going on, and, on this score, two features of the twenty-first-century theory commons and of literary world-systems broadly must be acknowledged. Both are political or, more exactly, geopolitical, given that they reflect a certain hierarchy, which, we have stressed, has been consolidated historically and casts on theorists' ground the shadowy contours of a tilted geography of the central and the marginal, the originator and the imitator, the producer and the consumer, and so forth.

Thus, on one hand, culturally, politically, and territorially isomorphic to the theory enterprise itself, this commons maps out and perpetuates, not unlike other world-systemic ensembles ranging from economy to literature, a history of inequality, a narrative of "combined and uneven development."[5] As suggested above, this history carries over into practice too. *How* theory is done and valued, its cultural capital and capitals, and its overall leverage are still a function of theory's *where* (most of theory's institutional and prestige centers lie in the West), as they are of its *who('s who)*—which theorists and what kind of theorist have been promoted, translated, quoted, influential, and so on. This has been the traditional complaint of prominent East European theorists and comparatists such as Adrian Marino. But, in a nutshell, this is also what the Warwick Research Collective submits in its 2015 elaboration on the Trotskyte formula quoted above, and this, too, is the first theory commons characteristic we want to highlight here.[6] Less marked at this juncture in the field's modern biography, the second is in play in the Collective's work as well. Starting out with its J. G. Ballard epigraph— "The periphery is where the future reveals itself"—*Combined and Uneven Development* allows, in effect, for a peripheral condition susceptible to overcome in a not-too-remote future the traditionally subsidiary status of knowledge production originating in "marginal" or "semi-marginal" areas such as Latin America and Central Europe.

In the same vein, then, we maintain that, on the other hand, the material-intellectual endeavor currently unfolding in existing or alleged less-than-central zones of the theory world-system—what we designate below as theory *labor*—entails a two-pronged, reproductive as well as productive, re-creative and creative algorithm of engagement with theory itself, its tenets, and forms. Accordingly, while this ambivalent travail will continue to concomitantly shore up said system and benefit from its geocultural motherboard, the cultural peripherals where this work takes place will also apply, for a number of reasons, a growing pressure on the system's overall political setup. Successively employing and redeploying the system's hierarchical wiring and overloading it with the kind of information and conceptual energies that ultimately demand a rewiring of the system itself rather than periodic status quo-preserving updates, the manufacturing and rerouting of theoretical discourse in and via places such as the Indian subcontinent, China, Japan, Australia, Slovenia, the Maghreb, the Caribbean, and even "provincial" France—the French universities outside Paris—may someday successfully contest the geography of unevenness embedded in this discourse itself as well as in the world apparatus of theory production, dissemination, and recognition that lies behind it. In this sense, from Routledge's 2013 *Global Literary Theory: An Anthology* to the 2017 edition of Wiley Blackwell's *Literary Theory* anthology, the 2018 version of *The Norton Anthology of Theory and Criticism*, the landmark 2019 *Bloomsbury Handbook of Literary and Cultural Theory*, and a host of other theory surveys, readers, and dictionaries published inside and outside the Anglophone world, our basic textbooks and reference instruments keep painting and nuancing a somewhat encouraging—because evolving—picture of the field.[7]

But *Theory in the "Post" Era* is not just looking ahead. In an equally significant sense, it also looks back into the past, specifically into the modern tradition of theoretical reflection in an important if lesser-known East European corner of the theory commons, Romanian critical culture. The book does so not to legitimize itself before national or international audiences, nor to brand exotically its jumping into what we deem as the defining if sometimes dauntingly diffuse theoretical conversation of the present, namely, the retooling of a key set of modern concepts for the twenty-first century's post regime of theory. It does so because the discriminating yet non-apologetic recycling of local knowledges into broader dialogues where the former does not dissolve into the latter's accredited and historically capitalized epistemologies, methodologies, and jargons is and has been endemic to East European theory all along. Summoning the idiomatic, the popular, the oral, and the exemplars of national culture from folklore to the Romantic era's "classics" in pronouncements on prosody, narrative, literary change, and the like has been a hallmark of modern theorizing in this part of the world. Bearing the imprint of their locations, these theorizations from Europe's geographical "peripheries" *have not been, however, "peripheral" at all* in the overall economy of the theory system under scrutiny here. Hence our reluctance to buy Wallerstein's developmentalist, three-tier world scheme wholesale and to treat cultural sites that happen not to be crossed by the Greenwich meridian and other "prime" coordinates of finance and geopolitical leverage as marginally meaningful and otherwise inescapably ancillary or derivative—in brief, as *effectively peripheral*. Economy and geography are vehicles of worldviews tainted by histories of empire, exploitation, and inequality, and, as such, the descriptive systems into which they can be and have been formalized are hardly self-evident axiologies, as Carmen Muşat notes in her chapter included in our collection. In other words, modern-era economic and geographical systems, more precisely their cartographic *renditions* of the world's locales, make for an unreliable value guide.

The story of modern theory as we know and, by and large, still do it today is a glaring case in point. Now, stories, like theories themselves, rarely stem from a single place. Nor do they achieve that memorable, canonical sheen without crossing other contaminating and transformative narrative habitats. The spatial, linguistic, as well as broadly cultural "translational" logic critics such as Rebecca L. Walkowitz locate at the core of contemporary literature is certainly characteristic of theory also, and eminently so of what has come to be known as "Continental theory." We would in fact claim that, more than literature, theory is "born in translation." While some theoretical concepts do pose the challenge of Barbara Cassin's philosophical *intraduisibles*,[8] theory is, as Andrei Terian has suggested with a nod to

David Damrosch, "the literary genre that undoubtedly stands to lose or gain the least in translation" and so has been massively translated from one language into another.[9] Moreover, prior to its renditions in new idioms, before being what it is and in order to be just that, to exist *tout court*, theory must "translate," move (see Lat. *translatio*) physically, in space, across countries and regions. Assuming, though, for the argument's sake, that stories—and, again, theory stories no less—originate in *a* place somewhere, and that their origin coincides with the center of a geocultural system built over time and over ethnolinguistic and territorial divides by reiterated negotiations and applications of theoretical models worked out elsewhere by "centrally" situated scholars, then a few things are pretty clear: Pascale Casanova's Paris, not to mention London, Zurich, Berlin, or New York, was for decades relatively marginal in the genetic saga of literary theory and on the intellectual map this narrative unfolds after World War I across the northern hemisphere and Europe in particular; then, if theory comes, say, to the European Southeast from a distance in decades after World War II, that is only because that distance had been covered half a century before in the opposite direction;[10] and last, acting and reacting at a distance and distance itself ultimately bring together, de-distance, and weave scattered stories and voices into modern theory's polyloquial history.

This is another way of repeating, as we are here, that the "Continent" in "Continental theory" and the very genealogy of this theory itself have never been what many of us might think nowadays, to wit, just a Western (principally West European) exploit—to be more exact, mainly Parisian, with allowances made for the German philosophical and psychoanalytic sources of French structuralism, poststructuralism, and feminism, and later on for the British beginnings of cultural studies. Instead, as a prominent historian of the discipline such as Galin Tihanov reminds us in a 2004 article and then again recently in a 2019 book, "modern literary theory was born in the decades between the World Wars, in Eastern and Central Europe—in Russia, Bohemia, Hungary, and Poland—due to a set of intersecting cultural determinations and institutional factors." "The contributions of Eastern and Central Europe to later developments," Tihanov insists in a passage worth reproducing *in extenso*,

> would be difficult to overemphasize. Indeed, the supposed advances in literary theory in its second "golden age," the 1960s and 1970s, were hardly more than elaborations and variations on themes, problems, and solutions played out in the interwar period in central and Eastern Europe. French structuralism, however refined (and sometimes reluctant to acknowledge its predecessors), was of course made possible by the work of Ferdinand de Saussure. But structuralism also depended on the achievements of Russian Formalism and the Prague Linguistic Circle, as well as on the formulations of the principles of phonology by

Nikolai Trubetskoi and Roman Jakobson in the 1930s. Narratology—notwithstanding the differences discernible in its later versions (those of Claude Lévi-Strauss, Algirdas J. Greimas, Claude Bremond, Gérard Genette, Eberhard Lämmert, Dorrit Cohn, Mieke Bal)—never quite severed itself from the legacy of Vladimir Propp, whose *Morphology of the Folktale* appeared as early as 1928. The continental version of reception theory in the 1970s was anticipated in works of the Prague Circle, above all those of Felix Vodička, who borrowed somewhat freely from Ingarden. Finally, Marxist literary theory in its later heyday was deeply influenced by the work of Georg Lukács in the 1930s.[11]

The phenomena Tihanov's historical sketch surveys are anything but "peripheral." To the contrary, these theoretical pronouncements have been trailblazing in a range of theoretical subfields from narrative studies to literary sociology. Tremendously consequential to this very day, they were absolutely epoch-making and remain central to an entire world-system of theoretical activity and innovation, which is why whenever it comes to "margins" and such in these pages, we reach for qualifiers like "putative," "presumptive," and their cautious brethren.

At the same time, neither were St. Petersburg, Moscow, Prague, and Budapest the absolute hegemons Paris, London, Konstanz, New York, New Haven, or Irvine failed to be, in spite of their claims. If "modern literary theory originate[d] in Central and Eastern Europe," as the Bulgarian critic's essay title asserts, that does not mean that the origination in question occurred monoculturally, *in vitro*, as it were. Romanticism, neo-Kantianism, and phenomenology—all of them of German extraction—were among its external catalysts.[12] Thus, whether we talk about the "Transylvania[n] ... birthplace of Comparative Literature," the OPOIAZ group, or "Circles" such as those of Prague in the 1930s and around Mikhail M. Bakhtin in the former USSR, the ambiance of theory's birth was—also with a Bakhtinian reference—broadly heteroglossic.[13] But these sites, groups, and projects were largely heterotopic, too, neither of one lexicon nor of a single place: intertextual, copiously intercultural, an ethno-linguistic medley of traditions shaped by interactions, transfers, transits, displacements, and exilic episodes of all sorts. "Modern literary theory," concludes Tihanov, "developed at the intersection between national enthusiasm and a cultural cosmopolitanism that transcended local encapsulations and monoglossia," in "a climate of enhanced mobility," first across and among countries of this European sector, then throughout the rest of the continent and the world.[14] "The unique, mind-opening possibility of 'estranging' the sanctity and naturalness of one's own literature by analyzing it in another language or by refracting it through the prism of another culture," he adds with a wink to the *ostranenie* notion Viktor Shklowsky introduced in the 1917 "Art as Technique" essay, "seems to be of paramount significance for the emergence of modern literary theory."[15]

The World Theory Commons

This historical process is a travel narrative: long-winded, full of twists and turns, its end—or absolute origin, for that matter—nowhere in sight. As with food, so with theory: no cuisine, "national" or not, without foodways; no theory without theoryways; and no common space without differences and distances. This is a story of travelers, of their portable knowledges, of their transferrable and translatable ideas, approaches, and tools, as well as of the fluid and roving cosmopolitan commons into which peripatetic intellectual actors and their homes, itineraries, workplaces, shelters, host universities, books, influences, terminology, and lingua franca have coalesced over the last one hundred years. Surely not *the* world or overlapping with it, this commons is nevertheless a world-system. "Putting in the hyphen was intended," Wallerstein explains the spelling of his concept, "to underline that we are talking not about systems, economies, empires *of the* (whole) world, but about systems, economies, empires *that are* a world (but quite possibly, and indeed usually, not encompassing the entire globe)."[16] In this respect, theory is, in its own way, a world too, and, following in the footsteps of scholars such as Thomas O. Beebee, we offer up World Theory as a construct analogous to and yet definitely more integrated, discursively more streamlined, and possibly less contested than its elder sibling, World Literature. World Theory's rise parallels, for better or worse, the last chapters of the story Wallerstein himself tells throughout his work. This is the story of the world as modern world-system or, with a term the sociologist is not very fond of, the story of recent ("late") globalization.

As a world-system, the theory commons finds itself, much like World Literature and virtually any twenty-first-century cultural phenomenon of planetary scope, in a double bind with respect to the wider, material-economic world-system. One offshoot of this predicament is that our commons, including the political labor obtaining in it, is bound to reenact, even in its presumably critical or dissenting moments, the global ensemble's logic and instruments of commonality and with them the late-global age's leveling drive, which have all made the theory world-system possible to begin with. This reenactment, however, need be and usually is neither inexorable nor complete. Prime international cultural precipitates of the modern era, theory and its practice are not doomed to further internationalize the world indiscriminately. It is therefore by no means a foregone conclusion that the increasingly worldwide diffusion of theoretical scholarship done in a certain way, language, style, or place will lead automatically to the co-optation of that work, way, language, style, or place into other corpuses, ways of doing theory, theoretical idioms, styles, and cultural environments or, vice versa, to that work's encroaching, invasive species-like, on the indigenous theoretical traditions it happens to be reaching.

This is what James Clifford and Vivek Dhareshwar point out in their update of Edward Said's well-known twin essays on theory as travel, "Traveling Theory" and "Traveling Theory Reconsidered."[17] Published more than a quarter of a century ago, Said's texts pursue the world migration of works by theorists like Lukács to show that as it journeys from Budapest to one European, American, and, with Franz Fanon, North African city after another, the Jewish-Hungarian thinker's Marxism morphs into "localized" varieties such as Lucien Goldmann's sociology, Raymond Williams's non-totalist approach to the old "base-and-superstructure" problem, Michel Foucault's genealogy, and so on; that these morphings have been either "reconciliatory" or "transgressive," more markedly oppositional politically, "develop[ing] *away* from [the] original formulation of ... [Lukácsian] traveling theory";[18] that, accordingly, a breakthrough in place X may travel to and translate into a "domesticated" and reified orthodoxy in place Y (and conversely); and that such transpositions and transplants, "the geographical dispersion of which the theoretical motor is capable," are crucial to theory's coming into its own, to a genetic phenomenology whose fruition shows off the chief role held in theory's life and operations both by location and distance, origination and reiteration, acceptance and resistance. These and cognate dyads make up the overall cross-cultural and cross-geographical dynamic through which theory completes itself, and the bottom line of Said's account is, first, that this completion frequently comes about elsewhere rather than at (its initial) home, in one Montaignean *ailleurs* after another actually, and, second, that the ecumenical web of such elsewheres—theory's whereabouts, its "hetero-domicile" in the modern era—established a theorists' community of sorts by the end of the previous century. Said is very clear about these two intertwined points: Theodor Adorno and Fanon, and Vienna (or Pacific Palisades) and French Algeria, respectively, do not come "after" Lukács but rather carry him over a cultural terrain that marks out the theorists' world commons. "When Adorno use[d] Lukács to understand Schoenberg's place in the history of music, or when Fanon dramatized the colonial struggle in the language of the manifestly European subject-object dialectic," writes Said,

we think of them not simply as coming after Lukács, using him at a belated second degree, so to speak, but rather as pulling him from one sphere or region into another. This movement suggests the possibility of actively different locales, sites, situations for theory, without facile universalism or over-general totalizing. One would not, could not, want to assimilate Viennese twelve-tone music to the Algerian resistance to French colonialism: the disparities are too grotesque even to articulate. But in both situations, each so profoundly and concretely felt by Adorno and Fanon respectively, is the fascinating Lukácsian figure, present both as traveling theory and as intransigent practice. To speak here only of borrowing and adaptation is not adequate. There is in particular an intellectual, and perhaps moral community of a remarkable kind, *affiliation* in the deepest and most interesting sense of the word. As a way of getting seriously past the weightlessness of one theory after another, the remorseless indignations of orthodoxy, and the expressions of tired advocacy to which we are often submitted, the exercise involved in figuring out where the theory went and how in getting there its fiery core was reignited is invigorating—and is also another voyage, one that is central to intellectual life in the late twentieth century.[19]

The study of theory, the "exercise" Said invokes, is fundamentally comparative. It must be so because how we understand theory must honor, we believe, how theory has developed historically. In a fashion similar to Walkowitz's "comparison literature"—third-millennium literature that travels in the multifaceted, formal and thematic ways in which "Lukácsianism" does here—we might talk in the post–Cold War decades about "comparison theory" should the phrase not be utterly redundant, as Said's analysis implies.[20] For not only studying theory but also doing it now— and doing it creatively, with attention to nuance, *originally*—is comparative work. As we see in *Theory in the "Post" Era*, today's theorists are—must be, we think—comparatists too. This is the quintessence of the labor we take contemporary theory to be, as well as the inherently affiliative vector Tihanov, with reference to the dawn of Formalist poetics, and Said himself in his discussion of the "nomadic" Lukács pin down as the organizing thrust of the modern world's cosmopolitan community of theorists. Both narrate intellectual histories that reveal the transnationally coalescing culture of theory as "travel culture," to recall here the anthropological concept Clifford brings to bear on Said's travel theory of the theory commons.[21]

Recognizing that "Said's ['Traveling Theory'] is an indispensable starting place for an analysis of theory in terms of its locations and displacements," Clifford further retouches the picture of Said's "intellectual, and perhaps moral, community" of theorists. This is an image that, we hasten to add, would get only tangentially modified in "Traveling Theory Reconsidered" by the extension of Lukácsian West European inroads into the Maghreb.[22] Clifford sets out, basically, to retool Said's "cosmo-theoretical" model for the postcolonial 1980s. The upgrade features, however, some intimations of the state of affairs that will become quickly a fixture of the theory commons in the multiply networked post-1990 world society of the internet, faster and faster travel, intensified communications, accelerated data sharing, digital publishing, and so forth. Not only is "theory," as Clifford says largely agreeing with Said, "always written from some 'where,'" and not only is "that 'where' … less a place than *itineraries*[,] different, concrete histories of dwelling, immigration, exile, migration," but these routes now branch out far beyond the largely European, "linear path" traced by Said, which, indeed, "cannot do justice to the feedback loops, the ambivalent appropriations and resistances that characterize the travels of theories, and theorists, between places in the 'First' and 'Third' worlds."[23] Nor is, aptly contends Clifford, exile *the* "distancing" factor it used to be prior to the fall of the Berlin Wall, when it forced so many theorists to complete their work "at" or "from" a distance and incorporate all sorts of distances, intervals, and differences between their native and adapted homes into their work while doing so. Likewise, while Adorno and Williams had "pretty clear notions of who would read them," where their work would end up, and how "discrepant" their publics' reactions would turn out to be, this is not the case anymore.[24]

On one hand, then, theory and theorists circulate more extensively than they did previously. On the other, while migration of ideas and people has dramatically gone up on a planet whose systemic complexity and integrated "oneness" are no longer captured by flattering and patronizing descriptors such as the "First" and "Third" world, one does not have to travel physically to obtain or grant access to scholarly-intellectual resources of all kinds, swap ideas, influence and be influenced, participate in all sort of projects, and otherwise bolster the theory commons. Thus, far from just preserving this commons' cosmopolitan constitution—one that remains burdened by cosmopolitanism's politically and historically mixed record—the concrete and complexly interconnected theory labor effectuated across the world community of theorists has upgraded and refurbished cosmopolitanism for the post–Cold War, internet and social media era.[25] The site or sites, rather, of this labor are what we designate as *conceptual laboratories* so as to capture the rich, material meaning of the *work* within them. Such labs scatter across the theory commons. They are microcommunities of theorists formally or informally organized, doing their job inside and outside and back and forth between various academic institutions as well as occasionally outside the academy altogether, variously connected to other similar groups across the world and constituting, together, our commons.

The Theory "Pandemic" and the Birth of a World Genre

The Romanian lab whose theory experiments are on display here is one such site. We write "experiments" advisedly because what we also want to convey is the experimental dimension of the conceptualizing and reconceptualizing labor going on in our lab. Day in and day out, this labor entails "growing" a large plate of traveling notions, methods, and theoretical models of wide circulation in the Petri dishes of the living environments of the lab personnel's surrounding culture, testing out the obtained varieties and hybrids in that culture's specific contexts, and then releasing, as the featured essays do, the conceptual products back into the world. Indeed, there is little doubt that these lab sites are "situated." This cultural situation is no less defining of literature's theoretical refraction in the post era. The early twentieth-century university may have provided, at least by some accounts, the New Critics with an enclosed space inside which "texts could be studied in a way" Alfred Kazin found "'equivalent to the scientist's escape from life into the laboratory.'"[26] But one hundred years later, criticism, theory, and the study they require do away, as Bruno Latour has underscored, with the ontological divide between "the culture of the laboratory" and the laboratory's circumambient material culture complete with its larger national archive, literature, and "mythology."[27]

At the same time, lab operations themselves—the labor of theory overall—break in the post age more resolutely through the actual or imagined barriers separating various national laboratories of earlier theoretical travail. This means that our theory lab is also "geo-situated," a site of intellectual "worldedness" as much as a place-bound subsystem of an ethnopolitical system. The labor performed in our lab today is, as both Latour and Itamar Even-Zohar would emphasize, heavily networked, plugged internally and externally, domestically and internationally, into extensive sets of transmission, translation, and relaying apparatuses. This post condition of theoretical work is unrivaled in history. As Even-Zohar would put it, this travail is not solely "intrarelational"—it does not get done exclusively inside that system no matter what—but also "interrelational," markedly "cross-systemic."[28] It does bear the imprint of a local or situational ethic,[29] but to quote Even-Zohar again, position or situation here must be understood in several ways at once so as to do justice to the wide spectrum of "interferences" and "contaminations" unavoidably going on between lab activities and cultural-theoretical labs and milieus close or remote, at home or in the bigger world.[30] The twenty-first-century post regime of theory fundamentally calls, in fact, for a "webbed" technology of theoretical pursuits, for a genuine engagement with similar work elsewhere. Actually, as our book makes it plain, the post work of theory *is* net-worked internationally—it is by definition a highly "contagious" international practice that further internationalizes its participants as well as their effort, instruments, and cultural adjacency. Since the end of the Cold War, "interrelational" contamination has radically increased its role in theory production. As we have noted repeatedly on various occasions, not only is this post-1989 world culture more interconnected, more contact-prone than before, but this integration also obtains frequently across, above, and oftentimes at the expense of nation-states. Populist–nationalist flareups, antiglobalist backlashes, and all sorts of Brexits notwithstanding, the geo-immune system of the nation-state-sponsored conceptual lab has been weakened worldwide.

This is or should be a commonplace by now. It is, in any case, worth reiterating here that, after the Berlin Wall's crumbling, people, capital, data, and discourse—theory, in our case—have been spreading, in print or digitally, over more and more permeable national frontiers. This is a general observation, and there are exceptions to it. Overall, though, it captures an axial *geocultural* aspect of the new millennium. This phenomenon becomes apparent in the spectacular, cross-, supra-, and, in some extreme situations, post-national revamping of theory—of its form, content, status, and relation to the theorist or author, language, audience, market, tradition it is expected to come from, and national archive it is supposed to add to. What many theory books and articles are these days, the way they look, how and where they are written, how they are produced, disseminated, traded, and read are less and less determined by the nation-state, by a *single* nation-state, by and within a cluster of regionally connected nation-states, or by a *symbolic capital-rich* center of theory accreditation. More and more theoretical texts are researched, composed, printed, digitized, distributed, translated, bought, lent, borrowed, promoted, and debated in *the world network* to various degrees. Nor is this world, to be clear, Casanova's *république mondiale des lettres* or the "republic of [the theoretical] imagination," to paraphrase Azar Nafisi.[31] All the same, theory is nowadays *"always already" born into a transnational and translational web of circulation and reception*, a situation, we maintain, best encapsulated by theoretical vocabularies and their wanderlust biographies. A "space between," theory space is indisputably a "translation zone." To theorize is to translate, to make, unmake, and remake these wayfaring concepts. The point or points are, first, not or not only that theory is translatable or that it travels more and possibly better than other discourse categories, but that doing theory is an exercise in translation and therefore involves the logic of translatability; and second and perhaps more importantly, former or still presumed "peripheries" of the theory world-system are today once again, and more noticeably than in the past, among the foremost such between spaces, theory hotbeds *par excellence*. Real or imaginary, "ex-centricity pays"—*in* theory yet not only theoretically.[32]

One thing seems, in any event, obvious: the evolving interplay of the *economy of territorial nationhood* and *the economy of theory production and reception* has been leading, step by step, to a new, "geotheoretical" order. Comparable to and overlapping with the geoliterary order brought about in a similarly systemic fashion by literature and its World-Literary spreading, layperson consumption, and specialized interpretation, this is the world-system of theory or theory as World Theory, as "geosystemic" practice inside the theory lab of our world commons. If we talk today, as we do here, about theory as a world genre, that is because the scholarship engendered by this practice has reached critical mass, which in turn is due, we suggest, to a panoply of revved-up, formal-thematic and cultural protocols whose spread nation-states, national cultural markets, and national literary and theoretical traditions and institutions have been less and less capable of corralling, quarantining, and harnessing. We write—again, quite apropos—"spread" so as to indulge a little the notion that, sometimes more than other fiction and nonfiction genres, theory and its influence expand, indeed "spread," like *influenza*, like some kind of both creative and implacable cultural symptomatology beyond the pathological, so much so that entire generations, groups, or schools (Chicago, Yale, Konstanz, Tartu, Geneva, Birmingham, and Ljubljana, among others) "come down" with various cases of theory—deconstruction over here, *la critique de la conscience* over there, etc.

As is well known, critics, comparatists in particular, have worked out all kinds of models of cultural influence. Thus, there is the anti-Voltairean horticultural model, the *tree* growing in the no less allegorical national garden; then, there is Franco Moretti's hydrological model of the *wave*, according to which certain forms propagate like ripples in a pond or tsunamis across oceans. And there is, we propose—or, more likely, we cannot *not* reach these days for—the epidemiological trope: the virus, the germ, or the theory "bug." In the late-global world, the ontology of separation, of discrete cultural experiments, and so on, takes a back seat to a predominantly flat ontology of perpetual, ever-escalating contact and contagion, of infection, dissemination, and horizontal accumulation. In this sense, the *ontological* gives way to the *oncological*, to a continuum of basically unquarantinable theory agents that all share an "infectious" nature. What they characteristically do is disperse across vast expanses of space, yet their movement is, again, less like the physical travel of, say, a plane, which gets to point B by leaving point A behind—or less like Moretti's wave, for that matter—and more like a plague that, in proliferating, can be in both places at the same time if not necessarily with the same intensity or in the same exact form. An "unhygienic," biodiscursive mess from the get go, culture generally and theoretical culture particularly develop in ways not very different from the microbiological cultures grown in a medical lab.

Originating in transmission and, literally by the same movement, in translation also, culture and theory remain transmissible and translatable, epidemic. They are triggered by, and *equal*, intellectual influence. They are a "sublime" influenza: non-pathological, multidirectional, life-giving. We "come down" with them despite our immune systems, no-go zones, and self-protection rites. And coming down with them inside our own sites of cultural and theoretical experimentation allows for a symbolic *germination* that, on one side, is enabled by the digital-humanities applications of new data storage and communication cybercapabilities and, on the other side, would be impossible without the germ of otherness, without others and their theoretical cultures. Hardly an *intra*cultural affair, theory obtains by way of contacts, *inter*culturally or, Jacques Derrida would say, "haptically," as it touches and is touched by other cultural and theoretical systems—as it touches on their themes, as it "touches up" their *Weltanschauungen*, and as its own proposals and conventions make an impact elsewhere.[33] This is what we mean when we submit that, "lab work" as it is, theory labor is never an *in vitro* procedure but, in all actuality, a transcultural *in vivo*, a matter of unavoidable, much needed, and far-reaching relationships and contaminations.[34]

Produced and reproduced all over the planet according to a more and more consistent set of formulas, topics, arguments, and counterarguments, World Theory belongs with a plethora of kindred discourse agents ranging from woollier aesthetic categories, morphologies, techniques, and enterprises to somewhat better structured literary movements, forms, and "genres." In literature alone, critics have identified: "World Bank Literature," "world-system literature," *littérature mondiale*, "comparison literature," "world poetry," the "planetary poem," "transcultural narrative," "world fiction," "the post-9/11 novel," the "cosmopolitan novel," "the world novel," "the international novel," the "geopolitical novel," and, more radically perhaps, the modern novel itself—with Moretti's title, "the modern epic."[35] While there is something to be said about the inflationary risks involved in such identifications, in the liberal stamping of the genre label on everything literature scholars might come across these days, and in genre studies broadly, a sizeable number of critics have taken these discourse modalities seriously and deem them "planetary" in terms of origin, circulation, and even structural patterns.[36] In essence, the Morettian "world texts" featuring these traits document thematically and enact formally the sharp, post-1989 upswing in Heideggerian, "pandemic" worldedness.[37]

Not unlike theory, what sets aside world texts beyond their mobility but related to it is a remarkable degree of fungibility, hence their superior translatability at least when compared to genres like poetry. This also accounts for a consistency that enables them to soak in and work over the clashes, movements, and intermingling of places, peoples, cultural habits, and values. For, by virtue of a "world-oriented" architectonics that combines "stock" structures and adaptability to culturally specific contents, these forms capture *the wide world-as-world* textually, topically (subject-matterwise), but they do so topologically as well, which makes a cursory comparison between the theory and novel of recent years quite instructive. Thus, the plots of today's world novel, for instance, obtain, indeed, "trajectorially" as they crisscross the planet, its continents, spaces, and times past, present, and future, weaving them all together narratively as, say, in David Mitchell's books. This happens, as it does especially in contemporary theory focused on globalization, world-systems, and comparative studies, with novels unusually sensitive to the world's worlding or coming together and, inside those works' fictional space, within "little worlds," communities, and locations no longer immune to the tug and pull of the planet. Deploying a feverish poetics of contagion, "world novelists" prompt us—and so do theorists themselves—to rethink a whole array of notions from national literature, history, and patrimony to the very dynamic of authorship and citizenship.

This reconceptualization drives the momentous textual and contextual change that has been affecting for a while now this novel category as well as theory and other world genres. This mutation, we venture, will likely be judged by future critics as the *second epoch-making shift* in modern literary and intellectual history, a turn temporally coterminous with and culturally akin to the post mutation charted by *Theory in the "Post" Era* across a range of theory discourses. The first, from the birth of modern realism through postmodernism, was—and we deliberately use the past tense here—instrumental to both the emergence of the nation-state, as Moretti observes in *The Modern Epic*, and to its weakening. In the post–Cold War network society of a *monde* increasingly shaped by everyday interrelational *mondanéité*, print culture and its postanalog avatar, digitality, are taking literary and non-literary forms such as theory itself into another era. Throughout the arts and the humanities, a whole new discursive model seems to be in the offing. We call it, also with a wink at Moretti's "world text," the "world-rich" paradigm. No less world-rich than a Haruki Murakami novel or a Yoko Tawada poem, twenty-first-century theory is a prime world genre and consequently part and parcel of this paradigm.

From Post-Theory to a Theory of "Posts": Conceptual Labor in the Third Millennium

This volume releases reports from one of the most resourceful theory labs of the postcommunist world, the Romanian collective known as the Critical Theory Institute (CTI), a post contingent itself, whose members came on the scene mostly after 2000. For, indubitably, our commons become much vaster after 1989: considerably more diverse, arguably more decentered, stretching far beyond the old "Continent" into its Eastern hinterlands, carrying on the worlding and "de-provincializing," postcolonial and multicultural critical revision of the European humanist legacy and thereby opening up the system of modern theory, it now incorporates the older Eastern Bloc.[38] A huge swath of the formerly and patronizingly named "Second" world, this whole area does not register, however, in Clifford's bird's-eye view of theory's planetary circuitries.

The omission strikes us as odd on several grounds. For one thing, virtually all Soviet "satellites" and "republics" were in 1989, when Clifford and Dhareshwar's volume came out, in a belatedly colonial situation: with some notable differences, Sovietization *was* colonization, much like the impending post-Soviet-postcommunist era would be postimperial and postcolonial. For another, as historians like Tihanov tell us, Central and Eastern Europe is, in a sense, "where it all began." For still another, it kept driving theory innovation throughout the Cold War years, with the Bulgarian and Romanian exodus of the 1960s and 1970s and Julia Kristeva, Tzvetan Todorov, Thomas Pavel, and Matei Calinescu among the illustrations of the now obsolescent Cold War exile model. To be sure, the Iron Curtain did not prevent this region from remaining a fertile contact zone, an attribute *perestroika* and, more decisively, the collapse of the Berlin Wall would greatly boost despite widening brain drain, asymmetries, and overall "unevenness" of the world-system under the neoliberal pressures of late globalization. Throughout this zone, from the Baltic states to the countries springing up from the ruins of what used to be Yugoslavia, theorists have been of late engaged, individually or in groups such as ours, in an endeavor—in a travail not always accompanied by travel and in travels not necessarily across physical space—that once again bodes well for theory's rejuvenation. Examples abound, from the Bulgarian collective led by Alexander Kiossev in the 1990s to the clusters of scholars affiliated with institutions and journals such as the Institute of World Literature of Bratislava (Slovakia), the Institute of Slovenian Literature and Literary Studies, the Institute for Literary Studies of the Hungarian Academy of Sciences, *Neohelicon* (Hungary), *World Literature Studies* (Slovakia), *Primerjalna književnost* (Slovenia), and *Euresis*, *Caietele Echinox*, and *Metacritic* (Romania). Like CTI, these are sites of assiduous and symptomatically local recalibrations of concepts in worldwide circulation such as contemporary critical genres (Poland), East European Orientalism and postcolonialism (Slovakia), and community, geocriticism, and "peripheral" status in World Literature research (Slovenia and Hungary). A steady flurry of volumes reuniting the outcomes of collaborative work on these topics proves that, in the East and elsewhere, theory was dead neither in or around 2000, when quite a few critics pronounced it so, nor today, when further efforts are being made to rethink its basics for the post stage of its history.[39] Unlike the sometimes insistent "post-theory" talk of the mid- to late 1990s—which, notably, was spurred by a 1995 *symploke* special-topic issue as well by the English essay collection the Kiossev group brought out the same year—our moment is "post-theoretical" only insofar as its sometimes parallel and sometimes intersecting reformulations of major tenets and approaches lead, as they have for a while now, to a theory of the "posts" or, differently put, to a proliferation of "post" concepts.[40] These are terms whose coining is by no means "post-" (read "non-") conceptual, though; post-millennial theory, or the theory practiced by our post-millennial theorists, is not taking us beyond theory, nor does it leave theory behind—the post in post-millennial hardly relegates theory to the past or marks theory as "passed." Involving as it does the prefix "post" or varieties of it ("neo-," "after," "meta," etc.), the hammering out of our "postist" lexicon channels the reflexive diligence typical of the theory revival now taking place across our commons. Firing on all cylinders, the Saidean engine of theoretical creativity is fueled, inside and outside CTI, by the kind of energy or activity we have called theory labor.

But what sets this travail apart from comparable work in the humanities or from other theory modalities, including those shaping the post–Cold War years? Which are its characteristics? Very succinctly, the chapters of this collection show that our labor is:

i. *reluctantly epochalist.* The standard, typically "post"-millennial question, we think, all contributions to *Theory in the "Post" Era* raise one way or the other is not "What comes after X?" but "What does X look like or mean after or in the wake of Y?" Organized into three thematic parts ("Aesthetics," "Temporalities," and "Critical Modes"), the book's chapters articulate this interrogation across these critical-theoretical domains in conjunction with various recent "ends" and "demises" (of the Cold War, Communism, the "Metaphysical Age," "aesthetics" [Alexandru Matei], postmodernism, "structure" [Corin Braga], the canon [Cosmin Borza, Braga], etc.) or, to the contrary, with certain "advents" and "onsets" (of the digital humanities, of populist politics [Ioana Macrea-Toma], of new eco-awareness, or of the Anthropocene as epistemological master framework). We recognize that these are watershed junctures and events in modern cultural or natural history. We note, too, that they have compelled theorists, as they do our contributors, to imagine new ways of thinking, for example, about criticism ("after" the internet, in Adriana Stan's chapter), comparative studies ("after" World Literature), modernism and the "contemporary" ("after" postmodernism), or traumatic memory ("after" East European Communism, as in Andreea Mironescu's piece). We also notice that these theoretical forays into such an unsettled conceptual territory have all the makings of an "epochalist" trend, but we hesitate to conclude, for instance, that the rise of "neocritique" is clear proof that critique and its objectives are *passé* (a reservation formulated by Mihai Iovănel in his chapter) or, vice versa, that renewed interest in ideology and politics in literary studies in Eastern Europe after 1989 signals a complete turn away from preoccupations of narratology (a problem taken up here by Alex Goldiş). The "sinces" and "afters" index, thus, an ample, multipronged but overall coherent mutation across theory compartments, conceptual-methodological sectors, national sites of theorization, and several decades of theory work, and yet, we also contend, this ongoing, pluridisciplinary, and geosystemic move past such posts has only occasionally made a clean break with the theoretical ideas, models, and positions about which the prepositional markers of posteriority, succession, and superannuation would urge us to think in the past tense. As chapters by Christian Moraru and others suggest, the "posts" may be signifiers of rupture, discontinuity, and opposition; they may imply, consequently, a timeline and even a "periodization," the end of a cultural and conceptual cycle and the beginning of a new one; they may also represent an ironic stance toward "what was"; or they may stand for a radical reexamination of the basic framework within which "what was" was indeed possible or, in a Latourian spirit, was *not* what we thought it was in the first place and so it may well be in the cards of a futural ontology.[41] On these and other grounds, the "posts" may also be symptoms and even vehicles of continuity, nostalgia, epigonism, and even replenishment of seemingly or effectively "exhausted" cultural and critical-theoretical forms. Thus, the "posts" lend themselves to translations that run the gamut from "anti-," "following," and "in the wake of" to "repeating" and "extending" something from the past to "retro-," as the case may be.

ii. *experimental and self-reflexive.* The lab results released in our book speak, then, to a situation still very much in flux, marked by the instability of extant notions and methods as much as by novel—established or emerging— concepts and by provisional verdicts and tentative steps forward. While we do not shy away from strong claims either, especially when they help us bring out in bold relief the meaning and scope of the paradigm shift to which the "posts," we trust, will have ultimately borne witness, our work is, as befits a laboratory like CTI, experimental to a considerable degree. As specified above, we view ourselves as an open subsystem of the theory commons. In this sense, we emphasize our inscription into worlds small and big. We open our lab windows to let in all sorts of "influences" and itinerant ideas so we can put these migrant agents to the tests of locally sourced cultural applications, regrow the traveling germs alongside native specimens, and reflect critically and self-critically on the conditions of possibility of that which various "posts" purport, as acts of critical assessment themselves, to leave behind, as well as on our own position in this evaluative process. What we have here is a situation where the "posts" are "anti-," in an avant-garde mode, that is, but this does not exclude a "meta-" component. This double gambit is part of our repertoire too: we do not simply describe orientations such as geo- and digicriticism; Stan and others who tackle these subjects in *Theory in the "Post" Era* also weigh their merit, examine their implications, and so forth.

iii. *nationally, transnationally, and ecologically affiliative.* CTI has joined in a collective, massive yet still incipient enterprise. Our book is a cross-section of this wider effort, or, better yet, a fractal representation of what has been afoot on a much larger scale in the world theory commons for more than two decades. This, we would like to think, does not make *Theory in the "Post" Era* derivative but only formally homologous to similar initiatives elsewhere. By way of fresh arguments and correspondingly ambitious terminological concoctions, we nominate new items for membership in the post family while weaving into the broader conversation local lineages and scenarios into which Latourian lab culture in turn remains, as we have said, simultaneously and fruitfully plugged. This culturally double-barreled move is instrumental to a travail of theory that views itself as both "sited" (apropos of Ștefan Baghiu's contribution), as our chapters routinely do, and worlded in terms of this work's foci, complex cultural logistics, as well as thematic interest in and epistemic reliance on matters such as "nature," "ecology," and, we shall see momentarily, "community," all of them conceived on a planetary scale. In other words, theorizing inside CTI requires a post kind of labor because what we think through is a whole constellation of post subjects and also because this thinking through's logistics is geosystemic and contemporary in a way itself "postist," to wit, decreasingly egocentric and incrementally post-centric or at least multicentric. Indeed, as Matei, Caius Dobrescu, Iovănel, and other CTI theorists have averred elsewhere, we are reaching a point where critical-theoretical thinking is *thinking with*—with others at a distance yet as involved as we are in the same "global dynamic" of reading, reflecting, and writing.[42] To the extent that it assumes and theorizes this dynamic, *Theory in the "Post" Era* is the second installment of a larger project that got off the ground with the 2018 essay collection *Romanian Literature as World Literature*.[43]

iv. *transdisciplinary*. What happens across locales of theoretical work occurs, at a comparable pace, over disciplinary boundaries as well. This is why the interdisciplinary nature of theory labor in the twenty-first century deepens, so much so that viewing post theory as *post*disciplinary may not be entirely farfetched. As this book shows, our field continues to borrow whole vocabularies and toolkits from other knowledge domains (environmental sciences [Matei], cybernetics and statistics [Stan], economics, psychology, and design [Teodora Dumitru], history [Bogdan Crețu], to name but a few) while lending neighbors like history and philosophy concepts and approaches that they too are, as just noted, adaptations of notions and principles fleshed out originally in linguistics, psychoanalysis, anthropology, or sociology. No doubt, today's humanities fully inhabit this multidisciplinary feedback loop and, as such, are safe neither from theoretical contaminations nor from theory's uninvited appropriations. In this respect, the CTI theorist is an industrious *bricoleur*. This is true argumentwise as well as terminologically. Flaunted in the chapters' titles themselves, a veritable disciplinary-epistemological *métissage* informs and unifies the post lexicon of our moment in theory.

Veritable building blocks of the contemporary idiom in theory, the terms of this vocabulary are networked inside, among, and outside themselves, and therefore require, as Cassin would insist, a similarly networked reading.[44] The volume's main segments zero in on their specific problematics, also in a typically post fashion, by traversing three knowledge force fields in a revisionary mode assisted by concerns, inquiries, and perspectives not indigenous to these areas. In the process, the aesthetic expands dramatically into post spaces like the "postaesthetic," as in Matei's environmentally minded ecoaesthetic discussion, in Goldiș's geopolitical rebuilding of narratology, in Macrea-Toma's and Andrei Terian's political and communal reinvestment of literature and theory after the resurgence of populist and anti-"PC" rhetoric, respectively, in Dumitru's "constructalist" reconstruction of literary evolution, and elsewhere in part one. Likewise, the temporal and its cultural affordances across time permit maneuvers in the present that attest to the growing porousness of the boundaries between "now" and "then." This historical frailty asserts itself in spite of the chronologies embedded in the "hard" or "soft" "posts" deployed here ("after Communism," "'after' Postmodernism," "'after' Postcolonialism") and once again aligns Romanian space and conceptual temporality with other intellectual time zones of the contemporary world—for which see the chapters by Carmen Muşat (on cultural "catchup" or "synchronism"), Creţu (on presentism and literary history), Mironescu (on "post-memory"), Moraru (on "postfuturism"), and Laura Cernat (on "biofiction" and the author's posthumous "return" in theory and fictional apocrypha), all of them in part two. Finally, if here historical categories and history altogether seem to dilate and overflow traditional rubrics and periods, the last sheaf of reports from our lab document, in part three, field shifts and transgressions across inherited critical modes into new disciplinary and cognitive approaches ranging from "geocritique" (Baghiu), "neocritique" (Iovănel), and "digicriticism" (Stan) to "somatography" (Dobrescu).

   v. *programmatic. Romanian Literature as World Literature* billed itself as a manifesto. It is, indeed, a platform of Romanian post-millennial criticism and theory. *Theory in the "Post" Era* has a similar aspiration. Above, we delineate not just what we do and, explicitly and implicitly, who we are, but also the implementing of an agenda that goes beyond criticism, theory, and our lab itself into the ethical, the political, and the communal. For, if theory, as we contend throughout, is done communally, in our commons and, on this account, needs community, the reverse is equally true: community needs theory too.

Why Community Needs Theory

There is no true, effective community without theory, more exactly, without a sense of itself, without some sort of generalizable, conceptualized, and sufficiently internalized grip on what it means to be just that—and to be *in* that—particular kind of community.[45] What we have just claimed holds true especially of our late-global world, given where we are at this stage in the modern transition out of the *Gemeinschaft* model into a less organicist, tightly networked *Gesellschaft*. Communities prove sociohistorically sustainable in the long run insofar as they develop and exercise ethical self-discernment, the capability of *seeing* themselves as structured groups, *sub specie theoriae*. Etymologically, this is, of course, what *theōria* means and what theory labor aims at practicing: an art of seeing, of discerning, and subsequently of becoming aware of the shared *langue*, of the coherence-inducing principles underpinning the *parole* of the myriad of sociocultural acts in which the group members engage day in and day out.

At the dawn of the twenty-first century, few if any communities can take this theoretical self-awareness lightly. Furthermore, we would submit that thriving communities will be those able to thematize, in the very texture of their everyday, their theoretical dimension, namely, a communal model warranting not only intellectual self-reflection but also a full-blown theoretical self-understanding, that is, an understanding of the communal self as articulated both with *other* communal understandings of themselves and with the selves attempting those understandings. It is in this sense that we pointed out earlier the quintessentially generalizable or, better yet, cross-communal, bridging, or *worldly* work of the theoretical, a work that becomes more and more visible and important today; it is in this sense too that we might stress now the same modus operandi of communal life—trans-communally, with the world, with its beauty and crises—after the Cold War, when communities are increasingly lodged at the crossroads of places, histories, and traditions, in overlapping geocultural landscapes of alterity; and it is in the same sense also that, accordingly, the communal and the theoretical reveal their isomorphic configurations and operations and perhaps their equivalence as well. If community and theory have grown into this homology or even synonymy, if they have been doing and meaning similar things, that is because they have been beholden for some time now to what Jean-Luc Nancy calls, with a wink at Carl Schmitt, "the law of the world." "The unity of the world," Nancy maintains in *Being Singular Plural*, "is not one: it is made of a diversity, and even disparity and opposition ... The unity of the world is nothing other than its diversity, and this, in turn, is a diversity of worlds ... the world is a multiplicity of worlds, and its unity is the mutual sharing and exposition of all its worlds—with this world." "The sharing of the world," he goes on, "is the law of the world. The world has nothing other; it is not subject to any authority; it does not have a sovereign. *Cosmos, nomos.* Its supreme law is within it as the multiple and mobile trace of the sharing that it is."[46]

Granted, we share our world in a geophysical sense. This is a given because, thus far, "we" have no more than one world as home. But we do not share it, as we should, in an ethical sense. This is, in our view, another given as well as *the* problem communities and theorists are facing today. Practically and theoretically, what compounds the problem, we think, is the notion of difference embedded in the still prevailing discourse of diversity. We posit, then, that "sharing" and, with it, the theoretical re-founding of the communal in the twenty-first century occur not as self and other "smooth out" their differences nor as these discrepancies and asymmetries prove superficial and our "common humanity" triumphantly shines through them, but precisely by means of such dissonances—due to them rather than despite them. From Kwame Anthony Appiah's self-described cosmopolitan ethics to Slavoj Žižek's bloviations on the world's flaws, cultural difference is made out to be something of a hurdle, to get in the way of ethical (Appiah) or political (Žižek) communality, to obstruct effective community. By other accounts, however, cultural differences may well be the solution. Neither an absolute, an intellectual fetish, nor something to put up with and eventually "get over," they are the "groundless ground" on which we could theorize and build, as Jürgen Habermas might label it, a "flexible-'we'" community across the more "entrenched" ones.[47] This community model is more inclusive of its "exteriority," in Maurice Blanchot's view, and therefore désoeuvrée, "inoperable" from the standpoint of a more descent-based, Gemeinschaft type of communal cohesion and "effectiveness."[48] This is, however, the kind of human association best positioned to operate in today's larger and vastly "diversal" world and tackle this world's equally diverse problems. Since the "go it alone" approach has been demonstrably the wrong way to go in this world, we—theorists, community members—can neither opt out of this community nor not grow into such a community ourselves.

In fact, it is imperative we do so. But doing so requires what we would call—with another "post"—a post-multiculturalist "politics of recognition" and, with it, a less conventional idea of identity "authenticity."[49] The motto encapsulating this idea would no longer be the autonomist "I want to be known for what I am" but the more humbly relational "I want to be known for what or whom I am with," because, to quote Timothy Reiss now, "I have accepted this 'co-definitional' world's 'challenge of knowing [my]self with others.'"[50] This kind of individual and communal stance can be theorized as post-multiculturalist to the extent that it recycles the Heideggerian being-with as a formula of authentic—because authentically self-conscious—being. "I know and am myself 'with' because I am and am known with and by an other"; "I can bear witness, to myself and the world, because I have borne with-ness," with "h": this is the cognition, the cognition as self-cognition community members attain more and more these days no matter where they are in the world, and also the recognition they demand for themselves no less than for those with whom they gain this knowledge. Thus, turning the tables on the traditional metaphysics of identity, Charles Taylor, Clifford, and other critics proclaim that to be authentic is to be "relational."[51] In this vein too, one could start thinking about a "theory of relational cultures," and more basically "of culture as relation,"[52] as stemming from and in turn "cultivating"—indeed, demanding—relatedness. In no way, though, does the Levinasian notion that "being is relation to the other than self" render the self's being less authentic.[53] Equally important, this does not make the other's originality and uniqueness less original and unique either. If effective existentially, culturally, or cognitively, the self's being with an other trades on this other's uncompromised otherness. This is the condition of possibility of relationality, of the self's being in relation, *tout court*, of being, communally and otherwise.

That is why, as our world sets self and other side by side with historically unmatched fervor, we must at least consider the notion of a *radically distinct cultural other* who need not be and in practice often is not hopelessly inaccessible to us and yet, at the end of our probing day, may still prove irreducible to our approaches, conceptual grids, and overall rationality. This is what we mean here by "other," "otherness," "alterity," and their cognates: somebody with whom we inescapably are *across* an undeniable and conceivably unbridgeable cultural gap. We lay emphasis on "being-with" as much as we do on "gap," with the proviso that the latter is less and less physical while the former is felt more and more: we are more and more with people who are *not* like us. For this other is not as "external" to us as he or she used or seemed to be. Differently put, this other's "externality" is these days best accounted for culturally rather than geographically or solely geographically. Everywhere nowadays, the other is a stranger *not so much out there but in our midst*, and he or she may remain "strange," as Habermas also observes, by personal choice, due to our epistemological shortfalls or cultural apprehensions, and for many other reasons. Not only must we allow for this strangeness of others theoretically. We must commit to it in our daily communal life as theorists and citizens because, if nothing else, it is as constitutive of them as it is of us. This is the originating scandal of "we," of our sometimes untheorized "authenticity." Others make up the paradoxically original ex-centricity that affords our recentering, self-identification, and self-aware identity and living. It is from such an extremely displaced position that we come home and get to have a home to begin with. Therefore, being with our kind, with our present and past, with our history and its meanings, in brief, with that which some deem a smooth continuum of selves and self-engendering rites brings to light a more diverse, genuine community. Make no mistake: "genuine" does not signify "pure" but original, where originality denotes, in turn, the original relationality or "primordial" inscription of otherness into the text and context of the communal self.[54]

Today's community theorists working in the Georges Bataille-Blanchot-Nancy and other lines do not invent communities' inherent heteronomy—"culture in the plural," as Michel de Certeau says—but only report with superior method and acuity on an identity structure already there although more bountiful and more salient now than yesterday and, they predict, more nurturing tomorrow than today.[55] Our communities, they stress, are both abodes and *vicinities*. As we may recall, the Greek *oīkos*, "house," is related to the Latin *vicus*, "row of houses," and *vicinitas*, which helps understand why the cultural-affective "oikonomy" of homeyness is shot through with the frissons of the "unhomely," why, if you "look internally [, you] discover [the] neighbor," and why this revelation is absolutely

"self-transforming."[56] A "proper" community, a community properly
theorized, less easily "identical to itself," more mindful of what it says whenever
it says "I" or "we" in the twenty-first century, lends itself to such a "discovery"
and "defamiliarization" as a less familial nation and familiar notion. For,
whatever cognition might arise domestically, locally, intra-communally, it
is predicated, as Homi Bhabha writes, on the "shock of recognition of the
world-in-the-home" as well as of "the home-in-the-world."[57] This "world of
ours" is or becomes ours because it also is a "world of others." It is therefore
incumbent on us, inside our communities of literature, culture, language,
faith, or theory, to relate to those others and their otherness as such, to the
different-as-different, along the lines of concern and responsibility and so to
"give back," respond to the "gift" ethically. This strikes us as a truly apposite
way of looking at the other, especially at this moment in world history: not as
something or somebody "fitting" the "I" from afar or in "my" neighborhood,
an apposition or reassuring footnote to the traditional subject and hearth of
communal discourse and culture, but as a sovereign and one-of-a-kind entity
whose "outlandish" singularity accredits mine.

There would be—and, as far as we are concerned, there are—no home
and homeland without the outland, no Heimat without Ausland and its
Ausländer, "foreigners." There is instead, Nancy explains, "only the 'with'"
of the worlds; there is "proximity" (topology, space) "and its distancing"
(cultural difference between entities dwelling at close quarters); there
is "the strange familiarity of all the worlds in the world" in which each
finds in the "encounter with another's horizon" its most "appropriate
horizon" of living, understanding, and self-understanding.[58] Promoting
"the general equivalence of all meaningful forms [formes de sens] in an
infinite uniformity," global capital's "un-reason" (sans-raison) is one of the
world phenomena that threaten to consume the world of "singularities,"
the world as world. For, pace Fredric Jameson, it is those singularities, the
unique, the one-of-a-kind, the a-serial—in brief, the cultural and its worldly
embodiments, the planet's cultures—that constitute the worldliness of the
world, that plurality defying integration into a "uni-totality" (unitotalité).[59]
By the same token, the ontology and topology of this world are also matters
of justice and ethics. What, how, and where we and our kin are obligate.
Next to "them" more than we have ever been, "we" are responsible to and
for them, more specifically, to and for what makes them other to us rather
than others like us.

Critics from Alain Badiou to Masao Miyoshi have argued for a
"postdifference" ethics allegedly better prepared to stave off "identitarianism"
by doing away with otherness altogether.[60] We are reluctant to join them.
We do not underplay the threat of "essentializing" and "parochializing"
"identitarianism." But the larger issues here are identity itself, how it comes
about, and what affords it. Identity cannot obtain outside difference, that
is, outside exchanges, barterings, and translations among distinct identities.

Moreover, once we grant this differential genealogy of being and visualize our "common ground" as Levinasian "relationship in difference," we must also abide by this vision both conceptually and ethically, at the level of understanding how things in the world come to be what they are, as well as at the level of how things are still not what they should be and where, against a Baudrillardian, "indifferent world," assenting to an eco-logic of difference no longer leaves us the option of "indifference."[61]

The "incongruity" and "discrepant" constitution of today's communities should thus appear as something to recognize and strive for, to foster in the world as well as to project into it imaginatively, theoretically, if you will. This is, as Nancy says, a desideratum of mundaneity, of our mundane "praxis" or being in the world.[62] In keeping with what the world consists in intrinsically—a relatedness domain where a relation *is* possible but, in it, the other must remain other, not effaced by the same—this imagining of the world sets itself up as a visionary bulwark against the assaults on the world's worldly pageant of nonpareil presences, events, and meanings, against the un-worldly (*immonde*),[63] "foul and festering 'immundity'" of flattening globalization, as Derrida puts it.[64] Seeking to provide an *alter* (to this) globalization, Nancy and Derrida's "mondialization" implies an ethics, mundane exchanges that reach beyond fashionable (*mondaine*) and often isolationist, unwittingly populist *alterglobalisme* to reinforce the world as mundus, as domain of a necessarily conjunctive ontology. Whatever and wherever we are in this world, we are with others—outside and inside our communities—because, as a character of Don DeLillo avers, there is nothing in it *but* others. What theorists like Nancy and writers like DeLillo do is redraw the picture of the world along these "alternate" lines and thus pose an other to late-global—be it neoliberal or populist—rationality quite literally: not only do they see the world as mundus, as a *being-with* realm; they also set off the "singularity," the otherness on which this relatedness is predicated, that other with whom we must be in order to be.

This is, we believe, what we need to keep in mind as we theorize our communities, the places they occupy in the bigger scheme of things, and what takes place in those places, in any other places for that matter, and in between them. For, as Giorgio Agamben explains, no matter where it happens, this place-taking occurs as one just "eases" into a place, into a residential "easement" that is both one's own lawfully and "always-already" an adjacency *within* the private property in which the proprietorial and the exclusive are consequently premised on an other's presence, on the shared, and on the right-of-way. Owners and the finite space where their ownership is exercised are predicated, as Levinas, Derrida, and other thinkers tell us, on hospitality (*hostipitalité*, writes Derrida), on its guests (others), and on the luminous infinity bathing the face-to-face of hosting. Innately *ek-static*, beings thus depend on—they rest on and have *a priori* internalized—a literally vital exterior. This exteriority is obviously a misnomer. A place where the cozy, organicist, culturally and ethically ingrown communal has not been theoretically, this outlying space is where our community theory should go and take hold in the twenty-first century. It is only befitting, we think, that *Theory in the "Post" Era* issues a call to such a place from a cultural geolocation itself deceptively external to the life, death, and rebirth of theory throughout the modern era and "after."

Notes

1   On such ongoing threats to the "world republic of theory," see Chen Bar-Itzhak, "Intellectual Captivity: Literary Theory, World Literature, and the Ethics of Interpretation," *Journal of World Literature* 5, no. 1 (2020): 79–110.

2   On theory's reproduction in the international arena and the cultural aspects of this process, also see Jean-Michel Rabaté's *Crimes of the Future: Theory and Its Global Reproduction* (New York: Bloomsbury, 2014).

3   See Revathi Krishnaswamy, "Toward World Literary Knowledges: Theory in the Age of Globalization," in *World Literature in Theory*, edited by David Damrosch (Malden, MA: Wiley Blackwell, 2014), 134–58.

4   See in particular Immanuel Wallerstein's *Geopolitics and Geoculture: Essays on the Changing World-System* (Cambridge: Cambridge University Press; Paris: Maison des Sciences de l'Homme, 1991).

5   The phrase, Leon Trotsky's originally, has been used by Franco Moretti to discuss *A Hundred Years of Solitude* in chapter 9 of *Modern Epic: The World-System from Goethe to García Márquez*, translated by Quintin Hoare (London: Verso, 1996), 243.

6   Warwick Research Collective (WReC), *Combined and Uneven Development: Towards a New Theory of World-Literature* (Liverpool, UK: Liverpool University Press, 2015).

7   Richard J. Lane, ed. *Global Literary Theory: An Anthology* (London: Routledge, 2013); Vincent B. Leitch, gen. ed., *The Norton Anthology of Theory and Criticism*, 3rd edn. (New York: W. W. Norton & Company, 2018).

8   Barbara Cassin, "Présentation," in *Vocabulaire européen des philosophies. Dictionnaire des intraduisibles*, ed. Barbara Cassin (Paris: Seuil, 2004), xx.

9   See Rebecca L. Walkowitz, "The Location of Literature: The Transnational Book and the Migrant Writer," *Contemporary Literature* 47, no. 4 (Winter 2006): 527–45, and *Born Translated: The Contemporary Novel in an Age of World Literature* (New York: Columbia University Press, 2015). Andrei Terian addresses theory's translatability in his book *Critica de export. Teorii, contexte, ideologii* (Bucharest: Muzeul Literaturii Române, 2013), 7.

10   Adrian Tudorachi, "Despre receptarea foarte târzie a teoriei," in *Dus-întors. Rute ale teoriei literare în postmodernitate*, ed. Adrian Tudorachi, Madga Răduță, and Oana Fotache(Bucharest: Humanitas, 2016), 46.

11   Galin Tihanov, "Why Did Modern Literary Theory Originate in Central and Eastern Europe? (And Why Is It Now Dead?)," *Common Knowledge* 10, no. 1 (Winter 2004): 63–4. Also see Tihanov's book *The Birth and Death of Literary*

Theory: Regimes of Relevance in Russia and Beyond (Stanford, CA: Stanford University Press, 2019).

12 Tihanov, "Why Did Modern Literary Theory Originate in Central and Eastern Europe?," 61, 67.

13 On the Transylvanian roots of comparative literature, see Anca Parvulescu and Manuela Boatcă, "Discounting Languages: Between Hugó Meltzl and Liviu Rebreanu," *Journal of World Literature* 5, no. 1 (2020): 47–78.

14 Tihanov, "Why Did Modern Literary Theory Originate in Central and Eastern Europe?," 67.

15 Tihanov, "Why Did Modern Literary Theory Originate in Central and Eastern Europe?," 70.

16 Immanuel Wallerstein, *World-Systems Analysis: An Introduction* (Durham, NC: Duke University Press, 2004), 16–17.

17 Edward Said, *The World, the Text, and the Critic* (Cambridge, MA: Harvard University Press, 1983), 226–47, and *Reflections on Exile and Other Essays* (Cambridge, MA: Harvard University Press, 2000), 436–52. Tihanov refers both to Said's essays as well as to Clifford and Dhareshvar's "discussion of [Said's] 'travelling theory' in the present globalistic climate" in his essay "Why Did Modern Literary Theory Originate in Central and Eastern Europe?" (68). As for Clifford and Dhareshvar's revision of Said, see their edited essay collection *Traveling Theories, Traveling Theorists* (Santa Cruz: Center for Cultural Studies, University of California at Santa Cruz, 1989), especially Clifford's "Notes on Theory and Travel" (177–85).

18 Said, *Reflections on Exile and Other Essays*, 438–9.

19 Said, *Reflections on Exile and Other Essays*, 451–2.

20 Walkowitz, "The Location of Literature," 536.

21 On this concept, see James Clifford, "Traveling Cultures," in *Cultural Studies*, edited and with an introduction by Lawrence Grossberg, Cary Nelson, Paula Treichler, with Linda Baughman and assistance from John Macgregor (New York: Routledge, 1992): 96–112, and *Routes: Travel and Translation in the Late Twentieth Century* (Cambridge, MA: Harvard University Press, 1996).

22 Clifford, "Notes on Theory and Travel," 184. Of late, Lukács has "returned" to Paris, but via Eastern Europe, in the work of Romanian critic Nicolas Tertulian. See Tertulian's *Pourquoi Lukács* (Paris: Maison des Sciences de l'Homme, 2016).

23 Clifford, "Notes on Theory and Travel," 185, 184.

24 Clifford, "Notes on Theory and Travel," 184–5.

25 While describing our theory commons as cosmopolitan, we are mindful both of recent attempts to retheorize cosmopolitanism and its relation to community for the complex challenges of the late-global era as well as of the sometimes politically ambiguous history of cosmopolitanism as lifestyle, moral philosophy, and universalist notion of the human. One book that associates the cosmopolitan and the commons is Nil Disco and Eda Kranakis, eds., *Cosmopolitan Commons: Sharing Resources and Risks across Borders* (Cambridge, MA: MIT Press, 2013).

26 Sascha Bru, *Modernism Before and After Theory*, in *The Oxford Handbook of Modernisms*, ed. P. Brooker, A. Gasiorek, D. Longworth, A. Thacker (New York: Oxford University Press, 2010), 43. Bru quotes from Alfred Kazin's *On*

Native Grounds: An Interpretation of Modern American Prose Literature (New York: Reynal and Hitchcock, 1942), 357.

27 On "the culture of the laboratory," see Bruno Latour and Steve Woolgar, *Laboratory Life: The Social Construction of Scientific Facts*, intro. Jonas Salk (Princeton, NJ: Princeton University Press, 2013), 53–69.

28 Itamer Even-Zohar, "Polysystem Studies," *Poetics Today* 11, no. 1 (1990): 53–5.

29 See David Rabouin, *Vivre ici. Spinoza, éthique locale* (Paris: Presses universitaires de France, 2010).

30 Even-Zohar, "Polysystem Studies," 25.

31 Pascale Casanova, *The World Republic of Letters*, trans. M. B. DeBevoise (Cambridge, MA: Harvard University Press, 2004). As for Azar Nafisi, her "republic of [the] imagination" is the United States. See Nafisi's *The Republic of the Imagination: America in Three Books*, illustrations by Peter Sis (New York: Viking, 2014).

32 This point has been made repeatedly by East European critics, sometimes in response to charges of servile cultural mimesis of trends and fashions originated or presumed to have arisen in the West. See, for example, Adrian Marino, *Comparatism și teoria literaturii*, trans. Mihai Ungurean (Iași, Romania: Polirom, 1998), 5–6. For a more nuanced position on this issue, we refer the reader to the introduction and some of the essays in Adrian Tudorachi, Madga Răduță, and Oana Fotache, eds., *Dus-întors. Rute ale teoriei literare în postmodernitate* (Bucharest: Humanitas, 2016).

33 Jacques Derrida theorizes the "haptics" of touching in *On Touching—Jean-Luc Nancy*, trans. Christine Irizarry (Stanford, CA: Stanford University Press, 2005).

34 On the *in vitro/in vivo* distinction, the cultural oncology involved, and the relational dynamic derived from them, see Christian Moraru's work, especially his essay "Contagion, Contamination, and Don DeLillo's Post-Cold War World-System: Steps toward a Haptical Theory of Culture," in *Contagion: Health, Fear, Sovereignty*, ed. Bruce Magnusson and Zahi Zalloua (Seattle: University of Washington Press, 2012), 123–48.

35 See Moretti, *Modern Epic*.

36 Christian Moraru discusses these world literary formations and genres in *Reading for the Planet: Toward a Geomethodology* (Ann Arbor: University of Michigan Press, 2015), 72. For a balanced survey of the fast-growing interest in genre across literary studies over against the backdrop of twenty-first-century globalization and World Literature, see Florian Mussgnug's article "Planetary Figurations: Intensive Genre in World Literature," in *Modern Languages Open* 1 (2018), http://doi.org/10.3828/mlo.v0i0.204.

37 "World text" is a rough translation of *opera mondo*, which phrase Moretti used and defined in 1994. Two years later, *Opere Mondo* became available in English as *Modern Epic*. Also in 1996, Casanova published a little piece titled "World Fiction," *Revue de littérature générale*, no. 2 (1996): 42–5.

38 The pluricentric structure of the world theory commons attests to the latter's increasingly "open," "polysystemic" nature. On polysystems and pluricentrism, see Even-Zohar, "Polysystem Studies," 14.

39 Tihanov's 2004 essay closes with a reference to literary theory's "demise."
    See "Why Did Modern Literary Theory Originate in Central and Eastern
    Europe?," 81.
40 See Peter C. Herman, ed. and intro., "The Next Generation," special-topic
    issue, *symploke* 3, no. 1 (1995), one of the opening salvos of the "post-theory"
    debate and the first of a spate of individual and collective volumes on "post-
    theory"—and more recently "anti-theory"—that have come out since the
    late 1990s, some of them edited by Jeffrey R. Di Leo, a major participant in
    the discussion. See also the collective volume edited by Alexander Kiossev,
    Post-Theory, Games, and Discursive Resistance: The Bulgarian Case (New
    York: State University of New York Press, 1995). On the "end of theory" as
    a theory genre of sorts and the "posts" proliferating around this moment, see
    Alex Ciorogar, ed., *Postumanismul* (Bucharest: Tracus Arte, 2019), especially
    Ciorogar's introduction, "În loc de prefață. Întoarcerea 'lecturii teoretice': între
    postcritică și postumanism," 7.
41 See Bruno Latour, *We Have Never Been Modern*, trans. Catherine Porter
    (Cambridge, MA: Harvard University Press, 1995).
42 See Mihai Iovănel, "Oglinda spartă a României. În dialog cu Mihai Iovănel,"
    Oameni de poveste, June 26, 2017, available online: https://oamenidepoveste.
    ro/in-dialog-cu-mihai-iovanel-oglinda-sparta-a-romaniei/ (accessed September
    16, 2018), and Alexandru Matei, "Introducere în noua ecologie a criticii
    literare," *Observator cultural* 722, May 30, 2014, available online: http://
    www.observator-cultural.ro (accessed June 6, 2017).
43 Mircea Martin, Christian Moraru, Andrei Terian, eds., *Romanian Literature as
    World Literature* (New York: Bloomsbury, 2018).
44 Cassin, "Présentation," xvii.
45 Christian Moraru had made this argument previously, in a different context, in
    "Why Community Needs Theory: Rethinking the Communal in the Twenty-
    First Century," *Euphorion* 27, no. 1 (April 2016): 35–7.
46 Jean-Luc Nancy, *Being Singular Plural*, trans. Robert D. Richardson and Anne
    E. O'Byrne (Stanford, CA: Stanford University Press, 2000), 185.
47 On "connection" to others "*despite* differences" and Appiah's cosmopolitan
    ethics, see his *Cosmopolitanism: Ethics in a World of Strangers* (New York:
    W. W. Norton, 2006), 135; for Habermas, see his book *The Inclusion of the
    Other: Studies in Political Theory*, ed. Ciaran Cronin and Pablo De Greiff
    (Cambridge, MA: MIT Press, 1999), xxxvi; on the "space of difference"
    as "groundless ground," the reader should consult Scott Lash's *Another
    Modernity: A Different Rationality* (Oxford: Blackwell, 1999), 11.
48 Maurice Blanchot, *The Unavowable Community*, trans. Pierre Joris
    (Barrytown, NY: Station Hill Press, 1988), 12. Jean-Luc Nancy follows
    Blanchot in *The Inoperative Community*, ed. Peter Conor, trans. Peter Conor,
    Lisa Garbus, Michael Holland, and Simona Sawhney, foreword by Christopher
    Fynsk (Minneapolis: University of Minnesota Press, 1991).
49 We allude here to Charles Taylor's "The Politics of Recognition," for which see
    Charles Taylor, *Multiculturalism: Examining the Politics of Recognition*, with
    commentary by K. Anthony Appiah, Jürgen Habermas, Steven C. Rockefeller,
    Michael Walzer, and Susan Wolf, ed. and intro. Amy Gutmann (Princeton,
    NJ: Princeton University Press, 1994), 28. Also see a class-oriented revisiting

of Taylor's basic concept in Nancy Fraser's article "Rethinking Recognition," *New Left Review* 3 (2000): 107–20.

50 Timothy J. Reiss, *Against Autonomy: Global Dialectics of Cultural Exchange* (Stanford, CA: Stanford University Press, 2002), 67, 73.

51 Charles Taylor, *The Ethics of Authenticity* (Cambridge, MA: Harvard University Press, 1992), 91; James Clifford, *The Predicament of Culture: Twentieth-Century Ethnography, Literature, and Art* (Cambridge, MA: Harvard University Press, 1988), 12.

52 Paul Gilroy, *Against Race: Imagining Political Culture Beyond the Color Line* (Cambridge, MA: The Belknap Press of Harvard University Press, 2000), 275.

53 Emmanuel Levinas, *Proper Names*, trans. Michael B. Smith (Stanford, CA: Stanford University Press, 1996), 5.

54 On the other as "primordial," see Wolfgang Iser, "Coda to the Discussion," in *The Translatability of Cultures: Figurations of the Space Between*, ed. Sanford Budick and Wolfgang Iser (Stanford, CA: Stanford University Press, 1996), 298.

55 Michel de Certeau, *Culture in the Plural*, ed. and intro. Luce Giard, trans. and afterword Tom Conley (Minneapolis: University of Minnesota Press, 1997).

56 Lou Freitas Caton, *Reading American Novels and Multicultural Aesthetics: Romancing the Postmodern Novel* (New York: Palgrave Macmillan, 2008), 39. Mark Taylor discusses the "self-transforming" impact of the relation with an other in "Paralectics." See Robert P. Scharlemann, ed., *On the Other: Dialogue and/or Dialectics; Mark Taylor's "Paralectics,"* with Roy Wagner, Michael Brint, and Richard Rorty (Lanham, MD: University Press of America, 1991), 17.

57 Homi Bhabha, "The World and the Home," in *Dangerous Liaisons: Gender, Nation, and Postcolonial Perspectives*, ed. Anne McClintock, Aamir Mufti, and Ella Shohat (Minneapolis: University of Minnesota Press, 1997), 454.

58 Nancy, *Being Singular Plural*, 185.

59 Jean-Luc Nancy, *La création du monde ou la mondialisation* (Paris: Galilée, 2002), 58, 72; on a radically different singularity notion, which we do not endorse, see Fredric Jameson, "The Aesthetic of Singularity," *New Left Review* 92 (March–April 2015): 101–32.

60 For a rebuttal of Alain Badiou's "rejection of difference" and of the ethics rooted in Badiou's concept, see Shu-Mei Shih's essay "Global Literature and the Technologies of Recognition," *PMLA* 119, no. 1 (January 2004): 27–9. On Masao Miyoshi and "the problem with the logic of difference," see his article "Turn to the Planet: Literature, Diversity, Totality," *Comparative Literature* 55, no. 4 (Fall 2001): 294–6.

61 Emmanuel Levinas, "Ideology and Idealism," in *The Levinas Reader*, ed. Seán Hand (Oxford: Oxford University Press, 1989), 244.

62 Jean-Luc Nancy, *The Sense of the World*, trans. and foreword Jeffrey S. Librett (Minneapolis: University of Minnesota Press, 1997), 9.

63 Nancy, *The Sense of the World*, 9.

64 Derrida, *On Touching*, 54.

PART ONE

Aesthetics

1

CONSTRUCTALISM:
Literary Evolution as Multiscalar Design

Teodora Dumitru

In what follows, I take several steps toward a transdisciplinary and transsystemic approach to literary and critical-theoretical practices by drawing on the constructal theory physicist Adrian Bejan has formulated chiefly in his 2012 book *Design in Nature*. By virtue of its unifying power as a "primordial principle," Bejan's scientific theoretical model sets out to integrate the dynamics of living and nonliving systems from a perspective that takes its cue from thermodynamics while diverging from other "holistic" paradigms, be they classical systems theory similar to that of Ludwig von Bertalanffy or those of the more recent "network" type. I argue that, still untapped by literary and cultural theorists, constructalism may offer at this stage in critical theory history solutions superior to other scientifically minded theoretical ventures and thus overcome the epistemological polarities that usually accompany the importation of scientific modes of analysis into research taking place outside the traditional purview of sciences. In that sense, what I do here is assess the possibility of introducing constructalism into literary and cultural studies. To that effect, I will run a test of sorts, consisting in "constructalizing" some theoretical scenarios from literary scholarship and in evaluating the critical benefits accrued through this operation. The focus of this experiment is Franco Moretti's work, in particular his influential 2005 book *Graphs, Maps, Trees: Abstract Models for Literary History*.

The first two sections of my contribution turn to the basics of constructalism, which have to do with mechanics and thermodynamics.

Admittedly on the technical and "dense" side, this lays the groundwork for the remainder of the chapter. As I show there, constructal theory may prove capable of eliminating a series of rigid oppositions encountered in literary-cultural interpretation, most of which are derived from the nature/culture antinomy and its variations implicating predominantly Marxist determinism, the evolutionism of Charles Darwin and its descendants, as well as the theories of emergence and their emphasis on the geometric engendering of all reality, to list but a few. This "constructalist deconstruction," I suggest, is useful not only for revisiting Morettian analysis. More generally, and more significantly still, it can also participate in the ongoing, post-anthropocentrist and post-aesthetic *re*construction of modern aesthetics, which has been indebted to a humanism excessively anchored in the abovementioned nature-culture binary and, subsequently, in a mimetic philosophy of art.

A Scientific Model for Literary Studies

As is well known, modern literary theory, history, and criticism have attempted repeatedly to incorporate scientific concepts. The transfer of analytic models from sciences into literary research has been going on for roughly two centuries. It was, essentially, with Auguste Comte's positivist sociology and Jean-Baptiste Lamarck's, Herbert Spencer's, and Darwin's evolutionism that the sciences of life started joining or influencing theories of Hippolyte Taine, Ferdinand Brunetière, and other critics. By adopting such approaches, criticism and literary history began to represent literature as less idealistically and anthropocentrically grounded and, instead, more and more realistically and materially oriented, increasingly resembling scientific thinking, and moving away from the theological and the metaphysical. The classical "anthropomorphization" of nature was thus gradually replaced by the "naturalization" of humankind and human creations, and so, from *ancilla philosophiae*, literary scholarship became *ancilla scientiae*, a true knowledge form connected to the epoch's scientific advancements. Thus, criticism and literary history entered relatively easily into dialogue with biological, economic, and sociological theories, and, although more difficult to handle, mathematics, physics, and their theoretical applications such as chaos theory (Henri Poincaré, Edward Lorenz), the theory of relativity (Albert Einstein), the principle of uncertainty (Werner Heisenberg), catastrophe theory (René Thom), and the geometry of fractals (Benoît Mandelbrot) were, one after another, drawn into the orbit of literary studies as well. Thermodynamics would not remain an exception either, given that energetism has influenced not only Freudian psychoanalysis but also symbolism theories. Likewise, entropy has also made quite a career in postmodernism and posthumanism. Under these circumstances, if I pick out a model from the sciences—and one from a *hard* science such as physics to boot—so as to broaden the range of theoretical options with innovative potential in literary investigations, I do so, first and foremost, to provide the latter with a more realistic grounding, in Karl R. Popper and Steven Weinberg's tradition of overcoming various anthropocentric and relativist philosophies. For, by reducing knowledge to the incommensurable and infinitely subjective parameters of the sociohuman, these philosophies have often led to unproductive disciplinary isolationism, one that has been hostile to projects of objective unification of knowledge across disciplinary domains. And so the questions are: can one hope that the "post" moment in critical theory will overcome this isolationism? Should this happen, how might the constructalist paradigm be instrumental to this process?

To answer, I would like to point out that, in opposition to theories that cast haphazard and unpredictability as leading characters in physics, chemistry, and biology, constructalism affirms, through its *constructal principle* or *law*, the need for a heightened and steady efficiency of flow, movement, and transmission of matter and information across the terrestrial ecosystem. Once achieved, this improvement is likely to forge in a number of fields, including the arts, and at all levels of the world's "existents," a hierarchical multiscale design that, when seen from above, looks like a multiple overlay of tree-shaped flows with a network appearance. According to Bejan, this complex design is non-random, deductible, and predictable at all echelons of existence. The action of the constructal law is empirically evident in the plethora of designs with arborescent, divergent, or convergent patterns one comes across in the world. The shape of a thunderbolt in the sky, the forms of trees and river basins, the structures of respiratory, circulatory, and nervous systems, the architecture of an airport, the spatial configuration of urban traffic, and, in classical artifacts, the formal plays of the "divine" ratios derived from the "golden number" are only a few illustrations of such energy-, matter-, and life-molding circulation. An innovative insight of constructalism is, in fact, that life is born not with the first forms of organic matter, as biologists believe, but with *movement* in the inorganic world.

Now, if in the nineteenth century, biologists took the first step toward understanding the living as a unit by discovering that plant and animal cells had similar structures, and the advances in genetics made it more pertinent to speak, *à la* François Jacob, of a *"logique du vivant,"* physicists were even more forward-looking. In his 1917 *On Growth and Form*, D'Arcy Wentworth Thompson attempted, without buying into the theory of natural selection, a conceptual unification of the living and non-living by positing that the morphology of the organic world is ruled by the laws of mechanics. Bejan's contribution aligns itself with this view. In effect, he reopens the discussion around Darwin's evolutionism along the lines of Thompson's hypotheses. Yet constructalism "subsumes" both Darwinism and Thompson's theory to a scientific model that preserves the explanatory force of both—Bejan shows that "selected" (Darwin's term) are biological mechanisms that more effectively fit the laws of physics (Thompson) in a complex, long-term process called evolution.[1] Thus, constructal thinking leaves behind not only the theories based on the living/nonliving binary but also, within the living, the scenarios informed by the culture/nature dyad. Either by reducing the natural to the human or by rejecting the possibility of a realistic-objective cognition, constructal theory denounces anthropocentrism and relativism. If, to a relativist, science and, moreover, nature itself are "social constructs," Bejan sees things from a diametrically opposed angle. To him, the sciences, technology, the arts, and culture overall are nature and therefore operate *under the same laws as those governing nonhuman existents*. The constructal image of overlapping, network-like arborescent structures unfolding entire tapestries of divergences and convergences may thus reconcile the philosophers of the living—anthropologists, biologists, and theorists of culture—with physicists and with their discipline, which is conventionally understood as a science of the non-living.

On account of this revision, constructalism is well positioned to contribute to the post-anthropocentric turn affecting contemporary epistemology across a range of disciplines, including the study of literature. The premise of Bejan's joining this broad conceptual reform is in place. Sociology and neuroaesthetics have already come into contact with his writings,[2] and studies currently limited to introducing the thermodynamic model of entropy to information theory, neurobiology, and related disciplines are, in my view, highly compatible with the relaunch of knowledge pursuits on constructalist bases.[3] So is, I might add, research showing that thinking, language, and even music—until recently deemed the exclusive privilege of the human— also exist within the nonhuman realm.[4] Consequently, constructalism makes available theoretical tools in line with the realistic approach to literary research endorsed by my intervention. At the same time, constructal philosophy also argues for the overcoming of the anthropocentric sway over modern aesthetics. On this particular ground, the nature of literature and its forms—genres, processes, canons, and the like—could be seen as similar to the nature or "essence" of knowledge in general, which in turn could be viewed as consistent with the natural world's overall non-teleological evolution, that is, one geared toward a certain preestablished finality. Whether divergent or convergent depending on context, literature and literary theory can thus be approached in a novel way, namely, as *flow*—flow of information, of course, but shaping other kinds of material as well and following the same rigor of streamlined movement present everywhere in nature.

Multiscalar Architectures and Their Logic

The constructal law states that "for a finite-size flow system to persist in time (to live), its configuration must evolve in such a way that provides easier access to the currents that flow through it."[5] A major principle of physics, according to Bejan, this law regulates any matter-moving "flow system" on Earth, from inorganic to organic structures and from nonhuman to human-made designs. A flow system—viz., the matter to be carried *plus* the configuration or design obtaining through this transportation—can be recognized by its *predominantly arborescent shape*, specifically, by a certain well-proportioned ratio among the different dimensions of the channels involved. Technically speaking, the constructal law is a relationship between "engines" and "brakes," one by which useful energy converts into mechanical work, an efficient flow design enabling "more work for less useful energy."[6] Required by the second principle of thermodymanics, the natural tendency of systems toward balance triggers, further, a variety of *two-stroke movements*: one at low speed on short and overall small segments, and the other at fast speed on long, large stretches. This explains the multibranch appearance of flow systems. For example, the best possible irrigation of a surface or volume calls for both large-scale pipes and canals or capillaries; just capillaries or just long pipes would not cover the space in question as effectively as possible. Yet not any combination of "small-short-slow" and "large-long-fast" structures ensures the success of the movement; what is needed, from a quantitative viewpoint, is the quasi equality between the two categories. As Bejan and Zane insist, "The time to move fast and long should be roughly equal to the time to move slow and short."[7] The variation in the size of flow channels is then connected to the idea of pulsation or rhythm. The flow system gives rise to contrasts—ramifications, waves, regularities, wing strokes, etc.—to manage more efficiently the resistances it encounters, whereas the ramification or the rhythm indicates an attempt to distribute the matter as evenly as possible and to smooth out the system's flaws.[8] The struggle against forces of resistance yields divergences, separations, or, conversely, convergences and multidimensional channel unifications. The latter bring about over time increasingly complex structures that Bejan calls "multiscale designs,"[9] which occur on all planes of existence so that the map of the inorganic, organic, or sociocultural world looks like an inextricable overlapping of ramifications undergoing incessant transformation.

The thesis of superimposed tree-shaped flows is Bejan's stepping-stone to an alternative to network theory. Thus, he denies the existence of grid-like flow systems featuring equal-size links or holes. He recognizes, instead, structures that may look like networks but are in reality "superpositions of trees" and involve dimensional discrepancies that otherwise reflect certain proportions.[10] Compared to the elementary, single-segment form of motion, the equivalent two-stroke movement marks a qualitative leap, since rapid flow over long distances occurs *after* slow flow across short intervals. Efficiency increase is then a complexity effect according to which the broader the scale and scalar impact overall, the greater the efficiency of a system that, Bejan asserts, is improvable but never optimal. Therefore, according to the constructal law, the evolution from simple to complex has a deterministic, predictable, and progressist aspect to it—for, after all, progress means greater efficiency—but not a teleological character. Evolution has a sense but no purpose, and this concerns the living, whose development across time is a particular case of evolution.

In this context, one theory affected by the constructal law is that of natural selection. Constructalism does share with Darwinism the repudiation of teleology, but, unlike Bejan, Darwin refutes any determinism of evolution other than natural selection, nor does he conceive of evolution as a leap from inferior to superior. According to Darwin, biological variations occur randomly, and only those capable of adaptation survive; and yet, again, in his view, adaptation does not equate to progress. Also, Darwin dismisses any scenario capable of predicting the evolution of the living. Bejan shows, instead, that there exists an evolution vector in the world of the living, too, and that that evolutionary element depends on a general rule that favors the most effective circulation of matter and information possible, which rule, *qua* rule, defies randomness and proves, for instance, that the history of animal movement and the corresponding anatomic adjustments of various species from swimming and crawling to the bipedal walk characteristic to humans were neither haphazard nor unpredictable. Notably, this is not an anthropocentric argument, for it does not view human morphology as an *optimum* of evolution but as a situation *in progress*. It is along the same lines that Bejan views the developmental direction toward *complex*, *large*, and *powerful* as a necessary and foreseeable tendency underpinning everything that exists, including the universe of the living.[11] Vaster and more intricate structures, he offers, are more economic and better performing than simple structures, and the transition from the latter to the former, he also says, is an evolutionary thrust reigning supreme all over the animate and inanimate world. Thus, drawing from physics, Bejan proposes an important correction, more effective than Thompson's—which, quite wrongly, did not accept natural selection—to Darwinist theory.

The reliance on a physics principle valid at all levels of the living and non-living makes constructalism look with suspicion on theories of emergence also. Arising almost simultaneously in 1970s physics and biology and well synthesized by the title of Philip W. Anderson's 1972 article "More Is Different," theories of emergence claim that, as a general phenomenon, evolution can be neither traced nor predicted on the basis of principles whose nature is purportedly elucidated by elementary particle physics, as Weinberg, Stephen Hawking, and others believe.[12] One cannot deal with evolution this way, we are told, because more laws come into being unexpectedly with each new level of complexity of the world, and also because they are irreducible to a set of laws valid for all such levels. As long as they reject the guidance of the deductive-predictive principles of hard sciences in the chance-friendly line of Darwinism, both bio-philosophies (which distinguish the evolution of the living from that of the inorganic) and the philosophies of culture (which treat the evolution of humankind and human offshoots such as technology, culture, and literature as unique phenomena) become illustrations of emergentist thought. Under such circumstances, challenging as it does the notion of aleatory evolution and the separation of principles governing over the ranks of the existent, constructalism is rather a type of reductionism, one applying itself to the world that is observable with the naked eye. Further, constructalism is the basis on which Bejan criticizes works such as Richard Dawkins's 1986 *Blind Watchmaker* and Stephen Jay Gould's 1989 *Wonderful Life*, books that emphasize the unpredictability of the evolution of life. A result of a development understood as flow efficiency, multiscale designs implicitly evolve a hierarchical structure where various ratios of "long"/"large" and "short"/"small" combine with varying proportions between "many" and "few," so that *more* small channels, through which flow is slow, and *fewer* large channels of high-velocity flow are key to a growingly efficient movement of matter across all terrestrial systems (more capillaries and fewer large-diameter vessels in bodies; narrower and shorter streets and fewer boulevards in cities; more lower-ranking employees and fewer bosses in a business, etc.).

Bejan is keen on translating this multiscale hierarchy—the "cornerstone" of natural design[13]—into "interconnectedness," "interdependence," and other language describing how small-and-many and large-and-few entities work together to assist movement.[14] Not only do the small and the large and the slow and the fast coexist and team up, but "primitive" forms also find themselves alongside newer structures as long as the old design still does its job. Through this collaboration thesis, constructalism endeavors to reform the Malthusian residues of Darwinism as well as egalitarian ideologies such as Marxism, which Bejan identifies with the totalitarianism of the former Soviet Bloc and brushes aside as a rigid, inefficient system. On the other hand, the anti-Marxist stance of Communist Romania-born American academic makes constructal theory look, when applied to socioeconomic issues, like another philosophical spinoff of Western neoliberalism. This impression has been borne out by Bejan's insistence on the hierarchy and collaboration between the few-large and the many-small entities, which easily can be read as an endorsement of inequality, conservative policies, and the like. The parallel between socioeconomic stratification and "natural hierarchy," however, is debatable, for Bejan declines to work with the "few-rich" versus "many-poor" correlative dyads—which, in his opinion, have been tainted by various "practitioners of the politics of envy," namely, by the Left—and puts forth instead euphemistically designated and ideologically suspicious solutions such as the opposition between "leaders" and "trailers."[15] On this score, too, constructalism parts company with Marxism. Where Bejan translates the relationship between "small" and "large" into "collaboration," Karl Marx sees "exploitation" or "dialectical contradiction." It bears noting, nevertheless, that, insofar as they both approach natural evolution deterministically, by pulling it from the domain of arbitrariness and unifying the living and the non-living under the auspices of similar principles such as movement or dialectics, constructalism and Marxism (especially through its philosophical core, dialectical materialism) are not wholly incompatible.

To sum it all up: two-stroke, equivalent flow types, multiscale designs, hierarchy, collaboration, complexity, efficiency. This is evolution in constructal terms. Physics can account for, and anticipate, the evolutionary path of the non-living but also of life itself, of human society, and of artifacts such as technology, the arts, and culture at large. These, Bejan contends, as Weinberg also would, are not just "copies" of a *modus operandi* of nature but a true modality in which the natural order manifests itself—in both thinkers, beauty does not imitate nature; beauty *is* nature.[16] Bejan suggests, accordingly, that the dynamics of symbolic products, literature included, is no more than the constructal law in action. Whether the literary text itself makes for an object to be looked at through the constructal lens or not is an issue whose discussion has been made possible by Bejan's trailblazing work. Otherwise, scholarly genres such as literary history, criticism, and theory have always had clear potential in this direction. Thus, some theorists seem to view literature and culture as a tapestry of multiscale designs, while others have launched entire theories that, in hindsight, constructalism could engage with, refute, or radically revamp. For instance, the rhizome Gilles Deleuze and Félix Guattari famously talk about in their 1980 book *A Thousand Plateaus*, a trope still front and center to debates in network theory, could be revised *via* constructalism by doing away with the antinomy between root structures and rhizome structures and by conceptualizing the rhizomatic as part of a flow system. Similarly, the arguments of works drawing on the network concept in literary and media studies, such as Caroline Levine's 2015 *Forms: Whole, Rhythm, Hierarchy, Network* and Patrick Jagoda's 2016 *Network Aesthetics*, could be reframed theoretically by turning to notions of multiscale design and superimposed tree-shaped flows. A most relevant illustration of how literary studies might be cross-pollinated productively by scientific models in which distinctions such as living/non-living and culture/nature fall by the wayside would be, however, what I have called "constructalist deconstruction," one brought to bear, below, specifically on the theoretical scenario of Moretti's *Graphs*.

The scientific claims orienting most of Moretti's work, coupled with ambitious objectives in whose pursuit his brand of criticism strives to come closer to hard sciences, render him a prime candidate for a constructalist makeover. A prominent representative of the so-called "knowledge turn" in the Western humanities, Moretti explored, as early as in the 1980s, the possibility, via Popper, of a "'falsifiable' criticism"[17] and later on tried to overthrow an entire Diltheyan tradition in literary studies by calling on scholars to favor explanation over understanding and interpretation.[18]

Along the same lines, noteworthy is that theoretical models from world-systems analysis and World Literature to post-anthropocentric aesthetics, which are currently enjoying a wide appeal and are also highly compatible with a constructal view of the world, either got their impetus from Moretti or found in his books a firm point of convergence. His description of the novel's historical development in mechanical terms such as "acceleration" and "narrative flow," for instance, may remind one of Bejan's theses on the birth of design. Likewise, Moretti's work on literary forms (genres, species, and typologies) speaks to his passion for configurations, which is, one might say, also the driving force of any constructalist propinquities. Then, how about "distant reading" as a telescope or, more broadly, lens through which one might make out multiscale literary designs? In any event, his contributions have been extensively scrutinized, and so my aim here is not another assessment or critique. What I want to do, instead, is to work through some of the tensions, antinomies, and conceptual impasses still marking, I would contend, his oeuvre and possibly "solve" them or, better yet, integrate them into a constructalist solution to problems that, in Moretti, are, in my estimation, left unsolved.[19]

"Constructalizing" Moretti: Marxism, Darwinism, and Beyond

In *Graphs*, Moretti declares that dialectical materialism alone strikes him as unable to come to grips with the complexities of literature.[20] Stemming from his doubts about the explanatory power of a materialist notion of literary form, the book's theoretical eclecticism chimes with constructalism's. Attracted by combinations of philosophies and vocabularies that, heterogenous as they may strike us, are those constructalism is keen on questioning, Moretti prepares, in a spirit that itself might be called constructalist, an original cocktail of methods and solutions. Thus, *Graphs* weaves together not only Marxist materialism, which, as is well known, reestablished determinism's place in the history of ideas, and Darwinism, in which natural selection figures as *the* deterministic force in the evolution of the living, but also theories of emergence, even though they are in principle hostile to determinism. Along with what I label, for lack of a better word, "latent constructalism," these are the main four Morettian theoretical "models" or zones that I propose to remap below with an eye to either uncovering constructalist concerns, perspectives, and conceptual instruments that are already there but not visible enough or showing how they could be injected into those intellectual spaces and what the benefits of such "constructalization" might be.

 i. The Marxist Model. Descending from the tradition of Italian Marxism, Moretti is, unsurprisingly, particularly keen on the "sociology of literary forms," a phrase that went into the subtitle of his 1983 book *Signs Taken for Wonders*. However, in some of his Marxist analyses, Moretti's thinking runs on constructalist tracks while displaying no direct familiarity with Bejan's work, let alone any intention to follow it (one should remember, however, that, prior to 2012, when Bejan's more popular books started coming out, his scholarship had addressed primarily specialists). A chapter of *Graphs*, "Maps," for example, is the theater of a spectacular crossing between a quasi-constructalist vision and a conceptual scaffolding of Marxist type, and this intersection is all the more interesting since Bejan's position is *a priori* hostile to Marxism. Starting with the analysis of some West European "village narratives" from the first half of the nineteenth century, such as Mary Mitford's *Our Village* (1824–32), John Galt's *Annals of the Parish* (1821), and Berthold Auerbach's *Black Forest Village Stories* (1843–53), "Maps" relies on a deterministic approach that, in the footsteps of Marx and, subsequently, Taine, strives to draw up "[a] map of ideology emerging from a map of *mentalité*, emerging[, that is,] from the material substratum of the physical territory."[21] The basis determines the superstructure. Here is, apparently, one might conclude, a classical sample of sociology of literature, an undertaking presuming to capture, via fiction, the evolution of the relationship between urban and rural areas in German and English spaces at a given time.

The essay offers much more, though. Morettian literary cartography leans on Walther Christaller's 1933 study *Central Places in Southern Germany*, which unearths an "ordering principle heretofore unrecognized": "towns provide specialized services ... which in order to reach as many customers as possible are located in 'a few necessarily central points, to be consumed at many scattered points.' The more specialized a service is, the more 'central' it also is, and on this socio-geometrical principle arises the urban hierarchy."[22] This "ordering principle," which calls for a few major centers and numerous points of lower rank, down to the level of private residences, and also Christaller's "Central Places" figure, reproduced by Moretti, would get the attention of any reader of Bejan. The figure in question does not illustrate just a "spatial division of labor," as Moretti says, but also a type of architecture recognizable even at a nonhuman level such as the structure of a forest. Thus, the "ordering principle" invoked here is arguably the constructal law complete with its multiscale design and hierarchy-generating flows: a few large and long channels prompting rapid movement (in large centers or cities and other areas of dense informational and material traffic and of services as specialized as possible) plus a higher number of small and short channels constituting the slow segment (micro-centers, villages, peripheries, and commercial areas where shops and businesses are less specialized).

Inserting Christaller's "ordering principle" into a sociology of literature favorable to a deterministic-Marxist approach, Moretti actually lays down the premises of a dialogue between constructalism and Marxism. Thus, the map of centers large (few) and small (many) is a "social geography" but can also be a way of charting the antagonisms between the "'rough circle' of work" and the "ring of pleasure," between the big-[and]-few, i.e., *the rich*, leisure cruises, and other "frivolous superfluities," on one hand, and the small-[and]-many, i.e., *the poor*, "material labour," and "serious daily needs," on the other.[23] If one entertains the notion that *work* lives its fluid life on little arteries and back roads with access only to bare necessities, and the *loisir* revels, to the contrary, in the luxury supplied by the broad avenues of the center, the aortas of great capital, then one may very well conclude that "Maps" creates the conditions for rereading Bejan through Marx—and eventually Moretti through Bejan—so that "small" can finally be equated with *poverty* and "large" with *wealth*. If, in Moretti, it is sociopolitical processes that rule over the reconfiguration of societal and literary forms ("rural class struggle, the industrial takeoff, and the process of state formation"[24]), those shaping forces are, according to Bejan, in turn subordinated to ampler mechanisms and their own law, which stipulates that both social groups and society as a whole "move" by following the logic of a flow system. Therefore, the intricate social design and, with it, the conditions for class struggle are all offshoots of the diversification of flows, viz., of the transition from slow to fast moving types, when villages or urban peripheries become capillaries that *lead to* the products of the center and *toward which* such products flow. As long as they remain outside the processes of "nation centralization" or industrialization, the village narratives of "Maps" instantiate the slow and short flow typical of countryside trails and a capitalism still in its infancy. Instead, the turbulent, multibranched flow generated by various industrial, commercial, and other kinds of traffics marks capitalism in its full force, namely, the streamlining of movement in time and space as socioeconomic architecture becomes broader and more complex, regardless of whether the relations between the actors involved are of "collaboration" or "exploitation"—this is the deterministic narrative capturing the logic of flows away from local to national and international. This is also how the conceptual apparatus of "Maps"' Marxist reasoning could be reconstructed or, better yet, "constructalized." Vice versa, the core constructal principle could be revisited from a Marxist standpoint so as to sound something like this: the masses move from the self-sufficient rural to social consciousness and thus to the wider berths to which historical necessity carries them. The railroad as access to class struggle—this would be, in this case, the constructal law as formulated by a Marxist with an assist from Moretti.

ii. The Darwinist Model. The image of the tree that illustrates the evolution of species by selecting divergent characters in *The Origin of Species* is deployed in the homonymous "Trees" chapter of *Graphs* to support a set of hypotheses about the development of a literary genre—the

English detective novel at the end of the nineteenth century as instantiated chiefly by Arthur Conan Doyle and his competition. As Moretti writes, "evolutionary trees constitute *morphological* diagrams, where history is systematically correlated with form."[25] Gould, whose 2002 *The Structure of Evolutionary Theory* Moretti quotes, foregrounds in the Darwinian tree not the branching-offs but the extremes, to wit, nature's preference for the most divergent types. This reading of Darwin helps Moretti make a case for a similarly divergence-based historical trajectory of languages and "literary forms."[26] Relying on Darwin and Gould, Moretti thus works out a whole theory of "extinction" of works and genres, stressing that evolutionary processes retain just a few of them.[27] His position is that, as a fundamental law of the living, selection also operates in the sphere of literature, where it depends on "form."[28] His handling of literary developments as a subset of the living's evolution rather than as one of the latter's quasi-autonomous *levels* and requiring judgment criteria of its own is typically Darwinist.

All the same, it bears asking, how might a constructalist appropriate Moretti's argument? He or she would probably say that, to be more efficient, flows must occur in two equivalent times. Thus, our constructalist critic would insist on the primacy of branching structures and implicitly on bifurcation as the basic sort of branching-off, the premise here being that flow's pushing against various resistance forces leads to ramifications, be they divergent or convergent, as well as to separations or mergings of channels. Further, if it fell on a theorist such as Bejan, rather than Gould, to draw on the epistemological trope of the Darwinian tree, he might argue something like this: the structurally divergent appearance of character types is real and matters, but it is only an *effect* of branching-off, namely, of another reality, which tells us that selection boils down essentially to a branching-off movement, and that, accordingly, bundles of ramifications engender over time a multiscale design. The image of the literary forms that "don't just 'change,' but change by always *diverging* from each other," while very close to that of a tree, as well as of the configuration of an organ's blood vessels, is an eminently constructalist image. The growth of such forms from a common ancestor through differentiation of characteristics can, therefore, be reconsidered constructally: it is the particular arrangement of channels that, under certain circumstances, improves the transmission of genetic information.[29]

The logic of symbolic information's circulation is no different. Building on constructalism's forays into linguistics, Bejan shows that the birth of the alphabet and *lingua franca*—both design types that enable communication by unifying and simplifying previous procedures of verbal exchange—attests to the action of the constructal law also at the level of symbolic practices.[30] And yet, one wonders, does the evolution of languages and literatures occur by increasing dissimilitude, as Moretti thinks in following Darwin, or, rather, by convergence such as in the alphabet and *lingua franca*? The constructalist would likely answer that evolutionary trajectories are a function of the particularities of the environment, given that the constructal principle governs both converging and divergent flows as, for example, in a river basin or in the vascularization of an organ, respectively. If, in the evolution of living organisms, divergence occurs in the context of isolated ecosystems, convergence takes place where there are no obstacles to communication, as Darwin realized when he discovered that, depending on the degree of isolation of the areas where they had been evolving, species can become quite different from one another. Therefore, one can claim neither that divergent movements are *a priori* superior to convergence phenomena as far as efficiency goes nor that these two categories are at variance as structures geared to distinct aims that would set the evolution of the living apart from that of symbolic artifacts. All these movements embody, simply speaking, various degrees of adequacy of the flow as a whole to the specifics of the environment.

If this is true, then we would have to reopen other previous Morettian cases, such as the distinction Moretti draws in his 2000 article "Conjectures on World Literature" between the "tree" model marked by a divergent, discontinuous stream characteristic of the gushing forth of the literature of a nation-state and the "wave" model, a convergent and ongoing flow befitting a transnational paradigm such as World Literature.[31] Notably, Bejan's integrative—rather than disjunctive—outlook would of necessity rule out the hypothesis of a radical difference ("absolutely nothing in common"! exclaims Moretti) between "tree" as flux of the national and "wave" as flux of the global.[32] In the same view, the two models would appear as flows of different sorts, and yet not as antinomies; they would be in fact indicative of a "consensual" movement quite literally, in that they move in the same direction, driven by the ontological imperative of a more efficient circulation of matter on Earth.

iii. The Emergentist Model. Although Moretti maintains that "maps … will possess 'emerging' qualities, which were not visible at the lower level," in "Trees"—rather than in "Maps"—he comes significantly closer to an emergentist take on literature.[33] There are, emergence thinkers maintain, no fundamental laws that would make up a red thread running through the world of the living and non-living from the simplest to the most complex forms. The existent, they believe, is subject to different rules at different levels of complexity, which are thus achieved unpredictably, in a way that renders forecasts and deterministic calculations fallacious and makes room for happenstance. When he invokes positions that dissociate the trajectory of the living from that of the non-living or accentuate the exceptional nature of the evolution of the human within the former, Moretti opens widely the gate to emergentism. Accordingly, on one hand, he approaches the rise and spread of literature just as emergence biologists would the birth and blossoming of life, that is, without any deterministic presumptions, and so notions of genre and World Literature look in "Trees" like emerging life forms, which Moretti describes by leaning on Ernst Mayr, a prominent advocate of emergence in biology. On the other hand, Moretti—ever the eclectic—throws into the mix references to scholars who have distinguished the general evolution of organic matter (a process achieved through the diversifying of biological characteristics) from the technical and cultural evolution specific only to the human and accomplished rather by convergence phenomena such as amalgamation, syncretism, and the like. He finds in Alfred Kroeber's 1963 *Anthropology*, in George Basalla's 1989 *The Evolution of Technology*, and in Gould's 1996 *Full House* support for his own reservations about the Darwinian tree, which, he suspects, accurately as it may capture the evolution of natural life, does little justice to cultural developments.

What really concerns Moretti here, though, is how literature should be viewed as language "technology." Does literature evolve according to a logic of diversification, as Darwin claims that life itself does? Or, to the contrary, are literatures defined by a convergent evolution, as anthropologists deem typical of technoculture? Moretti frames this dilemma in a way reminiscent of Hegelian dialectics. "Divergence," he remarks, "prepares the ground for convergence, which unleashes further divergence—this seems to be the typical pattern."[34] Nevertheless, at this point literature remains typologically indeterminate. So, once again, what kind of clarifications can constructal theory bring to the table? More precisely, how would constructalism react to emergentist attempts to approach literature? To respond, it would help to remember that, to a constructalist philosopher, technology, language, and culture are *nature*, much like the rest of the organic and inorganic universe—they are all governed by the same basic principles. The "Trees'" indecision between seemingly antinomic models—divergence in the evolution of the living as understood by Darwinist tradition, on one side, and convergence in the development of culture and technology, on the other—can thus be overcome with help from constructalism and integrated into a new conceptual apparatus. In my assessment, this would be superior to the rationale underwriting the traditional split between the principles of the non-living and living, a rationale not only stemming from, and ostensibly biased toward, the latter but also bespeaking an eminently anthropocentric vision meant to showcase, excessively and dysfunctionally, the "singularity" of humankind and its creations. At any rate, as soon as technology, culture, as well as living and nonliving organisms are conceived of as nature developing according to the same laws of physics, the theoretical disagreements subside. The constructalist image of the overlapping trees that look like networks and tapestries of divergences and convergences is the solution to the predicament Moretti has reached in following not only Darwin but also scholars such as Kroeber and Basalla. This is the compromise that reconciles anthropologists and the philosophers of culture with biologists, and all of them with scientists in disciplines studying the inorganic, insofar as they all agree that cultural evolution cannot but abide the same laws that regulate the increase in movement efficiency across nature.

iv. The "Latent" Constructalist Model. Literary genre, writes Moretti, is a structure "where flow and form meet."[35] This is just one of the numerous formulations in which the Italian critic sounds like an expert in multiscale designs. Yet Moretti inches even closer to constructalism when he discovers the work of D'Arcy Wentworth Thompson, the thinker who claimed that the evolution of life follows the principles of mechanics. The place of this theoretical rapprochement is "Maps," the *Graphs* chapter where Moretti attempts to ground his Marxist materialist approach to the relationship between "form" and "force" in the determinism of Thompson's *On Growth and Form.* In this section of his 2005 book, Moretti assigns both "social geography" and literary-aesthetic form a constitutive or ordering pattern in a way similar to how Thompson used mechanics to explain the evolution of organisms. The mere reference to Thompson in a study pursuing the transition from rural to urban and from provincial to national in the Western prose of the nineteenth century bears out Moretti's assent to the constructalist tenet according to which the phenomenology of sociocultural forms funnels down, in the final analysis, to the workings of physics laws. "Maps" even features a passage that seems written by Bejan: "for me geometry *'signifies'* more than geography. More, in the sense that a geometrical pattern is too orderly a shape to be the product of chance. It is a sign that something is at work here—that something has *made* the pattern the way it is. But what?"[36] The answer to Moretti's question is: *the constructal law.* Is this Moretti's answer too? Not quite. It is not the first time the author of *Graphs* suspects that an "ordering principle" for real and fictional geography alike is at play, but what he comes up with in "Maps" is, if not a constructalist way of solving the mystery, then something as close as possible to such a solution, namely, a notion of form—including literary form—as a Thompsonian "diagram of forces." "Deducing from the *form* of an object the forces that have been at work: this is the most elegant definition ever," thinks Moretti, "of what literary sociology should be."[37]

Among the Marxist, Darwinist, and emergentist models, all of them variously consequential for Moretti's literary-historical project, Thompson's work is the pinnacle of the theoretical pyramid, as it were, pointing directly as it does to the constructal law. The latter dwarfs and, theoretically speaking, subsumes all the other influences, at the same time boosting their epistemological thrust. According to this law, while evolution works through selection, haphazard, which cannot be ruled out either, is controlled by and subordinated to a primary principle of physics in turn operating in the sphere of the living and non-living alike, an ontological gamut whose extent Thompson himself, truth be told, did not suspect. Looking out from the Thompsonian summit, Moretti may then see in the distance a way of handling his conundrum—determinism, selection, or emergence?—by surmounting the shortcomings of old approaches as well as the latter's incongruent mix. This may well be the constructalist way. In building new arguments for a unifying understanding of the living and the non-living, constructalism could assist—more efficiently than Thompson's theory—the sociology of literature, just as it would sponsor any post-anthropocentric aesthetics.

Let us not forget, though, that the "forces" Moretti takes up here are, as a Marxist would ascertain, social classes locked in struggle, premodern structures dislodged by the advance of the bourgeoisie. Along these lines, it is somewhat ironic that Moretti resorts to Thompson—a kind of historical alter ego of Bejan's—in the most Marxist essay from *Graphs*, the book chapter that addresses "the direct, almost tangible relationship between social conflict and literary form."[38] In any case, does constructalism provide better solutions than Marxism in "Maps," or than Darwinism and emergentism in "Trees"? Does it account more effectively for the literary practices analyzed by Moretti in *Graphs*? In my opinion, the answer is a qualified "yes." The deterministic analysis of socio-literary geography in "Maps" lays a fairly solid ground for a Marxist understanding of the development of social classes in Western Europe from relative rural autarchy to internationalism. What constructalism furnishes is an awareness that the social dynamics of Mitford's *Our Village*, Galt's *Annals of the Parish*, and Auerbach's *Black Forest Village Stories*, with all its geohistorical specificities, follows a general law of circulation of matter and information on Earth. The image of Paris as "a diagram of forces" in Honoré de Balzac's novels ("Balzac's divided Paris, the battlefield between old wealth and ambitious petty bourgeois youth"[39]) and in Gustave Flaubert's, as well as the configurations and reconfigurations of such forces, narrative instances, and values in writings by Daniel Defoe, George Eliot, and Henrik Ibsen—which Moretti subjects in his 2013 *The Bourgeois: Between History and Literature* to the same socio-deterministic, Marxist and neomarxist scrutiny—are too, in *Graphs*, part and parcel of the constructalist revitalization of literary sociology.

To be sure, much like chemistry and biology retain their effectiveness as sciences even without incorporating the "ultimate theory" Weinberg dreams of, the book's analytic machinery works without having reached an awareness of how it might profit from a thorough, deliberately constructionalist refurbishing. Yet, just as an ultimate theory of elementary particles covers the very foundations of traditional sciences but cannot be reduced to any of the latter, constructalism does not merely replicate "Maps"' socio-deterministic conclusions either. It is more than a theory that puts basically the same things in fancier words. It can explain, instead, this very determinism more deeply while aligning it with a range of phenomena that is far more extensive than sociologists, anthropologists, and economists thought and shows that socioeconomic design is only a subset of the *arch-design* obtaining ceaselessly in the vast process geared toward sustaining movement on the planet. Similarly, in "Trees" and "Conjectures on World Literature," too, constructalism is well positioned to help recalibrate some of our notions. Whether one thinks of them as developing alongside the living or as technologies distinct from the organic, genre and, more specifically, literary "species" such as Doyle's English detective novel or free indirect-style narrative techniques may be investigated more successfully if one views them primarily as context-dependent, efficiency-oriented models designed to pass literary information along rather than as "living" forms or artifacts. In this vein, then, the rise of free indirect style, which "Trees" and *The Bourgeois* consider a "socialization" technique and analyze in Jane Austen and other nineteenth-century Western fiction authors, could also be seen as an index of discourse mutation. The shift here is away from the slow type of information transmission characteristic of premodern cultural autarchy, of "unilinear" literatures that neither branch off nor take in tributaries, to a faster and faster type that favors a language more and more "convergent," shared by all, belonging first and foremost to the community and only then to the individual, and in which even differentiating and individualizing marks come about in response to the pressure of collective discourse. Likewise, the narratives of the national and of World Literature in "Conjectures on World Literature" would gain in critical effectiveness if one were to treat them not as antinomies having "nothing in common" but as sub-ensembles of a larger circulatory system governed throughout by one of the most important laws of physics.[40]

A *Natural* Solution for a Post-Aesthetic World

In brief, constructalism is, analytically speaking, superior to Moretti's conceptual mix. The basic rationale behind my contention rests, simply put, on Bejan's integrative, cross-systemic outlook. To my mind, this is preferable to epistemological paradigms that, grounded as they stand in disjunctive regimes of knowledge, prove at odds if not utterly incompatible with each other in various respects—*Graphs* brings together, for example, the determinism of class struggle in Marxism (dominant in "Maps") and the intra-species and *chance-friendly* competition in Darwinism (prevalent in "Trees"), and this is worth noting given that they remain hard to reconcile even in more mutually accommodating recent avatars of the two philosophies. The problematic cohabitation between, on one side, deterministic theoretical models such as sociology, Marxism, and Thompson's physics, and, on the other, evolutionary schemes such as Darwinism and emergentism, in which the unpredictable carries a lot of clout, largely accounts for the unsystematic vision, conceptual indecision, permanent dissatisfaction, and overall search for better solutions in Moretti. Instead, constructalism makes available a better way of framing, elucidating, and projecting the future of literary phenomena than Marxism and Darwinism, not to mention, again, that the explanatory purview of its postulates, whose overarching scope remains invisible to both Marxist and Darwinist enterprises, encompasses the scope of all its theoretical competitors combined, just as Einstein's work integrates Isaac Newton's and Johannes Kepler's. This is also why one profits from "constructalizing" Moretti not by revisiting his essays piece by piece but by taking them as a whole, weighing the causes and risks of his eclecticism, paying attention to when and why he turns to a certain theory, to what he seeks in it, to what he gets and what he does not get out of it, and so forth.

In all fairness, constructalism too could turn to account its encounter with literary studies, as literature and literary scholarship are, generally speaking, in position to deliver know-how to sciences also. Just as geneticists approach the universe of the living in terms used in literary, linguistic, and semiotic notions—they routinely refer to the cell's "information," "code," "language," "text," and "message," which must be "translated," etc.— constructal theory would gain, at least in its sociologically minded applications, from literary inroads such as those imagined above. As we have seen, Moretti's work proves for it an unexpectedly fruitful field of dialogue with Marxism, too summarily dismissed by Bejan as a political practice rather than as an economic doctrine. There is, I think, a substantial amount of compatibility with the latter in constructalism, which is precisely why Bejan's insights could be successfully applied to world-systems-grounded literary-cultural analysis—in this light, I might point out that a notable conclusion drawn along the lines of the constructal law is that, insofar as the energy and resources consumed by all literatures go, so-called "developed" literatures displace more mass than the "small" or "peripheral" ones. Relatedly, constructalism could rechannel the impact of network theory on literary disciplines, replacing the deceptively egalitarian network trope with the more realistic picture of overlaid trees. For, arguably, where *conveying* information as efficiently as possible is concerned, arborescence, rather than the grid, encapsulates more accurately the world-systemic geodynamic to which transnational, World Literature, big data/quantitative, and environmental studies have been attending of late. The bearings of the constructal law on design, form, and pattern across such macrosystems are incontrovertible.

Notes

1   Carl G. Hempel and Paul Oppenheim particularly use "subsumption" in their research of the logic of scientific explanation. "The explanation of a phenomenon consists ... in its subsumption under laws or under a theory," they write in "Studies in the Logic of Explanation," *Philosophy of Science*

15, no. 2 (April 1948): 152. Using the term a bit more freely, one may say that constructalism "subsumes" previous theories to a unifying theoretical framework relevant to a more extensive range of phenomena.

2   See Adrian Bejan and Gilbert W. Merkx, eds., *Constructal Theory of Social Dynamics* (New York: Springer, 2007); also see Darren Bridger, *Neuro Design* (London: Kogan Page, 2017).

3   For the application of the entropy model to psycholinguistics, see Silvia Rădulescu, Frank Wijnen, and Sergey Avrutin, "Patterns Bit by Bit: An Entropy Model for Rule Induction," *Language Learning and Development* 16, no. 2 (2020): 109–40, https://doi.org/10.1080/15475441.2019.1695620.

4   See Eduardo Kohn, *How Forests Think* (Berkeley: University of California Press, 2013).

5   Adrian Bejan and J. Peder Zane, *Design in Nature* (New York: Anchor Books, 2012), 3. Zane is a specialist in journalism and communication.

6   Bejan and Zane, *Design in Nature*, 34.

7   Bejan and Zane, *Design in Nature*, 148.

8   Bejan and Zane, *Design in Nature*, 56.

9   Bejan and Zane, *Design in Nature*, 131.

10 Bejan and Zane, *Design in Nature*, 163, 164.

11 Bejan and Zane, *Design in Nature*, 69.

12 Philip W. Anderson, "More Is Different," *Science*, n.s., 177, no. 4047 (August 4, 1972): 393–6.

13 Bejan and Zane, *Design in Nature*, 130.

14 Bejan and Zane, *Design in Nature*, 48.

15 Adrian Bejan, *Physics of Life* (New York: St. Martin's Press, 2016), 174.

16 Bejan and Zane, *Design in Nature*, 4. A possible relationship between Bejan and Weinberg can be imagined if one considers the latter's notion of the beautiful as "natural." "Through countless false starts, we have gotten it beaten into us that nature is a certain way, and we have grown to look at that way that nature is as beautiful," writes Weinberg in *Dreams of a Final Theory* (New York: Vintage Books, 1994), 158. Both authors put forth scientific arguments against the idea of beauty as *mimesis*.

17 Franco Moretti, *Signs Taken for Wonders* (London: Verso, 2005), 21–7.

18 Franco Moretti, *Graphs, Maps, Trees: Abstract Models for Literary History*, Afterword by Alberto Piazza (London: Verso, 2007), 91.

19 See Jonathan Goodwin and John Holbo, eds., *Reading Graphs, Maps, Trees: Critical Responses to Franco Moretti* (Anderson, SC: Parlor Press, 2011).

20 Moretti, *Graphs*, 91.

21 Moretti, *Graphs*, 42.

22 Moretti, *Graphs*, 42–3.

23 Moretti, *Graphs*, 42, 44.

24 Moretti, *Graphs*, 64.

25 Moretti, *Graphs*, 69.

26 Moretti, *Graphs*, 70.

27 Moretti, *Graphs*, 72. Also see Moretti's 2000 article "The Slaughterhouse of Literature," *Modern Language Quarterly* 61, no. 1 (2000): 207–27, which became a chapter in *Distant Reading* (London: Verso, 2013): 63–89.

28 Moretti, *Graphs*, 72.

29   Moretti, *Graphs*, 69.
30   Bejan and Zane, *Design in Nature*, 190.
31   Moretti, *Distant Reading*, 60–1.
32   Moretti, *Distant Reading*, 60.
33   Moretti, *Graphs*, 53.
34   Moretti, *Graphs*, 80.
35   Moretti, *Graphs*, 14.
36   Moretti, *Graphs*, 56.
37   Moretti, *Graphs*, 57.
38   Moretti, *Graphs*, 64.
39   Moretti, *Graphs*, 57.
40   Moretti, *Distant Reading*, 60.

2

POST-AESTHETICS:
Literature, Ontology, and
Criticism as Diplomacy

Alexandru Matei

In episode 7, season 3 of the British series *The Crown*, Prince Philip welcomes to Buckingham Palace the first three men that had just traveled to the moon, in July 1969. Although this was, as is well known, a successful techno-scientific experiment, the highly mediated event is presented here in a rather aesthetic light. In the episode, Philip seems to be disappointed with the insufficiently "deep" conversation he is having with the three astronauts. His metaphysical curiosities—"What were you feeling?" "What were you thinking?"—remain unsatisfied, which is why he goes back to the spiritual discussions occasioned by the founding of a religious academy, led by Robin Woods, a conversation that he had seemingly despised at first. Prince Philip frames the moon landing in terms of Pascal's "silence of infinite spaces" rather than of technologies that enabled Neil Armstrong's "small step" on the moon. Philip views the astronauts as some kind of artists who have "created" the moon through a theoretical act of sorts, in the "contemplative," etymological sense of the Greek word *theoretikós*. The reality, however, is far different, for, as scientists, they are quite the opposite of such creative agents. Therefore, Philip returns to the preachers he had left in anger at their presumably aimless babble, having failed to grasp that, where religion is concerned, to speak is to preach, and, further, preaching is what a priest *does*, just as what an astronaut does is to rigorously carry out a technical plan in order to *accomplish* a mission.[1] Thus, one might say, Philip's thinking is oppositional, in that he does not "mediate" the relationship between two different categories of action. Preachers, he implies, talk instead of actually exploring the absolute, while astronauts explore without being able to adequately theorize the greatness of the object before them.

Prince Philip's disappointment stems, I would contend, from what Bruno Latour calls a modern type of thinking. If the relation among science, religion, and aesthetics seems to us today to be mutually exclusive, of the either/or type, this is because, the French philosopher argues, modernity has rendered it dependent on humanity's display of heroism in the struggle with Nature. Modernity thinks in exclusive terms.[2] In modernity, science reveals laws of nature. Religion, on the other hand, teaches us to discipline our body to save our spirit. In Kantian anthropology, aesthetics aspires to a universal principle that religion can no longer incarnate and science cannot materialize, a "universal communicability of the mental state,"[3] synthetic, vertical, according to a human—and humanist—ideal in which Man is philosophically speaking capitalized.[4] Along these lines, it is noteworthy that, despite the way in which the astronauts are portrayed in *The Crown*, the aesthetic perception of the moon is not entirely foreign to them, as reported in the media at the time. Buzz Aldrin, for example, expressed an aesthetic reaction when he declared that "The moon looks like a frozen beauty."[5] Earth's satellite can then just as well be a Romantic symbol and an astronomical entity at once.

Obviously, the alliance between aesthetics and science no longer surprises us today, when critics such as Steven Weinberg have shed a bright light on the aesthetic dimension of scientific theories.[6] Nor do we need to think like Jean-François Lyotard to recognize that this scientific sublime and, in particular, cognate heroic humanism and modernist humanism in general can no longer be embraced since their limitations have become apparent. The moderns have "triumphed" over Nature, and no one is going to question this victory—ironically enough, except for life itself, which shows the opposite is the case. Of course, the moon would have never become an aesthetic object and a material object at the same time if the *Apollo 11* mission had not succeeded, with the help of television, to "explicate" the moon for earthlings. As the Western Enlightenment process of mass education has advanced, more and more clearly accompanied by another process, that of "elucidating" the determinants of reality, the realm of aesthetic perception had broadened greatly. That is why we can no longer talk about a discursive field that is *exclusively* confined to aesthetics and that continues, by means of notions such as disinterest, indeterminacy, and freedom, to integrate the exceptional regime of autonomy that Immanuel Kant prescribed to and foisted on the aesthetic. The idea of a special domain, that of aesthetics, in which the human subject can display its ontological excellence and moral supremacy is of course justified in the context of modernity's onset and plays a decisive role in the rise of what I would call "the national human." The latter emerges as a privileged aesthetic object of Romantic discourses on being insofar as the nation accedes, as an ontological theme, to the *Da-* status that gives birth to Being. Martin Heidegger's 1933 infamous "Rektoratsrede" features a memorable phrase, *geistig-volkliches Dasein* (Dasein spiritual-popular). This is rooted in the idea of a humanized earth, a soil, flesh, and human blood mix defined as an essence of the world, an essence that also determines the world's shape, which then language—poetry in particular—makes manifest in its singularity, that is, in its originality as human world.[7] Although the idea of the nation is not explicit here, it can be inferred from this Heideggerian dialectic of art that activates a mechanism fashioned from soil, humans that "grow" from it, and language that, in its turn, "grows" from people to "speak" their Being.[8]

In contrast to this vertical movement, the idea of *explication* as embodiment of modernity's dynamic succeeds in making modernity *a single ontological, ecological, and aesthetic node*. Aesthetics becomes now both object and environment. "Explication" or, with a less usual English term, "explicitation" is a term that Peter Sloterdijk borrows from Heidegger, who, through "Unconcealment," translates Greek *alétheia* (un-forgetfulness), by which the German philosopher means, first and foremost, the fact that the task of philosophy is that of wresting Being from the forgetfulness in which modern everyday life engulfs it.[9] Sloterdijk takes up the notion of "explicitation" but inscribes it into another context, that of "modernization," where he infuses the Heideggerian concept with the kind of materiality that Latour defines ecologically. According to the French philosopher, "as we moved on, through our technologies, through our scientific inquiries, through the extension of our global empires, we rendered more and more explicit the fragility of the life support systems that make our 'spheres of existence' possible."[10] As part of this historical process of explicitation, the moon landing and the discourse surrounding it, including TV shows such as *The Crown*, have facilitated access to an "intersectional" perspective on the world and its constitutive elements, and so it seems to me that the unfolding of this process would be impossible without expanding the aesthetic interface with the world.

Even though the terms in which aesthetics has been traditionally formulated have become limiting, this limitation, serious as it is, is not without remedy. Before it brings aesthetics to a grinding halt altogether, the situation can be corrected. In line with similar recent attempts at "de-limiting" aesthetic practices and conceptualizations, my chapter proposes—a necessary and perhaps inevitable move in the post era of theory—a *post-aesthetics* that, on one side, can reformulate the largely discredited, humanist, and heroic discourse of a Kantian aesthetics reclaimed by national-humanism and always narcissistically self-centered, and, on the other side, can be understood not as a gratuitous form of theoretical voluntarism but as a practice or field work deeply "diplomatic" in a Latourian sense.[11] More to the point, the post-aesthetics I have in mind should give up the status of synthetic human faculty and implicitly of eagerly self-conferred universality to take, more modestly but also more "tactfully," and by the same token more "strategically" and efficiently, on a diplomatic function through which registering sensibility mediates discourses and values in the wake of experiences that are both linguistic and practical, undergone "in the field." In other words, the hypothesis I want to advance here is that of an aesthetician and, more precisely, of a literary critic *as* an aesthetician who is willing and capable to operate like a diplomat on a constant mission, always in the field of concrete practice. Let us not forget that the diplomat *mediates*, but only to change existing beliefs and to generate new decisions and actions. For this reason, I turn first to the speculative poetics of German critic Armen Avanessian to reaffirm the diplomatic dimension of aesthetics. Then, drawing from Graham Harman's *Object-Oriented Ontology*, I seize on the concept of "object" as very useful in arguments on diplomatic aesthetics, with some caveats that I will explain in due course. But if this diplomatic aesthetics has been illustrated, both in commentators on Latourian modes of existence and in Harman, primarily through recourse to contemporary media and the arts, its attention should now turn more systematically to literature.[12] Therefore, the last section of my intervention discusses, from the perspective of diplomatic aesthetics, a few "literary objects" that both the proponents of object-oriented ontology (OOO) and ecocritics seem to have overlooked despite the steps that all of them have taken toward a better understanding of what brings together and connects the human and nonhuman worlds. I should also add that I borrow the term "diplomatic" specifically from the Latourian ontology of "modes of existence," taking my cue, once again critically, from the way in which Latour eschews the modern dialectic of critical discourse to restage "descriptions" and "arguments" that are circulating in modern society, which he then analyzes in terms of whether or not they succeed in protecting the values that this society's members— that is, we, the moderns—"hold dear." And so, much like Latour, I could tell my reader that "My goal for this inquiry is to create an arrangement that I call diplomatic, one that would make it possible, if I could make it work ... [,] to help our researcher who has been attacked in the name of 'rationalism' by offering him an alternative definition of what he holds dear."[13]

Aesthetics, Poetics, Praxis

A diplomatic aesthetics would therefore be an alternate aesthetics. As such, it should take into account the habits of those who, when running across the term "aesthetic," think immediately about "the sensitive" or about "the ugly" and "the beautiful," but who also try to channel these associative reflexes so as to determine the extent to which they have managed to deliver on the promises that propelled these conjectures at the forefront of modernity—namely, the creation of a "better human being" and the possibility of a "good life." Precisely because modernity has not kept these promises, it is incumbent on post-aesthetics, I would maintain, to recouple "the sensitive" with the ontological and the ecological. Last but not least, though, a diplomatic aesthetic ought to be a discourse attentive to *all* arguments in favor of rethinking the aesthetic. Among them, especially noteworthy seems to me that which calls for a transformative post-aesthetics that not merely describes but actually produces, reformulates, and reconfigures the given objects and the surrounding world. On the grounds that, unlike poetics, aesthetics re-produces, rather than produces, and fails to "other" the given, Avanessian announces the end of aesthetics. "Signs," he alerts us, "are mounting that the hegemony of the aesthetic, a specific regime of defined practical and discursive rules on how to talk about and assess art, is coming to an end ... We are not just approaching the line separating the aesthetic from a post-aesthetic regime but may already have crossed it."[14] Aesthetics, Avanessian believes, must therefore be replaced with a speculative poetics that operates through *Überschreiben* (overwriting). "The reality of a thinking that has undergone dialectical negation is," Avanessian says, "a speculative reality; its facts have changed or transformed. In this respect, speculative poetics goes beyond and overwrites traditional poetics (and its focus on genres)."[15]

Incorporating a poetics thus understood, aesthetics can assert itself—rather than die off, it seems to me—as a diplomatic ontological mode and overcome the dichotomy between creative action and theoretical passion. Avanessian's speculative realism, then, should not necessarily bury aesthetics but instead assert and reassert it, or assert it *differently*, as a crossroads at which theory entails another practice, which in turn fuels another theory. A diplomatic aesthetics then need not be understood as a discourse about the one-way relationship between a "magical" aesthetic object and a *numb* subject, but as a coaction of four *agencies*: environment, object, "author," and "spectator." From this perspective too, I think that a diplomatic aesthetics should be seen as rooted in speculative realism as a theory of the *trans-formative* real. This is, in fact, how the "Fiction" mode of existence in Latour's landmark 2012 *An Inquiry into Modes of Existence* should be approached. Once he has situated aesthetics within Fiction, Latour places the latter as a "mode of existence" between "Technology" and "Reference," that is, among "quasi-objects,"[16] and at the same time as close as possible not just to the hylomorphic definition of "art objects"—"vacillation between material and form"[17]—but especially to the common notion of "aesthetics" as receptivity to beauty or to "the splendors of works of art."[18] Speculative realism is noteworthy here insofar as it brings about a first recalibration of the Latourian fictional mode of existence. There is still, of course, the "work of art," just as the epithet "splendid" has not vanished from the vocabulary, yet this kind of aesthetics lacks, I would venture, precisely the poetic function that can offer access to the transformation Avanessian has in mind. As the proponents of this newly emerged realism insist, there is no "given" aesthetic object, nor an already constituted subject who receives from this object what he or she "expects" to. Likewise, the "environment" is nothing else but an ongoingly transformed product, the ever-fluid ecology of our everyday actions, even though ontological experience varies from person to person. Oriented by poetics, diplomatic aesthetics is or can become reflexive, capable of listening "in the field" and of learning from praxis. At the same time, this aesthetics can seek the transgressive as a generative pattern, according to Avanessian, who observes that "Poetic experience is nothing other than this transgression: The experience of what is transgressed, of how it is transgressed, and not least of the boundary this very transgression brings into being. In other words, the possibilities of our senses are not intrinsically limited and cannot serve as a yardstick for the limitations of what can be thought."[19]

One of the benefits of diplomatic aesthetics is flexibility or, better yet, the opening up of space for the relationship between art and aesthetics. Not only can one not posit, in post-aesthetics, an "aesthetic truth" as an artistic truth, a truth pertaining to art and opposed to the scientific and socioeconomic truth, as well as to their technological and profit "worlds," but one cannot relate aesthetics only to art either, as long as the artistic domain can no longer be circumscribed by classical aesthetics. In fact, the artistic-aesthetic correlation has more to do with a reflex of thinking that has been denounced as such not just to argue for the expansion of aesthetics beyond art, as we have seen, but also to free art from the "terror" of aesthetics.[20] Still, it does not suffice to merely accept as a premise of post-aesthetics the idea of an all-encompassing, "generalized" aesthetics, for the very reason that this would involve, among other things, a sort of "anything goes" politics. As the reader will remember, people have talked for decades about "aesthetic capitalism," a regime in which hegemonic power exerts itself, according to Eduardo de la Fuente and Peter L. L. Murphy, through "soft" aesthetic and cultural methods, and an aesthetics *sans rivages* can be nothing else but a neoliberal instrument of control.[21] From this vantage point, a "relational" aesthetics has to be conceived in such a way that it will avoid the trap of instrumentalization, as Svenja Bromberg points out when she writes that

> if capitalism wants us to be ever more alive, happy, and truly engaged in shaping our own lives on the basis of the endless possibilities this world has to offer, then the critique offered by vitalist theories, aesthetic modes such as Bourriaud's "relational aesthetics," and more critical forms of emancipated spectatorship against an objectifying and alienating capitalist reality appear assimilated and defused.[22]

The challenge facing aesthetics today, a test the diplomacy of the post-aesthetic can, in my view, pass, is therefore twofold. On one hand, aesthetics thus reconceived becomes a theory of action. As such, it can be narrated (practiced) like a story with characters (inquiry objects) of all kinds, be they "things" or "beings," in relation to which one might ask questions such as "What is the moon?" "Is it beautiful?" On the other hand, we need an aesthetics that can be repositioned in the contemporary world, in a social, political, and economic context that encompasses and affects both minority identities and global flows. Contemporary art will undoubtedly be useful on this global stage, but on two conditions, both of them multiply illuminating, critically speaking, transdisciplinary, and ultimately empowering. One would be "purely" aesthetic or, if you will, aestheticist in an autonomist, old-fashioned sense, and it would require we not reduce the artistic domain to a market of commodities while rethinking aesthetics in a larger, anthropological sense, as a "poetics of the object," one that integrates the notion of explicitation as a producer-creator's form-generating act, as well as the concept of "vibration," of a receiver's active resonance. The other condition or premise of our work as critics would be ontological, and, if we started from it, we would succeed, I believe, in putting diplomatic aesthetics to work so as to show that contemporary literature and art are not the only domains of the aesthetic.

OOO and Literary Criticism as Art

A mode of existence in its own right and entrusted with a delicate mission of negotiator in the "Moderns'" anthropological project to boot, "Fiction" and its "network" constitute in Latour key elements of an insufficiently articulated diplomatic aesthetics. This is, first of all, because he does not clarify the historicity of the aesthetic vibration nor that of "support systems"—the media and the technological accoutrements—through which such vibration occurs. Unlike Avanessian, for whom only poetics is capable of creating, or rather re-creating and altering, Latour seems to reformulate the Jakobsonian "poetic function" of language, corroborating it with the "magic" of Timothy Morton's hyperobject but without showing a preoccupation with historicizing the forms.[23] Indeed, by glossing over forms' historicity at the expense of their functions in general, Latour avoids the biases that would have blocked the line of argument about the fictional "mode of existence." This line then does not hinge on intrinsic dichotomies—such as Roland Barthes's distinction between "readerly" and "writerly"[24]—but rather on the intention to explicate the ecological dimension of fiction and the fictional, on the precariousness of aesthetic vibration as proof of the uncertainty of living existence in general. From this perspective, it does not matter, for Latour, if we talk about Sidney Sheldon or James Joyce, or if we refer to Bollywood viewers or Latour readers as long as there are people and fictions that can make them all "vibrate." But the Latourian tenet of a "symmetry" between subject and object falls short of helping us really get a grip on how the coactive dynamic of various "agencies" has evolved historically; at the same time, post-aesthetics cannot ignore the fact that the very historicity of this vibration reflects the extent and especially the direction of "explicitation" on which we are embarking. As a result, the fictional mode of existence Latour proposed mainly to elaborate an aesthetic semiology related to, yet distinct from, other modes of existence with an "irrational" connotation (psychology and religion, in particular) has led in recent years, besides the speculative realism illustrated by critics such as Avanessian, to the birth of an aesthetic ontology of the OOO kind. Harman, the latter's main proponent, shares with Latour the principle of ontological equality between "actants" but departs both from him and from Morton in that he privileges the object over the "network" or "system." OOO and system-oriented ontology (SOO) are essentially working then with two types of "object"; whereas OOO posits that the object possesses an essence that aesthetic perception can access, SOO lays emphasis on the dynamic and constructive aspects of the speculative process, which provide, says Morton, access to conglomerates, networks, and "meshes" of objects.

The diplomatic aesthetics hypothesis and the idea of certain "objects" similarly inspired by Latourian symmetrical anthropology help and ultimately force us to acknowledge the importance of an aesthetic practice in which I am particularly interested here, namely, literature. In a famous article, Jane Bennett has called our attention to the exaggerations of an ontology that privileges a phenomenology of the object in itself, cut off from the productive dynamic of forms and the objects this dynamic generates and, at the same time, alters and transports, while re-generating other objects, just as fragile and vulnerable to change. "I find myself," Bennett confesses, "living in a world populated by materially diverse, lively bodies. In this materialism, things—what is special about them given their sensuous specificity, their particular material configuration, and their distinctive, idiosyncratic history—matter a lot. But so do the eccentric assemblages that they form."[25] At the end of the article, the author further qualifies these "assemblages" by referring to texts as objects but also media—a text cannot, obviously, be but woven, *textum* (to recall Barthes again), a fabric made up of words. The poetic object constituted by the text is itself a network, even as that text is also part of a network that includes it. Harman's attempt to adapt the OOO to literary studies does not translate, however, into an insight about the text as an object whose meanings change depending on the historical context in which it is placed; what he does, instead, takes the form of a confrontation of OOO tenets with those of literary theory, especially the immanent New Criticism, on one side, and Derridean deconstruction, on the other. Although he proposes an "object-oriented literary criticism," the only concrete recommendation the philosopher makes along the lines of his proposal is to subject the literary text under scrutiny to certain changes and then evaluate how substantially they have altered the text's identity. "The critic," Harman suggests, "might try to show how each text resists internal holism by attempting various modifications of these texts and seeing what happens. Instead of just writing about *Moby-Dick*, why not try shortening it to various degrees in order to discover the point at which it ceases to sound like *Moby-Dick*?"[26]

Thus, it seems to me that not only is there a confusion here about two different notions of "object," but also that each of the ways in which the "textual object" is defined depends on the orientation of the critic and theorist in question. Bennett is more of a cultural critic, whereas Harman and Morton are philosophers concerned with contemporary art rather than literature. A diplomatic aesthetics needs to take into account such differences, and yet my literary background leads me to agree with Bennett that literature lends to the notion of object an indeterminacy that should not be ignored. Is literature merely "storytelling," a Stendhalian mirror carried along a road? When it comes to literature, modern and contemporary in particular, can this object not be a textual object or some sort of aesthetic *dispositive* or device? That is why, I think, Francis Hallsall had a very good idea when he tried to approach *Inquiry into Modes of Existence* as an object of contemporary art. His point is quite simple and also relevant to our discussion. "There is an equivalence," he says, "between the way that Latour works and contemporary art practices. In short, Latour works like an artist."[27] Hallsall's argument rests on a fairly broad notion of art—one that transcends, it bears repeating, the *market* of contemporary art—and is predicated on the idea of a "conceptual rhyme" that he actually practices in his own demonstration, an idea which in turn evokes the aesthetic dimension of analogy as articulated by Andrew Ginger.[28] No doubt, Hallsall is onto something here. The "diplomatic" character of the aesthetic component is obvious in *Inquiry*'s narrative form itself. Let us recall, apropos of it, that Latour resorts not only to narrative but to contemporary art as well in the exhibits he has curated. If *Inquiry* now has a bilingual site whose versions can be accessed for free, *Reset Modernity!*, the sequel of Latour's 2012 book, is a contemporary aesthetic object comprised of text and image.[29]

Now, considering this Latourian perspective on art as praxis and on criticism that, *like art and through its engagement with it*, approximates or should approximate the same status of praxis, what might the condition of literature and, subsequently, of literary criticism be? To answer this question, it is time to state explicitly what I have only suggested or implied in my glosses to various thinkers, namely, that the domains of literature and art should no longer be separated because, even as an artistic activity circumscribed primarily by a symbolic function that is less apparent in any other practice, literature can in turn be an object in an OOO sense. Literature's objectuality becomes more and more evident historically as we near the contemporary moment in literature and theory. As Pascal Quignard put it in 2005, a novel is an "object of language,"[30] and, more generally, writing is a unique object for a theorist such as Lionel Ruffel precisely because literature *cannot* be narrated, summarized, or reduced to a paraphrase or allegory.[31] As a post-aesthetic, trans-formative object, however, the literary text can also function differently than in the suspense regime so sweepingly described by Latour or in the anagogical regime post-Romantic poetry sometimes requires from the reader. Furthermore, literature inheres in much more than a mere fictional pact that can help us experience a hero's adventures vicariously; nor are people generally so gullible to believe that anyone who has made it to the moon has been touched by the divine eidos and turned, *deus ex machina*, into an angel. The opposition between OOO and SOO is false insofar as each side tries to privilege one of the two dimensions of Latourian anthropological modernity. Thus, OOO echoes the ontology treated in *Inquiry*, where Latour does not seek different names for existence but rather a demonstration of ontological pragmatism, laying out a whole spectrum of ways of being and deploying for this purpose a homogeneous vocabulary and not the other way round, which is exactly what happened throughout modernity, whose "manners of speaking" enunciate the same ontology albeit in different ways.[32] "The Object" is then a generic name for things that "are"—the "ontic"—so that "objectology" might be another name for the OOO theory in the versions proposed, for instance, by Harman and Morton. The diplomatic aesthetics I put forth here pairs with OOO because the latter manages to turn aesthetics into a "liberated" perception mode, one intentionally emancipated from modern dichotomies and as such capable of retooling aesthetics as *the main knowledge vehicle*—with a caveat, though: to the extent that the role of aesthetics is to bring forward objects and to plead the causes of some in front of others, Harman's recourse to metaphor as an essential aesthetic trigger is, to my mind, a cop-out as simplistic as Latour's convenient pressing into service of fictional narrative as an aesthetic epitome. The shortcomings of this procedure cannot be ignored because, when he claims that the aesthetic, metaphorical perception of the object grants access "in person" to or for an "I-subject" and "object-zero-person," Harman runs the risk of fetishizing aesthetics itself.[33]

Such risks abound in his work because, like Morton, Harman turns to contemporary art, especially when he dwells on "strange" and "weird" objects and more broadly on a "*weird* realism in which real individual objects resist all forms of causal or cognitive mastery," which somehow creates a hierarchy between "classical" objects and the "objectological" entities of OOO.[34] Discussing the way in which a critic like Cleanth Brooks has approached literature, Harman allows that poetry cannot be ontologically different from science, but only because, in the wake of Latourian philosophy, science and poetry are not two ways of bringing reality into being any more but two ways of talking about the same reality, one allusive (poetry), the other "straightforward" (science). Thus, like science, poetry can tackle any object, taking it up as a versatile-transformative entity. Accordingly, the moon is simultaneously a planet when you step on it and a "star" you can see every night. Therefore, what Harman says about the "literal" and "non-literal" can become, I believe, a tenet of diplomatic aesthetics insofar as aesthetics is no longer a "dedicated" domain of existence, limited by exclusionary parameters, but rather a sort of supplement stretching across ontic domains. Just as digital hardware gadgets need USB ports or Wi-Fi setups to be connected, any object is equipped with a sort of aesthetic device for capture or "connection." This connective "clinamen"[35] has become increasingly explicit as the possibility for the object's exposure to the world has increased, also throwing into question the distinction between the noumenal and the phenomenal, which is nothing but an epiphenomenon of the dichotomous methodology of modernity itself.[36]

Literary Objects: *Le Nouveau Roman* and After

To avoid destroying the pragmatic character of literature and, at the same time, to account for the literary object in terms of a diplomatic aesthetics that traverses and co-articulates, as maintained above, the ontological, ecological, and traditional aesthetics, the so-called contemporary *descriptive turn* urged by Heather Love may come in handy. I find it odd, however, that Love forgets to mention an essential moment of this turn and, by now, of literary history more broadly, a moment and movement that, after being initially overrated, was consigned to oblivion precisely because the aesthetic discourse within which it operated had been unable to conceive of it based on traditional categories.[37] I am referring to the French *Nouveau Roman*, from which, in closing, I pull a few examples by way of putting some exemplifying meat on the theoretical bones of my "diplomatic" proposal. I do believe, actually, that, even though the *Nouveau Roman* benefited, in the decades right after World War II, from great critical support, which otherwise ensured its success among critics, theorists, and a fairly large audience outside the academy as well, a diplomatic aesthetics would succeed in revisiting two of the constitutive elements of its poetics, namely, the critique of realist narrative and the privilege conferred on description. In the New Novel, the text and the narrative no longer are, as has been noted, two pathways the reader can follow as they overlap, one being the copy of the other. From this perspective, and to put it very plainly, we could classify the works of authors such as Nathalie Sarraute, Alain Robbe-Grillet, Michel Butor, Robert Pinget, Jean Ricardou, and Claude Simon as "textualist" novels whose interpretive code lies not only in certain places in a carpet *pattern* but also in their recognition as textual montages and "visual" "novels," respectively, in which a *background* narrative, presumed rather than conspicuous, becomes a display window of objects.[38] A closed world made up of objects that are allowed to linger in perception, to become "charged" with the emotion of the viewer/reader, was already present in Robbe-Grillet's first novel, *Un régicide* (*A Regicide*). Worth mentioning is that when he finished writing it, in 1949, the novelist was a scientist, more precisely, an engineer with the Institut Français des Agrumes Coloniaux (IFAC), where he had researched the parasites of the banana tree in the French Antilles.[39] Beyond a professional life marked by the concrete realities of a research lab, the future writer did not work within a specific rhetorical tradition, and the literature he started writing was slightly influenced by the modernist-humanist politics of French literature as a national and social institution. Perhaps without realizing at first, Robbe-Grillet had already initiated a descriptivist shift that attempted to capture the very aesthetic clinamen of objects *qua* literary objects and would be carried on by an entire literary direction, the "Minuit School." The narrator of *A Regicide* does not actually display an object as such, with a Barthesian "reality effect," but instead "explicates" a monotonous landscape that, he maintains, is not worth seeing.[40] It is the very description that renders an object what it is, namely, an object. But all his novels trace, up to a certain point, such descriptive trajectories, which I bring up here mainly because their legacy represents today one of the most important trends in contemporary French prose. Half a century after Robbe-Grillet's *Les Gommes* (*The Erasers*), *La Clé USB*, one of Jean-Philippe Toussaint's latest novels, seems to pay homage to it, at least in the title.[41]

Robbe-Grillet's "objectual" literature loses momentum in the 1980s in the context of the end of the second French literary avant-garde and the resurgence of traditional narrative categories. In a 1954 memorable article titled "Littérature objective,"[42] Barthes picks up insightfully on Robbe-Grillet's objectualist procedures, noting that the novelist depicts the visible surface of objects without ever pointing to a hermeneutics, viz., without subjecting them to what Harman would call "undermining" and "overmining."[43] In fact, a few years later, in 1959, Robbe-Grillet himself asked the reader, in the warning that opens *Dans le labyrinth* (*In the Labyrinth*), to avoid any allegorical readings.[44] Harman, otherwise a self-declared Heideggerian, like many other critics inside and outside OOO, seems to ignore all this *literature of the object*, here confined neither to Robbe-Grillet and the Minuit School nor to the novel, and let us not forget that Georges Perec's novel *Les Choses* came out in 1965, and Francis Ponge's poetry volume, *Le Parti pris des choses*, in 1942. Also worth recalling is that the first issue of *Tel Quel* features a poem by Ponge, "La figue (sèche)," which opens with a heuristic comparison between poetry and a fig so as to illustrate precisely the diplomatic character of aesthetics as a linking and support element for the perception of things—the dry fig is, indeed, a metaphor, but one that tends to be reabsorbed in metonymy, which is likely to happen more and more often in a contemporary French literature whose genre boundaries have become increasingly porous.[45] This is the case, for instance, in *Chaussure*, by Nathalie Quintane,[46] not to mention that an entire direction of contemporary French poetry deals with the making of "verbal objects."[47]

To this "diplomatic" ontological tradition of the visual novel we might add that of a poetic avant-garde whose international, literary and theoretical-philosophical impact hardly needs to be underscored here, as well as intersections of these two directions such as the 1979 novel *Le Méridien de Greenwich* (The Greenwich Meridian), the objectualist debut of Jean Echenoz. Working from the narrative template of a spy plot, the writer imagines in *Le Méridien* a Pacific island crossed by the Greenwich meridian. The island is real or quasi-real, for it is located in the Marshall Islands, an actually existing geographical site comprised of atolls on which atomic experiments were conducted.[48] On this island, the protagonist has built, underground, a strange "vehicle" that appears to be useless and that we may now call a sort of "object-in-itself." His plan is to blow up his machinery in a suicidal act and in the very cave in which he had descended to check out his invention together with his lover, Vera. The contraption does look like a strange object that befits the descriptor "weird" and could be compared to the time machine from Robert Zemeckis's first movie *Back to the Future*, except that, in the latter, the emphasis falls on the precarity and deformity of the object. Recently, in fact, on the occasion of the release of his latest novels, Echenoz credited Joseph Conrad for the method of humanizing objects and objectualizing beings, a ploy one comes across in all of his novels published in the last decades of the last century.[49] I might add that he is not the only great novelist who has done this. While it is true that all of these authors draw on narrative elements more explicitly than Robbe-Grillet did, this does not keep these writers from leaving ample space to depictions of objects and beings, whether small and placed, after a fashion, under a magnifying glass or big and looked at through a telescope, and adjusting their narrative perception according to scale. Consequently, their reader is forced to perform what we should really call a superficial or "on-the-surface" reading, because the disjointed chronology of narrative syntax—analepsis, prolepsis, and the like—no longer matters much, just like when we find ourselves in a museum of contemporary art and try to grapple with what we see and what takes place there, and so we look at the objects on display in succession even though the temporal sequence in which those items were created may have been different.

From the perspective of modern, post-Kantian aesthetics, all of these examples seem less provocative if we take into account the rather modest scope of the imaginary invested in them as well as the ensuing deflation of narrative suspense. However, it is for this very reason that I talk, apropos of them, about a diplomatic aesthetics—because, that is, every one of the objects that has been textually reconstructed through explicitation and likewise, the texts themselves as verbal montages all flaunt that aesthetic, connective "hook" without being *transfigured* allegorically or analogically, without undergoing an interpretive conversion that is ultimately dependent on a human cognitive agent and can rescind their ontological belonging to the material world in which we find erasers, bizarre machines, figs, and so forth. These literary objects are aesthetic or, if you will, *post*-aesthetic objects. But they are so, and, as I insist, must be considered so not because you have to "take" the metaphor—as you would "take" the plane or train to reach a destination—to get to them, nor because they no longer exist unless they are charged with the "vibration" of the one who reads or reconstructs the text. Diplomatic aesthetics places at once literary objects and itself *amid* the worlds animated by values that circulate via technology, fiction, religion, and other ontic and discursive domains, but such an aesthetic does not pull the objects in question from these worlds to push them into an aesthetic-oriented world and lock them there. Herein lies a fundamental "ontological" humbleness and lesson that literary criticism should learn from the diplomacy of post-aesthetics. The moon, erasers, USB micro hard drives, and shoes remain, if they are not "hooked" aesthetically for a while, where they have been all along. What can happen to them is only a "meeting" of sorts—they can meet their textual alter-egos through various practices of production and perception. The role of criticism as artistic *and* diplomatic praxis consists specifically, I submit, in facilitating—in negotiating and mediating—such a meeting.

What post-aesthetics proposes under the name of diplomatic aesthetics must be then grasped, first, as an alternative to the still dominant aesthetic-cognitive paradigm, not as a *critique*. It is true that one's sensibility does not change overnight and, further, that individuals, not just groups, are different from one another. It is time, however, to recognize that, what with the university becoming a mass institution and the technology of video communication reaching digital-era performance levels, aesthetics has emerged as a way of understanding and coexisting with *any* entity of this world. Let us note that Paganini's violin from Palazzo Tursi in Genoa may be a fragile object, but so is *any* object that, in order to be a part of this world, triggers an attachment inside us and therefore participates in the live universe. Thus, a literary text is all the more fragile that, beyond its story—which can circulate from one individual memory to another—it demands to be reread, looked at, and "contacted" through that connective device it possesses and that needs to be discovered as an aesthetic object, as *une chose*. In effect, herein lies the difference between aesthetics and post-aesthetics: if, for somebody like Jean-Paul Sartre, the prose writer deals with significations ("ideas"), while the poet, painter, or musician trades in "things," as if only words could engage ideas and attitudes, post-aesthetics holds that any com-position, textual or not, and any ex-position of something—of an "object"—engage a position and create a situation in which the affect and intellect register, comprehend, and conceive the world anew.

Notes

1 Bruno Latour, *An Inquiry into Modes of Existence* (Cambridge, MA: Harvard University Press, 2013), 136.
2 Bruno Latour, *We Have Never Been Modern* (Cambridge, MA: Harvard University Press 1995), 36.
3 Immanuel Kant, *Critique of Judgment*, trans. and intro. Werner S. Pluhar (Indianapolis, IN: Hackett Publishing Company, 1987), 61.
4 Kant, *Critique of Judgment*, 164.
5 Buzz Aldrin, quoted in the official newspaper of the Romanian Communist Party, *Scânteia*, no. 8133, July 22, 1969, 8.
6 In *Dreams of a Final Theory*, Steven Weinberg observes that "in this century, … the consensus in favor of physical theories has often been reached on the basis of aesthetic judgments before the experimental evidence for these theories became really compelling" ([London: Vintage Books, 1994], 105).
7 Martin Heidegger quoted in Karsten Harries, *Art Matters: A Critical Commentary on Heidegger's "The Origin of the Work of Art"* (New York: Springer, 2009), 43.
8 "Art helps us save our own humanity," Harries concludes her interpretation of "The Origin of the Work of Art" in *Art Matters* (184).
9 For a recent analysis, see Katherine Withy, "Concealing and Concealment in Heidegger," *European Journal of Philosophy* 25, no. 4. (2017): 1496–513.
10 Bruno Latour, "A Plea for Earthly Sciences," in *New Social Connections: Sociology's Subjects and Objects*, ed. Judith Burnett, Syd Jeffers, and Graham Thomas (New York: Macmillan, 2010), 74.
11 Lately, an ethics of "diplomacy" as ecological militancy has been developed by Baptiste Morizot in *Les Diplomates. Cohabiter avec les loups sur une autre carte du vivant* (Marseille: Wildproject, 2016).
12 See Yves Citton, "Fictional Attachments and Literary Weavings in the Anthropocene," *New Literary History* 47, nos. 2–3 (2016): 309–30; Francis Halsall, "Actor-Network Aesthetics: The Conceptual Rhymes of Bruno Latour and Contemporary Art," *New Literary History* 47, nos. 2–3 (2016): 439–62; Patrice Maniglier, "Art as Fiction: Can Latour's Ontology of Art be Ratified by Art Lovers? (An Exercise in Anthropological Diplomacy)," *New Literary History* 47, nos. 2–3 (2016): 419–38.
13 Latour, *An Inquiry*, 7.
14 Armen Avanessian, "The Speculative End of the Aesthetic Regime," *Texte zur Kunst* 24 (2014): 52–3.
15 Armen Avanessian, *Ethics of Knowledge: Poetics of Existence* (Berlin: Sternberg Press, 2017), 54.

16 Bruno Latour, *Enquête sur les modes d'existence. Une anthropologie des Modernes* (Paris: La Découverte, 2012), 488. The table is simplified in the English edition, where the classification of modes into quasi-subjects and quasi-objects disappears (Latour, *An Inquiry*, 516). The fact that fiction is a "quasi-object" speaks to the materialism of Latourian aesthetics, but precisely this notion, introduced as early as in *We Have Never Been Modern*, is absent in the English version.

17 Latour, *An Inquiry*, 516.

18 Latour, *An Inquiry*, 407.

19 Avanessian, "The Speculative End of the Aesthetic Regime," 58.

20 See Carole Talon-Hugon, *L'Art victime de l'esthétique* (Paris: Hermann, 2014).

21 See Eduardo de la Fuente and Peter L. L. Murphy, eds., *Aesthetic Capitalism* (Leiden: Brill, 2014).

22 Svenja Bromberg, "The Anti-Political Aesthetics of Objects and Worlds Beyond," *Mute*, July 25, 2013, https://www.metamute.org/editorial/articles/anti-political-aesthetics-objects-and-worlds-beyond (accessed February 19, 2020).

23 Timothy Morton, *Hyperobjects: Philosophy and Ecology after the End of the World* (Minneapolis: University of Minnesota Press, 2013), 88.

24 Roland Barthes, "S/Z," in *Œuvres complètes III*, ed. Eric Marty (Paris: Seuil, 2002), 122 and after.

25 Jane Bennett, "Systems and Things: A Response to Graham Harman and Timothy Morton," *New Literary History* 43, no. 2 (2012): 431.

26 Graham Harman, "The Well-Wrought Broken Hammer: Object-Oriented Literary Criticism," *New Literary History* 43, no. 2 (2012): 201–2.

27 Francis Halsall, "Actor-Network Aesthetics," 440.

28 Andrew Ginger, "Comparative Study and the Nature of Connections: Of the Aesthetic Appreciation of History," *Modern Languages Open* 1 (2018): 18, http://doi.org/10.3828/mlo.v0i0.191.

29 See Center for Art and Media Karlsruhe, "GLOBALE: Reset Modernity!," April 16–August 21, 2016, https://zkm.de/en/exhibition/2016/04/globale-reset-modernity (accessed February 22, 2020).

30 Pascal Quignard, *Ecrits de l'éphémère* (Paris: Galilée, 2005), 236.

31 Lionel Ruffel and Olivia Roenthal, "La Littérature exposée," *Littérature* 160, no. 4 (2010): 8. Ruffel has also published an entire book in which he refers to the contemporary moment as one in which art and literature interpenetrate (*Brouhaha: Worlds of the Contemporary* [Minneapolis: University of Minnesota Press, 2018]).

32 Latour, *An Inquiry*, 20.

33 "Ortega," writes Harman, "is effectively saying that Kant's noumenal realm is not inaccessible, but that art consists precisely in giving us this noumenal realm in person." See Graham Harman's *Objected Oriented Ontology: A New Theory of Everything* (New York: Penguin Books, 2017), 71.

34 Harman, "The Well-Wrought Broken Hammer," 188.

35 The clinamen is an aesthetic quality in the sense defined by James J. Gibson in his essay "The Theory of Affordances," in *The People, Place, and Space Reader*, ed. Jen Jack Gieseking and William Mangold (New York: Routledge, 2014), 56–61.

36 As Harman writes, "The literal and the nonliteral cannot be apportioned between separate zones of reality but are two distinct sides of every point in the cosmos" ("The Well-Wrought Broken Hammer," 190).

37 Heather Love, "Close but not Deep: Literary Ethics and the Descriptive Turn," *New Literary History* 41, no. 2 (2010): 371–91.

38 Such is the case in Claude Simon. See Mireille Calle-Gruber, *Les Tryptiques de Claude Simon ou l'art du montage* (Paris: Presses de la Sorbonne Nouvelle, 2008), 13.

39 The fragment of the interview is featured on the site of the publishing house Minuit at http://www.leseditionsdeminuit.fr/livre-Un_r%C3%A9gicide-1794-1-1-0-1.html (accessed April 7, 2020).

40 Alain Robbe-Grillet, *Un regicide* (Paris: Minuit, 1978), 20, 21, and 23.

41 Jean-Philippe Toussaint, *La Clé USB* (Paris: Minuit, 2019).

42 Roland Barthes, *Œuvres complètes II*, ed. Eric Marty (Paris: Seuil, 2002), 293–303.

43 Harman, *Objected Oriented Ontology*, 41–52.

44 Alain Robbe-Grillet, *Dans le labyrinthe* (Paris: Minuit, 1959), 4.

45 Francis Ponge, *Le Grand recueil, III: Pièces* (Paris: Gallimard, 1961), 204.

46 "*Chaussure* is not a book that, under the guise of shoes, talks about boats, sausage, Darwinism, or about how we fell in love when we were kids. *Chaussure* really talks about shoes," warns Nathalie Quintane on the back cover of her novel *Chaussure* (Paris: POL, 1997).

47 See Pierre Alferi and Olivier Cadiot, "La Mécanique Lyrique," *Revue de Littérature Générale* 1 (Paris: POL, 1995): 3–22.

48 Jean Echenoz, *Le Meridien de Greenwich* (Paris: Minuit, 1979), 10.

49 Jean Echenoz, "Grand Entretien," *Lire* 482 (February 2020): 49.

3

EASTETHICS:
The Ideological Shift in
Narratology

Alex Goldiș

The historical overlap between the rise of the modern novel and of modern democracy has been noted by a host of theorists, from Mikhail M. Bakhtin, who formulated the notion of the polyphony of novelistic discourses and axiological perspectives, to Jacques Rancière, who has called attention to the waning of a rhetoric grounded chiefly in discrepant styles and tones, a process that, according to the French philosopher, led to the onset of the aesthetic regime of art. Along the same lines, more recent critics such as Nelly Wolf see the novel not only as a space that "reflects" democratic setups or their absence but also as one where the very dynamic of democracy is redefined, in an ongoing renegotiation of the "pact" that affords community itself.[1] All these efforts have been keyed to reframing the genre, as well as its scholarship, through a theoretical approach capable of capturing the ways fiction addresses, as *expression*, issues of social and political import. And yet, as has been also pointed out, we still lack a theory designed to paint a comprehensive picture of the complex relationships between the novel and society. This is, first, because Marxist-oriented criticism tends to ignore the forms of the literary, attending instead to the deterministic bearings of social situations on novelistic ideas, and second, because, at the other end of the spectrum, formalist analysis, rooted as it is in Gérard Genette's narratology, has basically decoupled literary fiction from referentiality, dismissing as irrelevant issues of intentionality and authorial ethos.

Taking my cue from *The Political Unconscious*, where Fredric Jameson posits that "form is immanently and intrinsically an ideology in its own right," my chapter argues for a study of narrative forms and for narratology broadly as tools for a political reading of the novel.[2] Important steps in this direction have already been taken by critics such as Susan Rubin Suleiman, who lays out the general typology of the "novel with a thesis" (*roman à these*), and Vincent Jouve, who, to elaborate "an ideological supersystem that organizes the story and renders it meaningful," dwells on the "democratic" (or "polyphonic") novel, in which points of view cannot be reduced to a unique, authorial perspective.[3] More recent contributions have reclaimed literary discourse as a form of pragmatic communication so as to reconnect the figure of the author, seen as a series of complex social negotiations, to the text's intentional system through concepts such as "posture" and "attitude" (Jérôme Meizoz),[4] the "moral responsibility of the author" (James Phelan),[5] and "authorial ethos" (Liesbeth Korthas Altes).[6] Presuming that, far from being universally applicable, theories are always context-dependent and historically situated, and, further, building on Revathi Krishnaswamy's notion of "world literary knowledges," which belies the assumption that non-Western cultures can be sources of cultural phenomena but not of theory production, I propose that an effective, ideologically minded narratology, my ultimate objective here, stands to benefit a great deal from the experience of East European literatures under totalitarianism.[7]

The most compelling argument in this sense, to begin with, is a matter of literary-historical reality: a moral and social *contract*, fiction constituted a multiply significant phenomenon in the former Eastern Bloc, where, most often, what Wolf calls "the internal democracy of the novel" responded to and even *made up for* the social absence of democracy.[8] This is because the official attempt to control literature not only in terms of "content" but also of expressive means ended up endowing form in the East with political substance and impact. This complex interaction between *aesthetic* form, on one side, and the *ethical* engagement with democratic values under a harsh censorship regime, on the other, was widely discussed by Romanian critics inside and outside Romania during and after Communism. One of the outcomes of this discussion was the notion of *eastethics* (*est-etică*). Itself "aesthetic"—a play on the paronymous intersection of *est* and *estetic* (Romanian for "East" and "aesthetic," respectively)—and no less typically "Eastern," the *estetic* was defined by Romanian critic Monica Lovinescu as a particular literary formalism, one derived from literature's deliberate *retreat into the aesthetic* through an "over-the-top" cultivation of forms.[9] As Lovinescu recalled in Paris in 1990 her reactions to her native country's Cold War literature, in Romania

> resistance took on a mostly aesthetic form. The ethical and political dimensions of literature were not held in high esteem during the post-1960s

period of pseudo- or quasi-liberalization given that, during the Socialist Realist past, they had been "compromised" by the Socialist Realist agenda, which had no doubt abused them and yet had been nonetheless served by them. The result of this suspicion of an ethically and politically invested literature was a body of work of very good quality, much more in line with what was being done in the West ... I do believe, though, that something was missing. This disdain for ethics that I could sense from afar was somewhat damaging ... I think Romanian literature is one of the most aesthetically refined Eastern literatures, whose repertoire, however, lacked, by and large, a strong ethical fiber.[10]

Long overdue, a revision of Lovinescu's eastethics concept would both respond and add nuancing elements to the ongoing international conversation around the socially "contractual" affordances of fictional prose. It is with this in mind that I would basically upend Lovinescu's argument and redefine eastethics as an *ethos* specific to Cold War East European literatures. Present and, in effect, deliberately assumed rather than absent or disregarded, this ethos was, I submit, one of form—of ethical and political form. This ethos sponsored the crafting of literary devices and techniques susceptible of serving as *sui generis* conduits of a political message.

Rancière's analysis of the larger epistemic systems of literary representation can help shed light on the mechanics of this sponsorship although, *nota bene*, the shift the French philosopher famously describes is *away from* an ethical regime of literature to an aesthetic, modern regime. The move entails giving up on the existing hierarchy of themes and on didacticism in favor of a formal politics that he fleshes out through a whole string of aporias. As is well known, Rancière credits Gustave Flaubert with sparking off this literary "revolution." "The new principle," Rancière writes,

> was stated in all its crudity by Flaubert: there are no high or low subject matters. Further, there is no subject matter at all, because style is an absolute way of seeing things. This absolutization of style may have been identified afterwards with an a-political or aristocratic position. But in Flaubert's time, it could only be interpreted as a radical egalitarian principle, upsetting the whole system of representation, the old regime of the art of writing.[11]

Under the new regime of writing, literature is "muted," much less declarative. In it, the relationship between writer and reader become "abstract," less guiding.[12] Synthetized by Rancière but shared by virtually all critics of modernism, this conception of literature renders the ethical *content* of the text hard to pin down. The new politics of the literary is not tantamount, Rancière clarifies, to precise ideological directions inside the text but is instead a matter of the "dissensus" effects of form and is understood, accordingly, as a "re-framing of the real," a new structuring of the "sensible." "The politics of literature," he adds, "thus means that literature as literature is involved in this partition of the visible and the sayable, in this intertwining of being, doing, and saying that frames a polemical common world."[13]

In my view, this conclusion poses two major problems. On one hand, a work's democratic indeterminacy entailed by the "absolutization" of style Rancière refers to does not necessarily follow from the work's intrinsic features, which would render any fiction a vehicle for ethical values, but rather from the inadequacy of the interpretive instruments one depends on to uncover that "système de sympathie du texte" (the text's sympathy or "approval" system), as Jouve dubs it.[14] On the other hand, it bears recognizing that the ways and degrees to which literature exerts its role of de-hierarchizing the sensible are very difficult to assess in Western society during the second half of the twentieth century, when, as Simon During observes in *Against Democracy*, democracy "as we know it" became basically synonymous with social and political normativity across all spheres of public and private, cultural and sexual life.[15]

Negotiating Novelistic Form under Totalitarianism

The situation of literature throughout the Soviet Bloc is, as noted above, illuminating for the insight it provides into politically charged aesthetic forms and how the novel's "internal" democracy—the novel *qua* novelistic art—contributes to the reframing and reinscription of represented reality. Imposed through ruthless administrative measures throughout Joseph V. Stalin's sphere of influence, the poetics of Socialist Realism can be defined as a both formally and thematically homogenizing tendency precisely because the utopia, never achieved, of this literature was to convey the Party's univocal message. Instrumental to this artificial homogeneity, the author's perspective was supposed to coincide entirely with the official line as well as with the reader's take on things, thus turning the audience into a passive recipient of the "message." Within the framework of Stalinist aesthetics, all of these different entities make up and are expected to speak with one voice. Or, one of the most profound changes the "ideological thaw" brought to East European cultures after Stalin's death was to eliminate the very unitary dimension of narrative perspective and instate, or reinstate, dialogism. In Soviet culture, the diversifying of narrative voices, a first step in the democratization of the literary message, was undertaken by leaning on Bakhtin's *The Problems of Dostoevsky's Poetics*, a revised edition of which came out in 1963. As journalist Maia Kaganskaia reminisces in a 1990 text, one can hardly overestimate the significance of Bakhtin's work in the negotiation of freedom in the Soviet era. "Our relation to Bakhtin," discloses Kaganskaia,

> was not disinterested; his texts, already so packed, were overloaded with a subtext, and the criticism of the monologic form of artistic expression we took as the negation of a single ideology in general, and of the one that occupied us in particular (or, more exactly, that occupied itself with us); we read *The Problems of Dostoevsky's Poetics* like a novel: in L. N. Tolstoy, for example, we divined an allegory of Soviet power (which, speaking honestly, is not such a strained interpretation, if one keeps in view a structure whose basic categories, not political but aesthetic, are "the people," "simplicity," and "moral benefit"). Dostoevsky was our positive hero (a symbol of spiritual freedom), and a personage by the name of "Polyphony" stepped forward as an allegory for "pluralism" and "democracy." Ridiculous?—Well, ridiculous. Painful?—Yes, painful.[16]

Around the same time, the need to diversify the means of expression in prose was being debated in Romania, which had been a satellite of the USSR for a decade and a half. Those disputes are especially significant because at stake were not merely some aesthetic formulas but writers' very right and ability to exercise their freedom of expression. The statement made at the ruling party's official Congress in 1961 by Stalin's Romanian counterpart, Gheorghe Gheorghiu-Dej, that "Socialism favors a variegated spectrum of styles provided they share the same political and philosophical premises" opened a Pandora's box by shifting the emphasis away from the aforementioned message or "content" to narrative perspective.[17] Where the Socialist Realist novel started from the assumption of narrative omniscience, which bestowed its own authority on a particular reading of the book in question, the formal decentering of this authority was bound to complicate or muddle that reading. With whom does credibility rest within a novel once the central narrative voice takes a back seat to the characters' many voices, each with his or her view of reality? Further, what type of character can be trusted with furnishing the kind of privileged focal point that would not twist the Party's sacred message? Answering these questions can help not only distinguish between courageous and conformist authors but also get a handle on an emergent *politics of forms*, one in which writers were increasingly and conscientiously engaged in literary praxis. The risk of losing the politically authorized focal point, a threat symptomatic of a deeper crisis of power in the modern novel, was clearly pinpointed at the time by Ovidiu S. Crohmălniceanu, one of the most influential Romanian critics of the era and a supporter of the Socialist Realist platform. "There is," he warned,

> under the pretext of introducing in the novel a non-privileged perspective—the kind offered by everyday life itself—a tendency to set

up the most backward mentality as a benchmark of narrative reliability ... The all-knowing "secretary of the epoch" from the Balzacian novel and the seasoned psychologist of the Proustian novel are giving way to the primitive, desperate, and semi-articulate being of Samuel Beckett's *Comment c'est*.[18]

The abandoning of a single narrative perspective and the mushrooming of viewpoints of sick or irrational characters, or even of dramatis personae who do not embrace the Marxist–Leninist ideology wholeheartedly, made critics loyal to Socialist Realism wary of the narrative machinery of the polyphonic novel. At any rate, in the first stage of the thaw, while fictional content remained untouched, indisputable, and strictly regulated by the Party, this minor formal liberalization represented an unexpected opportunity for writers to reclaim the autonomy of the literary field. Although this literary reformism came from the top, it was incumbent on them to feel out the regime and test the limits of this permissiveness. As they did so, they realized quickly that forms are not merely means of expression but also political vehicles.

It is not a coincidence that Marin Preda's novel *Risipitorii* (Wasters), published in 1963, the year of Gheorghiu-Dej's statements and of the polemics surrounding the rhetoric of fiction, was subject to one of the most intense exchanges between a Romanian author and censorship.[19] Overall, the book did not seem to pose a threat to Stalinist ideology. In fact, *Risipitorii* took up themes already sanctioned by propagandistic literature—for instance, one of the main characters, a steel mill worker, keeps breaking his own Stakhanovite records by overcoming the resistance of the plant's bureaucrats, who, unlike regular workers, were on the approved list of villains of propaganda literature. Nonetheless, the novel's fragmentary and polyphonic drive, which constantly shifts narrative focus away from one character to another, turns the book into a narrative at odds with the constraining poetics of Socialist Realism. This fluidity of perspective translates into a complication of a plot whose relentless branching out makes it hard to restore—and, notably, judge the whole from the ideological angle of—the novel's narrative core, thus engendering a fictional environment in which Preda can more easily sneak in "subversive" references and episodes that offer glimpses into the brutal realities of 1950s Stalinism. One of the most effective techniques of this subversiveness is ellipsis. Thus, although the narrator cannot quite talk openly about political repression, its presence in people's lives is laid out in detail. There is, in all actuality, no character in *Risipitorii* who does not suffer from the political abuses inflicted by the Communist Party. Dr. Munteanu, one of the novel's protagonists, gets suddenly fired from his position at Romania's embassy in Rome; a teacher (Constanța) who has done an excellent job in the classroom is "rewarded" by being sent out "in the field" to spread propaganda in disadvantaged communities; and Vale, who comes up with revolutionary techniques in the workplace, is transferred to another department without explanation. All these things occur out of the blue, and the narrator's *withholding* information on the reasons behind such disruptions in the characters' personal and professional lives is a tactic of calling attention to all these events.

In addition to the complex system of ellipses and the mobility of narrative focalization, a principal component of the ideological narratology in play in Preda and other writers is what Jouve refers to as the text's "sympathy system," namely, the set of ideas and options the work appears to be favoring and that materializes in the narrator's attitude toward his own characters. Remarkably, the "lack of ideological commitment" of narrative voice allowed by the Soviet censors following wave after wave of political thaw does not become ideological neutrality and, by the same token, "transparent" story but requires instead a painstaking decoding of the values inscribed into the text. For instance, in a "democratic" novel, all characters may be free to express themselves before the reader without being reprimanded or corrected by a central narrative actor, but that does not mean that what each of them says carries the same weight. As Suleiman points out in *Le Roman à thèse ou l'autorité fictive*, "certain characters 'are always right'—their comments (foresights, analysis, judgments) are always borne out by events. Such a character plays the role of an accurate interpreter of or spokesperson for the work's values. Once such a character has been created, all comments of this sort enjoy the status of authorized commentary."[20]

Like any other "debate" novels of the liberalizing years, Preda's book too centers around the conflict between two characters. Indeed, Doctors Munteanu and Sârbu embody two opposing stances toward the authorities. The former represents Stalinist ideology, in whose name he sets in place a repressive system in the hospital he runs. At one point, he even denounces his fiancée for her lack of ideological "involvement." The other character, instead, hesitates to join the Communist Party, admitting that the "desire to build a new world had been instilled in him rather than being already there, born in his heart." Moreover, Sârbu is out of place at the political meetings held at the hospital, and his handling of the clichés of the era is awkward. The narrator spends two pages on Sârbu's putative "ideological weaknesses," but they are rather sympathetic:

Dr. Sârbu was himself striving to adopt this style, in which the slogans on the walls or in the papers had to be included and uttered in such a voice as to give the impression that the speaker came up with them all on his own, but he noticed that the hospital's porter was more successful at this than him, and that's when he remembered he was an intellectual and thus had to speak like one, and when he succeeded, he was indeed appreciated, except that it happened once in a blue moon. Most times, when he made up his mind to speak up, even half an hour into the meeting, while listening to those presiding or to those who had already given their little speeches, he would realize that his own viewpoint fit the course of the gathering like a square peg in a round hole.[21]

Going a long way toward unearthing the text's implicit system of values, the frequent face-offs between Munteanu and Sârbu pit political commitment against professional autonomy. Whereas Munteanu argues that no profession "can be exercised freely ... independent of the economic and political laws that govern its society and era," Sârbu takes to task the attempts to co-opt professionalism through actions that have nothing to do with it. "You're setting yourself up," he says, "to be despised and turned into the plaything of social forces that have no interest in allowing professional psychologies to crystallize and acquire relative independence in social struggle."[22] At stake here is not only an issue of professional ethics confined to the academic and medical fields but also the very ethical problem of the intellectual's dealings with an abusive and illegitimate political regime. Granted, the main narrator avoids taking sides explicitly, and yet heroes' actions leave little doubt as to what the novel puts stock in and to what it does not. The characters' "intentional portraits" (*portrait intentionnel*, writes Jouve), which articulate the relationship between how they act and what they believe in, flaunt a glaring discrepancy between the two characters.[23] Sârbu is an accomplished professional capable of highly principled behavior as far as work relationships go, while Munteanu is a parvenu who takes political jobs well outside his expertise and leaves his first wife to marry a Communist high dignitary's daughter, whom he physically abuses. An upstart as he may be, his trajectory throughout the novel is steadily declining and culminates, quite apropos, with an attempt to take his own life.

Although the narrator never passes moral judgments in the course of the novel, he conspicuously endorses Dr. Sârbu's pushback against ideological bullying. Besides the hero's intentional portrait, the novel resorts to a number of narrative techniques to convey this endorsement not *expressis verbis* but, again, *formally*. Pivotal episodes in Munteanu's downfall such as the political meeting where he is exposed as a "reactionary" and his attempted suicide are narratively filtered through Sârbu, who takes them in and comments on them with empathy and bitterness. Thus, at the end of the novel, the narrator decides to yield narrative agency to one character, while distancing himself from the other, and this move indexes an ideological and political choice impossible to overlook. It becomes clear that *Risipitorii*'s *porte-parole* or authorial "spokesperson" is Sârbu, who, without representing a dissident's position with respect to the regime, declines to yield to ideological pressures. The novel's plea for the intellectual's moral and professional autonomy in a world where everything appears to be shaped by monolithic ideology emerges as the book's lesson. Not only is the latter central, but it is also subversive in a context that was still demanding, in no ambiguous terms, an equally unambiguous commitment to Marxist–Leninist politics. Yet again, the complex negotiation that went on between the writer and censorship of the era always took literary form into account. The most serious objection the censors raised to Preda's novel was that, while treating fairly the problem of "straying" from the Party's teachings, the frequency with which *Risipitorii* returns to them in the course of the story is likely to totally trivialize those teachings. Thus, one censor took issue with "the presence in the book of a host of facts that, together, amount to a very negative image, the positive aspects being easily overlooked, indeed barely mentioned so as to make room for the negative ones ... the numerous negative details are not warranted by the exigencies of the composition; they are just additions."[24] In other words, the novel's "negativity"—the subversive thrust the censor's antennae picked up on—inheres in its formal characteristics, that is, in a certain distribution of narrative matter, not in "content" per se. But, to reiterate, the procedure is hardly politically innocent. If, after the official condemnation of Stalinism, some deficiencies of Marxist-Leninism could be exposed, the moment they were spelled out and foregrounded as a book's central "compositional" principle they were denounced as a threat to official ideology.

The publication of the first volume of *Risipitorii*, we can say in hindsight, kicked off in Romanian culture the cat-and-mouse game between authors and censors. The game made available something vital, namely, a mechanism for *negotiating aesthetic forms*. The workings of this complex apparatus are insightfully described by semiotician Lev Loseff in his foundational 1983 study, *On the Beneficence of Censorship: Aesopian Language in Modern Russian Literature*. As Loseff explains, the overall dynamic of literary communication under Communism, one radically different from what was going on in democratic countries, unfolded along these lines:

> The text as it is created by the Author includes a segment to which the censorship is agreeable (Tc); a segment which the censorship will find objectionable, a taboo segment (Tnc); and a segment of noise (N), an authorial deficiency. As it passes through the filter of effective censorship (C), the text loses Tnc (blacked out by the censor) but retains Tc (understandably) as well as N, this being the province of aesthetic criticism, not the censorship (ideological censorship in its ideal State is not concerned with whether a work is well or poorly written, but only with whether that work contains information which has been forbidden to spread).[25]

Loseff observes that commenting on the background noise effect falls within the purview of literary criticism rather than of censorship. The latter is not so much preoccupied with the quality of the work in question as with whether or not said work contains information that could pose a threat to official politics. Loseff's abstract model, which does not apply to all situations, accounts, however, for the ways literary forms became hard currency on the aesthetic "black market" of anti-totalitarian ideology.

One must recognize, on the other hand, that the "anti-" prefix somewhat overstates the case. For, in the broader scheme of the intricate equation of official messages, the more or less significant deviations from them, and purely literary signals, the literature playing this game made for an ambiguous mixture of conformism and non-conformism. At best, these texts enacted what Wolf calls an "internal democracy" system, one geared to a departure from the hierarchy of representations in circulation in societies under totalitarianism, or, in Rancière's terms, to a redistribution of the sensible. This operation is not very different from the "transformation" Evgeny Dobrenko, perhaps the subtlest critic of Stalinist aesthetics, talks about. Remarkably, Dobrenko does not view Socialist Realism as a phenomenon limited to totalitarian art but as a fundamental mechanism of converting raw reality into ideological fiction. "Soviet society," Dobrenko comments, "was precisely and above all a society for consumption: ideological consumption. Socialist Realism was a machine for transforming Soviet reality into socialism. That is why its basic function was not propagandistic but aesthetic and transformative by excellence."[26] As Dobrenko understands it, Socialist Realism was not a literary current but rather a complex mode of reorganizing the substance of the sensible into new ideological categories. This mode boiled down to a redeploying and ideological rescreening of reality through the Party doxa and ultimately brought about a "de-realization" of existence in its most basic, quotidian as well as historical ramifications.[27] In the ample process of redefining all aspects of life, from social relations (e.g., the polarization of progressive and reactionary classes) to tradition (for instance, the erasure from public memory of major historical events or efforts to bestow new meanings on them) and even everyday language, reality as such fizzled out to make room for its Socialist construction. It is on this account that, in *L' écrivain et le dictateur*, Luc Rasson approaches both totalitarianism and purportedly "anti-totalitarian" writing as fictional projects. "The relationship of totalitarianism to the literature that claims to denounce it," Rasson maintains,

> is then one between one fiction and another. That is to say, individual fictions, i.e., novels, which acknowledge their own fictional status, push against a collective fiction, i.e., ideology, which seeks to pass itself off as reality. The function of criticism is activated when literary fiction exposes the fiction that wants us to take it for reality, law, and truth.[28]

Such considerations alert us to the elaborate interplay of fiction and reality both inside totalitarian ideology and the literature that sought to counter it. More often than not, fictional prose reacted to totalitarian fiction's assault on the sensible by restoring reality, whether that involved protecting the present, recovering a past untainted by ideological makeover, or casting doubt on Party dogma. In short, the efforts to democratize the novel in Romania and other East European countries during the 1960s strove mainly to do away with Stalinist fiction's hierarchical makeup of ideological, "de-realizing" representations. A massive infusion of variegated, complex, and concrete reality was called on to destabilize this edifice of unreality.

Retrieving the truth underneath its fictionalizing ideological veneer hinges, in Loseff's terms, on writers' ability to sell non-conformist content as noise effect, mere stylistic ornament, to censorship officials. Two Romanian authors stood out in this respect during Communism. One of them is Dumitru Radu Popescu. In Popescu's novel series *F*, the noise effect is so powerful that it completely drowns out—or, better yet, supplies the perfect "static" cover for—the meanings the novelist wants his readers, in all likelihood, to come away with.[29] Inspired by William Faulkner's formal innovations, in *F*, as well as in the 1973 novel *Vânătoarea regală* (Royal Hunt), Popescu "keeps changing the narrative forms," "experimenting with all the epic modes" from outward presentation to inner monologue, playing with multiple perspectives, and shifting away from the fantastic to the comic and the grotesque.[30] Thus, the novel both forefronts certain truths about the sociopolitical dramas of the Stalinist years and makes it all but impossible to pin those truths down and blame their enunciation on the writer. To make the censors' lives even more difficult, the characters are caricatures or paradoxical figures, "twisted people" who speak in parables and behave irrationally. Attributing politically unorthodox views and conduct to such unreliable oddballs is here an essential ploy of narrative eastethics. Over and against this confusing backdrop, political activists' brutal treatment of the country folks, if not of the "enlightened" few among the Communists themselves, in the name of building the perfect society is concurrently less salient narratively and *there* nonetheless. The noise effect at once conceals, protects, *and* relays the taboo information as narrative presentation scours the ideological varnish off historical reality.

The other writer who managed most efficiently this literary hide-and-show game and who lies, surely not by accident, at the top of the 1960–1980 Romanian prose canon is Preda. He had an unparalleled grasp of the rules and what it took to win. It was no secret to him that key to success was good command of the techniques of symbolic representation. Where Popescu's "method" was to build up narrative noise and use it as decoy and camouflage, Preda's consisted in cutting it down to a minimum. The second volume of *Moromeții*, possibly the most successful political novel of the liberalizing decades, virtually puts on trial Romanian Communism by enlisting the formal apparatus of the polyphonic novel. Both fiction

and political argument, the book seems, at first blush, to strike a balance
between the old, pre-World War II world and the new one. But a closer
examination of the text's "system of sympathy" goes to show that, in
Morometii's second volume, the pivotal narrative voice sides decisively
with the former, which is on the verge of vanishing. Furthermore, a look
at how Preda develops his characters reveals that the author caricaturizes
the Communists, be they true believers or not, while also subjecting to
ridicule a hero such as Niculae, the genuine spokesperson of the new
society. Preda goes back here to a technique already tried out in *Risipitorii*.
Absolutely essential to the practice and critical understanding of the
politics of literary form in East European totalitarianisms, this technique
is subversion through "fictional mandate" or "delegation." Again, Preda
keeps "background noise" low. Its source is the dialogical setup and,
inside it, the portrayal of the main character, Ilie Moromete, as a bizarre
type who enjoys waking up his son late at night to argue about politics.
Moromete critiques the very foundations of the regime, and his charges,
which basically remain unrebutted, are peppered with references to the
confiscation of private property, the destruction of meritocracy, and the
curtailing of free-expression rights.

The ethos of literature under Communism took shape, as it does
in *Morometii,* inside the novel, through an overlap of the text's moral
"voice-over" and the perspective of a protagonist such as Moromete, but,
interestingly enough, could be corroborated outside the storyworld by
the author's public sanctioning of characters' opinions. Worth noting is
that such authorial "sympathies" for a certain hero or heroine mattered
a great deal both during the Socialist Realist years, when a writer
could be held responsible for a character's words and acts, and during
liberalization. This identification, which gave writers so much headache
in the 1950s, would be turned into a dissensus ploy for taking shots at
official politics starting with the second half of the 1960s, when, as critic
Sorin Alexandrescu comments, the "narrator's protest replaced the protest
of the writer-as-citizen."[31] Thus, such subtle connections and equivalences
between the real author's stance and his or her narrators' and characters'
constitute the most complex aspects of the politics of the novel under
totalitarian censorship. In Preda's case, things are even more complicated
because the writer's ideas have been routinely, if sometimes too quickly,
treated as echoing the protagonist's. "Why are the writer's thoughts
deemed 'morometian' even in articles or books that do not even mention
Moromete's name? Why are his attitudes toward events compared to
those Moromete would have had in similar situations? Why is Moromete
not a 'Marin Preda type,' as it would seem natural? Who is the father and
who is the son?" wonders Florin Mugur in the introduction to his volume
of interviews with Preda.[32]

An East European Fictional Pact?

Exploring how the ambiguous relationship between the authorial self and textual voices fashions meaning, Susan S. Lanser has proposed five criteria for what she calls implied reading, that is, a reading that aims to connect the worldview of narrative voice with the author's.[33] Among them, at least one bears on the poetics of narrative form under totalitarianism, namely, the one pertaining to "reliability" and referring to the compatibility between the author's values and perceptions and the narrator's or protagonist's. Such meaning transfers and inferences from author to character and the other way around, unwarranted as they seem to those of us beholden to the basic conventions of what has been called the "fictional pact," occurred frequently in the literary and political arenas of Communism. Available evidence tells us that Preda actually benefited from the moral capital his characters accrued in the public eye. Thus, he belongs to a category that, to paraphrase Iulia Zaretskaia-Balsente, I would label "integrated nonconformists," that is, a class of cultural actors "who are keen on doing their jobs by inserting themselves into the extant societal structures imposed on them ... but who, in their everyday activity, place emphasis on the role of what we have called social critique."[34] This "social critique" is part and parcel of Preda's image as "unofficial public consciousness" and "moral symbol" in Romanian literary milieus. Whether or not Preda protested, among his associates, against official attempts to re-Stalinize culture in the early 1970s, the image in question was not painted in such meetings but through a subtle—and subtly formal—negotiation between fiction and the author's conduct *outside* the book's covers. Needless to say, Preda's case is anything but isolated; writers' symbolic authority under Communism generally depended on this interplay, which was in turn a function of the political management of literary forms *inside* texts.

All in all, we are dealing here with a fairly unique situation, which may allow for a theoretical recalibration of the venerable problem of the thorny relationships between aesthetic and ethical or political acts. Bound up with this issue, specifically with the fictional pact built into it, was another, "reading contract," which generally regulates the interface among the members of the author-work-reader triangle. What must be underscored here is that Cold War East European literatures have—quite literally—rewritten the compact that, in modern prose and, again, from within literature itself, stipulates the moves readers are to make so as to respond to works successfully. If the "fictional pact" of Western modernity was largely predicated on the notion that, very simply put, it would be a "fallacy" to read a fictional text as a reference to the "real world," that was certainly not the meaning-making premise here. The difference stems from the role the text in question assumed or was assigned in that world.

Sorting out the functions a text can perform according to its public status, Dominique Maingueneau employs the criterion of a "framing scene," which defines, he says, a work as fictional or non-fictional discourse, as literary, religious, philosophical, and so forth.[35] These classifications determine the text's relationship with reality and subsequently the need, plausibility, and overall relevance of conjectures about the text's ethos. Or, in the pre-1989 East European context, the fictional nature of literature was permanently under pressure—treated with suspicion, discounted, regarded as cover for political allegory, and so on—by censors, ordinary readers, and the authors themselves. Under these circumstances, the "religion of the aesthetic," which, according to critic Mircea Martin, characterizes post-Stalinist Communist Romania, needs to be rethought. It does not testify, I think, to a reluctance to deal with ethical and political themes, but, quite the contrary, to an eagerness to take them up but to do so formally.

This decision, this moral commitment, required, however, a tactical dissimulation of the fictional contract in effect, a disguising ploy that allowed ethical and political meanings to be articulated *and* shared with the public.[36] Ultimately, this dissimulation made it possible to Preda, Augustin Buzura,[37] Constantin Țoiu,[38] and other Romanian writers of the time to bring to light in their novels most of the political system's deficiencies. While stopping short of confronting the Communist regime head-on, these works contain essential information about the repressive Stalinist system, the mechanisms of the secret police (the infamous Securitate), the social injustices ironically brought about by Communism, and the persecution of intellectuals. For this reason, when the autonomy of the *aesthetic* was threatened, and this complex contract was rescinded by authorities, both writers and readers felt deprived of their right to truth, history, and the relative democracy couched, let me reemphasize, in the *aesthetic* form itself. On this ground too, the very concept of easethics as presumably betraying an absence of ethical concerns and an understanding of literature as a gratuitous, carefree pursuit must be reconceived so as to do justice to what actually drives this notion and practice, that is, a subtle if less apparent dialectic of the ethical and the literary.[39] Thus, the claim Lovinescu made in 1990 should be nuanced to the effect that ethics (understood as a writer's moral engagement) and aesthetics (exercised as an art of literary expressiveness) need not be and, in our case, were not opposites, as she thought. They are correlatives, and, again, their dynamic is dialectical, accompanied all along by the authors' constant reflection on its formal operations, on the means of artistic expression that enabled them to voice certain political positions at a time of censorship. It is precisely the aesthetic pact of fiction that, encoding the core provisions and affordances of the politics of form, permitted the fostering and publicization of social and ethical stances and values.

The fictional contract made allowances for a particular relationship between authors and readers. The relationship rested on a cultural capital whose accumulation depended on how well the writer played the game of politics and form—and of politics *as* form—and assumed what Alexandre Gefen has called, following Roland Barthes, "the responsibility of forms" so as to designate, within the politically engaged literature of the twentieth century, the shift away from questions of theme to the problem of expressiveness.[40] In his essay on Stalinism as "total art," Boris Groys reminds us that "the basic tenets of the socialist realist method were developed in extremely evolved and highly intellectual discussions whose participants often paid with their lives for an infelicitous or inopportune formulation, and this of course increased even more their responsibility for each word they uttered."[41] To be sure, writers were expected or, out of a desire for recognition, felt compelled to speak out on important public issues, and when they did not do so, their very silence was deemed telling. But it was not just their conduct that was supposed to reflect a distinct ethos; the readers' behavior *as* readers was subject to similar anticipations and demands. Joseph Brodsky noted that the rise in literacy standards under Communism turned virtually the entire population into a massive audience capable of fairly sophisticated perusal and of adeptly reading between the lines.[42] So what Eastern Europe witnessed after World War II was the ethics of citizenship *play out as an ethics and politics of reading*. This conversion enabled citizens-readers to work through the ellipses, paraphrases, and other forms of indirect language of an "Aesopian" narrative system bent on taking apart and complicating democratically the hegemonic one-story of the regime. A highly intense dialogue between writers and readers thus took place for decades in this part of the world. As a result, the presence and political significance of literature in the public consciousness became quite acute; conversely, the literati were fully aware of this reality and catered to it.

This all translated into a clear sense that writers did have views, expressed them, albeit obliquely, and were otherwise "engaged" and present, in brief that who they were and what they thought made a difference no matter how ambiguously their being there and opinions were conveyed. This authorial presence may explain, said ambiguity notwithstanding, why East European criticism never really gave up on the idea of the author figure as a repository and reflector of the text's "moral authority." In a book published in 1981 and titled *Întoarcerea autorului* (The Return of the Author), Romanian critic Eugen Simion rebuts the "death of the author" argument in French literature and criticism from Arthur Rimbaud and Stéphane Mallarme to Phillipe Sollers and Maurice Blanchot, contending—no doubt prompted by his dealings with Romanian literature—that "not only does the author create the work, but a work also starts to create an author in its own image."[43] Likewise, the most influential theory of the Romanian novel, namely, that put forth by Nicolae Manolescu in the three-volume monograph *Arca lui Noe* (Noah's Ark, 1980–3), revisits the Romanian history of the genre as a process in which the omniscient narrator's authoritarian "voice" gradually dies out while an entire polyphony comes about and boosts characters' agency, thus hinting at the novel as a democratic form and anticipating some of the debates on rhetorical and contextual narratology initiated by Altes and Seymour Chatman and Ansgar Nünning, respectively. In this vein, one must understand eastethics as the shortest route not only between the writer's intent and the reader's horizon of expectations but also between the text's sociopolitical "baggage" and the author's narrative choices. And so, if today there still is a gap in narrative studies between literature and social commitment, a "chasm," as Mieke Bal says, between narratology and politics, I think it can be bridged.[44] To do so, we would be well advised, first, to bring back into conversation concepts such as *intentio autoris* (the author's intent), *intentio operis* (the work's intent), and *intentio lectoris* (the reader's intent)—a triad long fallen by the wayside in the aftermath of structuralism and poststructuralism—and, second, to draw from the formal, and yet so substantial, engagement of East European novelists such as Preda, Popescu, and Buzura. This engagement, I suggest, reopens with concrete and rich evidence the case entered by Rancière on behalf of a literature determined to remain both literary and *engagé*.

Notes

1 Nelly Wolf, "Le roman comme démocratie," *Revue d'histoire littéraire de la France* 105, no. 2 (2005): 343–52.
2 Fredric Jameson, *The Political Unconscious: Narrative as a Socially Symbolic Act* (New York: Routledge, 2002), 141.
3 Vincent Jouve, *Poétique des valeurs* (Paris: Presses Universitaires de France, 2001), 34.
4 See Jérôme Meizoz, *Postures littéraires. Mises en scène modernes de l'auteur* (Geneva: Slatkine, 2007).
5 See James Phelan, *Experiencing Fiction: Judgments, Progressions, and the Rhetorical Theory of Narrative* (Columbus: Ohio State University Press, 2007).
6 See Liesbeth Korthals Altes, *Ethos and Narrative Interpretation: The Negotiation of Values in Fiction* (Lincoln: University of Nebraska Press, 2014).
7 Revathi Krishnaswamy, "Toward World Literary Knowledges: Theory in the Age of Globalization," *Comparative Literature* 62, no. 4 (Fall 2010): 399–419.
8 Wolf, "Le roman comme démocratie," 343.
9 Monica Lovinescu (1923–2008) was one of the most important voices of the Romanian exile during the Communist years. Having emigrated to Paris in 1947, she became an editor with Radio Free Europe, where she commented on the Romanian cultural scene. Collected and published beginning with the volume *Unde scurte* (Short Waves, 1978), most of her interventions focus on the Communist censorship of Romanian literature, decrying the atrocities

committed under Stalin's and Ceauşescu's regimes while also often lamenting writers' timid dissent.

10 Monica Lovinescu, "Răspuns la o masă rotundă a Grupului pentru Dialog Social," 22 15 (1990): 8.

11 Jacques Rancière, *Dissensus: On Politics and Aesthetics*, ed. and trans. Stevan Corcoran (New York: Continuum, 2010), 156.

12 See Jacques Rancière, *La parole muette. Essai sur la contradiction de la littérature* (Paris: Fayard, 2011).

13 Rancière, *Dissensus: On Politics and Aesthetics*, 152.

14 Jouve, *Poétique des valeurs*, 121.

15 Simon During, *Against Democracy: Literary Experience in the Era of Emancipations* (New York: Fordham University Press, 2012).

16 Maia Kaganskaia, "Shutovskoi khorovod," quoted in Joseph Frank, *Through the Russian Prism: Essays on Russian Literature and Culture* (Princeton, NJ: Princeton University Press, 1990), 32.

17 Quoted in Paul Georgescu and Matei Călinescu, "Probleme ale poeziei actuale," *Gazeta literară* 7, no. 46 (1961): 16.

18 Ovidiu S. Crohmălniceanu, "Romanul fără autor," *Gazeta literară* 10, no. 35 (1963): 7.

19 Marin Preda (1922–80) is one of the most discussed post-World War II authors in Romania. His body of work illustrates all the transformations that Romanian literature has undergone since Socialist Realism, when Preda wrote fiction that served Stalinist propaganda, such as *Ana Roşculeţ* or *Desfăşurarea*, until the so-called period of liberalization, when he recovered, in part, his freedom of expression. His greatest accomplishments as a prose writer are the novels *Moromeţii* (vol. 1: 1955; vol. 2: 1967), which takes place in a rural setting and whose protagonist, Ilie Moromete, is portrayed as a subversive figure, rejecting both ruthless capitalism (vol. 1) and Communist propaganda (vol. 2), and *Cel mai iubit dintre pământeni* (*The Most Beloved Earthling*, 1980), one of the most ambitious novels written under Communism, a book that denounces Stalinist atrocities.

20 Susan Rubin Suleiman, *Le Roman à thèse ou l'autorité fictive* (Paris: Presses Universitaires de France, 1983), 201.

21 Marin Preda, *Risipitorii* (Bucharest: Curtea Veche, 2011), 246.

22 Preda, *Risipitorii*, 303.

23 Jouve, *Poétique des valeurs*, 73.

24 Ioana Diaconescu, *Marin Preda: Un portret în arhivele Securităţii* (Bucharest: Muzeul Literaturii Române, 2015), 263.

25 Lev Lossef, *On the Beneficence of Censorship: Aesopian Language in Modern Russian Literature* (Munich: Verlag Otto Sagner in Kommission, 1984), 45.

26 Evgheny Dobrenko, *Political Economy of Socialist Realism*, trans. Jesse M. Savage (New Haven, CT: Yale University Press, 2007), 5.

27 Dobrenko, *Political Economy of Socialist Realism*, 14.

28 Luc Rasson, *L'écrivain et le dictateur. Ecrire l'expérience totalitaire* (Paris: Editions Imago, 2008), 14.

29 The prose of Dumitru Radu Popescu (1935–) is revealing in terms of the Faulknerian narrative techniques it introduces into Romanian prose. If his early books *Fuga* (Running Away) and *Zilele săptămânii* (Weekdays) are

beholden to Socialist Realism and propagandistic literature, he distanced himself gradually from their schemas in favor of more complex formulas. Novels such as *F* (1969), *Vânătoarea regală* (1973), or *O bere pentru calul meu* (A Beer for My Horse, 1974) have been critically acclaimed for subverting the realist conventions of traditional prose.

30 Gheorghe Perian, *Pagini de critică și istorie literară* (Cluj-Napoca, Romania: Ardealul, 1998), 127.

31 Sorin Alexandrescu, "Intelectualul ca mediator social," 22 15 (1991): 14–15.

32 Florin Mugur, *Convorbiri cu Marin Preda* (Bucharest: Albatros, 1973), 10.

33 Susan S. Lanser, "The 'I' of the Beholder: Equivocal Attachments and the Limits of Structuralist Narratology," in *A Companion to Narrative Theory*, ed. James Phelan and Peter J. Rabinowitz (Malden, MA: Blackwell, 2005), 206–19.

34 Ioulia Zaretskaia-Balsente, *Les intellectuels et la censure en URSS* (Paris: L'Harmattan, 2000), 21.

35 Dominique Maingueneau, "Ethos, scénographie, incorporation," in *Images de soi dans le discours*, ed. Ruth Amossy and Jean-Michel Adam (Lausanne: Delachaux et Niestlé, 1999), 75–100.

36 Mircea Martin, "Despre estetismul socialist," *România literară* 37, no. 23 (2004): 18–19.

37 Augustin Buzura (1938–2017) is one of the most popular prose writers of the Communist era, appreciated both by the public and literary critics for novels such as *Absenții* (The Absents, 1970), *Fețele tăcerii* (The Faces of Silence, 1974), *Orgolii* (Prides, 1977), and *Vocile nopții* (Voices of the Night, 1980), where he decries allusively the ills of the Communist system, from generalized corruption to repressive institutions.

38 Constantin Țoiu became known following the publication of his novel *Galeria cu viță sălbatică* (The Ivy Vine Screen, 1976), where parable, symbolism, and a bookish style mobilize references to the surveillance system and the concentration camps of the Stalinist era.

39 Monica Lovinescu, *O istorie a literaturii române pe unde scurte 1960–2000*, ed. and preface Cristina Cioabă (Bucharest: Humanitas, 2014).

40 Alexandre Gefen, "Responsabilités de la forme. Voies et détours de l'engagement littéraire contemporain," in *L'Engagement littéraire*, ed. E. Bouju (Rennes: Presses Universitaires de Rennes, 2005), 75–84.

41 Boris Groys, *The Total Art of Stalinism: Avant-garde, Aesthetic Dictatorship, and Beyond*, trans. Charles Rougle (Princeton, NJ: Princeton University Press, 1992), 9.

42 Joseph Brodsky, "Jazyk — edinstvennyj avangardist," interview given to V. Rybakov, *Russkaya Mysl* 3188 (January 26, 1978), 8, quoted in Lossef, *On the Beneficence of Censorship*, 19.

43 Eugen Simion, *Întoarcerea autorului. Eseuri despre relația creator-operă*, afterword and critical bibliography by Andrei Terian (Bucharest: Univers Enciclopedic Gold, 2013), 7. The book has been translated into English as *The Return of the Author*, ed. and with an introduction by James W. Newcomb, trans. Lidia Vianu (Evanston, IL: Northwestern University Press, 1996).

44 Mieke Bal, "Introduction to Volume III," in *Narrative Theory: Critical Concepts in Literary and Cultural Studies*, vol. 3, *Political Narratology*, ed. Mieke Bal (London: Taylor & Francis, 2004), 2.

4

METAPOLITICS:
Recommitting Literature in the
Populist Aftermath

Ioana Macrea-Toma

A strange convergence in political debates across the world is currently taking place between liberalism and populism, which both appear intent on contesting the cultural paradigm of multiculturalism and minority politics. While countries in Central and Eastern Europe as well as from the Euroatlantic region have witnessed the combined resurgence of nationalism and anti-liberalism, some political pundits have hastened to include liberalism itself in the genealogy of newly violent rhetoric targeting racial, ethnic, religious, or sexual minorities. It is worth asking, in this context, how can literature recommit itself politically as the emerging identity-related pathologies are affecting political landscapes from Brazil and France to the United Kingdom and the United States? Answering this question is my chapter's goal. To that effect, I take my cue from Alain Badiou and principally from Pierre Rosanvallon, who, following Pierre Bourdieu's 1993 book *La Misère du monde* and Michel Foucault's 1978–9 *Les vies parallèles,* has recently pointed to the necessity of a civic and intellectual project susceptible to foreground multiple ways of being and to *render visible* the critique of those categories that appear to be underrepresented in society's political structures.[1]

According to Rosanvallon, the latter should articulate the aspirations of the politically "anonymous"—the unrepresented, underrepresented, and therefore nameless politically—and channel those desires into the labor of "intercomprehension," of coming to grips, that is, with the composite ethnocultural makeup of the social body so as to prevent frustrations and potentially extremist backlashes at the ballot box and otherwise. I would claim, however, that, had he taken into account the literatures from the former Communist Bloc, Rosanvallon would have drawn somewhat different conclusions. It is noteworthy, in this vein, that the sociologically minded post–Cold War literature of the region has been aesthetically *and* politically invested. Its authors have composed more than just fictional ethnographies even though, in postcommunist Central and Eastern Europe, since 1989 identity politics has been bouncing back and forth between a Western understanding of multiculturalism and a multiethnic reality experienced as divisive and disruptive. Nor have the region's political elites really taken up the multiculturalist agenda whose implementation European integration required. At the same time, minorities' newly developed self-perception has run an entire identity gamut from ethnic and territorial identification to social affiliation with and across excluded and marginalized categories such as women, migrants, and religiously and sexually discriminated groups. Thus, and despite the conceptual pressures sometimes applied by Western-funded NGOs, "multiculturalism never took palpable roots," as critics have underscored, "in ... postcommunist political cultures."[2] Instead—and this is what I am basically contending here—the deeply political thematics of multicultural interactions and minority rights has asserted itself in the already existing, "intellocentric" cultural modality typical of this part of Europe, namely, availing itself of intellectuals' and especially fiction writers' work as a site for vigorous representation and dissection.

On this account, I turn, in what follows, to Romanian authors such as Radu Pavel Gheo, Dinu Guțu, Bogdan Suceavă, Adrian Schiop, and Gabriela Adameșteanu, and I revisit their narratives as a twofold reflective enterprise, that is, as reflection or representation of a certain social environment as well as reflection *on* it, or *meta*reflection, meditation on the whole entanglement of identity-related political tensions and issues of the world portrayed in the books of these novelists. Instrumental to my analysis is the notion of *metapolitical* literature. The italicized term is not my coinage. Among other things, Badiou's 1998 book *Abrégé de métapolitique* comes to mind right away.[3] However, where the French philosopher deploys the metapolitical in his rebuttal of what he views as a rather socially disengaged liberal political philosophy that has relegated politics to a matter of "freely expressed" opinions, I see metapolitics as a literary, primarily fictional form enabling Central and East European and Romanian authors to present and think critically about a wide array of political topics ranging from multicultural to regional and ethnic situations and political rights, social aspects that have been inadequately addressed by right-wing and left-wing activists and politicians alike after 1989. Let us also remember that critics such as Badiou end up proposing a radical reconceptualization of democracy itself, which they fault for being too obedient to the state, and that this rethinking favors a non-consensual political emancipation from the bottom up. Instead, the writers I am considering here, critical as they prove of postcommunism's political morass and lingo, are hardly for doing away either with liberal democracy "as we know it" or with the statal structures affording its workings. Yet again, they do not "theorize" this and related positions; they *stage* or narrativize them as writers, in and as their art. This is why metapolitics designates below a *literary practice*, one that has the makings of a "transitional" genre or sorts, for it consists of fictional writings produced during the transition out of Communism, which outgrow quickly the phase of superficial engagement with political events and subjects and enter into an effective dialogue with political sciences and activism by tackling "marginal" themes systematically. As I will demonstrate, such works, and Romanian novels in particular, show interesting, perhaps surprising affinities with a segment of world literature expanding of late in the West and its former colonies and which a growing number of critics have identified as "post-postcolonial." What sets aside this corpus is its critique of contemporary identity discourses. Comparable thematically and otherwise to this zone of post-postcolonial fiction, the novels in question typically pursue, I submit, broader sociopolitical objectives, marking programmatically, openly, and thoroughly the civic-political engagement of fiction writers. This directness speaks to a passion for truth and a commitment on the part of authors who distance themselves both from the allusive-formalist literary style dominant before 1989, which basically sought to dodge censure, and from the clichés of post-1989 political analysis and public discourse, which were often out of touch with social realities.

"Post" Alignments: Postcommunism, Postcolonialism, Post-Postcolonialism, and Literature as Politics

After the Cold War, the resurgence of rhetorics and social behaviors suggestive of an entire pathology of identity and, at the same time, the assault on cultural pluralism, perceived as being imposed by the West, appear to be in Central and Eastern Europe both nationalist aftershocks of Communism and anti-globalization reactions. Compounding the situation has been the incoherent and largely undependable political culture of the new elites. The anxieties triggered by the decline in living standards determined by the flux of transnational capital, coupled with the loss of trust in liberal politics in the early 1990s, initially led to an acknowledgment of the contradictions between economic liberalism and democracy and subsequently to growing skepticism about the whole ideological-institutional edifice of liberalism, including the modern state and its legitimacy, the integration into Euroatlantic structures, and individual cultural rights, and eventually to a decreased interest in political participation altogether. Over and against this gloomy backdrop, the populists stepped in, claiming to reinvigorate political life by eliminating taboos presumably linked to "political correctness" and by appealing directly to constituencies neglected by precedent policies—"the people."[4] Even though Romania has not experienced the populist phenomenon in its extreme forms, the 2018 referendum on the constitutional definition of the family, along with the assault on the judicial system, sent a strong message about a possible anti-liberal backsliding similar to what was going on not just in neighboring states but also in Europe and beyond, where the rise of Donald J. Trump and other leaders like him refocused the conversation on the role liberalism, and not just conservatism, had played in the revival of racist and xenophobic nationalism.

Now, as critics such as Mark Lilla have insisted, liberal governments have appropriated leftist vocabularies of freedom of expression of marginalized socioethnic categories but have got bogged down into a sort of particularism of identity that has obscured a more unifying social vision.[5] The discrimination experienced by minorities would thus be reproduced, Lilla suggests, by the very discourse meant to eradicate it. His *The Once and Future Liberal: After Identity Politics* documents, in fact, a larger distrust in multiculturalism as a political ideology. The latter's critique and ensuing weakening have been taking place in the West at a time when, at the Eastern end of Europe, multiculturalism remains either poorly conceptualized or, worse, treated with suspicion as an "import." Besides the classical conflict of the early 1990s between the pro-Western elites and the former Nomenklatura's Communists, now attempting to reinvent themselves as "autochthonous" voices, the "culture wars" in Romania attest to an overall adherence to the diversity ideal. Romanian critic Sorin Antohi has pointed out, though, that the EU accession-related reforms became a bone of contention among the liberal elites themselves once they came into power in 1996.[6] This demonstrated, according to Antohi, that their ideology was abstract, incoherent, and "literary." The launch of the Bucharest-based magazine *Observator cultural* in 2000 brought about, however, a significant change of tone in the ongoing disputes through its explicit embrace of multiculturalism and "PC" but without raising the intellectual level of "culture wars" rhetoric. This remained confined, as Antohi would also have it, to the realm of personal, non-doctrinal conflict, following a polemical scenario not unlike those in Hungary and Poland, except that Romanian neoconservative groups did not become radicalized in an ethno-nationalist and anti-liberal sense.

To rephrase my earlier question, then, what role does literature play in a cultural field where the problems of disadvantaged and marginal identities have been neither politically examined nor sufficiently explored by alternative social histories and, more generally, by rigorous scholarship? Furthermore, can East European fiction supply a political rather than just literary solution worth considering at a time marked worldwide, on one hand, by renewed and multiple civic and ethnoracial challenges, and on the other, by increased efforts to move the entire discussion into a "postmulticultural" stage? My argument is that Romanian literature has served, for two-odd decades now, as *political analysis by default*, to wit, as metapolitics. In this capacity, it has taken up the hot-button issues of a culture struggling to come to terms with its own social and ethnic complexity, and it has done so by resisting the pressures of the commonplaces of traditional multicultural critique while not losing sight of local realities. To be sure, the authors I summon here have more than a theoretical relationship to issues of national, regional, and transregional identity, migration, gender, and sexual orientation. Some of them are transnational actors who, inside and outside their country of origin, have been exposed to multicultural environments and controversies. This is one reason they appear well equipped to resonate, quite critically, to this whole thematics at home. As they do so, they respond to everyday situations pertaining to multiculturalism, diversity, and minority rights. In a more oblique yet highly instructive way, they also react to the clichés peppering more mainstream, political takes on these issues in scholarship on better-known writers such as Zadie Smith and Chimamanda Ngozi Adichie, who have also dwelled at length on such matters. Not only that, but Smith, Adichie, and others have done so oftentimes in the same metapolitical spirit as their Romanian counterparts, thus foregrounding interesting similitudes between postcolonial and postcommunist literatures.

In effect, Smith's and Adichie's fiction seems poised, as if echoing Lilla's objections, to critique identity discourses and reassess their relevance in societies in which ethnocultural *hybridity* has provided strong competition to *diversity*, multiculturalism's initial *mot d'ordre*. The two women writers illustrate, in fact, a recent postcolonial experience in which this shift is conspicuously in play and, as such, instrumental, as some say, to the fast-expanding logic of "post-postcolonialism." Born in the mid-1970s to parents of color (Adichie in Nigeria, and Smith, whose mother is Jamaican, in England), both writers pursued humanistic studies in the United States (Adichie) and Great Britain (Smith), respectively, in the late 1990s and drew public attention as postcolonial realities and scholarship were tested by the new dynamic of late globalization. Furthermore, they seem to have absorbed the kind of theory, or at least, feminist worldview, arising after the heyday of postcolonialism. According to these new theoretical developments, the focus on peripheries and local cultures must avoid reproducing the "essentialist" thrust of dominant reading models, metropolitan or not, and throw light instead on the mutual and complicated exchanges and contaminations between centers and margins, as well as among margins themselves, in the current phase of globalization.

Thus, Adichie manages in her 2013 novel *Americanah* to develop a nuanced critique of racism through the depiction of various forms of discrimination to which people of color are subjected.[7] What has been less noticed by critics, however, is that she is also subtly dissecting only apparently nondiscriminatory progressive discourses. As we learn, the novel's protagonist, Ifemelu, a Nigerian woman who prefers to identify as Igbo and is studying in America, feels out of place in the activist atmosphere of the Yale campus. The academic world strikes Ifemelu as awkward, hypocritical, and superficial in its grievances, indulging its self-righteousness and annoyingly nitpicking knack for the "deeper" meanings underneath the obvious. For academics, racial violence, Ifemelu suspects, appears as a mass of things constantly in flux and calling for endless "interpretation" rather than as hard material realities. Likewise, the progressive Londoners present at the gathering where Obinze, Ifemelu's boyfriend, is invited, have embraced just causes to flaunt their own moral virtue, and so have the academics surrounding Ifemelu, as they come up with research topics and wage ideological battles. In the same vein, in many of her public interventions, Adichie has taken issue with the "single stories" and stereotypes that, while sympathetic to the plight of Africans, deprive them of the dignity the West usually grants the individual. In *Americanah*, she does not just bring nuance to her in-depth inquiry into the complex histories of people of color, nor does she merely gesture to alternate accounts. She also explores how histories flatten out and become univocal, how competing reality versions become monolithic when confronted with social complacency or with hostile ways of acting and thinking. Moreover, her work does not only describe the injustices committed against minorities; it also captures the extent to which the latter as well as the white majority have normalized such injustices whether by accepting or by ignoring them. Adichie does not hesitate to expose the reality of racism in a clear, matter-of-fact manner at odds with the multicultural stances and tactics that often end up watering down and entangling the problems at hand in confusing analysis, vacuous theorizations, and de rigueur indignant posturing.

Smith's 2000 novel *White Teeth* mobilizes an even broader spectrum of subjectivities in the globalizing crucible of identities and identity discourses.[8] The novel follows the intersecting destinies of three families in the London of the last decades of the twentieth century: Jewish immigrants who have changed their names from Chalfenovsky to Chalfen, the English-Jamaican Joneses, and the Bangladeshi Iqbal family. The book has been read as a manifesto for multiculturalism, but the author has rejected this "ideological term."[9] Remarkably enough, she associates both multiculturalism and fundamentalism with a kind of sentimentalism of abstract causes, for which immediate reality—such a pivotal concern for metapolitical literature— makes for an impure antidote. For her, the postcolonial subjects of Jamaican or Bengali descent who arrived in England after World War II are in a constant state of becoming, their ethnic or fundamentalist traditionalism being nothing more than self-defensive reactions against the assimilating tendencies of their children or partners. Thus, the Islamism of the Bengali immigrant's son from *White Teeth* is just one of the avatars in his juvenile and violent self-search, whereas the Muslim father's traditionalism is belied by his adulterous behavior and paraded as a "self-purifying" routine. In her turn, the daughter of the Jamaican Jehovah woman rejects the cultural ways of her ethnoracial group and is bent on joining the London middle class. Race is here either fetishized when associated with the dominant class or conflated with class when it comes to the English family. The latter feeds on the erotic exoticism of the Jamaican-British and Bengali youth while also availing themselves of presumably "purifying," race-neutral sciences and, I might add, pseudosciences like eugenics as well. Opposed to such dubious experiments as it may be, leftist activism comes off as shallow. Inspired by Guy Debord, the militant radicalism of animal rights activists in *White Teeth* stems from a bizarre kind of sectarian, non-human neo-Marxism. As for right-wing extremism, this is largely prompted by misreadings of the Koran and in that equally questionable. Multiculturalism remains, under these circumstances, the specialty of high-school teachers, a kind of idealistic pedagogy cut off from the woolly materiality of surrounding identities and ideologies. Smith's solution, and Adichie's too, is, in a nutshell, a critical cosmopolitanism endorsing not only widely shared values but also a historical grasp of identity formations and of their violent and aberrant expression.[10]

Metapolitics in Contemporary Romanian Literature

If a multicultural praxis and consciousness failed to take shape during the 1990s culture wars, postcommunist Romanian literature has become a fertile ground for exploring identity, thus picking up a pre-1989 documentary thread. After all, the literature of the marginalized and underprivileged is not just about them. It also allows literature as a whole to overcome the aesthetic formalism of allusive writing typical of the Communist years and to plug itself into a wider, transnational network of interrogations about the status of the underprivileged in the age of planetary flows of people and capital. By focusing on aspirations[11] rather than on the social status of different kinds of marginalized people constantly changing in terms of who and where they are, some contemporary Romanian novels, as I detail below, call not so much for multicultural readings as for a *post*multicultural approach, by the same token resisting or complicating responses traditionally received from Romanian critics.[12]

As they trek across continents (Africa, North America, Europe) and social spaces (bourgeois, working class, liberal-academic), Adichie's protagonists, a man and a woman, undergo a racial coming of age of sorts, a gradual awakening into an awareness of their race, as well as of their emotional and professional lives. Gheo's books share many features of this narrative scheme. His characters, both those in *Disco Titanic* (2016) and in the earlier, 2010 novel *Noapte bună, copii!* (Good Night, Children!), are followed from childhood into adulthood as they cross all kinds of borders, symbolic and less so.[13] The heroes and heroines are, always, boys *and* girls who grow up passing *across* and *over*, leaving behind Communism and crossing into the West or falling for the "classical" demons of capitalism (pornography) and Socialism (collaboration with the secret police). In Gheo, the returns to Romania or the trips to other countries take place in a permanent historical relation to an ahistorical childhood mesmerized by pop music (from "over there") and vague longings for a promised land ("over there" also). Unlike Adichie or Smith, Gheo adopts a more comprehensive historical perspective, for his characters are representative of an entire generation born around the mid-1970s and carrying with it the evolution and existential questions of Romanian society over thirty years.

Most significantly, the historiographic reconstruction undertaken by Gheo works by means of a detailed examination of social reality and discourses. The reflexive component operates through the perspective of a fiction writer embedded in both novels' storyworlds, an author-figure who takes up, from an ironic distance, a whole array of themes, including the fate of literature in Eastern Europe. The only character in *Noapte bună, copii!* who does not emigrate becomes a writer in Romania, wins a scholarship from a foundation and is advised to write, for Western audiences, an ironic and critical book about Romanian Communism and Communist leader Nicolae Ceauşescu. His sponsor makes a point to remind him that the "big" historical and philosophical subjects fall within the purview of Western literature, and that Eastern authors have no choice but to entertain with works of exotic appeal. Quite apropos, Gheo has written the very opposite kind of novel, sweeping and problematic, which combines the metaliterary and the metapolitical to comment ironically and self-reflexively on the marginal world it comes from as well as on the relationship with the society and literature of the bigger world. Questions of cultural identity are also pursued at both micro- and macro-social levels in relation to the discrimination against the Roma population, the manifestations of ethno-nationalism in the former Yugoslavia, and the regional culture of Southwestern Romania (Banat). When a character accuses the city of Timişoara's real estate mafia of being "Gypsy," the author intervenes through another character who mentions the long history of multiethnic expropriations in the city, thereby turning the discussion into one about inequality. Gheo has in fact been criticized for the "political correctness" of his authorial alter-ego, who pops up, as has been claimed, *deus ex machina* into the story.[14] It is well known, though, I might add in passing, that the author himself has decried the attempts to censor opinions and police exchanges about identity. His position, I should also specify, has little to do with the neoconservatism otherwise typical of the right-wing public intellectuals in today's Romania, reflecting instead his own, brief experience as an immigrant in the United States.[15] What the reader witnesses, then, is a sensitivity sharpened across continents and liable to react strongly not only to racial stereotypes. Peremptorily proclaimed by the protagonist of *Disco Titanic*, Banat's alleged cultural superiority over the rest of the country is queried by the book's investigation into the tragic consequences of such parochial particularisms in the Balkan Wars of the early 1990s. This narrative move is all the more significant as Banat and its urban center, Timişoara, have been, on the contrary, spaces of harmoniously multiethnic coexistence, having been modeled on the "hybrid cultural Central-European regions" of the Habsburg Empire such as Lemberg/Lwow/Lviv and Cernăuți/Chernivitsi, both located in the Bukovina region currently split between Romania and Ukraine.[16]

Gheo's fiction constitutes, then, a transcultural, metaliterary, and last but not least, metapolitical experiment. To carry it out, the author breaks out of the framework of a literature concerned mainly with the nation's transition out of totalitarianism and engages with the transnational history of political ideas, following the trajectories of people and concepts in Eastern Europe and reflecting on the urgency to rethink civic projects through literary forms capable of widening the postcommunist-nationalist thematics of the literatures in the region without losing sight of their concrete ethnocultural conditions. This is no small feat given that unlike writers such as Adichie and Smith, the Romanian authors who have tackled the themes of cultural and ethnic identity and, in particular, the problematic of a social and ethnic "other" rarely belong to minorities. Schiop and Guțu are, in fact, anthropologists by training who have, for a few good years, immersed themselves in the marginal socioethnic communities they are writing about, namely, the Roma from Bucharest's largely ghettoized Ferentari district and soccer fan groups (the Ultras), respectively. Gheo has even done a PhD thesis on literature and ethnicity, and if his scholarship on fiction's relationship to such topics in an increasingly mobile world complements his novels about political transitions and geographical translations, Guțu's and Schiop's literature, one might say, is their way of "redeeming" themselves for having previously "objectified" their characters into research subjects.

Romanian scholar-authors' background in scholarship and theory indexes more than just their outsider status with respect to the lives they study or narrate. While positioning themselves within a literary practice shaped for decades by evasive-allusive styles, these writers shed new light on issues and notions that have informed not only their country's exit from Communism but also the entry into a vaster geocultural field of social commentary and literature, a world domain marked by rising consumerism, gender and, more broadly, left-wing politics, expanding ethical concerns, and so forth. In this fast-evolving and sometimes disconcerting environment, the marginalized and the disenfranchised show up in literature not as thematic foci but because they are instrumental to a redefinition of public activism and to thinking through specific social issues. The 2014 Ferentari novel, *Soldații: Poveste din Ferentari* (Soldiers: Story from Ferentari), allows Schiop not only to get close to an ethnosocial world different from his but also to revise self-ironically his own knee-jerk reactions and, on occasion, idealistic and aery political notions.[17] Thus, the book maps out metapolitically an entire "political"—inefficiently activist and speculative-academic—field of action and thought. Going against the grain of most fiction on such themes, *Soldații* also mounts a critique of nonfiction by a whole cohort that has appropriated these subjects "interdisciplinarily" yet superficially and with an eye to the next stipend. While the novel devotes tens of pages to Ferentari residents in an attempt to open a window into their "warm hearts" and "disturbed minds," the left-wing, intellectual and academic crowd is treated to sketchy portraits that capture their ethical and existential fragility in an age of professional crisis and conceptual confusion.

Similar attempts to carve out a distinct space inside this field of ethnographic and sociopolitical analysis drive Guțu's 2017 novel *Intervenția* (The Intervention).[18] Having been himself involved in the writing of EU-funded grants, Guțu sets the rough world of soccer fans up against academic hypocrisy, which he views as ultimately self-serving and less genuinely interested in the issues at hand. He describes at length the corruption plaguing multicultural projects and dwells on the jargon of applicants versed in failproof clichés and in not much else. Intimate knowledge of the research object does not suffice in this case, and one could maintain, as I would, that Schiop succeeds whereas Guțu appears to be headed into a dead end. Through a rather harsh personal introspection and by drawing on the interactive theories developed by Erwin Goffman, *Soldiers* problematizes the author's attraction to social milieus of so-called "ill repute." Here, people's conduct is not presented as fitting preexisting, social or ethnic classifications and clichés but in concrete situations and as derived, accordingly, from a steady stream of fleeting perceptions and reactions. Thus captured, the underworld of human degradation is plugged into the history and pulse of the world outside.

The novel does not bring out, then, Ferentari's "authentic" human reality, even though this reality is, sociologically speaking, as undeniably objective as the existence of comparably marginalized groups in writers like Adichie. Having internalized the others' gaze, the ghetto's inhabitants put on the show of their own alterity, perform *and* understand their own condition, contextually and historically, better than the activists and critics who "empathize" with them from a safe distance. At the same time, historical causality also accounts for the differentiations *within* the Roma community, some of its members retaining the reflexes of the 1990s due to the time spent in prison, while others, on their way up socially, have adopted an odd mix of "civilizing" and authoritarian habits. The "soldiers" referred to in Schiop's title embody the grim side of this complex reality, while also revealing that in this world racial differences are superseded by those involving status and behavior, the most discriminated against—and by the people of Ferentari— being the ghetto's drug addicts. Where Schiop's realism limns an "interactive" world of overlapping worlds, Gheo's focus on underworld, subcultural, and "other" themes brings into the spotlight a narrative conglomerate of ordinary facts, while Guțu's writing is one long ideological outburst. Thus, one of Gheo's heroes returns home, after many years spent in the West, to a Bucharest where corruption is rampant and petty crime takes place in the open. He is in fact robbed by a Roma hard-currency dealer and witnesses the maltreatment of a prostitute. By contrast, Guțu's alter ego enjoys soccer fans' faux-macho and sometimes violent fellowship, which he finds more comforting than the company of bleeding-heart academics.

This goes to show that the presentation of the marginal world of ethnoracial categories mechanically associated in the Romanian mind with the Roma and other minorities turns out to be a delicate undertaking that risks fetishizing them as schematic objects of oppression or seeing them through the covertly racist clichés about the "degradation" of mores. In other words, metapolitical fiction authors too struggle with the representation of a human subject under threat of being objectified—oversimplified qua subject and thus misrepresented—by the very narrative gaze that purports to account for and possibly do justice to it. In this vein, it bears recalling that, building on the Foucauldian description of the diffusive forms that power can take, Yves Citton has insisted on the prevalence of expressive codes and styles over substance in the development of social attitudes.[19] In his work, Citton does not pursue head-on an ethos of equality, which is bound to remain an abstract notion in a spectacle society where inequities derive to no negligible degree from access to the media. Instead, he urges the academic Left and the Left in general to come up with an approach likely to provide this society's underprivileged with means to escape the frameworks and schemes of public recognition and scholarly analysis prescribed by others. The idea is less to encourage self-expressions and self-definitions, as Lilla would say, by the marginalized themselves, and more to foster an awareness of the possibilities of transgressing dominant narratives by altering the conversation about the very issue of marginality, a problem often reified, trivialized, and otherwise mishandled both by the Right and Left. It is probably fair to say, in fact, that the Romanian intellectual Left finds itself still at the stage of denouncing positions perceived as conservative, "small-bourgeois," and elite, having yet to develop analytical protocols capable of grasping these issues from within their own socioethnic realm. Given this situation, fictional writing understood and practiced metapolitically, as a form of political knowledge and exploration of human reality by literary means, makes up for the shortcomings of a scholarship in which the subaltern and the forgotten, who they are and what they represent, are foregone conclusions and pedantically rehearsed stereotypes.

Identity Dilemmas, Civic Conundrums

Thus, just as *White Teeth* deflates idealistic pathos and rock-solid certitudes, the post-2000 Romanian novel casts a skeptical shadow on political commitment. In Adameşteanu's *Fontana di Trevi*, for instance, the critique of Western feminism and the pro-democratic actions of the 1990s go hand in hand.[20] The Morar family's anti-Communist fervor in the political group Forum—which, most likely, alludes to the Romanian Group for Social Dialogue (GDS)—is followed in the novel, two decades later, by gender studies-inspired activism, all against the backdrop of generalized, revved-up upwards social mobility among the time's entrepreneurs and intellectuals alike. The author's critique calls to mind Lilla's taking to task of liberal identity politics, but, in all actuality, also bespeaks skepticism about pro-democratic liberalism in a post-totalitarian society, a platform Adameşteanu herself backed up in the 1990s as an editor of *22*, GDS's center-right weekly. The disintegrating social environment is symbolized in *Fontana di Trevi* by the disease that afflicts the immigrant daughter of anti-Communists turned cultural activists who in the 2000s discover the serviceable lingo of minority rights. More generally, the characters' lives appear shaped by perfunctory engagements and gestures, with the tossing of the coin in Rome's Fontana di Trevi the book's apposite and overarching allegory.

Schiop's work too bears witness to this aleatory identity dynamic, along with a persistent sense of relativism and haphazard in the world of civic and political values. His fiction translates the distrust of the academic Left into concrete politics, into a particular political plot, more exactly. He intimates that democracy is a fragile pursuit in a society where the secret police—the infamous Securitate of the Communist era—clings to its former prerogatives and aggressive capitalism has weakened key components of social life while condoning the mushrooming of mafia-style structures. In a society whose memory of underhanded manipulation and control is still vivid, the cynicism of the new generation of social observers, writers, and anthropologists also extends to the possibilities opened up by liberal democracy, education, and the judicial system for alleviating inequalities. This is why, much as authors like Schiop are familiar and even sympathetic to various minority-oriented, left-wing theoretical and political agendas, they approach socially marginal categories from positions that are neither necessarily intellectual-theoretical nor progressive-collective but driven by a desire for an unmediated knowledge and an authentic solidarity at loggerheads with the closed system of intellectual prestige and showy leftist rhetoric. In this regard, it is quite telling that Schiop succeeds as an author but fails as a character, as it were, for, inside the novel, the narrating authorial alter ego's relationship with the protagonist does not change the latter's life. Schiop admits that, instead of freeing his Ferentari friend from the cycle of poverty and degradation, he merely "immortalized" him in a book quite literally, cooping him up forever in an ancillary social identity.

There is no coincidence that in Gheo's novel *Disco Titanic*, too, the motif of identity transformation ties into the more political theme of the democratic ideal's erosion, which is hinted at by the protagonist's partnership with a Mephistophelian character modeled after the classic type of the Securitate agent. Like the Morars' daughter in *Fontana di Trevi*, Gheo's hero participates in the 1989 anti-Communist uprise, although he does so out of guilt for having been an informer, and later becomes a venal businessman under the protection of the former Securitate officer who goes by the Dantesque name of Mr. Vergil. Unlike in Adameşteanu's novel, though, the moral relativism and existential plasticity that define the characters of *Disco Titanic* have nothing condescending or blasé to them. The ethical and political conversions are not reported from an outsider's perspective either. Gheo exposes the mechanisms behind the watering down of values and the exacerbation of cultural psychoses and then moves on to relay the emotions triggered by various twists and turns in people's lives. Vlad Jivan's, for example, is indeed scarred by brushes with the Securitate, and yet the anti-Communist revolutionary turned entrepreneur remains capable of honorable aspirations. Gheo does not comment ironically or cynically on Vlad's situation, as Adameşteanu sometimes does on her heroes.' Instead, he reviews the chain of events that, under Communism and after its official demise, lead individuals, sometimes tragically, to all manner of compromise and thus perpetuate the subservience to their Securitate handlers.

A number of analogies can thus be drawn between Adichie's postcolonial Nigeria and Gheo's postcommunist Romania. In both worlds, capitalism makes characters more pragmatic while also touching off moral crises, which in turn reveal untapped resources of ingenuity and dignity. The protagonists decline to conform to hackneyed perceptions and expectations of "local specificity" not only through their broader aspirations as world citizens but also by making choices that place them at odds with the increasingly mercantile surrounding realities. Consequences of homogenizing globalization, these are illuminated, among other things, by sex work in the West, a heavily gendered subtheme that brings the two novels together and concomitantly pulls them apart. Thus, whereas Ifemelu refuses, after a humiliating experience, to sell her body to survive, the heroine of *Noapte bună, copii!* cannot free herself, unlike her male friends, from a cycle of fateful degradation, and, with her Romanian boyfriend's approval, becomes a porn actress. The narrative of an immigrant's sometimes degrading "adjustment" to his or her new home has its own commonplaces by now, if one may call them that, but what Gheo accentuates is the background that makes this episode less of a cliché, namely that the heroine's self-confidence was traumatically shaken back under Communist rule, when she was raped by a group of border guards during a failed attempt to cross the border without official approval. When her boyfriend abandons her later on in the United States, she commits suicide, after a long period of disillusionment with the West she had dreamed of as a child. But the similarities between the postcolonial South and the postcommunist East end here. Rampant corruption in the native country, on one side, and, on the other, the self-centered individualism of adopted culture erode Gheo's characters, far from steeling them. Thus, both writers unsettle the West/East antithesis predicated on the no less clichéd dichotomy dehumanizing capitalism/integrative community. Not only that, but Gheo suggests that in the countries of the former Eastern Bloc, social ills and community disintegration predate post–Cold War assimilation into global capitalism.

Where Schiop and Gheo formulate critiques of contemporary society by reworking aspects of their biographies, Bogdan Suceavă hews closer to the memoir formula by claiming total honesty in his 2018 autofictional novel, *Avalon. Secretele emigranților fericiți.*[21] In Suceavă, identity amounts to a complete identification between author and protagonist, and so the authenticity effect no longer hinges on the narrative craft that went into the character's "revelations" and "confessions" of the tragic or opportunistic exploits and metamorphosis he has gone through. The dilemmas of acculturation and multiculturalism are overcome from the get-go as the author professes openly a sort of cosmopolitanism of mathematical universalism. The protagonist of *Avalon* is an immigrant mathematician for whom science opens the door to a world that values learning and ensures it dignified pursuit. As in Smith, the university professor is a cosmopolite whose critical antennae have not been desensitized by success, and so he comments, for instance, on the natives' condescendence toward East European doctoral candidates, a reaction hardly justified by the former's cultural horizon, which compares unfavorably, Suceavă notes, to the latter's. Unlike in Adameşteanu, immigration is conveyed from within the character's inner, conflicted world rather than from the blasé, outside perspective of an author who has not lived through what the hero has and for whom, to make matters worse, migration, relocation, and the like are rather fuzzy notions simplistically associated with failure, "uprooting," and cultural disorientation. The book views the political as a stage for clichés-brandishing opportunists but salvages the larger concept of an ethics understood as foundation of civic life. Suceavă looks ironically on Romanian political activists' anti-Communist tirades as well as on the vulgar language of the media, and, notably, his ironies are metapolitical in a moral kind of way. Moreover, the moral radicalism asserted in relation to the world left behind ultimately mobilizes the hero professionally in the new world. Most likely, Suceavă's *Avalon* marks the author's next step in his fictional yet more direct engagement with Romanian ethnocultural fixations. Having also penned allusive novels that capture, as in the 2004 *Venea din timpul diez*, the grotesque of religious and nationalist extremism, the author shifts gears and opts for a less postmodern and more straightforward self-expression.

Not unlike Gheo's, Schiop's, and Adameşteanu's recent work, Suceavă's testifies to an entire metapolitical turn in post-2000 Romanian literature. This corpus seeks to both chronicle the postcommunist changes and reflect on the efficiency and inefficiency of various conceptual apparatuses having to do with methodology, ideology, and public policies. As we have noticed, such fictional undertakings are often accompanied by research projects in anthropology and history of ideas, and this is not without significance. For, analyzing Central and East European writers' concern about preserving their relevance as producers of social knowledge in the context of a diminishing audience and appetite for literature, Andrew Baruch-Wachtel has pointed out that authors increasingly choose their themes depending on potential audiences, which leads them to a steadily growing panoply of subjects and ways of treating them.[22] The writers discussed above seem to move in the opposite direction, however. That is to say, they are trying to *unify* the potential public of their books by bringing together a whole range of topics whether inside a single novel or across several novels by the same author, and so ethnic themes intertwine with those pertaining to gender and sexual orientation, and the remembrance of the past unfolds almost necessarily alongside recollections of the 1989 "Revolution" and of subsequent political regimes. Nourished by this thematic amalgamation is a substantial body of metapolitical literature in which multicultural and, in particular, post-multicultural analysis combines with the fictional genealogies of immigrants, women, Roma, and other socioethnic categories on which contemporary Romanian writers are characteristically keen.

Notes

1   Pierre Rosanvallon, *Le Parlement des invisibles* (Paris: Seuil, 2014), 49–50.
2   Balázs Trencsényi, Michal Kopeček, Luka Lisjak Gabrielčič, Maria Falina, Monika Baár, and Maciej Janowski, *A History of Modern Political Thought in Eastern Europe*, vol. 2, *Negotiating Modernity in the Short Twentieth Century and Beyond*, pt. 2, *1968–2018* (Oxford: Oxford University Press, 2018), 272.
3   Alain Badiou, *Abrégé de métapolitique* (Paris: Seuil, 1998).

4   Ivan Krastev, "The New Europe: Respectable Populism, Clockwork
     Liberalism," *Open Democracy*, March 21, 2006, https://www.opendemocracy.
     net/democracy-europe_constitution/new_europe_3376.jsp (accessed January
     29, 2019).
5   See Mark Lilla, *The Once and Future Liberal: After Identity Politics* (New
     York: HarperCollins, 2017).
6   Sorin Antohi, *Războaie culturale. Idei, intelectuali, spirit public* (Iaşi, Romania:
     Polirom, 2007), 18–33.
7   See Chimamanda Ngozi Adichie, *Americanah* (New York: Knopf, 2013).
8   Zadie Smith, *White Teeth* (New York: Random House, 2000).
9   Stephen Bates, "Zadie Smith Dismisses Big Society and Multiculturalism
     Policy," *The Guardian*, May 21, 2010, https://www.theguardian.com/
     books/2010/may/21/zadie-smith-big-society-multiculturalism (accessed
     December 25, 2019).
10   Paul Jay, *Global Matters: The Transnational Turn in Literary Studies* (Ithaca,
     NY: Cornell University Press, 2010), 154–76.
11   Rosanvallon has recommended that today's literature reflect the aspirations of
     individuals rather than their social status (*Le parlement des invisibles*, 22).
12   "Small-bourgeois" is the label Mihai Iovănel has applied to Gheo's novels.
     See Iovănel, *Ideologiile literaturii în postcomunismul românesc* (Bucharest:
     Muzeului Literaturii Române, 2017), 145–7.
13   Radu Pavel Gheo, *Disco Titanic* (Iaşi, Romania: Polirom, 2016), and *Noapte
     bună, copii!* (Iaşi, Romania: Polirom, 2010).
14   Cosmin Borza, "Un roman occidental," *Revista Cultura 5* (561), February 2,
     2017, https://blog.revistacultura.ro/2017/04/08/radu-pavel-gheo-disco-titanic-
     review-de-cosmin-borza/ (accessed January 31, 2019).
15   Radu Pavel Gheo, "Rezerva de comisari politici," *Suplimentul de cultură* 235,
     July 4–10, 2009, http://suplimentuldecultura.ro/5134/romanii-e-destepti/
     (accessed January 31, 2019).
16   Victor Neumann, "Multi- şi inter-culturalitate. Moşteniri imperiale în Banatul
     Timişoarei," *Punctul critic* 2, no. 24 (2018), https://www.punctulcritic.ro/
     victor-neumann-multi%E2%80%91-si-interculturalitate-mosteniri-imperiale-
     in-banatul-timisoarei.html (accessed December 30, 2019).
17   Adrian Schiop, *Soldaţii. Poveste din Ferentari* (Iaşi, Romania: Polirom, 2014).
18   Dinu Guţu, *Intervenţia* (Iaşi, Romania: Polirom, 2017).
19   See Yves Citton, *Mytocratie. Storytelling et imaginaire de gauche* (Paris:
     Éditions Amsterdam, 2010).
20   Gabriela Adameşteanu, *Fontana di Trevi* (Iaşi, Romania: Polirom, 2018).
21   Bogdan Suceavă, *Avalon. Secretele emigranţilor fericiţi* (Iaşi, Romania:
     Polirom, 2018).
22   See Andrew Baruch-Wachtel, *Remaining Relevant after Communism: The Role
     of the Writer in Eastern Europe* (Chicago: University of Chicago Press, 2006).

5

COMMUNALITY:
Un-Disciplining Race, Class, and Sex in the Wake of Anti-"PC" Monomania

Andrei Terian

On October 6 and 7, 2018, Romanians participated in a referendum on Constitutional "reform." The issue was a change in the definition of family. The modification, its proponents hoped, would have specified explicitly that marriage can only take place between a man and a woman. Legally speaking, such a change would have been redundant, for the country's Constitution did not even acknowledge the possibility of same-sex marriage. Furthermore, Romania had only decriminalized homosexuality in 2001 as a result of pressures put on lawmakers by civil society and by the European Union, to which the nation aspired to adhere. In this context, the referendum seemed rather a sort of preemptive strike, a result of Romanian conservative voices coming together and especially of efforts by Coaliția pentru familie (Coalition for the Family), a conglomerate of more than forty organizations, which had managed to gather no less than three million signatures (a little over 16 percent of the country's voting population) in 2016 in support of this Constitutional stipulation. Subsequently, a segment of the Romanian political spectrum, including the country's ruling party, started pushing for the amendment, and growing official support eventually led to the referendum. This was not surprising, nor were the actual results. A total of 93.4 percent of the valid votes were in favor of the modification—that is, for a temporary halt of legalization of same-sex marriage—whereas only 6.6 percent of voters expressed disagreement with the proposal.

The referendum outcomes make even more sense when set side by side with polling data on the role of religion in Romanian society. A survey taken by the Pew Research Center, also in October 2018, concluded that Romania is "the most religious out of 34 European countries," with 55 percent of the adult population considering itself "highly religious."[1] Given how unfavorably various faith-based groups—in particular the Christian Orthodox Church, Romania's main religious institution—looked on homosexuality, no wonder voters so strongly supported the proposed amendment. Yet the referendum was a painful defeat for Romanian conservative forces. The overwhelming "for" 93.4 percent is misleading; merely 21.1 percent of vote-eligible Romanians bothered to go to the polls. To get a sense of what happened, let me point out that the 2016 parliamentary elections had a voter turnout of 39.4 percent, while in the 2019 presidential elections, the turnout was 51.2 percent in the first round and 54.8 percent in the second.[2] What this means is that the referendum failed to elicit at least half of the interest Romanians ordinarily show in political issues, not to mention the considerably low turnout threshold—30 percent, with a two-thirds valid votes ratio—and the government's extension of the voting period to two days to make sure the legal threshold was reached. Nonetheless, four out of five Romanians boycotted the referendum by refusing to vote. Now, speculating as to why 80 percent of Romania's population more or less refused to back the amendment initiative may not get us too far. The reasons behind voters' reluctance to endorse it were, it seems, diverse and complex.[3] As noted, some voters simply cast a negative vote. Considerably more treated the referendum with the same indifference with which they had met national elections and other forms of public consultation during the postcommunist era. It is also clear, however, that at least 20 to 25 percent of the country's voters boycotted not only the referendum's proposition but also the latter's very subject or "theme," if you will. In other words, instead of giving an answer, whether negative or positive, they declined to play into the official premise and overall narrative of the referendum and thereby legitimize the notion that a certain social matter or *state of fact*—the existence of same-sex couples—should be treated, if I may keep on using the same Latourspeak, as a matter of concern or "social issue" negotiable and adjudicated on at the ballot box. That is to say, voters refused to misuse their authority and limit the rights of sexual minorities. More importantly still, they did not want to recognize and adopt, by their sheer presence at polls, a language that both afforded and reinforced questionable definitions of notions such as "right," "society," "family," "gender," and "minority."

A "lesson" critics, theorists, and even activists should learn from the referendum, this resistance and what it tells us about the dynamic of theory and social practice in the "post" era inform the argument of this chapter. With this episode in mind, I propose that an efficient way of standing up to politically disenfranchising and philosophically reductionist ideologies, politics, and policies such as conservatism ("old style" or "neo"), nationalist chauvinism, xenophobia, populism, fundamentalism, racism, classism, and sexism—all of which variously underpin neoliberalism's global agenda and purport to head off any criticism by throwing around the presumably disqualifying charge of "political correctness"—is building not so much, and certainly not in the first place, a counter-discourse, irrespective of how progressive and rhetorically appealing this may be, but a community willing to engage, *qua* community, in counter-political and, indeed, counter-narrative acts such as the Romanian referendum.

My argument has three implications. The first is that the bedrock of this community is neither theoretical nor ideological but ethical; consequently, its hallmark is not a subversive or revolutionary vocabulary but rather a communally shared language fostered in a socio-professional zone less beholden to preexistent ideological, disciplinary, and academic lingos. The second is that such a community's linguistic identity and ultimately this community *tout court* are, as pressing projects—because I do believe they are so—more readily feasible in those democracies presumed to occupy "peripheral" world locations, for in such geocultural areas the political boundaries and divides of all sorts, including those between the various stances, actors, and conceptual-ideological investments at play in so-called "political correctness" and the controversy around it are far less marked than in North America or Western Europe. Following from the previous, the third upshot or aspect of this entire discussion has to do with the sites of this project. As we have seen, these venues or forums are actually existing communities. What about their representation though? As I show in the last half of my intervention, and as other contributions to *Theory in the "Post" Era* demonstrate, the community language I am talking about is best shaped in literature and, I might add, in literary criticism as well. Especially in the new millennium, poets, fiction writers, and critics have become keener and keener on politics as well as more and more open to the political insights supplied by domains and ways of knowing well outside literature and its reading. The rise of "PC" as a contested topic across these knowledge fields and its treatment in contemporary Romanian literature are a case in point.

"Recent Man" to "Sexo-Marxism"

Bandied about in the cultural press since the first postcommunist years, the "PC" mantra becomes a staple of public debates during the early twenty-first century.[4] Two literary events were behind this spectacular if belated impact. One was the February 2000 founding of the *Observator cultural* magazine in Bucharest. This weekly was and remained for a while the postmillennial platform of the "1980s Generation," which had basically marked Romanian literature's turn to postmodernism during the Cold War. Actually, the very article that laid out the publication's program, authored by critic Ion Bogdan Lefter, offered up as a cultural recipe for the entire country a conceptual potpourri of "terms such as *postmodernism, poststructuralism,* and *cultural studies, Europeanism* and *pro-Americanism, antinationalism, antifundamentalism,* and *anti-Orthodoxism, liberalism* and *multiculturalism, prodemocracy* and *political correctness.*"[5] No less significant was the 2001 publication of Horia-Roman Patapievici's book *Omul Recent* (Recent Man), which mounts a comprehensive critique of postmodernity and of its presumed offshoot, "PC." According to Patapievici, "recent man" is nothing else than the modern and, by extension, postmodern individual that has "wasted" his essence, his tradition, and his individuality—incidentally, attempting to explicate the masculine pronoun would be pointless here. This man, opines Patapievici, has done so because he, said man, has been caught in the "ever-changing temporality of simulacra."[6] This definition would also accommodate, as the critic fancies, the explicitly revisionist tendencies of "PC," which he deems, from a standpoint typical of domestic Christian neoconservatism, "a totalitarian movement of Leninist inspiration, the greatest threat to the ideals of a free society since the fall of left-wing totalitarian regimes."[7] It must be noted, however, that Patapievici's claims are derivative. They are hardly grounded in a direct engagement with works presumably advocating "PC." In fact, his sources are a combination of hearsay and extracts from anti-"PC" crusaders such as Allan Bloom, Warren Farrell, Camille Paglia, and Edward Behr.

Be that as it may, the clash between the postmodern and conservative camps was inevitable in Romania as well. The polemics reached boiling point in the 2002–2004 interval, when *Observator cultural* published a series of opinion articles signed mainly by Romanian émigrés and public intellectuals educated abroad, who contributed direct or indirect rebuttals to *Omul recent*, rejecting it for being half-baked, reductive, and not backed up by research. Among these articles, Christian Moraru's stand out. Commenting on a collection of essays by Mircea Cărtărescu, the 1980s Generation's quintessential figure, whom he ranks as "the most important author to have written in Romanian after World War II," Moraru identifies a cultural model quite different from—in effect opposed to—the one described and promoted by Patapievici.[8] In contrast to the latter's way of seeing things, which Moraru describes as a "combination of ignorance, vaguely Marcusian Jeremiad, anti-modernism, and anti-liberalism,"[9] Cărtărescu illustrates the embodiment of a "cosmopolitan transculturalism" that recommends him as "a European or, better yet, Euro-Atlantic spirit, open, pluralist, and genuinely multicultural."[10]

Moraru's intervention drew a swift and *ad hominem* reply from Andrei Pleşu, former Minister of Culture, art critic, and editor-in-chief of the weekly

Dilema, which, alongside *România Literară*, was and has remained one of the Romanian publications most relentless in their denunciation of "PC."[11] While contributing little of substance to the actual polemic, Pleşu's attack prompted Moraru to formulate one of the most persuasive arguments in the entire debate. "If we agree," writes Moraru,

> that a poem, a drawing, or an essay cannot take shape wholly independently from other texts and discourses floating around in social space and belonging to the intimate structure or the "identity" of the author ... who writes or paints, it then makes sense to analyze how said poem, film, or painting enters into a dialogue with those texts and discourses. What is the latter's "subject"? What do they focus on? In short, they shed light on the fundamental categories fashioning at once sociopolitical and private space: sexuality, gender, ethnicity, race, age, etc .... It is, in all actuality, the responsibility of criticism to take on such an investigation, whose consequences are "revisionist." In practice, this undertaking inevitably becomes interdisciplinary; its forms are called feminism, gender studies, postcolonial studies, and so on, and can combine in all kinds of ways.[12]

The first culture war of postcommunist Romania ended in 2005, following two institutional developments. First, in January, the country's recently elected president, Traian Băsescu, appointed Patapievici at the top of the Romanian Cultural Institute, which had been playing a crucial role in the promotion of Romanian culture abroad. Second, in February, in the aftermath of the scandal ignited by *Omul recent*, Ion Bogdan Lefter was forced to resign from his position as chief editor of *Observator cultural*. This way, even if the publication continued to promote, albeit in a more moderate tone, the values of the cultural left, "PC" supporters saw themselves deprived of a high-impact publishing venue. Nor did Cărtărescu rush to own up to the countermodel role assigned to him by Moraru. In the following years, he became not only the author with the largest number of translations subsidized by the Romanian Cultural Institute but also—and alongside Patapievici—one of President Băsescu's admirers. As for "PC," Cărtărescu was, and is, ambivalent at best. "The concept," he declares in an interview, "is legitimate: it was born out of the need for peaceful cohabitation of a multi-ethnic and multicultural world such as North America yet is more difficult to grasp in a European cultural climate still dominated by significantly more ethnically homogenous national states. But even Americans find it hard to put up with 'PC' excesses sometimes."[13]

In any case, "PC" no longer represented a hot button issue in Romanian society during the decade that followed. When the subject resurged—unsurprisingly, in conjunction with Donald Trump's victory in the 2016 US presidential elections—it did so as a series of campaigns orchestrated by conservative forces against "sexo-Marxism." The moniker was coined by journalist and movie director Iulian Capsali, whose ideological options span Christianity (anti-secularism), traditionalism (anti-modernity), and anti-Occidentalism (Russophilia). As a matter of fact, it is not by accident that Capsali launched the "concept" in an interview with the Russian news agency Sputnik in 2016. On that occasion, he warned that in Romania, "through sexo-Marxism and aggressive peddling of LGBT ideologies, a social revolution is being pursued, by which the minority wants to impose its views on a people whose Christian ethos must be erased for all time."[14] The real theorist of sexo-Marxism, however, seems to be Adrian Papahagi. "Sexo-Marxism," he contends, "preserves ... Marx's classical socioeconomic discourse but enhances it with Freudian additions from Reich and Marcuse, or with Fanon's views on race. Another component of the New Left ... is ecologism."[15] There is an attempt at a definition here, but the latter carries less weight than the bizarre term itself, which suggests, or hints at, more than its description—the pseudo-concept is rhetorically effective even though it designates less than what Papahagi covers. For, although he sees sexo-Marxism as operating in four dimensions (class, gender, race, and the environment), the term itself names no more than two—"sexo" is intended to render Marxism somehow frivolous by association. At any rate, the invention of sexo-Marxism coincided with a new flurry of attacks directed by Romanian conservatives against "PC." The loudest among the new detractors appears to be literary critic Mircea Mihăieş, who has devoted tens of articles to the fight against the so-called doctrine, which he regards as "the most devastating ideology that could possibly come about at the end of the twentieth century."[16] His crude and vituperative comments on the subject reached a new low during the 2020 wave of racial unrest in the United States, a phenomenon Mihăieş blamed on the spread of "political correctness," which is made out to be a "combination of Socialism and Fascism," "one of the manifestations of extremism," and a promoter of "lecture-hall racism."[17]

As with Patapievici's contentions two decades prior, Papahagi's and Mihăieş's bloviations have triggered a series of responses in the Romanian cultural press. Among these, one of the most compelling was the dialogue between Christian Moraru and Mihai Iovănel, which came out in the special issue *Euphorion* magazine published on "PC." Two ideas appear to be key in their conversation: on one hand, "PC" is not "a 'political philosophy' articulated as such—it is neither an object that is taught or discussed in universities nor a 'goal' for the achievement of which those who pursue it meet up in cigarette smoke-filled back rooms," but rather just "a notional specter that acquires reality and becomes a fetish in right-wing discourse";[18] on the other hand, ideological fiction and battle cry as it is, "PC" does point to a set of problems and stringent issues Romanian culture cannot avoid addressing anymore. "What truly exists," Moraru tells Iovănel, is an *ethical* rather than just political preoccupation for certain problems, as well as an inclination, *an activist practice* of critique and intellectual work generally interested not only in discussing but also in correcting exclusivist or simplistic reading patterns and, more broadly speaking, actual historical injustices committed especially during modernity throughout the world, not only in the United States. It is high time we admit that this world includes Romania too.[19]

Adrian Schiop: A Case for Hypermarginality

Interestingly enough, progressive Romanian intellectuals' reactions to charges of "sexo-Marxism" have been relatively different from how they responded when they were vilified as "recent men" back in the early 2000s. First off, direct rebuttals have been significantly fewer this time around. There has not been much to refute either, for, over the previous two decades, during which anti-"PC" inquisitorial rhetoric had been churning around in Romanian publications, the campaign seemed to have exhausted all its arguments and started sounding like a broken record, rehashing the same clichés over and over again. At the same time, feminism, gender studies, and the systematic study of racism, anti-Semitism, xenophobia, and despite the still open wounds of the Communist past, Marxism as well have been making deeper and deeper inroads into higher-education curricula and programs. More notably, a younger, postmillennial generation of Romanian humanists has come on the scene and, with them, an entirely new mindset.

Bearing witness to this shift is the critical reception of Romanian anthropologist and fiction writer Adrian Schiop's most recent novel, the 2013 *Soldații. Poveste din Ferentari* (Soldiers: Story from Ferentari).[20] Since Ioana Macrea-Toma analyzes the "metapolitical" dimension of the book in the preceding chapter of this volume, I will limit my discussion to the author's representation of group identities in 2010s Romania. Thus, let me note that, at first glance, Schiop's overall position as an author and individual appears to bespeak a double if not triple minority status. For one thing, his 2004 autobiographical novel *pe bune/pe invers* (straight/queer) presents its author as the first representative of queer Romanian literature, shortly after homosexuality was decriminalized in the country.[21] For another, his 2009 *Zero grade Kelvin* (Zero Kelvin) combines the depiction of queer milieus and of microcommunities of New Zealand immigrants.[22] For still another, his 2013 novel tells the story of an anthropology PhD student who moves to Ferentari, one of Bucharest's poorest neighborhoods, where he has a relationship with an ex-convict named Alberto and does research on *manele*, a music genre considered specific to the Roma minority and on which Schiop would publish a monograph in 2016, the first of its kind in Romania—a mere four years later, I might add, Schiop would be the screenwriter and lead actor for his novel's film adaptation, which has been very well received at international festivals and has been streaming on Netflix.[23] Moreover, the various facets of the protagonist's minority standing at play in the novel's protagonist reinforce each other. "In the aggressive environment of Ferentari men," he reveals, "most of them figured out that something was amiss in my sexuality."[24] Thus, he finds himself in a marginal position even within the groups he aspires to become a part of. As a homosexual, he sees himself forced to accept not being able to engage sexually with other homosexuals, but with heterosexuals solely;[25] and as a new Ferentari resident, he is an outsider in the eyes of the locals, who tolerate his presence as long as they drink his beer and smoke his cigarettes. This is as much as saying that Schiop—the actual author, his autofictional alter ego, the actor, the anthropologist, and so on—instantiates and brings into play, inside and outside his storyworld, a particular kind of positionality that I would call *hypermarginality*, namely, a sociological category or condition where an individual's outsider standing as a member of one or more minority groups is reinforced and further complicated by his or her marginal place in those communities. As Ovio Olaru suggests,

> *Soldiers* has been successful for three reasons: 1) Because it takes place in Ferentari, an ill-famed Bucharest neighborhood, a place that has been, on one hand, stigmatized in the extreme and, on the other, kept in symbolic inferiority to the downtown, for which it remains, by force of circumstances, *terra incognita*. The problems touched on apropos of Ferentari are impoverishment, social ostracism, crime, shabby living conditions, discrimination against the poverty-stricken, and so on. 2) Tied into the neighborhood's destitution are the racial issues the novel also raises: the protagonist's lover is of Roma ethnicity, and the residents are … mostly majority Roma as well. To address the racial aspect, Schiop lapses neither into melodrama nor left-wing rhetoric. 3) Finally, the protagonist's homosexuality makes a difference here as the gay element bolsters the narrative's subversive force by setting the story against a complex Romanian backdrop where racism and the middle- and upper-classes' contempt for *manele* intersect homophobia.[26]

The hypermarginality for which Olaru provides evidence does not become in Schiop subject to elaborations and "militant" theorizations. As Macrea-Toma also stresses apropos of Schiop, he is wary of social-justice journalism, academics, and left-wing activism and is not very keen on the gay Bucharest Pride Parade either. Nonetheless, it is obvious that, its subdued political tone notwithstanding, the book calls, through its very controversial subject and authorial self-positioning, for a certain politics. And yet, when it came out, the novel was quasi-unanimously acclaimed, no matter the ideological positions of the publications where it was reviewed and sometimes even against the reviewers' own political orientations. What is more, in their over forty reviews of the novel, commentators neither dwelled exclusively on what I have defined as hypermarginality nor turned a blind eye to it.

It bears noting, in this vein, that in the first piece of this sort dedicated to the novel by *Observator cultural*, which, as pointed out earlier, had introduced "PC" into Romanian critical culture, Adina Diniţoiu remarks that "the novel revolves around a love story—homosexual, but it hardly matters, for its significance is universal—where the relationship between the two partners is also one of ... unequal power."[27] Granted, shifting focus away from the same-sex relationship to the political, as if the two were unrelated, may be a problematic move, but this does not stop Diniţoiu from closing with an unambivalent value judgment: "Adrian Schiop's *Soldaţii* is ... one of the best fiction books of the year."[28] One can witness a similar shift, this time to the social, in an analysis by critic Costi Rogozanu, who, in an article published in left-wing *Gazeta de artă politică*, appreciates the book not necessarily because it deals with homosexuality, but because it does not shy away from "old-fashion realism."[29] Nor are narrative style and politics dimension at loggerheads. Quite the contrary. As Rogozanu explains the dynamic of literature and ideology,

> We need social literature not to enlist it in ideological campaigns but precisely because this kind of literature can provide more refinement, nuance, and depth to current debates. A good novel on migration would have to be more than commiseration with the destitute or an NGO report. A good novel addressing rural poverty would have to reach beyond inept urban sarcasm as much as beyond syrupy pseudo-philanthropism. To *this* end, then, artists would have to get in the habit of ideological fights.[30]

Truly surprising is the open-mindedness with which Schiop's book was received in *Dilema*. One of the magazine's editors, Marius Chivu, penned one of the most enthusiastic reviews of Schiop's novel. In his opinion, the book is "an impressive social-milieu novel," a "moving love story," and "an exemplar of linguistic innovation," all of these qualities making it "the Romanian novel of 2013."[31] The reviewer also observes that the homosexuality issue builds up, rather than exclusively accounting for, the novel's psychological significance:

> The queer novel the book seems to be at first blush is actually much more than that, namely, a love novel teeming with episodes equally appealing to a heterosexual reader because, despite the social environment and the type and sexual identity of the characters, the story picks up on, and repaints, the standard picture of every relationship: seduction and

intimacy, dependency and suspicion, breakups and reunions, betrayals and regrets, all of this going slowly and implacably downhill.[32]

Stimulating the debates around the novel without monopolizing them altogether, the queer problematics is later taken up by Ștefan Baghiu and Alex Goldiș in the *Cultura* magazine, whose politics is a non-militant leftism of sorts. In his review, Baghiu maintains that one of the novel's great merits is having avoided "the ostentatious flaunting of homosexuality, which would have diverted critics' attention," he thinks, "from the book's aesthetic value."[33] According to him, Schiop manages to convince readers that the plot, particularly the protagonist's personal predicament, is not merely rehashing conflicts in Western literature and public discourse. The novelist, Baghiu argues, lays out a genuine "ontology of the outskirts," by the same token bringing to fruition "one of the most arduous projects of recent literature"—"a brick thrown at literature's window."[34] The social immersion in the characters' environs also intrigues Goldiș, who emphasizes that "instead of expounding on the ghettoized world, Schiop prefers to spell out its basic rules," which the protagonist, a "self-aware outsider," agrees to play by.[35] The critic insists, though, that the novel's depth has little to do with "Ferentari's dark anthropological underbelly," deriving instead from the "love story lying at the book's core," "one of the best" one comes across in Romanian literature in recent memory.[36]

"Un-Disciplining" Our Vocabulary, or Commonality and Communality

Two patterns are visible across these and other comments on *Soldații*. The first pertains to vocabulary, which reiterates terms such as "queer," "sex," "love," "power," "society," "real," "reality," and so on. Needless to say, these are not innocent words but "archeconcepts" around which thought has been orbiting throughout the ages in the West and beyond. And yet none of these critics references any of the texts, foundational or not, from the mountainous bibliography on such subjects. Nor do they feel compelled to engage with Marxism, constructivism, queer studies, or any other theoretical and political paradigms coalesced around these notions in modern times. A cavalier, "journalistic" (as Adriana Stan says in this volume), or, perhaps better still, "trivial" treatment seems to be de rigueur. I propose, however, that while this "trivial" aspect is real, there is more to it than meets the eye. I suggest that, etymologically and otherwise, the trivial, the *trivium*, and the social "triviality" derived from it must be understood as sharing a certain physical, social, and notional space, as commonality. This commonality is here paramount, and the journalistic venue and presentation mode of this sort of literary criticism are best suited for staging such commonality. What this kind of approach to the plethora of concepts tackled by Schiop reminds us is that before being fleshed out conceptually, theorized formally, and maneuvered terminologically, sex, power, class, and the like are facts of life irreducible to specialized jargon, doctrine, and theory, irrespective of how rigorous and nuanced obtaining terminological, political, theoretical constructs may be. Queer identities neither come from nor live in gender and queer studies, much though feminism and gay and lesbian criticism and theory have gone a long way to helping us come to grips with the array of questions swirling around sexuality, heterosexuality, homosexuality, and so forth. Likewise, the historical development and roles of various social classes neither stem from nor span Marxism's otherwise capacious analytical purview. Having said all this, let me also underscore that this sort of criticism does not simplify, naturalize, standardize, and otherwise "co-opt" the terms and social realities in question. None of the reviewers is impervious to the subversive potential of the play these notions and their semantic worlds get in Schiop's novel.

How is this possible, though? How can one write about race, class, gender, or sex and, at the same time, steer clear of the usual phraseology and, by the same movement, of the traps laid out by neoconservative anti-"PC" vociferations? The answer strikes me as disarmingly simple: we can do all this not by replacing rhetorics and, in particular, concepts (that we do not like) with other concepts (that we like) but by un-disciplining all this lexicon, by *"rediscovering" this terminology as everyday language and reality* through community practices susceptible to disseminate and "trivialize," extend socially the use and engrained ethics of these notions. One of such practices, I propose, is, alongside Schiop's literature, criticism on it. Resulting from this practice is the community of literary critics, one that, notably, forms here across political divides. It is no happenstance, however, that criticism is a hotbed of communality. Even when its declared focus is aesthetic, what this criticism actually accomplishes in practice is to remind us that "aesthetics ... is not a depoliticized discourse or theory of art, but a factor of a specific historical organization of social roles and communality ... [A]esthetics and politics are imbricated in the constitution of specific orders of visibility and sense through which the political division into assigned roles and defined parts manifests itself."[37] This is as much as saying that the shortest pathway to commonality takes us through communality. This is, it seems to me, an aspiration writers, scholars, and other citizens of the world republic of letters should work tirelessly to turn into a reality and thus give new meaning to Pascale Casanova's well-known title. As *Soldații*'s reception goes to show, the communality ideal finds fertile ground in critical praxis. Literary critics appear best positioned not only to acknowledge the specificity of identity parameters such as "queer," "Roma," and "homeless," but also to interrogate, *together*, the various ways in which such elements can ultimately be assimilated into, and in turn transform, the larger communities constituted around race, gender, sex, and class.

Notes

1   Jonathan Evans and Chris Baronavski, "How do European Countries Differ in Religious Commitment? Use Our Interactive Map to Find Out," Pew Research Center, https://www.pewresearch.org/fact-tank/2018/12/05/how-do-european-countries-differ-in-religious-commitment/(accessed October 9, 2020).

2   See data posted at Biroul Electoral Central, "Voter Turnout," 2018, http://referendum2018.bec.ro (accessed October 11, 2020); Central Electoral Bureau, "Attendance, Provisional Results, Partial Results," December 11, 2016, https://parlamentare2016.bec.ro (accessed October 11, 2020); and Biroul Electoral Central, "First Page," 2019, http://prezidentiale2019.bec.ro (accessed October 11, 2020).

3   See Sergiu Gherghina, Alexandru Racu, Aurelian Giugăl, Alexandru Gavriș, Nanuli Silagadze, and Ron Johnston, "Non-voting in the 2018 Romanian Referendum: The Importance of Initiators, Campaigning and Issue Saliency," *Political Science* 71, no. 3 (2019): 193–213.

4   See Mihai Iovănel, *Ideologiile literaturii în postcomunismul românesc* (Bucharest: Muzeul Literaturii Române, 2017), 24.

5   Ion Bogdan Lefter, "Pentru refacerea coerenței culturale naționale. La început de *Observator cultural*," *Observator cultural* 1, no. 1 (February 29, 2000): 1.

6   Horia-Roman Patapievici, *Omul recent. O critică a modernității din perspectiva întrebării "Ce se pierde atunci când ceva se câștigă?"* (Bucharest: Humanitas, 2001), 131.

7   Patapievici, *Omul recent*, 291.

8   Cristian Moraru, "'Modelul Cărtărescu' versus 'Modelul Patapievici': Discursuri culturale și alternative politice în România de azi," *Observator cultural* 4, no. 177 (July 17–23, 2003): 32.

9   Moraru, "'Modelul Cărtărescu' versus 'Modelul Patapievici,'" 32.

10 Moraru, "'Modelul Cărtărescu' versus 'Modelul Patapievici,'" 32.

11 Andrei Pleșu, "Vigilența resentimentară," *Dilema* 11, no. 541 (August 15–21, 2003): 3.

12 Cristian Moraru, "Cultură, politică, resentiment: Fișe pentru un dicționar spectral," *Observator cultural* 4, no. 187 (September 23–29, 2003): 17.

13 Marius Chivu, "'Nu mă tem de tehnologie, ci de oameni': Interviu cu Mircea Cărtărescu," *Dilema veche* 16, no. 785 (March 7–13, 2019): 14.

14 Iulian Capsali, "De ce au ajuns românii să-l regrete pe Ceaușescu. Interviu exclusiv" *Sputnik – Moldova*, https://ro.sputnik.md/politics/20161226/10518482/interviu-ceausescu-capsali.html (accessed October 9, 2020).

15 Adrian Papahagi, "Ce este sexo-marxismul?," *Dilema Veche* 16, no. 801 (June 27–July 3, 2019): ii.

16 Răzvan Chiruță, "'Corectitudinea politică este cea mai devastatoare ideologie care a putut să apară.' Interviu cu Mircea Mihăieș," *Suplimentul de cultură* 12, no. 505 (December 5–11, 2015): 9.

17 Mircea Mihăieș, "Rasismul de amfiteatru," *România literară* 53, nos. 29–30 (July 17, 2020): 4.

18 Mihai Iovănel and Christian Moraru, "Corectitudinea politică între realitate și fetiș," *Euphorion* 30, no. 4 (October–December 2019): 19.

19 Iovănel and Moraru, "Corectitudinea politică între realitate și fetiș," 19.
20 Adrian Schiop, *Soldații. Poveste din Ferentari* (Iași, Romania: Polirom, 2014).
21 Adrian Schiop, *pe bune/pe invers*, Foreword by C. Rogozanu (Iași, Romania: Polirom, 2004).
22 Adrian Schiop, *Zero grade Kelvin* (Iași, Romania: Polirom, 2009).
23 Adrian-Ion Schiop, *Șmecherie și lume rea. Universul social al manelelor* (Chișinău, Republic of Moldova: Cartier, 2016).
24 Schiop, *Soldații*, 25.
25 Schiop, *Soldații*, 46.
26 Ovio Olaru, "Teorie gonzo," *Vatra* 48, no. 3 (March, 2018): 32–4.
27 Adina Dinițoiu, "O poveste din Ferentari," *Observator cultural* 14, no. 447 (December 19, 2013–January 8, 2014): 8.
28 Dinițoiu, "O poveste din Ferentari," 8.
29 Costi Rogozanu, "Unde-s marginalii în literatura nouă?," *Gazeta de artă politică*, January 22, 2014, http://artapolitica.ro/2014/01/22/unde-s-marginalii-in-literatura-noua/(accessed October 9, 2020).
30 Rogozanu, "Unde-s marginalii în literatura nouă?"
31 Marius Chivu, "Ferentari love story," *Dilema Veche* 11, no. 522 (February 13–19, 2014): 14.
32 Chivu, "Ferentari love story."
33 Ștefan Baghiu, "Nașterea tragediei din spiritul manelelor," *Cultura* 9, no. 6 (February 20, 2014): 10.
34 Baghiu, "Nașterea tragediei din spiritul manelelor."
35 Alex Goldiș, "Realismul hardcore," *Cultura* 9, no. 34 (September 18, 2014): 10.
36 Goldiș, "Realismul hardcore."
37 Beth Hinderliter, William Kaizen, Vered Maimon, Jaleh Mansoor, and Seth McCormick, "Introduction: Communities of Sense," in *Communities of Sense: Rethinking Aesthetics and Politics*, ed. Beth Hinderliter, William Kaizen, Vered Maimon, Jaleh Mansoor, and Seth McCormick (Durham, NC: Duke University Press, 2009), 1.

6

ANARCHETYPE:
Reading Aesthetic Form after "Structure"

Corin Braga

Especially in the modern era, literature has evolved a set of traits that, in contrast with those defining previous literary traditions, stand out as anarchic, iconoclastic, antinomic, anti-systemic, and anti-canonical. These unconventional features have constantly drawn the attention of critics, some of whom have taken the trouble to catalog them. So has done, for example, Brian McHale in *Postmodern Fiction*. Here he lists items such as the literary equivalent to the Aristotelian "excluded middle" (*tertium non datur*) but also the "Included Middle" notion developed in logic after World War II by Stéphane Lupasco, Basarab Nicolescu, and others; the self-erasing story; narrative forking paths; violations of linear sequentiality; strange loops, or metalepsis; multiple and circular endings, as well as non-endings; Chinese boxes and Russian dolls; infinite regress; mimetic *trompe l'œil*; and techniques of "variable" reality.[1] Elsewhere, I have submitted that this entire panoply of formal characteristics can be subsumed under a single structural and morphological category, which I have called "anarchetype."[2] In what follows, I build on my previous work to revisit this notion so as to place it in the broader conversation currently surrounding notions of form, genre, and value in the world theory commons.

To that effect, I start out by tracing briefly the evolution of this concept throughout literary history, highlighting a world literature corpus of works and genres that I view as predominantly "anarchetypal." In the first part of the chapter, I question the traditional correlation, inherited from Aristotle, between archetypal configurations and aesthetic value. Why is it, I ask, that, to this very day, we tend to assume that a work's significance and value are a function of that work's necessarily "centered" form? At issue here, I suggest, is neither so much formalism per se nor the focus on form or structure generally, but the understanding of the latter—and the implicit appreciation of textuality—as *centeredness*, as following from and being deployed around some kind of center or core. In search for an answer, I revisit relevant post-World War II-era arguments, which, one way or the other, posit that literary works can acquire aesthetic value only insofar as these texts are reducible to a *cogito, ratio*, synopsis, or *Gestalt*. These all are, I contend, privileged terms participating in the setting up of critical judgment as founded on an *aesthetic of centeredness*. Questioning the soundness of this position, I ultimately propose divorcing aesthetic value from the structural coherence of form. Severing the umbilical cord between the two allows, I submit, for a revaluing of underappreciated works and generic forms as well as for a "democratization" of genre theory through the rehabilitation of certain types of text that have been long marginalized. Notably enough, the moves I make here are part and parcel of a more extensive revisionist effort that, only loosely coordinated with respect to method, terminology, and focus, has been in full swing since the start of the third millennium. Although the literary anarchetype is a more complex formation than genre, critics' and theorists' straight-on or oblique engagement with it has yielded of late, I maintain, an entire anarchetypal genre or discourse of sorts inside and across various national traditions in criticism and theory.

Archetype and Anarchetype

The term "anarchetype," to begin with, is made up of three Greek etymons: the prefix *a, an* ("a-," "anti-," or "contra-"); *árkhaios* ("old," "original," or "primitive") or *arkhê* ("beginning" or "principle"); and *týpos* ("type" or "model"). Grouped in pairs, these roots can be found in "anarchy" (comprised of *an* and of the verb *árkhein*—"to lead" or "guide") and "archetype" ("first type," "original model"). Depending on how we combine all three of them, the anarchetype would denote, then, either an "anarchic model" of text, which rejects and destroys structure, or an "anti-archetype," to wit, an "exploded" or fragmented archetype. Thus, the archetype and anarchetype signify two organizing principles that are conflicting and complimentary. The archetype, along with all its avatars (*arché, télos, eídos, ousía, enérgeia, idéa, alétheia*), marks those works that have a central, hierarchical, harmonious, and organic structure, whereas the anarchetype fashions and helps describe works that are decentered, disjointed, anarchic, chaotic, and devoid of a unified meaning. I should, however, point out from the outset that these definitions do not align with any of the theoretical camps involved in the debate over the "structural center" and its avatars, a controversy launched by Jacques Derrida at the landmark 1966 Johns Hopkins conference[3] and dismissed by neo-evolutionists and neuroscientists as a false problem and a sophism.[4] I therefore do not intend to take issue, as a "postmodern" critic might, with the notion of archetype seized as an ineffable essence that underwrites the Grand Narratives denounced by Jean-François Lyotard, but rather to analyze it as objectively as possible. Nor do I attempt to demonstrate, in a fashion one might call "maximalist," that centered structures dominate all creativity fields, whether philosophical, literary, or artistic, or that such structures are merely artificial, forcefully imposed conceptual constructs. Instead, I want to see if, alongside these centered forms, there are other, less logocentric and more freely moving textual configurations, perhaps even decentered and disjointed works that no longer operate paradigmatically, that is, according to set patterns and models.[5] As indicated above, I define all these structural "leftovers" as anarchetypes.

Now, if one applies the archetype and anarchetype concepts to literature, one can distinguish two types or categories of works. On one hand, archetypal works behave in an organized, centered, and unified manner, resting as they do on a homogeneous, finite, and complete scenario, which provides their meaning with a "backbone," as it were. A classical tragedy characteristically exhibits a unified structure, in keeping with the rules Aristotle and Boileau laid down on unity of place, time, and action. In contrast, anarchetypal works behave anarchically and chaotically. They adhere to no central, totalizing meaning, developing instead in surprising and contradictory directions that cannot be subsumed under a single scenario. An alexandrine novel or a Jules Verne "extraordinary voyage," for example, tends to feature any number of adventures and divergent, centrifugal episodes that could go on endlessly, without fitting neatly into a closed, structured form. To use a cosmological metaphor, the archetype may be compared to a solar system where the planets harmoniously revolve around a central sun, the *logos* of the whole, while the anarchetype could be likened to the galactic dust that precedes the birth of a planetary system or to the cloud of debris left over by the explosion of a supernova. The presence of such open, incomplete, or fragmented configurations throughout literary history has already been noticed by contemporary theorists and critics such as Gilles Deleuze and Félix Guattari, who set up in *A Thousand Plateaus* an opposition between root-like structures and the rhizome. Thus, the root-based, "tree-like" book presents a totalizing image of the world, a cosmos of hierarchically and genealogically interconnected forms. The "rhizome-like" book, on the other hand, branches out in multiple, aleatory directions, lacking a point of origin, a trunk, or a center, and projecting a chaotic picture of the world.

Rhizomes resist both encoding and totalizing meaning and are otherwise resolutely anti-genealogical, connecting any points within the network arbitrarily. Where the tree-like structures have been invoked to explain a range of different systems from Darwinian evolutionism to linguistics, the rhizomatic forms are better suited to describe, for instance, the workings of synapses in the human brain or a-centric social arrangements. Likewise, whereas the mechanism for establishing a center depends on "the power claimed by a signifier," rhizomatic formations preclude any such structured or generative model.[6]

It is worth noting, along the same lines, that as far as literature and the arts go, the anarchetype accounts for the configuration—or lack thereof—that, according to Umberto Eco, defines what he calls "open work." In both music and literature, the Italian philosopher shows, "to aim for maximum unpredictability is to aim for maximum disorder in which not only the most common meanings but also all possible meanings turn out to be impossible to organize."[7] Contemporary art, in particular, tends to work against, and to constantly disrupt, worn-out models and schemes, thereby serving as a liberating pedagogical tool.[8] Furthermore, in *Six Walks in the Fictional Woods*, Eco points out that "open works" are malleable, infinitely "breakable," devoid of message, and "as ambiguous as life itself." In them, the lack of organization opens up the possibility for their going haywire structurally speaking. Films such as *Casablanca* or *The Rocky Horror Picture Show* have turned, Eco says, into "cult works par excellence, precisely because they lack form, and as such, they can be infinitely dismantled and deformed." Confronted with open works, readers find themselves in a "narrative forest" that morphs into a true labyrinth right under their own eyes. The limitless demands, in terms of encyclopedic knowledge, texts like *Finnegans Wake* make on readers turn these texts into "infinite forests" impossible to penetrate and map out.[9] To define such open configurations, literary analyses have borrowed from sciences such as mathematics, physics, and informatics concepts as diverse as fractals, networks, and chaos theory. Gordon E. Slethaug, for example, has examined works of American authors like Thomas Pynchon, John Barth, Michael Crichton, and Don DeLillo through the lens of entropy, stochastics, feedback loops, bifurcation, flow, dynamic theory, and strange attractors. If some contemporary texts deploy such techniques in rather subtle ways, others flaunt them explicitly and deliberately.[10]

Unlike anarchetypal works, those that can be said to be archetypal follow an orderly narrative structure and develop a coherent, unified scenario regardless of how they are built. Thus, the modern novel, as opposed to *romance*, came into its own when it began to trace the evolution of an individual destiny from a certain moment in the protagonist's life to a final, conclusive point. Johann Wolfgang von Goethe's *Wilhelm Meister's Apprenticeship* pursues a life trajectory that literally "makes sense," builds or cobbles together meaning, in that personal and historical experiences add up to a biography, namely, to a story with a beginning, middle, and end. One can generalize and argue that the plot of an archetypal novel is built as an initiation path according to a unifying, meaning-engendering scenario. Such works are conceived and written around a structuring, cosmo-genetic core that makes the narrative material gravitate along concentric orbits, just as a magnet shapes iron filings on a sheet of paper. For instance, Dante's *Divine Comedy* is modeled on a cosmological and metaphysical structure, within the rigorous limits and hierarchy of Christian theology. Even though the protagonist's journey is marked by twists and turns through the inferno, purgatory, and paradise, launching, in the process, new storylines about the past lives of the dead he encounters, these deviations never veer from the "backbone" of the work's central vision. *The Neverending Story* by the German fantasy author Michael Ende is also archetypally constructed, for while the direction in which the events unfold may not be immediately apparent, the influence of mythical formulas and Jungian archetypes is strongly felt, shaping the characters' destinies. Dante's poem exemplifies an ostensibly theological archetype, "a bright star" hovering above the work, if you will, and meant to illuminate its overall, unified structure, whereas Ende's novel is rooted in what one might call a psychologically liminal archetype, a kind of *soleil noir*, subterranean and invisible but equally capable of focusing and organizing the imaginary universe.

Gravitating around this enlightening source, and alongside works dominated by a single, central authorial subject, an alternative set of works has emerged, featuring a multiple, decentered subject and departing from the archetypal model, which is thus left suspended in the void, as it were. These works are likely to confound readers who try to summarize them or grasp their gist. They cannot be reduced to a sentence or an "abstract" not because they are deliberately dense or sprawling so as to test the reader's predictive skills, as in some detective novels, but rather because their substance eschews the logos—the organizing rationality that endows them with meaning. Their poetics behave anarchically or anarchetypally, pushing in centripetal directions that fail to cohere around a central meaning.[11] From this standpoint, one can discern in the history of European culture a parallel series of works and forms that no longer share a unifying scenario, a magnetic framework of sorts that structures the narrative iron filings. If the episodes, scenes, and imagery of an archetypal work succeed one another and build up to a totalizing meaning, no such straightforward arrangement and predictable conclusion can be found in an anarchetypal work, where each scene or setting may be self-sufficient, fully integrated, and meaningful, and yet the overall narrative lacks coherence and fails to yield an organic signification. Such texts are driven not merely by a baroque or avant-garde desire to shock and intrigue through their disarticulation, which would in and of itself constitute a paradoxical orientation in how they have been articulated and what they suggest, but rather by a disinterested or indifferent attitude toward any single and unified meaning scenario, which is perceived as normative, prescriptive, reductive, and sterile.

Thus understood, the archetype and the anarchetype could be compared to chains made up of LEGO® pieces. In the former, the chain is propped up by a solid scaffolding; in the latter, although the links of the chain are strong, the chain itself goes in all directions, in disarray and without the firmness of a mechanical apparatus, of a prosthesis, for instance. The anarchetype is a culturally invertebrate animal—or, to pursue my zoological analogy further, an animal with an atypical skeleton—a creature that may look like a monster to those used to the world of vertebrates. And yet this literary monstrosity may open up venues and possibilities unsuspected by canonical poetics, even though the anarchetype's driving force seems to be an allergy to "high-brow" literature, imposed norms, standard rules, inherited schemes, and "beaten paths" whether within or without the works themselves. Inside texts, archetypal mechanisms oversee the choice a writer makes when, reaching, say, a narrative crossroads, he or she strays from a preestablished trajectory of known facts and predictable or familiar meanings, thus unsettling the reader's horizon of expectations. The anarchetype might then be defined as a creative instrument, be it epic, lyrical, dramatic, and so forth, an entire apparatus, in fact, that spontaneously or deliberately—no matter how the author sees or theorizes it—*blocks, jams, and otherwise eschews* those associations and connections, as well as the sequencing of images, scenes, and situations leading to a "holistic" meaning. An anarchetypal work, in other words, is one in which a single, unified meaning-making scenario of a literary cosmos has been pulverized into a meaningless nebula. In this universe, the classical laws of Aristotelian physics no longer apply, having been displaced by quantum logic, and so this art world's impact on audiences is all about quantity and mass. No longer revelatory and illuminating meaningwise, the effect produced by this kind of art is cumulative, precluding Aristotelian *anagnórisis*, too ("recognition"), and amounting instead to an affective, sensorial, and imaginative assault. The fragments, meteors, asteroids, and leftover scenes, imagery, and symbols make up a figurative cloud that engulfs the reader not by evoking the archetypal star from which it originates but rather by its massive presence, which overwhelms the imagination and destroys conventional modes of perception. Anarchetypal poetry, prose, and drama use images, characters, situations, and myths the same way builders recycle older buildings' bricks and other material, which are part neither of the former dwellings' overall structure anymore nor of the composition of a new architectural project either—they find themselves in a *de-composition* stage.

Granted, labeling a work anarchetypal can be problematic, and where one critic sees an anarchetype another may identify an archetypal scenario that the former overlooked, or conversely, a critic who discerns a partial meaning included in an anarchetypal ensemble may unjustifiably elevate its status to an archetypal, all-embracing meaning. To be sure, there are works, from François Rabelais's *Gargantua and Pantagruel* to Roberto Bolaño's *2066*, which feature emblematic, allegorical, and symbolic elements, such as monster figures, metamorphosis, sacrifice, crime, or love. To decide whether a particular work is archetypal or anarchetypal, one should determine first if a certain theme permeates the entire text, or if it represents an isolated iteration, leftover symbol, or partial archetype that explains, alongside other such archetypes, only one narrative segment rather than the entire ensemble. Anarchetypes do not necessarily involve the total disappearance of archetypal themes but only the disintegration of complete scenarios into fragments of meaning, just as—to return to the cosmological analogy above—the nebula caused by the explosion of a supernova consists of vapors and meteors left over from the original star. The risk lies in mistaking a partial archetype for the organizing principle behind the whole work; and, vice versa, there is always a chance that a work initially identified as anarchetypal may ultimately reveal its hidden archetypal nature. I would nevertheless point out that there is still a sufficient amount of works that clearly and demonstrably illustrate the anarchetypal category, as their meaning fragments fail to cohere into, or gravitate toward, a single, unifying understanding.

World Literature and the Anarchetypal Corpus

The anarchetype is, then, a morphological class that describes a certain way of building literary works; it is neither a historical category that defines a particular literary current or cultural paradigm nor a generic rubric that provides norms for this or that literary or artistic genre. All major cultural epochs and genres can include both archetypal and anarchetypal works, even though the number of such works varies depending on the paradigm holding sway at the time. Thus, cultural moments dominated by a single, unrivaled model of understanding the world have often yielded archetypal works that follow the ontological scenarios sanctioned by their mainstream religions or ideologies. On the other hand, the more convulsive and revolutionary intervals that have seen an overhaul of their *Weltanschauungen*, when explanatory narratives have multiplied and come to compete against one another, have given rise to disjointed and fragmented works, torn between convergent and centrifugal tendencies. Roughly put, such works' formal and thematic configurations are anarchetypal or, more broadly, anarchic.

Chronologically speaking, the ancient epic and its surrounding mythology are probably the first to come to mind in this historical context. Interestingly enough, Claude Lévi-Strauss admits, at the beginning of *The*

Raw and the Cooked that, in his attempt to classify the Amerindian myths, he failed to impose a unifying scheme on a "fuzzy" narrative nebula that kept multiplying and diversifying depending on narrator, audience, place, and time. Although built around certain nuclei of meaning, the Indigenous mythology of Latin America tends to proliferate anarchically, foregoing an all-encompassing meaning. As Lévi-Strauss says,

> There is no end to mythical analysis, whose work of decomposition does not uncover a secret unity. Themes duplicate themselves infinitely. Just when you think you have separated them and can keep them so, you realize they have merged again, driven by unpredictable affinities. Consequently, the unity of myth is only tentative and projective, always reflecting just a state or moment of myth.[12]

Thus, lest he force on myth a meaning center that is otherwise absent in it, Lévi-Strauss adopts an *anaclastic*, or, I would say, "anarchetypal" approach that involves a refractive or, better yet, spiral development, as opposed to a linear and hierarchical one. Without a beginning and an end—or, rather, starting from any one of the myths "floating" in the narrative mass of the mythological body—his book maps out its subject through "star-shaped configurations" or organizing grids, constructing the semantic fields of each myth and arranging them into a network of meanings, for "without aiming to set out from or arrive somewhere, the mythical thinking never runs its course. There is always something left unfinished."[13]

Unlike the primitive epic, classical mythologies are archetypal because they are the result of systematic labor performed by Babylonian, Egyptian, and Jewish scribes or by a masterful compiler such as Hesiod. Classical myths did not start off as, but have become over time, what Mircea Eliade calls "exemplary histories" that have provided religions with narrative and ideological foundations.[14] Stereotyped through tradition, fixed and sustained through dogmas, underwriting rituals and liturgies, these myths have emerged as "final models" or, as I have called them elsewhere, "eschatypes," a concept that refers to works or bodies of work that have ended up, as a result of their centuries-long evolution, closing themselves up into an overarching scheme. Such mythical structures were first pulled from primitive narrative amorphousness and then turned into "original models" or archetypes throughout the period dominated by a certain religion, be it henotheist, polytheist, monotheist, or of another type.[15] Later on, canonical myths would in turn begin to shed their archetypal structure once the numinous fascination they exerted was challenged by other myths, and the traditions as well as the religious and political institutions that guaranteed their status and stability lost their normative power. This kind of anarchetypal dismantling of mythological structures is evident, for instance, in the fantastic tales of North Asian origin analyzed by V. I. Propp, who sees them as acculturated avatars of local shamanic religion;[16] in the orally transmitted Irish Celtic tales, which were transcribed, adapted, and altered by Christian ¡monks between the seventh and fifteenth centuries;[17] in the neo-Platonic, occultist (astrological, alchemical, kabbalistic, magical, etc.) "interpretations" of Christianity during the Renaissance;[18] and in the numerous syncretic cults and religious trends of the last two centuries.[19]

Another cluster of texts that favor anarchetypal forms consists of alexandrine novels from late antiquity such as Petronius's *The Satyricon*, Apuleius's *The Metamorphoses*, Heliodor's *Aethiopica*, Chariton of Aphrodisia's *Chaereas and Callirhoe*, Achilles Tatius's *Leucippe and Clitophon*, and Lucian of Samosata's *A True Story*. As already stressed, the archetype and the anarchetype are not generic but structural categories, which is why the group above includes examples from both types. Thus, Apuleius, a neo-Platonic philosopher initiated in mystery cults, constructed his novel around the scenario of a mystical evolution: coming into contact with witchcraft, the mysteries of the Great Syrian Goddess and Isis, and the cult of Bacchus, Lucius goes through all initiation stages, from the subhuman stage of an ass to the divine phase of a triple initiate in the rites of Isis, Osiris, and Sarapis. Moreover, to foreground this journey from animal nature to the divine, Lucius's story is placed in a *mise en abyme* fashion within the three chapters that make up the tale of Amor and Psyche. Apuleius fills this tale with a neo-Platonic allegorical meaning about the human soul that transcends the mortal condition and reaches the divine through Eros. But this unifying scenario is heavily interrupted by episodes and digressions that, as Apuleius explains, have to do with the conventions of the "Milesian" novel, which are aimed at arousing the reader's curiosity and pleasure, while also enriching the imaginative fabric of the text. Granted, this alluvial narrative material does not change the course of the novel, which runs like a red thread through digressions. What happens, though, when the archetypal scaffolding, the mystical backstory, disappears, leaving behind only the collection of "marginal" episodes? Illustrating this very process, *The Satyricon* shows that the author may have intended to end Trimalchio's adventures with an initiation or some other resolution, but since the novel is unfinished, the narrative scheme is incomplete, and the text itself remains unstructured. A similar process characterizes the other alexandrine texts, where the adventures and journeys no longer serve to anchor an overarching framework, a *ratio* for the whole, developing instead hedonistically through the free association of more or less fantastic episodes, which yield "novels" such as Lucian's and are perfect examples of anarchetype. In *A True Story*, after passing by the Pillars of Heracles, the protagonist travels through miraculous places, encountering rivers of wine, trees that look like women, seas of milk, earth made of cheese, the Islands of the Blessed heroes of old, the belly of a whale, and the Dreamland, even climbing up to the Moon. The novel ends with the promise, never redeemed, that the next volume would tell the story of the main hero's adventures on a continent across the Atlantic.[20] Such a narrative trajectory could go on forever, zig-zagging all over the planet and beyond, refusing to adhere to any rule of unity, place, or time, to any sense of bounded space or meaning.

Worth mentioning here is another predominantly anarchetypal corpus of texts, which comprises seventeenth-century chivalry novels, beginning with *Amadis de Gaula* by Garci Rodriguez de Montalvo. In the case of the "Round Table" novels, one can show that, over almost three centuries, from Chrétien de Troyes to Thomas Mallory, the proliferating collection of stories and episodes underwent an incremental structuring process, from the initial narrative nebulosity we have noticed elsewhere to a final "recapitulation" (*anacefalesis, recapitulatio*) centered around the Holy Grail symbol, which brings the cycle to an end. Renaissance novels, on the other hand, lack a meaning center susceptible of sustaining an overarching structure. Their protagonists set out on increasingly exciting travels and exploits that lack logical unity and are linked only by free-wheeling associative fantasies. Not even the hero's death puts an end to the saga, as Amadis's epic task is taken up by his son Esplandian, then by his grandson Lisuarte of Greece, followed by Florisel of Niquea, Rogel of Greece, Felixmarte of Hircania, and Palmerin of England, to name but a few. While the Round Table novels can be seen as constituting an eschatype, Renaissance chivalric romances proliferated anarchetypally until they exhausted the associative schemes, which would lead, a century later, to the collapse of the entire genre at the hands of Miguel de Cervantes.

A similar evolution characterized other genres of early modernity, such as picaresque novels, adventure novels, travelogues, *voyages extraordinaires*, and generally what British and American criticism calls *romance*. Although picaresque novels parody chivalric romances through burlesque realism, as opposed to the flamboyant fantastic, and feature ordinary anti-heroes, as opposed to noble knights, such novels retain the open form that allows for unlimited sequels. As Alma Rosa Mar Serrano has observed, one of the generic traits of the picaresque is the "open structure" or structural "pluralism."[21] Not only did *Lazarillo de Tormes*, for example, inaugurate a subgenre but, under the powerful influence Lucian's writings exerted during the Renaissance, also generated all kinds of fanciful sequels, such as the anonymous *Segunda parte de Lazarillo de Tormes,* in which the protagonist visits a utopian realm under the sea. A picaresque character like M. Bigand in Chevalier de Mouhy's *La Mouche ou les Aventures de M. Bigand* goes through a rich assortment of extravagant adventures from the fantastic to the trivial in a universe ruled by arbitrary laws. Likewise, the travelogues invented by armchair travelers, starting with the famous *Travels* by John Mandeville, crisscross the era's territories on zig-zag routes that defy reality. The *voyages extraordinaires* of the seventeenth and eighteenth

centuries, from which Charles-Georges-Thomas Garnier included only a
limited sample in his anthology *Voyages imaginaires*, are often "polytopias"
that string together, on an almost infinite thread, real and imaginary topoi,
ideal or nightmarish kingdoms, human beings and monstrous creatures,
which together make up a kaleidoscope of the human race in all its varieties.
Some examples include Béroalde de Verville's 1610 *The True Story, or the
Journey of the Fortunate Princes*; Jonathan Swift's 1726 *Gulliver's Travels*
and Pierre-François Guyot Desfontaines's 1730 sequel, *The New Gulliver,
or The Travels of Jean Gulliver, Son of Captain Gulliver*; Henri Pajon's 1740
Histoire Du Prince Soly, Surnommé Prenany & De La Princesse Fêlée; the
1778 *Travels of Hildebrand Bowman, Esquire*; and Nicolas-Edme Rétif de
La Bretonne's 1781 *La Découverte Australe Par Un Homme-Volant, Ou Le
Dédale Français*.
  During the modern era, the rise of a polymorphous capitalism, along
with the accompanying unprecedented fragmentation of the self, set the
stage for the disintegration of inherited forms and genres, making room
for ambitious experiments. Literary anarchetypal configurations began to
be adopted deliberately, albeit they were not identified as such, by authors
intent on avoiding coherence-prone schemes and scenarios, the center, and
even the *logos* of the very works they were completing. Initially, this rupture
occurred in poetry, where the shock of the self's dissolution into Charles
Baudelaire's *homo dupplex* was felt most strongly. As Melvin Friedman,
among other critics, has demonstrated, symbolism prefigures the stream of
consciousness novel by rendering interior life in all its chaotic spontaneity.[22]
Indeed, suffice it to compare modern masterpieces such as *Faust, The
Tragedy of Man*, or *The Legend of the Ages*, on one side, and the poetry
of Arthur Rimbaud or Stéphane Mallarmé, on the other, to understand
the distinction between archetypal and anarchetypal poetry. Such poets'
metaphorics no longer employs figures of speech at the level of meaning
so as to construct an allegorical universe but at that of form broadly, as a
mere figurative representation of psychological states. As for prose, Mikhail
M. Bakhtin proposed the concept of the "polyphonic novel" to describe
the new narrative apparatus created by one of the founding fathers of
the modern novel, Fyodor Dostoevsky.[23] It should be noted, though, that,
breaking with the tradition of the monophonic or monological novel, the
Dostoevskian novel foregrounds the notion of musical polyphony not so
much as a choir of divergent voices belonging to several characters, nor as
a panoply of different authorial styles, as Franco Moretti seems to think,
but as *multiple inner voices or personalities within the same character*.[24]
After all, the vocal polyphony of distinct characters was present in earlier
literature already—in Goethe's *Faust*, for example—but there, one might
argue, the author projects his multiple selves onto various characters. From
this perspective, the literary work constitutes a giant interior arena where
the author's identities clash and interact: Faust personifies his active self,

Mephistopheles his shadow, Margaret and Helen the *anima* side of his soul, Homunculus his spirit, while Euphorion and the redeemed Faust embody the divine child.[25] By contrast, Dostoevsky does not displace different aspects of his personality onto different characters. Instead, he conceives of each individual character as a psychic whole, with all its contradictory sides, and therefore problematic, divided, and doubled—a reflection, in other words, of the dichotomous, agonic condition of modernity.

To convey this polymorphism of Western civilization, modern novelists have returned to the forms and revived the ambition of old epics and writings, developing what Edward Mendelson calls "encyclopedic narrative." This subgenre includes, to name but a few, *The Divine Comedy, Gargantua and Pantagruel, Don Quixote, Faust, Moby Dick, Ulysses,* and *Gravity's Rainbow*. Like Homer's poems and the Bible, such works aim to reflect an entire culture and the encyclopedic knowledge of an era. To this end, encyclopedic narrative is cumulative and heterogeneous, analytical and synthetic at the same time, "monstrous" in construction, offering a mythical history or the history of a civilization, a complete account of a science or technology, deploying a set of literary styles, and positing a polyglot dimension of language.[26] The encyclopedic genre can encompass texts that are put together both archetypally and anarchetypally. Four of the seven works inventoried by Mendelson (*The Divine Comedy, Faust, Moby Dick,* and *Ulysses*) revolve around an overarching architecture and the symbolic meaning of initiation, and so they are archetypal; the other three are decentered, fluid, open-ended, and thus anarchetypal. One could add to the latter premodern works (*Orlando Furioso* and *Lazarillo de Tormes,* for instance) that have been canonized despite their open configuration. Comparing an anarchetypal work such as *The Faerie Queene* and the archetypal *Paradise Lost*, which are organized according to the principle of free association and of the biblical narrative archetype, respectively, it becomes clear that aesthetic value cannot be—and in fact, has never been—derived strictly from the presence of a centralized, totalizing, and systemically enforced meaning.

The absence of such a meaning characterizes, I would propose, that which recent genre theory and World Literature critics have called "world texts." As is well known, Moretti has built on Mendelson's argument and theorized those kinds of works "whose geographical frame of reference is no longer the nation-state, but a broader entity—a continent, or the world-system as a whole."[27] The modern epos, contends Moretti, has abandoned organic, centripetal structures and has embraced instead the principles of mechanical accumulation, collage, and juxtaposition. These "centrifugal novels" have "a form that may be cut at will. Above all, one that may be *added to* at will ... A form in continuous growth,"[28] with "weak, indecisive endings, [which] neither conclude the text nor settle its meaning once and for all." They often remain, however, "an ensemble devoid of unity, an archipelago of 'independent worlds.'"[29] Still, once again, while driven by anarchical impulses, the world-text genre does not coincide with the anarchetype. First, as I have already indicated, not all encyclopedic or world texts lack the backbone of a *logos* or overarching meaning. Even if he wrote his poem in fragments, through an accumulation of episodes elaborated over his lifetime, Goethe followed Friedrich Schiller's recommendation to organize the text around an allegorical scenario. Following all the roads, "from heaven, across the world, to hell," Faust's evolution becomes a great parable of entire humanity's destiny, a variation on the Adam archetype. Likewise, although experimenting with a wide range of polyphonic and stream of consciousness techniques, James Joyce keeps *Ulysses* tied to the archetypal scheme of *The Odyssey*.[30] Moreover, alongside this historical or temporal narrative scheme, a spatial nexus also obtains in *Ulysses*—what Rudolf Arnheim describes as a Dublin "synopsis."[31] Thus, the best example of an anarchetypal work in Joyce's oeuvre is not *Ulysses* but *Finnegans Wake*, where we can no longer find any system of references or cartographic grid that could help us orient within a minimally centered system.

Postmodernism has further intensified the centrifugal tendencies already so prevalent in modernists such as Joyce and in modern literature generally. Starting with Friedrich Nietzsche, the questioning of Grand Narratives and founding myths is, of course, not only a hallmark of Lyotardian thought but also of postmodern literature broadly, which has reproduced ontologically, psychologically, and formally the great critique of meaning, the polymorphism of culture, and the identity crises of the contemporary human self. Again, many of the anarchetypal traits are obvious in several subgenres of both modernism and postmodernism, most notably in the *systems novel*. Thus, in *The Art of Excess*, Tom LeClair shows that, to get a grip on the outside world, to wield narrative devices effectively, and to make an impact on readers, postmodern prose has drawn on the theories and techniques of complex systems from biology.[32] According to Stefano Ercolino, however, the *systems novel* is "torrential, chaotic, labyrinthine, long-winded, shrouded in obscure symbolisms, and structured by such rigid and often hard-to-unravel logic."[33] In his turn, Frederick R. Karl has singled out one of the post-War World II American narrative subgenres, which he dubs the *mega-novel*, and which is characterized by anarchetypal traits such as length, openness, incompleteness, chaos, disorder, experimentalism, and decentering. This form, Karl maintains, "is long but lacks any sense of completion; while it has no boundaries for an ending, of course it does end; it seems to defy clear organization—it seems decentered, unbalanced—yet has intense order; it is located outside traditional forms of narrative" but "still employs some conventional modes. Its aim posits disorder, messiness, the chaos of our existence and by extension of our times."[34]

A more recent theoretical contribution in this direction is Ercolino's *maximalist novel*. Synthesizing all of the concepts mentioned above, Ercolino catalogs the following traits associated with novels driven by totalizing ambition: length ("chorality, digressions, the polycentric multiplication of narrative threads"); encyclopedism (literature as archive, or the attempt to "digitalize" the world through literature); polyphony and fragmentariness ("the fragment is the morphological part of the rhizomatic cognitive structure of the maximalist novel"); diegetic exuberance ("the narration is hypertrophic and ultra-dense"; "the idea of unitary and unifying narrative action explodes into a thousand pieces, flooding into a large number of stories"); completeness (the presence of an all-integrating structure); narrative omniscience; the paranoid imagination; intersecting semiotic systems; ethical engagement; hybrid realism.[35] As one can see, the first four features characterize anarchetypal forms (*narrative entropy*), while the next three are mostly archetypal—actually, Ercolino himself shows that the maximalist novel struggles with an inner dialectic between chaos and cosmos. This does not mean that anarchetypes, as a formal category, do not define certain literary genres and subgenres, even if some of the latter tend toward narrative entropy more than others. Moreover, just as not every systems novel, mega-novel, or maximalist novel is necessarily anarchetypal, some of them being clearly logocentric, so too length or size is no guarantee of literary anarchy. Anarchetypal configurations are as likely to occur in short texts and in novels of average length. In modernism, a text such as *Alice in Wonderland* by Lewis Carroll is perfectly open and so infinitely expandable according to a logic of oneiric-anarchical associations. Short novels, such as *L'Arache-cœur* (Heartsnatcher) and *L'Automne à Pekin* (Autumn in Beijing) by Boris Vian, or *Molloy* and *The Unnamable* by Samuel Beckett, display the same refusal of meaning, structure, and center as maximalist novels, engaging deliberately in narrative deconstruction and rejecting inherited schemes and traditions. Nor does Pynchon need *Gravity's Rainbow*'s bulk to craft the anarchetypal *V.*, which, despite its more modest dimensions, shares with the 1973 masterpiece the same freedom of formal and logical constraints.

Anarchetype and Canonical Value

As the above discussion suggests, while anarchetypal formations have been programmatically and massively adopted in contemporary art and literature, they are not exclusive to modernism and postmodernism. Rather, they are—to reiterate—transhistorical; we come across them throughout cultural history, except that, if they are currently appreciated, in premodern times they were oftentimes viewed as failures or abnormal deviations, which stripped them of aesthetic value and placed them outside the canon and implicitly outside the realm of "high-brow" literature. To my mind, utilizing the descriptive category of the anarchetype could help restore status to certain works and even whole genres that have traditionally been deemed inferior, minor, or worthless. The anarchetype allows us, in fact, to distinguish a structural criterion that has been imposed by dominant poetics as a benchmark of value and success. Thus, the question is, how do we deal with those writers, particularly premodern, whose objective in their work is not a coherent *cogito* or an all-inclusive scheme? Indeed, how are we to treat authors who settle for the fluidity of the imaginary instead of striving to infuse their texts with a *ratio* or synopsis, who cannot or would not, even, organize systematically their texts around a meaning center, who prefer the vegetative chaos of a jungle to a cathedral's architecture and rhizomes to a tree, and who, finally, due to the traditional dogma that says "value equals *centered* structure," have almost invariably been banished from the canon? I offer up the anarchetype as a solution to at least some of the problems foregrounded by these important and timely questions.

The use of the structural criterion as a measure of aesthetic accomplishment goes all the way back to Aristotle and has been carried on by various theorists working in the classical tradition. In *Poetics*, Aristotle set out to "inquire into the structure of the plot as requisite to a good poem."[36] Of the six parts that make up a work (plot, character, diction, thought, spectacle, and music), the most important is "the arrangement of events." "A beautiful object," the philosopher writes, "whether it be a picture or a living organism or any whole composed of parts, must not only have an orderly arrangement of parts, but must also be of a certain magnitude; for beauty depends on magnitude and order" (Arist., *Poet.* 7.31). To observe this principle of order (*táxis*), first, "the plot, being an imitation of an action, must imitate one action," and, second, the work as an integrated whole must be preserved, "the structural union of the parts being such that, if any one of them is displaced or removed, the whole will be disjointed and disturbed" (8.35). A unified plot must, accordingly, develop only a single plot line, not two or more (13.47); furthermore, a work should have for its subject "a single action, whole and complete, with a beginning, a middle, and an end," so that it "will thus resemble a single and coherent picture of a living being and produce the pleasure proper to it" (13.89). To the organic development criterion Aristotle adds rationality, stipulating that "the tragic plot must not be composed of irrational parts" (24.95). In other words, structure functions as a *logos* that lends the work a cosmos-like, integrative character. Absent the latter, the work would simply fall through—the least successful subjects, exemplifies Aristotle, are "episodic," and they doom those works in which "episodes or acts succeed one another without probable or necessary sequence" (9.39); tragedy authors who combine several subjects "either fail utterly or meet with poor success on the stage" (18.67); and, finally, tragedy is superior to the epic also because it explores no more than one subject (26.111).

The Aristotelian aesthetic canon remained dominant up until modernity. The rules of unity and consistency were proclaimed throughout the ages by Horace, Quintilian (*Institutiones Oratoriae*), Cicero (*Rhetorica ad Herennium*), Venerable Bede (*De arte metrica*), Dante (*De Vulgari Eloquentia*), Antonio Sebastiano Minturno (who criticized new genres, such as romance, for failing to conform to Aristotle's rules), Scaliger (who held up the Aristotelian ideal of a "unified structure" to the Pleiads poets), Boileau (who prescribed the rules of action, time, and place for classical literature), John Dryden, Alexander Pope, and John Milton, all the way to Matthew Arnold (who, at the height of the Victorian era, affirmed his Aristotelian beliefs), Rosalie Cole, Northrop Frye, and the members of the "neo-Aristotelian" Chicago School of Literary Criticism.[37] And even if *Gestalttheorie* schools, especially Prague formalism and French structuralism, seemed to have cast aside the Aristotelian mode of thinking and liberated themselves from its influence, they too emphasized structured form. Likewise, as Patrick Sériot has shown, the Russian formalists too, despite the appearance of conceptual innovation, worked from *a priori* post-Romantic and non-Darwinian premises that subordinated "structure" to "the whole."[38] Or, Aristotelian generic norms also presuppose, as we have seen, a hierarchy of genres. From ancient to modern times, distinctions have been made between high and low styles, high-brow and mass-audience genres (the *Bildungsroman* vs the detective novel, for instance), and those works that have not complied with the rules for unified and coherent structure have been relegated to the subcultures and lower genres of popular culture.

Elsewhere, I have discussed some of the most important modern theorists who continue to derive a work's value from the "organic" development and structural coherence of form.[39] Worth mentioning here is that, in his 1971 book *The Critical Consciousness*, Georges Poulet contended that the task of the literary critic is to reveal the *cogito* of the texts and authors he or she is analyzing. Borrowed explicitly from Descartes, the notion refers in Poulet to the organizing principle of the fictional universe; it is this *cogito*, posited the Belgian critic, that allows both the author and the reader to have an insight into a text's overall meaning.[40] Similarly, Roman Ingarden believed that literary works manifest themselves as organisms whose principle of coherence or vital "soul" is a *ratio*, the work's *idea*. The implication here is that in the absence of this structural inner logic, the work lacks not only coherence but aesthetic significance too.[41] In his turn, Rudolf Arnheim draws a connection between *Gestaltpsychologie* and cognitive sciences, maintaining that a work's "proper form" lies in the harmony among its parts, in its dynamic unity, which allows it to be taken in as a totality. He calls this dynamic scheme that captures a work's unifying and hierarchical structure *synopsis*.[42] In the same vein, Romanian theorist and comparatist Adrian Marino argues that only a coherence-inducing makeup and an overarching meaning can ensure the cohesion, importance, and relevance of an artistic text.[43]

It is over and against the backdrop of this longstanding theoretical tradition that I propose to decouple the archetypal and the anarchetypal from the valuable and the worthless, respectively. To my mind, binary terms such as structured vs unstructured and centered vs amorphous cannot function as criteria for distinguishing between valuable and worthless and, by implication, between canonical and non-canonical. In short, and the Aristotelian canon notwithstanding, archetypal coherence is no guarantee of aesthetic success. Although the archetypal-anarchetypal distinction has been part of the Western aesthetic vulgate for more than two millennia, it is time to recognize, I think, that the dyad and the privileged structure notion embedded in it carry no axiological cachet, serving merely as descriptive and morphological categories. By continuing to impose norms of structural unity on anarchetypal texts, we risk distorting their nature and message, judging them on extraneous grounds or, better yet, dismissing them as failures because we misjudge what their "structure" is or whether there is one at all. It is true that our appreciation of open configurations and polymorphous works is the merit of modern developments. But we should extend this kind of receptiveness to entire literary history so as to recover and restore value to individual works, bodies of work, and whole genres that have been underappreciated by Aristotelian poetics and its followers. At the same time, a caveat against the other extreme is probably in order too: reclaiming any anarchetypal work as aesthetically valuable just because it meets an anarchetype's structural parameters is not acceptable either. The aesthetic success or failure of both archetypal and anarchetypal works will continue to depend on an author's skills, as well as on the assessment system in place. Nevertheless, it seems to me that we have reached the historic moment when we can finally remove from this system the centered-structure prerequisite—an operation that has been underway for decades now but is far from over. The very existence of a large corpus that functions in a "Brownian" mode, centrifugally or, as I put it, anarchetypally, calls, indeed, for value judgments, which have been ordinarily couched in the language of the success-failure antinomy, to be replaced with a more typologically neutral analysis to which descriptive terms such as archetype and anarchetype could be of real use at a time our theory commons is taking another look at "form."

Notes

1   Brian McHale, *Postmodernist Fiction* (London: Routledge, 1987), 106–16.
2   Corin Braga, *De la arhetip la anarhetip* (Iași, Romania: Polirom, 2006), and "Despre anarhetipuri," in *Concepte și metode în cercetarea imaginarului. Dezbaterile Phantasma*, ed. Corin Braga (Iași, Romania: Polirom, 2007).

3   Jacques Derrida, "Structure, Sign, and Play in the Discourse of the Human Sciences," in *The Structuralist Controversy: The Languages of Criticism and the Sciences of Man*, ed. Richard Macksey and Eugenio Donato (Baltimore: Johns Hopkins University Press, 2007), 247–73, originally published in French in *Écriture et la Différance* (Paris: Seuil, 1967), 409–29.

4   See, for example, Joseph Carroll, *Evolution and Literary Theory* (Columbia: University of Missouri Press, 1995), 396.

5   As my book *10 Studii de arhetipologie* (Cluj-Napoca, Romania: Dacia, 2007) makes it clear, I use the concept of the archetype in a cultural sense, as an artistic constant or recurring model, and not in a metaphysical sense, as in the case of Plato's Ideas, nor psychologically, as Carl Gustav Jung does.

6   Gilles Deleuze, Félix Guattari, *Rhizome* (Paris: Éditions de Minuit, 1976); Gilles Deleuze, Félix Guattari, *Mii de platouri*, trans. Bogdan Ghiu (Bucharest: Editura Art, 2013), 7–37.

7   Umberto Eco, *Opera deschisă. Formă și indeterminare în poeticile contemporane*, Preface and trans. Cornel Mihai Ionescu (Bucharest: Editura pentru Literatură Universală, 1969), 116.

8   Eco, *Opera deschisă*, 139.

9   Umberto Eco, *Șase plimbări prin pădurea narativă*, trans. Ștefania Mincu (Constanța, Romania: Pontica, 1997), 148, 150–3, 166–7.

10 Gordon E. Slethaug, *Beautiful Chaos: Chaos Theory and Metachaotics in Recent American Fiction* (Albany: State University of New York Press, 2000).

11 As I have already acknowledged elsewhere, I borrow the modifier "anarchetypal" from Bulgarian philosopher Boyan Manchev, who used the term during a conversation we had years ago.

12 Claude Lévi-Strauss, *Mitologice I: Crud și gătit*, trans. and preface Ioan Pânzaru (Bucharest: Editura Babel, 1995), 24.

13 Lévi-Strauss, *Mitologice I*, 25.

14 See Mircea Eliade, *Aspects du mythe* (Paris: Gallimard, 1995).

15 I have defined the concept of the "eschatype" in *De la arhetip la anarhetip*, 282–7.

16 See Roberte Hamayon, *La chasse à l'âme. Esquisse d'une théorie du chamanisme sibérien* (Besançon, France: Éditions la Völva, 2016), 705–27.

17 See Corin Braga, *Le paradis interdit au Moyen Âge II. La quête manquée de l'Éden occidental* (Paris: L'Harmattan, 2006).

18 See Ioan Petru Culianu, *Eros și Magie în Renaștere. 1484*, trans. Dan Petrescu, preface Mircea Eliade, afterword Sorin Antohi (Bucharest: Nemira, 1994).

19 See Mircea Eliade, *Ocultism, vrăjitorie și mode culturale. Eseuri de religie comparată*, trans. from English by Elena Bortă (Bucharest: Humanitas, 1997).

20 For the entire corpus, see Pierre Grimal ed. and trans., *Romans grecs et latins* (Paris: Gallimard, 1958).

21 Alma Rosa Mar Serrano, "Lazarillo de Tormes," Monografias.com, https://www.monografias.com/trabajos96/resumen-lazarillo-tormes/resumen-lazarillo-tormes.shtml (accessed November 23, 2018).

22 Melvin Friedman, *Stream of Consciousness: A Study in Literary Method* (New Haven, CT: Yale University Press, 1955).

23   Mikhail M. Bakhtin, *Problems of Dostoevsky's Poetics*, ed. and trans. Carol Emerson, intro. Wayne C. Booth (Minneapolis: University of Minnesota Press, 1984), 6–7.

24   Franco Moretti, *Graphs, Maps, Trees: Abstract Models for Literary History* (London: Verso, 2005), 83–5.

25   Braga, *10 studii de arhetipologie*, 132–48.

26   Edward Mendelson, "Encyclopedic Narrative: From Dante to Pynchon," *Modern Language Notes* 91, no. 6 (1976): 1267–75.

27   Franco Moretti, *Modern Epic: The World-System from Goethe to García Márquez*, trans. Quintin Hoare (London: Verso, 1996), 50.

28   Moretti, *Modern Epic*, 96.

29   Moretti, *Modern Epic*, 48.

30   "The parallels with the *Odyssey*," Ezra Pound wrote, "are mere mechanics, any blockhead can go back and trace them. Joyce had to have a shape on which to order his chaos." See F. Read, ed., *Pound / Joyce: The Letters of Ezra Pound to James Joyce, with Pound's Essays on Joyce* (London: Faber & Faber, 1967), 250.

31   Rudolf Arnheim, *New Essays on the Psychology of Art* (Berkeley: University of California Press, 1986), 79.

32   Tom LeClair, *The Art of Excess: Mastery in Contemporary American Fiction* (Urbana: University of Illinois Press, 1989).

33   Stefano Ercolino, *The Maximalist Novel: From Thomas Pynchon's* Gravity's Rainbow *to Roberto Bolaño's* 2066, trans. Albert Sbraglia (New York: Bloomsbury, 2014), 5.

34   Frederick R. Karl, *American Fictions, 1980–2000: Whose America Is It Anyway?* (Bloomington, IN: Xlibris, 2001), 155. See also Christian Moraru, "Meganovel," *American Book Review* 37, no. 2 (2016): 12–13.

35   Ercolino, *The Maximalist Novel*, 20, 28–9, 66, 71, 75. See also Nick Levey, *Maximalism in Contemporary American Fiction: The Uses of Detail* (New York: Routledge, 2017).

36   Aristotle, *The Poetics of Aristotle*, ed. with critical notes and trans. by S. H. Butcher (London: Macmillan, 1902), 7.

37   For this kind of historical overview, see Heather Dubrow, *Genre* (New York: Routledge, 2014).

38   See Patrick Sériot, *Structure and the Whole: East, West and Non-Darwinian Biology in the Origins of Structural Linguistics*, trans. from the French by Amy Jacobs-Colas (Berlin: Walter de Gruyter, 2014).

39   See Corin Braga, "Le centre structurel et ses restes," *Caietele Echinox* 33 (2017): 50–61.

40   See chapter 18 in Georges Poulet, *La conscience critique* (Paris: Librairie José Corti, 1971), 299–314.

41   Roman Ingarden, *The Cognition of the Literary Work of Art*, trans. Ruth Ann Crowley and Kenneth R. Olson (Evanston, IL: Northwestern University Press, 1973), chapter 13. a, "The combination of all the strata of the work into a whole and the apprehension of its idea," 72–89.

42   Arnheim, *New Essays on the Psychology of Art*, X–XI, 21.

43   Adrian Marino, *Introducere în critica literară* (Bucharest: Editura Tineretului, 1968), 77–9.

PART TWO

Temporalities

7

POST-SYNCHRONISM:
"Cultural Complex," or Critical Theory's Unfinished Business

Carmen Muşat

In the introduction to his 1993 book *Culture and Imperialism*, Edward Said describes culture as a "theater where various political and ideological causes engage one another."[1] As *Orientalism*'s readers would expect, the emphasis on culture as a dramatic battleground, as a scene of debates, clashes, and spectacular encounters at once agonistic and surprising, speaks to his preoccupation with rethinking the role geography and history play in the fashioning of cultural products. Keen on the give-and-take dynamic of culture and its spatiotemporal, economic and political contexts, Said recalibrates Bakhtinian theory of culture's intrinsic chronotopic nature. Although neither of the abovementioned books refers to Mikhail M. Bakhtin, Said's vision, according to which literary theories and ideologies have multiple spatial and temporal "roots,"[2] is strikingly similar to how Bakhtin approached "the intrinsic connectedness of temporal and spatial relationships that are artistically expressed in literature."[3] A key element in both theorists is the belief that "every entry into the sphere of meaning is accomplished only through the gates of the chronotope."[4] Yet, whereas Bakhtin focuses mainly on literature, Said seeks primarily to capture the impact of the geographical and historical on the cultural, as well as the modalities in which power relations in the geopolitical arena play out in literature.

I rehearse these basic notions and parallelisms as a way of laying the groundwork for my argument on what I call "cultural complex." Posed repeatedly throughout the twentieth century and very much with us today, the main question my chapter asks concerns spatial-temporal location as a determining factor in a culture's self-making and self-understanding. From Alois Riegl's 1901 theory about the way "space feeling" shapes certain styles to the ideas of ethnologists such as Leo Frobenius, philosophers such as Oswald Spengler, and historians such as Fernand Braudel to the theoretical constructs elaborated by Bakhtin, Said, and contemporary geocritics like Bertrand Westphal and Robert T. Tally Jr., the issue of cultural products' dependence on geographical situation has remained front and center. Moreover, if we examine closely dichotomies such as "center" and "periphery" and "central" and "marginal," which are frequently bound up with cognates such as "major" and "minor," "original" and "copy," "big" and "small," and "rich" and "poor," all of which used to qualify relationships among cultures, we notice how, in literary criticism and in intellectual history broadly, geography is never just physical expanse, landscape, or topography. "Culturally constructed," as we say, it also acquires, by association with historical experience, an axiological cachet—in plain English, *place* is set up as *value*. For centuries, the varying distance from the West, long deemed the center of the known world, and especially from economically, politically, and culturally powerful Western nation-states like France and England, has marked not only different historical evolutions of non-Western or non-West European countries but also their collective self-images, self-assessments, and, engrained in those, long-standing *cultural inferiority complexes*. The other and more important question to raise here is whether a post theory moment such as ours can complete its paradigm overhaul without also taking on such complexes so as to revisit the still influential view of national cultural poetics in non-European and "marginally" European zones as *synchronization, as "catching up" with Western culture's temporal regime.* As I submit, in "peripheral," "small," or "belated" cultures, the cultural complex functions not just as an inhibiting factor but also as a stimulus, as an incentive. More precisely, it can serve, and has served, as a catalyst of "culturogenic" energies geared not merely to a mechanical "updating" of local cultures by bringing them in line with, and up to the "level" of, European "centers" but also to opening up unique pathways of creativity.

It is probably worth remembering, to begin with, that marginal cultures, or cultures that have seen themselves as such, have frequently considered their position on the world map as a "curse of geography." To be peripheral with respect to Paris or London has meant, simply speaking, to be an outsider deprived of the advantages of civilization and consequently less able to join on equal footing the broader, transnational temporality of collective advancement.[5] Lucian Blaga, Emil Cioran, Vesna Goldsworthy, Dubravka Ugrešić, Peter Nádas, György Konrád, Slavenka Drakulić, and countless other East European writers have over and over again evoked frustrations and cultural psychoses triggered by belonging to spaces deemed outliers, "behind" spatially, temporally, and otherwise, and "second-rate" to the West. They have often invoked "the collective complex of a small nation"[6] and "the invisible wall between us and them,"[7] notions that are still lingering in national psyches even after the fall of the Berlin Wall and the expansion of the European Union. For this reason, taking another look at the concept of cultural inferiority complex put forth by authors such as Cioran, Ugrešić, and Drakulić and theorized by Mircea Martin in the 1980s may help fulfill one of the more urgent tasks of our theory commons at the beginning of the twenty-first century, namely, a better understanding and possibly a rebuilding of the exchange mechanisms through which cultures have related to one another and have thus made themselves inside and outside Europe for centuries. Literary geocriticism and cartography can be instrumental, I think, to this operation insofar as they provide new perspectives on the genesis and evolution of cultural complexes of inferiority and, particularly, on the bearings geography has on the configuration of planetary cultural landscapes. For talking about cultural interaction and contamination means, implicitly and explicitly, talking about place, about spatial constraints, about geographical opportunities and hurdles, and about their encoding in specific historical, economic, political, cultural, and religious temporalities. Undoubtedly, the ways a culture meets the challenges of its physical location, surroundings, and so forth are deeply rooted in what Joseph L. Henderson called in 1988 "the cultural unconscious," one marked by shared emotions, traumas, and historical experiences, as well as by a community's longstanding presence within geographical coordinates determined not only as bounded territory but also inter-territorially or relationally, as closeness or remoteness, adjacency, proximity, and interval— in space and time—from other territories and the cultural processes, prestige factories, and mimetic pressures effectively situated or imagined in them.[8]

Less frequently, the cultural inferiority complex has surfaced in "bigger" cultures also, except that, in them, its effect has been prevailingly emboldening. Consider, for instance, how Restoration-era British society related to French literature and civilization as a model to follow, given that "up to the 1680's France was the sole great power in Europe," its cultural dominance of Europe lasting until the years right after World War II.[9] Likewise, US culture experienced, until the first decades of the twentieth century, a strong European cultural complex due to America's "belated" development. The absence of tradition and the "youth" of America are recurrent themes in Ralph Waldo Emerson's essays. These bespeak, on one hand, the newcomer's frustration, and on the other, the excitement of someone who has a lot to accomplish and offer others, even though he arrived late on the scene of world culture. In fact, what the history of world literatures and history overall teach us is that, when they are attributed to cultural values, descriptors such as "big"/ "small," "central"/ "peripheral," and "old"/ "new" rarely amount to much besides mere perceptions and self-perceptions, all of them subjective if not outright biased, inevitably partial, and oftentimes ill-informed. During their historical evolution, cultures, like the societies engendering them, go through periods of flourishing and decadence, excelling in certain areas and less so in others. Furthermore, history also shows that when it comes to priorities, characteristics, and other defining elements of a culture's "identity," their *change*, and change generally, is precisely what makes that identity both unique and so hard to pin down. As Kwame Anthony Appiah reminds us, cultures "are made of continuities and changes, and the identity of a society can survive through these changes. Societies without change aren't authentic; they're just dead."[10] Appiah's "contamination" theory, then, accounts for those social, political, and economic mechanisms activated by the production, dissemination, and hybridization of cultures. The theory also suggests that, as far as influences and borrowings are concerned, they all have constantly worked both ways, not just from the West's "big" cultures outwards—hence another reason "marginal," "small," and "young" are not axiological handicaps. It is worth keeping in mind all these distinctions and nuances as I go back to my main questions, and ask: how does geography fashion power relations among cultures and the elaboration of cultural concepts and theories? How do cultural inferiority complexes inform certain worldviews? How might a more solid grip on such fixations and anxieties afford a better grasp of how cultures come about and, more specifically, of how cultural mimesis works?

The Complexes of Romanian Literature

In 1981, at a time marked by the Communist regime's terminal crisis and hardly propitious to innovative scholarship, Mircea Martin published *G. Călinescu şi "complexele" literaturii române* (G. Călinescu and the "Complexes" of Romanian Literature). Drawing on Romanian critic G. Călinescu's work, the book set out to theorize the "cultural inferiority complex" as the driving force of Romanian literature's development in modern Europe. Martin's premise is that what explains the relatively late birth of Romanian literature is the "literary" idiom this literature required for self-expressive purposes, an idiom that was slow in the making and came into its own only after 1800 as a result of groundbreaking work by the members of the "Transylvanian School" and following the increase in the number of Romanian publications, particularly periodicals. I might note that, with a few exceptions—Dimitrie Cantemir, who wrote the first Romanian novel in 1705, and Ion Budai-Deleanu, whose heroic-comic epic poem *Ţiganiada*, though written in 1812, came out only in 1875— an original literature fully emerged in today's Romania only after 1829, along with a whole generation of writers and intellectuals schooled in Paris and Vienna and later involved in the major events that marked Romanian modern history, such as the 1848 Revolution, the Union of the Romanian Principalities (1859), and the anti-Ottoman War of Independence (1877). The self-acknowledged mission of this generation was, as Romanian literary historian Paul Cornea has put it bluntly, to "actively contribute to the great work of assimilating the knowledge, techniques, and institutional forms of the West, seeking, through sensible instruction and reforms, to lift the Romanian people out of backwardness."[11] The cultural ideal to which this group aspired was Western, and the goal of its reformist work was to bridge the cultural gap between the model and its local version. Such ideas cropped up obsessively in all the programmatic articles published between 1820 and 1840 by representatives of this generation, who repeatedly and characteristically drew attention to the *underdevelopment*, *belatedness*, and *inertia* of Romanian society. For these "trail-blazers," as Cornea dubbed them, everything was yet to be done—a whole world awaited its building socially, economically, politically, and culturally. This "attempt at renewing entire Romanian society" stemmed from a powerful inferiority complex, later perpetuated and intensified under unfavorable geohistorical circumstances.[12] For Martin, it is clear that

> We are dealing with a "complex" when in the course of, or after, a negative assessment, there occur exaggerations or reductive, sweeping generalizations, compensating efforts in other areas, or downright reversals of proportions and, especially, criteria. The "complex" is evident not only in the ensuing distortions but also in its obsessive repetitiveness.[13]

Much like individuals, whole cultures are also affected by such complexes, at least within some of their segments and at certain moments in their history. Again, Emerson articulated such a complex in his 1837 lecture "The American Scholar." "We have listened too long to the courtly muses of Europe," Emerson declared and went on to complain that "the spirit of the American freeman is already suspected to be timid, imitative, tame."[14] It is worth noting that nineteenth- and twentieth-century Romanian writers such as Titu Maiorescu and Benjamin Fondane made similar claims regarding the derivative, imitative nature of Romanian culture, which they deemed, again and again, subordinated to its European models to the point that the obsessiveness of the complex, the "repetitiveness" highlighted by Martin, eventually became, in and of itself, subordinating and started doing independently, less and less in correlation with cultural realities, the kind of cultural work that was anything but emancipating. This is how, as Carl Gustav Jung suggests in *The Structure and Dynamics of the Psyche*, these inferiority complexes come to hold sway over—to "own," as it were—whole societies. As Martin, too, shows, such psychocultural anxieties have acquired a relatively high degree of autonomy, becoming before long, through language and cultural-historical practice, repetitions that foster further repetitiveness, self-fulfilling prophecies.[15] They "have accompanied Romanian literature," the critic stresses, "like a shadow," so much so that, "inevitably," this literature's "modern self-consciousness is inconceivable without them."[16] They have spurred and, at the same time, have been prompted by an odd mix of realities and feelings including, as he specifies, skepticism about and sometimes even open contempt for the very possibility of a national literature, the lack of knowledge and recognition of this literature in the international arena due to the quasi exclusively domestic circulation of Romanian, and the acute sense of Romanian literature's belatedness compared to Western literatures.

Martin employs only Romanian-literature examples, but many of his observations foreground a broader pattern of contacts and swaps between centers and peripheries, the West and the rest, and "major" cultures, which are created and propped up by widely spoken international languages and political and economic power, and "minor" cultures, which rarely boast such leverages. In the final analysis—and this bears emphasizing at this juncture in the history of comparative literature—Martin's intervention supplies all basic tools for configuring the dynamic of relations inside World Literature and for describing how cultural forms and ideologies have arisen from geohistorical, spatial and temporal experiences in which cultural complexes have held a determining role. As Martin comments, "the distance in space correlates with the distance in time, and both with lack of audience,"[17] a conclusion that can be extended to spaces and times beyond Romanian modernity. Both real and imaginary geographical and linguistic isolation, the obsession with being relegated to the periphery, with being exiled or abandoned in an everlasting *province* have been, at one time or another, mapped in American (US and Québécois), Australian, and Danish cultures—to exemplify at random—onto the axis of temporality and, in this dimension, have brought about the perception, at least, of cultural time lags or delays with respect to French, British, and other models. In turn, such disparities have translated and started being mobilized by various rhetorics essentially as axiological gaps, which "marginal," "belated," and therefore "inferior" cultures have experienced in the presumably "inherent" temporality of their praxis and have been therefore expected to "overcome." Both external and internal, these expectations have resulted in a certain handling of cultural differences (suspected of "delaying" progress) and collective self-esteem (undercut by meager or no international acknowledgment and a feeling of inferiority) that have fueled the "bipolar" cultural complex grounded in a simplistic advanced (imperial, central)-provincial (colonial, far-off) antinomy.[18] "Repetitive" and "autonomous," decoupled, that is, from cultural realities, the complex tends to "resist consciousness" (to wit, rational scrutiny) "and collect experiences that," predictably, bear out its tenets.[19] Whether the latter are true or not, the complex itself is real and does real work, which is why the entire histories of "small" literatures, European or not, can be read as national narratives of cultural inferiority.

Yet again, much like "later" or "imitative," "inferior" is a function of "remote" and is otherwise "inconvenient" locationwise. One should point out, in this vein, that, according to Romanian writers such as Cioran and, to a lesser extent, Blaga, Romanian literature has been forced to evolve in an unfavorable geopolitical context—"a Latin island in a Slavic sea," as the cliché goes—lodged as it has been at the crossroads of conflicting interests of ruthless empires such as Tsarist, Ottoman, and Austro-Hungarian. Now, it goes without saying, geopolitical "misfortunes" of this kind are also opportunities. The multicultural "thickness" of the area in terms of idioms, borders, religions, ethnicities, traditions, cultural horizons and their interactions, and so forth is quite unique in the world and has left its imprint on Romanian literature. However, being part of the Romance family of countries and languages has always trumped regional adjacency in the national imaginary, as it has made a huge difference, Martin argues, aesthetically, in terms of adopting certain standards of style, literary accomplishment, value, and form overall. Ever since the early fifteenth century, when they discovered Western civilization, Romanian intellectual and political elites have been keen on their country's "lagging behind," and their main goal has been to "import" culture, civilization, and their benchmarks from the West, not from neighbors. The *ex Occidente lux* principle has guided the formation of modern Romania, according to Martin, who also notes that this fascination with the West has always gone hand in hand with an inferiority complex. From the sixteenth to the eighteenth century, building a cultural identity in the Romanian provinces entailed, in effect, the internalization of such complexes in relation to French and Italian achievements, followed later by a fascination with German and English cultures, especially in the second half of the nineteenth century and the first half of the twentieth century.

A growing anxiety of the geographical, political, economic, and last but not least, linguistic "disadvantages" putatively "built into" Romanian culture and "Romanianness" lies behind what Martin calls "the tyranny of models," which has been often felt as a "terror of asynchronicity."[20] And how could one not feel this way, wonder Romanian critics, since, born late, in the whirlpool of European Romanticism, with few notable works written or in sufficient circulation before 1800, Romanian literature and criticism have been haunted by the specter of belatedness from the outset. In that, Romanian literature history is somewhat comparable to American literature history, or, more accurately, to the story of European presence in US literature, whose own presence also showed up belatedly on the world stage, comparatively speaking. In its case, however, the fast-shrinking distance from modernity's "center"—the West, which would include the United States before long—coupled with the geopolitical status of English,

North America's main idiom, made for a different evolution. In Romanian cultural space, the rapid succession and sometimes overlapping of literary movements and ideologies between 1820 and 1940 account for the fervor with which authors tried to make up for "wasted" time and "burn through the [developmental] stages"—as critic Eugen Lovinescu put it, translating, tellingly enough, a French phrase—so as to accelerate growth, catch up, and shake off the country's geohistorical and linguistic "curse." Take, for instance, the "gap" between the "national poet" Mihai Eminescu (1850–89) and French poet Arthur Rimbaud (1854–91), which, in Martin's opinion, is not "necessarily one of value" but has to do with the "ages of poetry." What the critic means is that, although the two writers were contemporary, Eminescu's work is Romantic, while Rimbaud, typically associated with Symbolism, is considered either a post-Romantic precursor of modernism or one of the first modern poets. "Adopting [a] Western model" like Romanticism, which, in the West itself, was no longer a model at the time of its adoption by Eminescu, explains Martin, modern "Romanian literature started off with a considerable handicap."[21] This has been the "disadvantage" Romanian authors have tried to "overcome" ever since.

Their success has grown steadily throughout the twentieth century, culminating with the writers of the "1980s Generation" and their channeling of creative energies into *original* forms across genres through dialogue with the Beat poets and other figures of international postmodernism. This is the result of what Martin calls, in echoing Lovinescu, "the *impersonal objectivization* of certain inferiority complexes felt toward Europe's more advanced literatures."[22] This "objectivization" of the complex—its conversion into its opposite in literary practice—took place in Romania after 1970 following the discovery of American and South American literatures and led to a double emancipation of Romanian literature from "tutelar" French culture and, more broadly, from the mimetic pressures of the European model. Expanding rapidly in the 1980s and, past the 1989 milestone, into the postcommunist 1990s, this process diversified a great deal in the twenty-first century in a context marked by an unprecedented opening of borders, the rediscovery of neighboring literatures, and ever more substantial, culturally empowering contacts with the world beyond.

It is this kind of conversation with the world that Lovinescu had in mind when he argued in *Istoria civilizației române moderne* (History of Modern Romanian Civilization [1924–1925]) for the indelible necessity to borrow from and develop exchanges with more "advanced" cultures. Notably, in his view, one should borrow "tactically": not at random but only those things that fit a national "specificity" already in place. The procedure is therefore *"differentiating"*—as it borrows, the successful artwork distinguishes itself both from its outside source and from internal (domestic) tradition. This appropriation logic also underwrites *synchronism* and *revision*, two concepts central to Lovinescu's critical thought and closely tied with his theory of the "mutation of aesthetic values." Since Bogdan Crețu also discusses this issue in this volume, suffice it to say here that this theory, a rationale for literary-historical change, is relational, much like most concepts one comes across in Lovinescu, Martin, and other Romanian critics who have mulled over the formation and repercussions of cultural complexes. These authors seize theoretical language and language generally as operating in systemic interface with history and geography, which supply not only the material backdrop but also the cultural poesis framework and, by the same token, a way of making sense of any critical and theoretical elaborations, including such psychocultural reflexes, representations, and self-representations.[23] The persistence of formulaic stereotypes such as "Balkans-like" or "from the Balkans"[24]—which, in Romania at least, are negatively connoted and contrasts symbolically to the more "central" ... "Central-European"— documents once again a process by which certain historical experiences that have caused, over time, not only collective suffering but also frustration and a nagging sense of inferiority and inequality have been internalized and have become ideology, unexamined yet serviceable concepts. Reiterated ad nauseam by historians, writers, critics, and theorists from different eras, they remain quite resilient. As Jung also underscores in *The Structure and Dynamics of the Psyche*, one can push back against them, but they can resurface at any time if the right opportunity presents itself. Recent history has offered plenty of examples in this sense, culturally and politically. A tragic case in point, the early 1990s Balkan Wars are what I would call, with a nod to Harold Bloom, a geohistorical stage of resentment—a murderous resentment, to be sure, that goes far beyond the theoretical version the American critic identifies in postcolonial scholarship.

Not just in the former colonies, but also in the more or less politically independent countries of Europe's "wild East," as the Balkan region has often been referred to, the relationship with Western cultures has been underpinned by inferiority complexes. Invoking William Blake's glosses on Joshua Reynolds's *Discourses*, Said highlights the major part art and culture have played in the consolidation of empires over the centuries.[25] Said's observation applies to Europe's "margins" as well. Never colonized by Western powers—or subject in a very loose sense to what has been called modern Europe's "internal" colonization—the small nations of the European Southeast have frequently positioned themselves in relation to the West as to a dominant culture, superior in terms of values and, consequently, worthy of imitation. In these countries, imperialism, while never directly and formally implemented as in colonies proper, has operated primarily in terms of culture and has frequently translated into the inferiority complexes I have been talking about.[26] These carry over into the insights, accounts, and narratives of representative writers of Southeastern Europe such as Nádas (Hungary), Cioran and Mircea Cărtărescu (Romania), Ugrešić and Drakulić (Croatia), and Goldsworthy (Serbia), to name but a few.[27] They all note, sooner or later, how the defensive reactions provoked in the public cultural unconscious by the frustrated desire for outside recognition and by otherwise real historical injustices have often been accompanied by overreactions in the opposite, nationalist direction. Interestingly, these involved the belatedness fixation, which their "priority complex" sought to turn on its head. A good example for this compensatory backlash is *protochronism*, a bizarre cultural-ideological and temporal formation typical of the late, nationalist stage of Romanian Communism and defined by certain regime-affiliated writers and historians' farfetched attempts to identify in the country's traditions precursors, priorities, and absolute firsts in the world history of art, medicine, aviation, mathematics, technology, and other fields.

Real Places, Imaginary Spaces, and Creativity

As Martin insists, "the history of Romanian literature is not the same as the history of this literature's 'complexes.'"[28] And yet the two intersect and overlap in ways that cannot be ignored. This is also true of other countries whose geohistorical situation is comparable to Romania, especially in the Balkans. Here, the double-edged fascination with the West and the obsession with participation in the Western cultural circuit have been, over the last two centuries or so, determining factors not only of the kind of general modernization that has made most if not all European nations look *like each other* institutionally and otherwise but also of a *differentiating*, creative emulation that has also helped them carve, at last, individual, recognizable profiles. True, former empires such as Austria-Hungary and France and imperial capitals such as Vienna and Paris, then London and other metropolises of the West have been inevitable frames of reference for Balkan and Romanian intellectuals. This attention has yielded, however, not only local iterations of Western humanism, the Enlightenment, Romanticism, and modernism but also "isms" that originated in this part of the world, including those instrumental to the birth of modern theory, as the Introduction to this volume points out. Thus, if "synchronization" originally boiled down to progress acceleration and "burning through stages," which Lovinescu peremptorily urged during the first decades of the last century, the years around and after World War I, when Romanian Dadaism, Russian Futurism and Formalism, Constructivism, and various high modernisms took off, were more than a moment of "synchronization" in this corner of Europe. This was, in reality, a time of cultural initiative, of influence exerted rather than just felt, when the tide seemed to have turned, and Europe was beginning to set its cultural clocks to developments in unlikely places such as Bucharest and St. Petersburg. Travels of books, ideas, and people, translations and criticism, interactions and exchanges of all sorts had by then thrown bridges over many of the abovementioned gaps.

The end of World War II put an end to this "corrective" chapter in the history of European cultural dynamic, and the installation of puppet regimes by the Soviet army all over the Eastern Bloc reopened and widened those discrepancies and disjunctions. There is reason to hope, however, that the process of cultural temporality adjustment can resume in the "New Europe" following the fall of Communism and, no less importantly, the democratization of power relations inside the EU. For three decades now, Europe's old cultural chronologies and stylistic-aesthetic time zones have been tested and reset by emerging political topologies less bounded by frontiers and constantly reshaped by historically unmatched circulation of people, goods, ideas, books, and so forth among member nation-states, between them and the bigger world, and on markets whose logic, sites, reach, and routes defy Cold War-era concepts, partitions, and hierarchies of time, space, and value. Former "centers" have not disappeared, but additional hubs, nodes, and networks of communication have appeared. Nor are "margins" what they used to be. All of them have been redistributed (inside Europe) and reconnected (to the rest of the world) by late globalization, which has altered the very condition of the cultural sphere on national and planetary scales alike, as well as the meaning and makeup of the "canon"—of what is read, distributed, and appreciated locally and, again, internationally as well. What it all comes down to is unparalleled *movement* across and interaction over or at a distance, which have been transforming the geography and distinct cultural temporalities without doing away with either. In all actuality, the opposite may be true. As Yuri Lotman remarked a while ago, "geography becomes a kind of ethics. So any movement in geographical space is significant in the religious and moral sense."[29] In this sense too, geography has been and remained relevant in terms of orienting and, by the same movement, helping "break the code" of the poetics of the cultural temporality that makes, say, Serbian literature Serbian and Bulgarian literature Bulgarian. Quoting Lotman in *La Géocritique. Réel, Fiction, Espace*, Bertrand Westphal also analyzes in his 2007 book exactly how the geography of "here," "there," and the spaces in between, on one side, and this symbolic temporality, on the other, are coarticulated. "Space and the world in which it unfolds," writes Westphal, "are the fruits of a symbolic system, of a speculative movement, which is also a glimmer of the beyond, and—let us venture the word—of the *imaginary*."[30]

Discussing how the spaces of the "real world" are taken in and reworked into representation, Goldsworthy proposes in her 1998 essay *Inventing Ruritania* such useful concepts as the *imperialism of the imagination* and *narrative colonization* to break down the workings of an imaginary geography of the Balkans in well-known British novels like Anthony Hope's *The Prisoner of Zenda* and Bram Stoker's *Dracula*. She notes that the people of the region relate to themselves and their cultures via mental pictures produced, reproduced, and distributed by literature and mass media from countries located far away from the Balkan Peninsula and Central-Eastern Europe. More often than not, real geography is thus overlaid by a thick lattice of fictions—some of them relentlessly exploited by the tourism industry—that explain why, for instance, Transylvania is nowadays "Dracula's land" not just to foreigners who have no knowledge of Romanian history and geography but, most revealingly, to Romanians as well. This goes to show what geography actually means in today's media-integrated world more than ever before: not just a real, material space but also one constructed, produced quasi performatively—*in situ* or at a distance—by means of images and narratives that, together, work to configure an identity whose religious, historical, political, and cultural ingredients may well be outsourced to British or Hollywood gothic. In a similar vein, Drakulić evokes in "People from the Three Borders," a short story from *Café Europa: Life after Communism*, the unique situation of inhabitants of the Istrian Peninsula, "a territory of ten distinctly different Slavic dialects and four dialects of Italian origin."[31] Although a "rather small and compact geographical unit," Istria has always been, culturally, and historically, politically, and, one is tempted to say, even territorially, fluid, in constant change, as "the most western part of Croatia, the most southern part of Slovenia and the most northern part of Italy." Istria "is on the edge of each of these countries, as it used to be on the edge of the Austro-Hungarian empire or Yugoslavia. The pressure to define, to categorise, to choose one particular nationality has been here before, and the same practice is part of the new political reality."[32] This reality, at once old and new, is the reality of geography as real and imaginary space in turn measuring local cultural time in conjunction with other temporalities. This reality is hardly an Istrian monopoly in Central and Southeastern Europe, as authors such as the Slovenian Boris Pahor and, just a bit farther away, the Italian Claudio Magris prove. But Italy and Istria, and on a larger scale, Western and Eastern Europe are still separated by a divide both visible and invisible in its accoutrements. The same geopolitical aggregate if not unit is threatened by the two discordant temporalities pulling apart its body—this is the disjointed, "two-gear Europe," as it is known among economists. Can critics and theorists perhaps imagine a scenario in which cultural difference, pace, and time might be pressed into the service of a more just, effective, and coordinated union?

Notes

1   Edward Said, *Culture and Imperialism* (New York: Vintage Books, 1994), xiii.
2   Said, *Culture and Imperialism*, xxi.

3   Mikhail M. Bakhtin, *The Dialogic Imagination: Four Essays*, ed. Michael Holquist, trans. Caryl Emerson and Michael Holquist (Austin: University of Texas Press, 2011), 84.
4   Bakhtin, *The Dialogic Imagination*, 258.
5   In his 1936 *Schimbarea la față a României* (Romania's Transfiguration), Emil Cioran dismissed off-hand all Romanian values and lamented the marginality and provinciality of Romanian culture. The very first chapter of the book is in fact titled "The Tragedy of Small Cultures." Giving voice to the frustration felt by his entire generation, Cioran equates "minor," "peripheral," and "anonymous," viewing a culture's destiny as predicated on what he calls "terrestrial grace," that is, its geographical situatedness. "Inferiority complexes," he states, "characterize minor life forms, whose development cannot be conceived without a model, without a prototype" ([Bucharest: Humanitas, 1990], 5).
6   The phrase belongs to Croatian writer Dubravka Ugrešić and can be found in *The Culture of Lies: Antipolitical Essays*, trans. Celia Hawkesworth (London: Phoenix House, 1998), 4. For more about the sense of inferiority felt by East Europeans traveling to the West and especially about the suspicion with which Western custom officers regard them, see Slavenka Drakulić's *Café Europa: Life after Communism*: "Any citizen from a communist country was by definition a suspect"; "precisely because we did travel, we knew that we were not welcome in Western Europe. But that inferiority complex was balanced by the fact that the citizens of other communist countries could not travel [either]" ([Bucharest: Abacus, 2008], 16, 17).
7   In *Café Europa*, Drakulić describes the humiliating experience she goes through as an East European when crossing into the West: "And I look at them for a moment, I know, they know and the police officers know that barriers do exist and that citizens from Eastern Europe are going to be second-class citizens still for a long time to come, regardless of the downfall of communism or the latest political proclamations. Between us and them there is an invisible wall, Europe is a divided continent, and only those who could not travel to see it for themselves believed that Easterners and Westerners could become equal" (21).
8   See Joseph L. Henderson, "The Cultural Unconscious," *Quadrant* 21, no. 2 (1988): 34–57. As Jung's disciple, Henderson defines the cultural unconscious as "an area of historical memory that lies between the collective unconscious and the manifest culture pattern." Thomas Singer and Samuel L. Kimbles elaborated on this definition a few years later.
9   See J. R. Jones, *Country and Court: England, 1658–1714* (Cambridge, MA: Harvard University Press, 1978), 95.
10 I am citing here from Kwame Anthony Appiah's article "The Case for Contamination," published in the *New York Times Magazine*, January 1, 2006. "Living cultures," Appiah also writes, "do not, in any case, evolve from purity into contamination; change is more a gradual transformation from one mixture to a new mixture, a process that usually takes place at some distance from rules and rulers, in the conversations that occur across cultural boundaries" (https://www.nytimes.com/2006/01/01/magazine/the-case-for-contamination.html [accessed May 31, 2019]).

11   Paul Cornea, *Oamenii începutului de drum. Studii și cercetări asupra epocii pașoptiste* (Bucharest: Editura Cartea Românească, 1974), 6.

12   Cornea, *Oamenii începutului de drum*, 27.

13   Mircea Martin, *G. Călinescu și "complexele" literaturii române* (Bucharest: Editura Albatros, 1981), 34. Leaning on Martin's discussion, Bogdan Ștefănescu develops the concept of "vacuity" to explain how Romanian intellectuals of various generations picture the "gap"—temporal and otherwise—between Romanian and Western cultures. On this problem, see his essay "Romanian Modernity and the Rhetoric of Vacuity: Toward a Comparative Postcolonialism," in *Romanian Literature as World Literature*, ed. Mircea Martin, Christian Moraru, and Andrei Terian (New York: Bloomsbury, 2018), 255–70.

14   Ralph Waldo Emerson, "The American Scholar," in *The Complete Essays and Other Writings* (New York: Random House, 1950), 66. In another lecture, "Literary Ethics," delivered before the Literary Societies of Dartmouth College on July 24, 1838, Emerson talks about the derivative nature of American culture, which he compares to an empty vessel or form without content. "But the mark of American merit in painting, in sculpture, in poetry, in fiction, in eloquence," he writes, "seems to be a certain grace without grandeur, and itself not new but derivative; a vase of fair outline, but empty—which whoso sees, may fill with what wit and character is in him, but which does not, like the charged cloud, overflow with terrible beauty, and emit lightnings on all beholders" (Ralph Waldo Emerson, *Literary Ethics* [New York: Thomas Y. Crowell & Company Publishers, 1900], 2).

15   This view is corroborated by Thomas Singer and Samuel L. Kimbles in the introduction to their 2004 edited volume, *The Cultural Complex: Contemporary Jungian Perspectives on Psyche and Society* (New York: Routledge, 2004), 1–10.

16   Martin, *G. Călinescu și "complexele" literaturii române*, 27.

17   Martin, *G. Călinescu și "complexele" literaturii române*, 47.

18   Thomas Singer and Samuel L. Kimbles develop the "bipolar complex" concept in the introduction to their 2004 edited volume, *The Cultural Complex: Contemporary Jungian Perspectives on Psyche and Society*, to distinguish between the cultural complex and notions such as cultural identity and national character. Singer and Kimbles draw on John Weir Perry's definition of this particular complex (which, in Perry, applies to the individual psyche) and apply it to groups. "Once the cultural complex is activated in an individual or a group, however, the everyday cultural identity can be," they argue "overtaken by the affect of the cultural complex, often built up over centuries of repetitive traumatic experience. At that point, the individual and/ or the group has entered the territory of what Perry called the 'affect-ego' and 'affect-object'—but at the level of the cultural complex rather than personal complex" (Thomas Singer and Samuel L. Kimbles, "Introduction," in *The Cultural Complex: Contemporary Jungian Perspectives on Psyche and Society*, ed. Thomas Singer and Samuel L. Kimbles [New York: Routledge, 2004], 6).

19   Singer and Kimbles, "Introduction," 6.

20   Martin, *G. Călinescu și "complexele" literaturii române*, 45.

21   Martin, *G. Călinescu și "complexele" literaturii române*, 15.

22 Martin, G. *Călinescu și "complexele" literaturii române*, 24.
23 I elaborate on the "rootedness" of concepts in particular spatial and temporal contexts in my book, *Frumoasa necunoscută. Literatura și paradoxurile teoriei* (Iași, Romania: Polirom, 2017).
24 Balkan stereotypes such as "Europe's powder barrel" can be traced back to the turbulent history of the region. So can German chancellor Otto von Bismarck's infamous words about the region, which is worth less, said Bismarck, than the life of one Pomeranian grenadier.
25 Here is Blake quoted by Said in *Culture and Imperialism*: "The Foundation of Empire is Art and Science. Remove them or Degrade them and the Empire is No more. Empire follows Art and not vice versa as Englishmen suppose" (13).
26 I draw here on Said's distinction between colonialism and imperialism. "As I shall be using the term, 'imperialism' means," specifies Said, "the practice, the theory, and the attitudes of a dominating metropolitan center ruling a distant territory; 'colonialism,' which is almost always a consequence of imperialism, is the implanting of settlements on distant territory" (*Culture and Imperialism*, 9).
27 Vesna Goldsworthy's 1998 book, *Inventing Ruritania: The Imperialism of the Imagination* (New Haven, CT: Yale University Press, 1998), is extremely significant in this sense, as it sets out to analyze how Western literature, especially British, creates imaginary territories starting from actual geographical spaces. Goldsworthy investigates, subtly and humorously, the negative perception of the Balkans abroad and, in particular, the effects this "empire of the imagination" has on the region's inhabitants.
28 Martin, G. *Călinescu și "complexele" literaturii române*, 37.
29 Quoted in Bertrand Westphal's *Geocriticism: Real and Fictional Spaces* (New York: Palgrave, 2011), 1.
30 Westphal, *Geocriticism*, 1.
31 Drakulić, *Café Europa*, 162.
32 Drakulić, *Café Europa*, 162.

8

POST-PRESENTISM:
The Past, the Passed, and "Now" as Critical Operator

Bogdan Crețu

Described by French historian François Hartog as that "category of the present" that "has taken hold to such an extent one can really talk of an omnipresent present," presentism has itself been more and more present in recent debates.[1] An increasingly important element in the theoretical vocabulary that, as the editors of *Theory in the "Post" Era* suggest, has progressively unified post–Cold War critical language, this concept holds a central place in the contemporary "post-lexicon" of temporality, especially in the polemical and antinomian forms of "counter-" or "anti-presentism." In what follows, I discuss how the Romanian critical culture of the last decades has intervened in the pro- and counter-presentism discourse that, for some time now, has infused our world theory commons with fresh historicist energies. To better understand the nature of this intervention, I first provide a succinct overview of the Romanian theoretical reflection, both explicit and implicit, on, and often in support of, presentist epistemology. To that effect, the opening part of this chapter surveys briefly the ways Romanian critical-theoretical thought has wrestled with the tensions between the past and the present, with the strategies of constructing and managing national identity and cultural memory and, ultimately, with how the past legitimizes the present and how, in turn, the present reinvents the past, sometimes in the name of a phantasmagoric future. In the same section, I also revisit Romanian theory's more recent forays into this problematics so that, starting from there, I can

then chart the reorientation they have brought about and that, as I maintain
in this chapter's second part, can be consolidated in the post-presentist
direction so defining for today's critical theory and practice. As I intend to
show, this direction, which I view as at least partially "historicist," is not
necessarily anti-presentist; it rejects only the reductive and assimilationist
"tyranny" of a present lacking in critical self-reflexivity, or what I define as
"classical" or "counterproductive" presentism. Otherwise, the tendency I
am tracking here is not incompatible, I would venture, with what American
neo-Victorian studies calls "strategic presentism." My post-presentism is, in
fact, an attempt to make presentism more—rather than less—historicist and
deploy it, thus historicized, pragmatically or, as the Victorianists of the V21
network put it, "strategically."

One question that bears raising right away is whether the classical
definition of presentism allows for this sort of retooling of the concept.
As is well known, Hartog claims that the contemporary period—which,
according to him, began in 1989, when the Berlin Wall came down and the
reign of totalitarianism in Eastern Europe and the USSR virtually ended—is
dominated by *presentism*. This, Hartog contends, has presumably established
itself as a Grand Narrative or master historiographic epistemology that
has transformed the relationship between past and present as well as the
building of the future. "The present, in the very moment of its occurrence,
seeks itself," the critic writes, "as already history, already past. In a sense, it
turns back on itself in order to anticipate how it will be regarded when it
is completely past, as though it wanted to 'foresee' the past, to return itself
into a past before it has fully emerged as present."[2] This *historicization of
the present* dominated the humanities for several decades, but I believe it has
run out of steam in recent years. If history and other disciplines are facing a
crisis, that is also because they have been hewing too close to the narrative
logic of Hartog's presentist regime, as well as to other explanatory narratives
that oversimplify the diversity of cultural and historical phenomena. On this
account too, we have entered a post-presentist stage.

Whether one thinks of it as a philosophical, scientific, or largely cultural
operator, presentism is usually understood by Hartog and others as a means
of projecting the perspective of the present onto the past, thereby molding
the past into the form of the present. Most definitions of the concept concur
in this respect. In a 1999 article, Theodor Sneider defined presentism as
"the doctrine that only the present is real."[3] As David Ingram and Jonathan
Tallant also argue, "presentism" is an ontological doctrine with "a view
that only present things exist."[4] In her turn, Sabine Cherenfant notes in the
opening of her introduction to the 2019 *Presentism: Reexamining Historical
Figures Through Today's Lens* that

> each year, decade, or century brings a new way of life that determines
> what society prioritizes as its moral standards. Likewise, what is upheld

as moral and immoral affects how the past is viewed from the vantage of the present. This practice is known as presentism. It refers to one's tendency to analyze the past with current-day attitudes instead of viewing history from an objective perspective.[5]

Thus, presentism has to do with how we relate to the past from our present positions, with our values, dilemmas, and identity conflicts, with our mindsets and cultural codes, and especially with our ideological interests. It is about the way in which the *now* determines the *then*, about the swap of standpoints, as the present is no longer a moment conditioned by the bygones, but, rather, the past becomes hostage to the present and echoes its needs. We are dealing with a retroactive vision of tradition, which is no longer already there, an accumulation of facts in the past but "under construction" in a present that decides what counts as tradition. *Presentism manifests itself particularly under the pressure of an ideology that has a stake in instrumentalizing the past.* In his study dedicated to "regimes of historicity,"[6] Hartog notes that there is always an ideological finality, a political *telos* in the relation between the future and the past, a symbolic goal or agenda redolent of an allegedly "scientific" outlook and bearing names such as Nation, People, Republic, Society, and Proletariat.[7] At any rate, in play here is one of these mythologizing narratives that ideologies draw from to legitimize both their presentism and "futurism," as it were, that is, the past's makeover and the refashioning of the present in the name of a "golden future."

A Critique of Presentist Reason

During the last hundred years, Romania experienced more than five decades of authoritarianism or totalitarianism, which meant, basically, a relentless political and ideological assault on social life, as well as on historiography, criticism, and not least, the arts. But even before World War II, Romanian culture had constantly fantasized about a "useful" past conveniently tweaked to cater to each age's interests. Without taking up this issue explicitly, Romanian literary criticism and especially historiography have plied presentism, sometimes aggressively and other times more discreetly. As elsewhere, national identity has been forged in Romania via literature and literary criticism, through a tug-of-war between the past and the present. This dynamic has alternated retrospective extensions of the present into the past and the latter's tendentious reconstructions, which have rendered it, more than once, an outdated version of the present. The nineteenth century had a special relation with premodern times, practicing presentism as a hegemonic cultural modus operandi that involved essentially discarding Eastern, post-Byzantine tradition and leaning on Western models. A primary tool for the formation of national culture, this presentism tapped liberally into the past to authorize the present's projects. This is why the time's presentist enterprise bears out the mainstream definition of presentism, which, according to Benjamin Morgan and others, inheres in "an unrecuperable distortion of the past."[8] In the same vein, at the beginning of the twentieth century, the nationalism that permeated a considerable part of the culture imposed a twisted—one might say presentist—relationship with the literary past, a dominion of "now" over "then" that rendered the present a cumulative stage, sum total of all previous endeavors, a climax of tradition and its only possible, "natural" version. Lasting for decades, this historical revisionism did not end with the coming to power of the Soviet-backed Communists after World War II. The new regime, too, encouraged various, oftentimes extreme forms of presentism, cooking the books of history to fit a Marxist perspective or, after the 1970s, the Socialist nationalist fantasies under Nicolae Ceauşescu, which all but *officialized* the past into an ideological fiction. Accordingly, the story of previous centuries, and *de facto* the entire pre-Communist story of the country, was rewritten as a tale of an unending class struggle or, in keeping with a nationalist mythology that promoted a bizarre exceptionalism *à la Roumaine* during the last decades of the Cold War, as a legitimizing narrative of Communist dictatorship and especially of the cult of the dictator's personality.

Now, Romanian criticism has favored at least three concepts pertaining to the intertwined temporalities of literature, literary reception, and national literature and culture. Some of these notions have sought to bring a literary work's originating moment, along with its surroundings, into the present and enlist that temporal context in the latter's ideologically and politically transformative maneuverings. The first concept of this kind is *the aesthetic*, more precisely, the ebb and flow of aesthetic value over time, a problem Romanian critic Eugen Lovinescu tackled systematically. His "mutation of aesthetic values," a theory he worked out as part of a critical platform designed to steer Romanian literature toward modernism in the first half of the twentieth century, posited that "the aesthetic is not a universal notion, everywhere the same, but rather only the expression of a shifty, individual perception" and further, that the variations in detecting and defining the aesthetic are conditioned by at least two factors: the cultural milieu and time or moment. National cultures, he also insisted, are neither sealed off nor self-sufficient. Rather, they actively influence each other and often "synchronize" to align with one another as they come about.[9] Parallel to, and in fact echoing, culture and literature's own synchronizing or catchup mechanisms is an appositely "synchronist" criticism that, if unchecked, can bring works from various literatures and eras under the same common denominator by discounting what makes them different while bestowing the same understandings on them on behalf of the present of evaluation. Such a leveling of cultural and historical differences is abusive, Lovinescu explains. For the contact between "us" now and, say, ancient and classical works never occurs directly, "through the aesthetic intuition, or sensibility," but "only through study, or intellectual means," a pursuit that is rarely innocent and uncolored by the agenda of nowness.[10]

There are similarities between the "mutation of aesthetic values" and recent theories about the "resonance" of literature and its meanings across time, aspects Wai Chee Dimock glosses on in a 1997 article.[11] It is noteworthy that both Lovinescu and Dimock employ the term "synchronism," although Lovinescu uses this notion in a positive sense and endows it with a meaning that is only partially found in Dimock. What carries most weight for the American critic is that the "synchronic model" she is critiquing "hardly acknowledges that the hermeneutical horizon of the text might extend beyond the moment of composition, that future circumstances might bring other possibilities for meaning."[12] She proposes instead the concept of a "diachronic historicism" that "allows texts to be seen as objects that do a lot of travelling: across space and especially across time. And as they travel, they run into new semantic networks, new ways of imputing meanings."[13] The aesthetic value of a poem or play originated in a culture A, Lovinescu maintained half a century before, grows or lessens depending on the overall ambiance and moment in which the text is received in culture B, while Dimock sees this change as taking place especially across vast intercontinental spaces and, to flesh out this theory, offers up the term "resonance." For Lovinescu, it is not the text itself that changes but our perception of it; for Dimock, the text is not a finite artifact but a process, and its literary nature (Lovinescu's "aesthetic value") refers to "that which resonates for readers past, present, and future."[14] In any case, noteworthy is that, beyond these distinctions, a still predominantly nationalist critical culture formulated in the 1930s solutions retrospectively compatible with post-2000 "transconceptual" or "transmethodological" theoretical proposals that, according to Eric Hayot, may supply viable alternatives to the impasse caused by "the institutionalization of the period as the fundamental mode of literary study at every level of the profession."[15]

A second concept relevant to this discussion is *retroactive interpretation* and was put into practice, most memorably, by George Călinescu. To this very day, Călinescu is the most influential critic and literary historian in Romanian culture, particularly due to his 1941 *Istoria literaturii române de la origini până în prezent* (History of Romanian Literature from Its Origins to the Present), in whose preface he bluntly states that "a literary history without a value scale is nonsense, an arbitrary social history."[16] His method of identifying "value" is *retrospective* and postulates the "influence" of the moderns on their predecessors. Analyzing Călinescu's method, Mircea Martin has called it "regressive assimilation from a distance."[17] He points out that, in Călinescu's opinion, earlier works steadily transform by accruing new meanings under the influence of new ones, and the former are remade by the latter rather than just mechanically making them possible; in a "young" literature, in which modernity was achieved through qualitative leaps, this is, Călinescu intimated, the only scenario that can fill in the gaps. What interested him as a critic, therefore, is imagining *a continuity unfolding in the opposite direction, from the present to the past*, once the more "natural" one—the chronology of tradition itself, running from the past to the present—proved historically untenable.

Călinescu's "retrospectivism" has quite a bit in common with R. G. Colingwood's theory of history. Both talk about *the imagination*, about the relation between *objectivity* and the inherent *subjectivity* of historiography, as well as about *narrative* as historiographic discourse. For Colingwood, historians—and literary historians no less—"must re-enact the past in [their] own mind[s]."[18] To him, as to Călinescu, literary history entails recreating the ideas of earlier writers in contemporary terms and systems of reference. Likewise, both draw on Benedetto Croce, who was keen on "philological history,"[19] on the past living in documents. Thus understood, history is no longer just a series of actions but rather a body of texts. Not only that, but before we accurately recreate events through archival research, we discover, decipher, and analyze texts. Thus, the focus shifts away from the event, which has passed and lies in the past, to the document *qua* text available for reading *now*—in other words, away from the past to the present. But histories of national literatures, which seize on the aesthetic as signifier of ethnic excellence, manipulate the archive to construe the past as an impetus for the present and a catalyst for a future that is envisioned as the most evolved form of national culture, a temporal container of the "essence" of collective identity. This past-present-future dynamic is precisely what Chris Lorenz foregrounds in his critique of Hartog's theory. "During the modern period," Lorenz observes,

> it had been the historian's task to clarify the past to an audience in the present in the light of the future—usually that of the Nation or of another collective identity. Modern histories were characterized by a progressive development because the past in the light of the future was the modern key category of self-understanding. The present was always conceived as a temporary station between the past and the future-in-the-making.[20]

The present's self-positioning as a controlling middle point and self-serving information dispatcher between the past and the future is, too, a symptom of the presentist mode of replacing history as a rigorous document-based discipline with the more subjective—more "imaginative" interpretationwise—domains of memory and patrimony, by the same token cultivating an attachment to those affective values whose historiographic "discovery" both shore up group identity and afford it a future. Călinescu's method is then definitely one with his nation-building times.

Finally, the third concept is a political-ideological concoction idiosyncratically named *protochronism*. Coined by Romanian critic Edgar Papu in the 1980s, the term is an explicit rejoinder to Lovinescu's concept of *synchronism* and so pits the fantasy of Romanians as trailblazers and pioneers in the history of inventions and of human civilization overall against the more modest notion of "progress" as imitation (possibly of the West) and curiosity about others, which, as the protochronists would have it, would foster a cultural style of delayed reaction (rather than action) and a self-perception (or "consciousness") of "belatedness."[21] This was the time Socialist nationalism marshaled various local myths into a faux-Hegelian narrative geared to presenting Ceaușescu as an apex of Romanian history, thought, and culture. Needless to say, there is, in principle, nothing that prevents the creative critic from revisiting the national past so as to align it with new, transnational chronologies. But in a context where propaganda and censorship controlled and made all public gestures foregone conclusions, Papu's theory was co-opted ideologically and became quickly its own caricature. An amusing attempt to put a Romanian stamp on major breakthroughs in literature, sciences, and so forth, it makes for one of the most extravagant presentisms on record.

The post–Cold War era, however, has witnessed a dramatic swing of the pendulum, with more and more critics pointing up the pitfalls of presentism. In this vein, a notable contribution is a 2011 article by Mihaela Irimia.[22] The author suggests that all historians are beholden to their various presents one way or the other. Presentism though, we are told, seems to "suspend time," the only clear coordinate of a "then," ignoring the past's vestiges, testimonies, and even reality altogether. The critic distinguishes between two forms of presentism. One is "essentialist," she details, insofar as "[it] see[s] 'human nature' as a perpetual given unmodified by spatio-temporal specificity, appealing to us as archetypally selfsame, applying to whatever culture." The other is "actualist," viz., of the "now," given that it "see[s] human nature 'there' as we see it 'here,' 'then' as we see it 'now.'"[23] Irimia also differentiates between classical historicism and the New Historicism. As she writes, "The Old Historicism … looks at the past as a box full of events. For the New Historicism, the past is a text full of words. Thus 'les mots et les choses' negotiate History, history, and histories."[24] Irimia goes on to survey a few theories about presentism without articulating, however, her own or referencing Romanian literature, a rather abstract treatment of the problem that would change with younger critics such as Adina Dinițoiu. In an essay on presentism and postmillennial Romanian fiction, Dinițoiu takes up Hartog's *regime of historicity* to show how contemporary Romanian literature "ignores, even denies the [Communist] past" or, alternatively, how writers from older generations "reclaim th[at] past, returning to it by tapping into the individual and/or collective memory." Analytical rather than theoretical, Dinițoiu's article focuses on a few recent novels and concludes that their "presentism" speaks to "a crisis of transition [from Communism to democracy and capitalism] to post-revolutionary disillusions."[25]

The Case for a New Presentism

Under presentist attack have come, in Romanian and other critical cultures, especially classical works, which have been thought to convey broader political, moral, and religious meanings. In short, the claim here is that such literature can be and de facto has been mobilized ideologically through interpretations, whether those have been intentionally presentist or not. The bulk of the theoretical corpus of anti-historicist pushback has coalesced, as is well known, around William Shakespeare's work in reaction to critical scenarios revolving around approaches and issues of gender, sexuality, race, class, ethnicity, and imperialism, some of these interventions challenging, or demanding changes in, the performance of Shakespeare's plays. For Terence Hawkes, a well-known advocate of the currently expanding presentist philosophy, owning up to one's presentist procedure is a sign of critical honesty. Not that presentist reading is something to feel apologetic about. The method is totally legit given that no matter what we read is technically in or comes from the past and is read *a posteriori*, in and from the viewpoint of our *now*. The presentist "project," Hawkes asserts,

> is scrupulously to seek out salient aspects of the present as a crucial trigger for its investigations. Reversing, to some degree, the stratagems of new historicism, it deliberately begins with the material present and allows that to set its interrogative agenda. Perhaps this simply makes overt what covertly happens anyway. In principle, it involves the fundamentally radical act of putting one's cards on the table. In practice, ... it calls for a heightened degree of critical self-awareness.[26]

It stands to reason, of course, that we cannot hold against classics and authors generally that they "failed" to consider the problems and solutions of our time. As long as they are openly assumed—as they should be, according to Hawkes—presentist protocols of analysis put the readers on guard so they know what to expect and what the critic's aims are. Therefore, in a democratic regime of reading, and in a democracy *tout court*, presentism could be a way to promote a valuable agenda. In cultures under strict political control such as Communist Romania, however, where classics were scrapped from the school curricula and libraries, and literary historiography itself was shoehorned into the official view of history, presentism was egregiously abusive. It not only fictionalized the past but also excised from it whatever could not be brought in line with the ideological script of the moment.

Literally opposed to presentism as censorship is presentism as problematization of contemporary dilemmas. Rejecting both old and New Historicism as too indebted to the "context" of the work under scrutiny, presentist criticism of the kind envisaged by Hawkes seeks to uncover the tensions and issues of the *critic's context* in earlier, particularly classical works. True, the critic may find himself or herself in a pickle when hypotheses or visions about the world he or she operates in are not borne out by the text. And then there is also the nagging question of the practical implications of misogynism in or of Homer, homophobia in or of Dante, Shakespeare's anti-Semitic characters, and Fyodor Dostoevsky's panslavism and ultranationalism. What are *we* to do with them? How might they affect our teaching and research? On the other hand, it bears acknowledging that there is nothing presentist about reading Shakespeare politically and thus treating him, for example, as an author invested in colonialism since imperialism *was* a reality of Renaissance England. But these all are distinctions one easily loses sight of amid the highly politicized controversies around presentism, a situation for which Romanian criticism after the downfall of Communism is once again a case in point. Such polemics heated up all of a sudden in the 1990s, when critics committed to anti-Communist politics began to revisit Cold War-era literature. This revisionism rubbed the wrong way both those for whom left-wing politics was not anathema *a priori* and who found post-1989 "ethical" and "political" readings of authors' comportment during the 1970s and 1980s unwarranted. Equally ham-fisted were and are considered, this time within Romanian conservative circles, genuinely or putatively presentist inquiries of gender, sexuality, and other disparagingly referenced "studies" of this sort.

Interestingly enough, the charge leveled from either direction has repeatedly alleged disregard for literature as an "aesthetic" object coupled with "undue" pressure on the latter to "yield" certain meanings and on the reader to buy them. For Evelyn Gajowski, however, the objection speaks to a wrong way to look at what is happening here. The point, she says, is not to disavow the position from which we read; to the contrary, it is our duty to recognize it and its role in how we read. "Capturing the moment we are in," Gajowski insists,

> is not an exercise in solipsism, navel-gazing, indulgence, or self-centeredness. It is, rather, a matter of ethical responsibility, of owning up to the meanings that we construct in Shakespeare's texts and culture rather than projecting the authority of those constructions—our authority—elsewhere, on the author, the author's culture, the author's monarch, the unbearable weight of four centuries of theatrical and critical tradition.[27]

Again, such "constructions" must walk a fine line between the cultural-historical realities *in* Shakespeare and those *of* the critic's "moment." One should also admit that these are quite different—on one side, Shakespeare's plays, which are not mere containers of messages from the Elizabethan age but also landmarks of European culture, around which aesthetic trends, traditions, and even group identities have flourished; on the other, the present's ideological tensions around all kinds of subjectivity categories and practices crystalized in entirely new cultural formations and discourses. One must keep in mind too that a presentist approach would benefit from attention to form and its literary effectiveness as it does from dwelling on politics, past or present, and not least from a nuanced grasp of the interface of the stylistic and the political. Thus, a Renaissance scholar would be quick to remind us that the Elizabethans had a complex understanding of gender; that Shakespeare both illuminates and flattens out such complexities throughout his work; that, most notably, these cultural operations are inseparable from his texts' formal articulation; and that, consequently, reading Shakespeare ethically and aesthetically are, similarly, one and the same thing.

Ignoring such intricacies has not gone unpunished. In a 2002 article-manifesto titled "Against Presentism," Lynn Hunt takes issue with presentism's presumption of its moral superiority. Arrogance, Hunt opines, is a big problem here, but still bigger is the gap it widens, instead of closing, between the past and the present. "Presentism," she argues,

> at its worst, encourages a kind of moral complacency and self-congratulation. Interpreting the past in terms of present concerns usually leads us to find ourselves morally superior; the Greeks had slavery, even David Hume was a racist, and European women endorsed imperial ventures. Our forebears constantly fail to measure up to our present-day standards. This is not to say that any of these findings are irrelevant or that we should endorse an entirely relativist point of view. It is to say that we must question the stance of temporal superiority that is implicit in the Western (and now probably worldwide) historical discipline. In some ways, now that we have become very sensitive about Western interpretations of the non-Western past, this temporal feeling of superiority applies more to the Western past than it does to the non-Western one.[28]

But not all hope is lost. "[It] is possible," Hunt allows, "to remind ourselves of the virtues of maintaining a fruitful tension between present concerns and respect for the past. Both are essential ingredients in good history."[29]

What the critic proposes here is not so much a concrete solution as an ideal. Is there a middle ground? I believe so. To my mind, it has to do with critics' adequate positioning in relation to the literary past, for, in my assessment, neither historicism, whatever its stripe, nor presentism in its

"classical" form has done justice enough to the "literariness" of literature—
to what makes a novel or drama what it is and thus different from other
discourse categories. To clarify what I mean, let me also say that, as far
as I am concerned, a major dilemma facing today's literary and cultural
scholarship has to do with the place a critic assigns himself or herself through
critical praxis inside the triangle of text, the text's context, and the present
of the text's interpretation. As far as I can see, there are three possibilities
here, all of them imperfect. The first is historicist and shared, incidentally,
by old and New Historicism. The second is formalist-structuralist-inspired.
And, presentist in essence, the third also affords a new type of presentism or,
if you will, a post-presentist modality of engaging with literature. If, below,
I deal with them together instead of taking them one by one, that is because
the discussion will be done with an eye to pinpointing what they fail to
accomplish but also—and this anticipates my argument—because they are,
in a sense, each other's antidote.

To get to the remedy, or to the solution missing in Hunt's presentist
critique, I would like to raise a series of questions, beginning with one about
"context." Would scholarship on classical authors, I would ask, restore them
to their genetic context? Is that their task? The effort is necessary, I argue,
but not sufficient, for their works are not born classical but become so over
time, and so they transcend said context. Hamlet does not mean to us what
he meant to those who saw him on stage for the first time; to most of us,
he probably symbolizes the fractured consciousness of *modernity*, that is,
of a cultural condition and time *after* the early seventeenth century. By the
same token, a Romanian "classic" such as Mihai Eminescu is not just his
oeuvre but also the sum total of all constructions so-called "Eminescology"
has put on it. Necessary as it is, formal analysis alone does not elucidate the
multiple, literary and ideological ramifications of the work either; criticism
cannot do its job independently from its own, *present* context, in a vacuum.
The aesthetic is not a fixed, transcendent quality; it is an effect, rather,
always variable, always negotiable, as Lovinescu already knew all too well.
A decontextualized criticism would be twice dehistoricized, from its own
time and space and from the time and space of its object as well. A-topian
and a-temporal, it would draw conclusions likely to be partial, abstract, or
idiosyncratic, of limited relevance *in the present* for, let us remember this
too, any interpretation has behind it, visibly or less so, a community, one
that, if real rather than allegorical, is formed and active primarily in this
present.

Elisabeth Fox-Genovese has astutely sensed the risks we run if we seal
the text off from its historical ambiance. Whenever they did so, she writes,
scholars "raised technique over substance, analysis over narrative, and critic
over author. Indeed, pressing the limits of credibility for all but the votaries
of fashion, they announced that technique had subsumed substance,
analysis narrative, and, most important, critic author."[30] Presentism as critic-

centered criticism lacks, then, an ethical balance between the interpreter's agenda and the work's "intent." And yet an "ethical" presentism, if you will, is not unimaginable.[31] Education and training—literary but not solely—presuppose a sense of continuity of cultural values no matter how variegated their spectrum, a tradition or traditions as well as a functioning mechanics of their transmission. But this mechanics is not or should not be purely reproductive. The present's dilemmas may play a discriminating role, "filtering" critically and problematizing whatever is being passed on over time. Directly and indirectly, they push us to ask ourselves: how do we map the past out? What kind of values does this mapping help us retrieve and bring into our time? It is not only within a critic's reach to assess the past. He or she also has the moral obligation to do so instead of "merely" describing it. This is neither because everything that has passed is part of "tradition" nor because the latter is automatically a role model for us, "now." But, once more, such asymmetries, which the presentist ethos encourages, are no license for revisions of the past whose primary goal, acknowledged or not, is to harness it to current political campaigns. The past, as I have said, is not to be cynically instrumentalized, to be "reinvented" and thus "weaponized" as useful past. Truth be told, the past is not to be reinvented but re-evented, rediscovered as hierarchy of events, facts, values, and ideas, and the critic's implicit yet salutary mission is to *present* it—in all senses—selectively.

Taken separately, each of these interpretive models leaves out something important; otherwise put, the answer to presentism's excesses and shortcomings is, I think, a combo model pooling strengths from all directions. The interpreter, to start with, cannot afford to pin himself or herself into the corner of a definitive, narrow position or exceedingly selective gaze. What presentists have understood is that the past lacks true value unless it enhances the present by adding a new, semantic, moral, or aesthetic layer to it. In turn—and this is also something they are fully aware of—the present does not acquire consistency just because it rewrites the past or presumes to "correct" it, to be its "improved" update or "evolved" stage. Generally speaking, in the arts and art criticism, "evolutionism" is a dead end. Postmodernity does not represent a more "evolved" cultural stage than the Renaissance; it is just another cultural *moment*, if this is the right word. There is a difference between the two, but it is not one of developmental "stages." Historicism remains necessary because it is sensitive to the nature of this difference, especially when we handle older material composed under the sway of an episteme distinct from ours. An early-modern genre such as philosophical and religious dialogue, for example, is based on precise symbolic codes that have meanwhile fallen out of use, so today's scholar has to know them to comprehend and appreciate what he or she is reading. Yet again, there is a flipside to this argument too: if historically remote works are to appeal to us now—if we are to really make sense of them, treat them as more than relics or museal items—then they must be rendered accessible through interpretations that links them up to our epoch. On this score, Shakespeare's evolving reception across history is once more instructive. Shakespearean plays have gained semantically with, rather than despite, the rise of modernity. Modern sensibility has enriched their meanings, has "modernized" and even "presentified" them, in the wake of or in direct response to developments defining our time inside literature and performance history, such as the theater of the absurd, new experiments in scenic production and directing, and an ever-increasing range of political controversies that seem to find their perfect echo-chamber if not anticipations in the Shakespearean corpus.[32]

A special case is the immediate past, which has not yet settled as a past in public memory and to which we, "now," are still attached psychologically. Particularly when dealing with a crisis or trauma, it is impossible to sort out what one recalls from what has actually occurred and witnessing from unbiased research, as Hartog would like. For what the French historian overlooks is that neither objectivity nor the "distance" attributed to history as a modern discipline nor, as noted earlier, "the aesthetic" itself, as specific feature of literariness, are ever qualities per se but effects of a certain positioning, whether methodological, ideological, or subjective-emotional, as the author reacts to stimuli from the present or from the emotionally charged past that lingers in the present. Thus, literature may respond to its time's dramas and, more broadly, to its contemporary *Zeitgeist*, which register thematically (as in writers such as Thomas Mann, Hans Fallada, and Kurt Vonnegut, who spoke directly to World War II in their novels), or formally, in authors such as Paul Celan, who rework literary language itself so as to showcase the impact of trauma. As Lorenz insists, this response participates in the collective effort of coming to grips with the past. "The notion of trauma," he notes,

> turns out to be the "missing link" between the state of general indebtedness in presentism and the victims of injustices: the indebtedness concerns the victims of injustices and of catastrophes, past, present, and future. No wonder that presentism also implies an inversion of the meaning of the modernist project of the Nation: the dead in the past have no longer died for the sake of the Nation, but because of the Nation.[33]

As modernist projects, "modernizing" highly "patrimonial" authors like Shakespeare and nation-building are then not entirely homologous. The difference is clearly marked in democratic societies and less so in countries like 1980s Romania, where being in the present and being present in the public eye had to be sanctioned by, and in turn endorse, a sacrificial, traumatic yet unacknowledged as such version of nationhood. Part and parcel of the vastly revisionist official agenda, this heroic version of history could be ignored by neither literary critics nor historians. I have designated this mandatory presentism as "extreme." What about the presentism I call "classic," though, namely, presentism in its questionable yet less zealous and excessive forms? Have we got rid of it? If we have not, should we? And why? Arguably, it is still around in the less successful zone of cultural studies that seems to expect literatures from past ages to resonate to contemporary conundrums. For that and other reasons, what we still need to ask is this: how should we read a literary work without cutting it off from its original milieu and from what it is *as* literature but *in such a way* that taking into account its own episteme and overall sociohistorical framework would add new and plausible meanings not only to the work itself but also to the world in which we do this reading?

The question already points to an answer by implying that a certain "de-historicizing" presentism exists and must be first cast aside before we update—retool for our own present—the presentist apparatus of literary and cultural analysis. I would maintain, in fact, that it is high time we do so. For we have reached, I propose, a post-presentist stage. At this point, the "regime of historicity" described by Hartog and others is not functional anymore. Following the crumbling of Eastern Europe's totalitarian regimes and the rise of a multifaceted, digitally enhanced world-system of communication and interaction in the early 1990s—a historical juncture, as we have seen, so important in Hartog's argument—truly major epistemological transformations have been by and large less and less touched off by isolated, national territory-bound political events and ideological hegemonies. As with other domains and forms of economic, social, and cultural life, the humanities have undergone decentralization. Most significantly for our discussion, this process has trickled down to how humanists think of their arguments, methods, interpretations, and generally of what they put out discoursewise over and against the backdrop of *extant* material of this type. In brief, they assume nowadays that their interventions only bolster an existing plurality of such critical narratives. Thus, critics are pursuing novel ways to overcome ossified temporal models such as periodization in literary history, and, as they are doing so, they are more and more adamant about the flaws of presentism as we know it. Hayot has actually recommended abandoning the presentist, "chronocentric" position altogether. "Imagine periods," he invites us, "as they might look from some moment other than the present (thereby at least attempting to mitigate chronocentrism)."[34] We should quit, we gather, narrating the history of literature from an angle that is limited and even falsifying temporally (as it injects retroactively into developments a logic otherwise absent in them) and spatially, territorially, or politically (as it coops up the dynamic of texts and contexts in the Ur-context of the nation-state). According to this narrative, Thomas Mann should have been influenced more by Heinrich von Kleist than by Dostoevsky, and mid-nineteenth-century Romanian poet Dimitire Boltinineanu should have impacted Eminescu's writing to a greater extent than Arthur Schopenhauer or Novalis.

Of course, that has been hardly the case. In Romanian and other cultures, critics took the first step in the post-presentist direction as they started querying more insistently their brief's narrowly national frame of reference around the end of the Cold War. But, apropos, again, of Eminescu, Romania's much-touted "national poet," and abovementioned "Eminescology," how can one reconcile the national (and even nationalist) drive of the nineteenth century and today's world-systemic tendencies? To deny or simply blame the constitutive nationalism of nineteenth-century literature will not do. Likewise, to read the era's texts as no more than aesthetic objects amounts to missing their cultural import. We would be better off, I believe, if, against both historicism, old or not, and old presentism, we looked, prompted as we are *by our own, globalizing present*, at the nineteenth century as the first clearly distinct transnational stage of Romanian culture as well as of other cultures in the area and beyond. This resetting of historical and geocultural perspective would befit East European nation-states as well as others that have formed following the weakening or breakup of empires inside and outside Europe. For *we can see better now, from our twenty-first-century vantage point*, that the mid-late nineteenth century marked the crucial point when Romanian culture got plugged into the larger European network of communications and associations that, powered as it was by various national energies unleashed by Romanticism and leaving behind the Enlightenment, was becoming more and more webbed and ready to write a new chapter of the modernity saga.

I have italicized the words in the previous sentence on purpose. They couch the perspectivist knack I am talking about—the kind of fresh, "contemporary-like" yet historically documentable things a reconstructed presentism is susceptible, I trust, to allow us to discern in times long gone. But the same presentism can help us ford the historical gulf between ourselves and what I have referred to as our "immediate" past and answer questions such as, how can we read the literature of the Communist years in the third decade of the third millennium? Can we do it outside the traumatic context in which were published the novels analyzed by Alex Goldiş in this book? Obviously, that corpus can no longer "capitalize" on those circumstances, nor can it benefit from the "complicitous" criticism that had supported it at the time. "We" no longer read Communism's "subversive" or "dissident" literature as "we" and others ("back then"), under Communist rule, used to read it. "We" do not read *against the interdiction* to read at all, nor do we look for political truth in fiction anymore. Or, if we do, if there is a political reality to be "deciphered" in that fiction, that is not Communist oppression, which that fiction still bears witness too, of course, but the more stringent reality surrounding *us*. To my mind, this response is both presentist and warranted.

What new possibilities might presentism open up? Conversely, what makes it possible today, in an era that seems at once epistemologically insurgent and blasé, both eager to experiment with untried methods and critical of them, rushing to revisit and even assimilate the past but reluctant or incapable of building something stable and coherent around it? Posthumanism, posthistory, post-postmodernism, post-memory, postnational—we keep switching our lenses and toolkits in our post era, and this fluidity of method and vantagepoint renders books, films, poems, old or recent, kaleidoscopic entities, composite, entropic, conceptually saturated, real and theoretical at the same time and in that bound up with a specific geolocation as well as with places and communities that have developed those theories without which the very reality of artifacts becomes hard to account for and get across. I write "places" and "communities" advisedly—the plural hints at a *decentralized* system of theory production in which there is little room for a master paradigm's inflexible temporal linearity and insensitivity to the living complexity of historical events. The current global, transnational literary theory is no longer dispensed—at least not to the extent it used to be—from a few centers out to "peripheries," and its field of circulation, disregarding older borders and barriers, natural and cultural, is ever-widening. Accordingly, its geopolitical footprint is bigger. Its social impact, however, across various communities is uneven. Because literature's own social relevance has diminished, this impact has concomitantly shrunk, in some cultures more than in others. This makes it even harder for theoretical microcommunities to gather around new, unifying Grand Narratives, presentism included. In this sense too, we live in post-presentist times. Also in this sense, such groups' chance to gel into and work together in a coherent and reciprocally beneficial community is not "narrative," or not narrative in a "Grand," epistemological way, but communicational. More to the point, it is linguistic, or lexical. It lies, that is, in a shared conceptual vocabulary. If this language is presentist, it is only in that it takes the pulse of the post ecologies of twenty-first-century theory.

It is within this new environment that the concept itself has radically morphed. Fundamentally, presentism—new presentism—is *not looked at with uniform suspicion anymore*. It is no longer taken to mean, as Dimock sums up classical presentism, "to be blithely unaware of historical specificities, to project our values onto past periods without any regard for the different norms then operative."[35] Themselves presentist, as it were, moments of ongoing crisis such as ours *unsettle* the past, make it intellectually intriguing once again, semantically provisional and fluid. Securing the future—the present's top priority in such times—hinges on getting a handle on that fluidity, which in turn depends on our ability to understand temporality in new terms. In Dimock's vision, presentism actually affords the relation with the future, and a future *tout court*, by disrupting chronology. "An orientation toward the future—an answerability to and a reparative impulse toward what is anyone's guess—might turn out," she hypothesizes, "to be the mediating ground on which presentism and historicism could meet, just as it might be the mediating ground on which different subfields of literary studies could be purposefully gathered."[36] Dimock's project of repositioning our work so that it faces intentionally, "methodologically," the future—a "turn" that, in my view, should capitalize on the critic's concepts previously mentioned in this chapter ("resonance," "elasticity of scale," and "alternating tenses")—strikes me as a decisive step in the direction of the middle ground in whose search I have been here. Historicism and the New Historicism, it can be said, set out to restore the past literally and *in toto*, "as is" ("was") by documenting it; mainstream presentism retrieves *from the past* those lessons that are relevant to, and interest, the present; post-presentism, or contemporary presentism, should, I think, *smooth out* the transition or the cognitive passage from one cultural moment to the next, put them in an "ontological" dialogue *with each other and with the future*. What Dimock, numerous theorists and theory communities, and others outside them are looking for, in the end, is an opening, a pathway to a plausible and acceptable future in whose building social sciences and literary-cultural studies are assigned a clearly defined and deserved role. Dimock singles out ecocriticism, an increasingly necessary and fast-growing field, as a response to the ecological crisis. The latter threatens not only the present but also the future, which it endangers so radically that it may cancel it altogether. This menace is such an urgency, so present, I suggest, that it makes that future both impossible as future, time to come, *and* brings that futures into the present, renders it present in the sense that that future forces us to act in certain ways because its fate is being decided now. Like other emergencies of our era, the environmental crisis calls for new ways of living, for new measures, as well as for a commitment to a new concept and practice of time. We must recognize that the past needs to be retrieved and known for its cautionary lessons, and that the present, with its sometimes shortsighted, "short-term" outlook, is hardly the sole repository of truth. A constant tension, a critical dialogue, and a constant commerce between various time zones of history are all necessary, I believe, if we are to keep the hopes for a certain future alive. A retooled, futural presentism could go a long way toward making sure the channels and bridges of such vital exchanges stay open.

Notes

1   François Hartog, *Regimes of Historicity: Presentism and Experiences of Time*, trans. Saskia Brown (New York: Columbia University Press, 2015), 8.
2   Hartog, *Regimes of Historicity*, 114.
3   Theodore Sider, "Presentism and Ontological Commitment," *Journal of Philosophy* 96 (1999): 325.

4	David Ingram and Jonathan Tallant, "Presentism," in *Stanford Encyclopedia of Philosophy*, ed. Edward N. Zalta (Spring 2018 Edition), https://plato.stanford.edu/entries.presentism (accessed May 4, 2020).

5	Sabine Cherenfant, "Introduction," in *Presentism: Reexamining Historical Figures Through Today's Lens*, ed. Sabine Cherenfant (New York: Greenhaven, 2019), 7.

6	A regime of historicity, writes Hartog, "is a tool for comparing different types of history, and also (or above all, I would now say) for highlighting modes of relation to time, and exploring forms of temporal experience here and elsewhere, today and in the past—in short, it serves to explore ways of being in time" (*Regimes of Historicity*, 9).

7	As Hartog writes in *Regimes of Historicity*, "The future illuminating the past and giving it meaning constituted a telos or vantage point called, by turns, 'the Nation,' 'the People,' 'the Republic,' 'Society,' or 'the Proletariat,' each time dressed in the garb of science. If history still dispensed a lesson, it came from the future, not the past. It resided in a future that was to be realized as a rupture with the past, or at least as a differentiation from it, unlike *historia magistra*, which was based on the idea that the future might not repeat the past exactly, but it would certainly never surpass it" (105).

8	Benjamin Morgan, "Scale, Resonance, Presence," *Victorian Studies* 59, no. 1 (Autumn 2016): 109.

9	E. Lovinescu, *Opere. II, Istoria literaturii române contemporane. Istoria literaturii române contemporane (1900–1937)*, ed. Nicolae Mecu, intro. Eugen Simion (Bucharest: FNSA, 2015), 334–5.

10	Lovinescu, *Opere. II, Istoria literaturii române contemporane*, 343.

11	Wai Chee Dimock, "A Theory of Resonance," *PMLA* 112, no. 5 (October 1997): 1060–71.

12	Dimock, "A Theory of Resonance," 1061.

13	Dimock, "A Theory of Resonance," 1061.

14	Dimock, "A Theory of Resonance," 1064.

15	Eric Hayot, "Against Periodization; or, On Institutional Time," *New Literary History* 42, no. 4 (2011): 739.

16	G. Călinescu, *Istoria literaturii române de la origini până în prezent*, 2nd rev. edn., ed. Alexandru Piru (Bucharest: Minerva, 1985), 4. The similarity Călinescu's theory shares with René Wellek's has been noted by Mircea Martin in *G. Călinescu și "complexele" literaturii române*, 2nd edn. (Pitești, Romania: Editura Paralela 45, 2002) and Andrei Terian, *G. Călinescu: A cincea esență* (Bucharest: Editura Cartea Românească, 2009), 278–80.

17	Martin, *G. Călinescu și "complexele" literaturii române*, 183.

18	R. G. Colingwood, *The Idea of History* (Oxford: Oxford University Press, 1946), 282.

19	Croce develops this theory in two studies, *Teoria e storia della storiografia* (1916) and *Storia come pensiero e come azione* (1938).

20	Chris Lorenz, "Out of Time? Some Critical Reflections on François Hartog's Presentism," in *Rethinking Historical Time: New Approaches to Presentism*, ed. Marek Tamm and Laurent Olivier (New York: Bloomsbury, 2019), 24.

21	Edgar Papu, *Din clasicii noștri. Contribuții la ideea unui protocronism românesc* (Bucharest: Editura Eminescu, 1977), 5.

22   Mihaela Irimia, "The Presence of the Present: Presentism?," *Euresis*, no. 4
     (2011): 147–54.
23   Irimia, "The Presence of the Present: Presentism?," 150.
24   Irimia, "The Presence of the Present: Presentism?," 151.
25   Adina Diniţoiu, "Prezentism şi mizerabilism în proza douămiistă românească,"
     Transilvania 2 (2015): 25–9.
26   Terence Hawkes, *Shakespeare in the Present* (London: Routledge, 2002), 22.
27   Evelyn Gajowski, "Beyond Historicism: Presentism, Subjectivity, Politics,"
     Literature Compass, nos. 7–8 (2010): 686.
28   Lynn Hunt, "Against Presentism," *Perspectives* (May 2002). https://www.
     historians.org/publications-and-directories/perspectives-on-history/may-2002/
     against-presentism (accessed June 10, 2019). I refer the reader to Hunt's article
     "The Problem with Presentism Is That It Blurs Our Understanding of the Past"
     from *Presentism: Reexamining Historical Figures Through Today's Lens,* ed.
     Sabine Cherenfant (New York: Greenhaven Publishing, 2019), 14.
29   Hunt, "Against Presentism," 16.
30   Elizabeth Fox-Genovese, "Literary Criticism and the Politics of the New
     Historicism," in *The New Historicism*, ed. H. Aram Vesser (New York:
     Routledge, 1989), 213.
31   See David A. Tomar, "Historical Narratives Offer a Skewed View of the Past
     That Presentism Can Fix," in *Presentism: Reexamining Historical Figures
     Through Today's Lens*, ed. Sabine Cherenfant (New York: Greenhaven
     Publishing, 2019), 76–81.
32   The classical reference here is Jan Kott's study, *Shakespeare, Our
     Contemporary*, first published in 1961.
33   Lorenz, "Out of Time? Some Critical Reflections on François Hartog's
     Presentism," 30.
34   Hayot, "Against Periodization; or, On Institutional Time," 747.
35   Wai Chee Dimock, "Historicism, Presentism, Futurism," *PMLA* 133, no. 2
     (March 2018): 257.
36   Dimock, "Historicism, Presentism, Futurism," 260.

9

POSTFUTURISM:
Contemporaneity, Truth, and the End of World Literature

Christian Moraru

There was no ordinary future any more, only this ecstatic tormented terrified present. The future has passed through the present like a sword.

—IRIS MURDOCH, *THE BLACK PRINCE*

The future is our resource of silence ...

—JEAN-MICHEL RABATÉ, *CRIMES OF THE FUTURE*

As one historian after another has pointed out, the modern experience of time has been shaped, in the West and elsewhere, by a progress narrative. In fact, "the idea of modernity itself is," according to Octavio Paz, "a by-product of our conception of history as unique and linear process of succession" in which one moment follows, improves on, and supplants another.[1] The arche-category subtending all these discrete intervals is the present lived as *modo*, "now." Under modernity, however, this nowness is also profoundly futural. It bursts at the seams with an array of impatient futures—it "sped toward the future," jots *post*modern scholar Ursula K. Heise on the critical ticket she has issued modernity.[2] Nor has postmodernity brought this forward-oriented sequentialism to a grinding halt. Whereas the modern, let alone modernist present set itself up as a stage of radical novelty, postmodern art has been restaging allusively, playfully, and satirically the past as present. Either way, though, "now" makes routinely allowances for a thereafter. "Presentist" in its annihilation or reanimation of history as it may be, such nowness nonetheless proves, with a term Wai Chee Dimock has employed in the debate around "presentism," "futurist." This present is a hotbed of further presents poised to supersede the obsolete now, or a medium visited by spectral pasts eager to reembody.[3] Whether one purports to start with modernism's proverbial clean slate or from a historical archive vulnerable to ironic rewriting, and whether one pictures, accordingly, the coming world as in modernist science fiction or as in postmodern cyberpunk, the present affording such projections remains largely ahead looking. "Future-heavy," it makes provisions for that which it faces and into whose territory it inches steadily, appropriating this futural domain, presenting to us, and thus presentifying, the world to be.

In what follows, I elaborate on my suspicion that we are approaching fast, if we have not reached already, the end of this futurogenous present and perhaps of an entire cultural paradigm. I do so, like other contributions to *Theory in the "Post" Era*, obliquely, in dialogue with the literature of our time, specifically with Ian McEwan's 2019 novel, *Machines Like Me*. For what this fascinating and disturbing book shines light on is precisely the opposite to what I have just described: not a present that leaves behind or rehashes the bygones to reemerge "new and improved" as future, but a future that has come—and gone—in and as our own present or immediate past. Indeed, this future, this *prospective* past, *passes* because the recent past or broader present also known as the contemporary is where the yet unborn future goes, or returns, rather, but solely to pass away by failing to make a difference and by failing *tout court*. As Reinhart Koselleck observed, moving forward and modernity as progress become conceivable when the present shakes off the burden of the "exemplary" past.[4] This past is still there but no longer inhibits, and this unleashes futurality, authorizing the cultural logic of futural poesis. McEwan's narrative is a mirror image of this futurogenous movement. In the novel, history "makes an example" of the future's failure, and this example or counterexample, rather, weighs down on the present to the point of blocking this logic. Thus, if modernity's present is pregnant with futures, the British 1980s, in which the novel is set, miscarries the future arriving in them. That is not simply because that future is born prematurely, technologically imperfect; in effect, this very imperfection, this technological flaw, renders the post- or, more exactly, trans-human superior to the human in whose time it lands, even though, as we will notice, this superiority has a dark side to it. Nevertheless, the asymmetry between this future and the historical juncture in which it materializes is so striking that the former winds up folding in the clutches of the latter. As it turns out, humanity is not ready to treat this technofutural disruption of its present as an *event* unsettling the cultural status quo and charting a new course for the world's history, including its *literary* history. An application of Alan Turing's trailblazing research in mathematics and computer science, the much-awaited invention of the decade—battery-powered machines looking, reasoning, feeling, and creating as "we" do, if not better—has all the makings of a transformative occurrence, but it comes to naught. Because they cannot fathom what triggers the robots' "suicides," people prove impervious to the epochal shift potentially ushered in by the new technology.

This sea change, this future that *will have not come to pass* and yet McEwan's storyworld must reckon with, is not so much a payoff of technological advancement but of a new, cybernetics-derived ethics that pivots on injunctions pertaining to truth as moral and social value. In that, the problem here—the problem of and with the future—is more cultural than strictly technological. If McEwan's androids are beholden to this *cybernethics*, the human dramatis personae of *Machines Like Me* and nonfictional "people like us" generally are not. "We" are like and therefore *with* other humans in the late twentieth–early twenty-first-century period—we are co-present, and our co-presence in this moment gives contemporaneity meaning—to the extent that we and the novel's cyborgs are ethically at loggerheads. Humans are inferior to machines insofar as, unlike them, we play fast and loose with truth. Instantiated for now by McEwan's nonhuman characters, another ethos, of complete honesty and sincerity, might one day be within our reach, though. That ethos would eventuate together with a Janus-faced "post" of the human, which would have to accede and assent to a "posthuman" ethics and implicitly to a "postcontemporaneity" of sorts with regard to itself, to other coeval humans, as well as to their inherently shared contemporaneity. If one is, as Martin Rueff insists, contemporary "to" or "of" and thereby always *somebody*'s contemporary, then postcontemporary humans would have to come up with new ways of being with one another, and they may just learn them from how the androids of *Machines Like Me* handle truth.[5] In this respect, then, McEwan's robots are the harbingers of a postcontemporary under whose cultural rather than narrowly temporal aegis the future seems once again possible if not necessarily in the linear, progressivist modality of modernity.[6]

On the other hand, that possibility is undercut, I argue, by machinic ethics' absolute, quasi-dystopian strictures, which in turn are sanctioned by the deaths of the androids themselves. McEwan's intimations of postcontemporaneity appear to open up new, truth-bound protocols of being with others, human and nonhuman, in the world—of being contemporary—but end up reinscribing the a-futural logic of a literally time-wasting contemporaneity that gobbles up one future after another and spews out stillborn undertakings, fruitless élans, and thwarted aspirations. Mounting as it may a valid critique of human ethics, cybernethics is, in the final analysis, a dicey proposition. If people do not come over to it, they will keep glossing, at their peril, over the present's tough truths; if they do, the risks would be no less ominous for individuals, their freedoms, and, interestingly enough, even for world literature. Jamming futurality, this ethical quandary makes the contemporary *a-* or, better yet, *post*futural, in McEwan's work and outside it as well.

Postfuturism and the Politics of Time

Along with other incidents peppering McEwan's "alternate" 1980s, what happens around and to the "inanimate" Adams and Eves built and sold to humans for companionship and other purposes—a theme whose "mannequin" version McEwan tried out previously in the short story "Dead as They Come"—is informed by the same imaginary undergirding a host of fast-diversifying, multimedia genres from the mashup zombie apocalypse to *The Simpsons*' meta-cartoonish musings on the zombie apocalypse.[7] No doubt, the modernist and postmodern arts feature plenty of social setbacks and outright disasters, but, especially in the wake of September 11, 2001, the catastrophic outlook has become disproportionately and characteristically dominant. Moreover, this is no longer solely a matter of "worldview" or *Zeitgeist* either, a thematization of end-of-times mood; the thematic fixation appears to be evolving its own, apposite formal mode too. I term this mode or story pattern "postfuturist" because, first, its narrative operations involve a chronological arc vastly different from our ordinary, sequentialist representation of the future; second, because this a-successional scheme is somewhat similar to the future perfect tense or, as the French would say, future anterior—things that might very well occur later on have already come into being during the overall realistically limned but historically amended current epoch, at a point prior to the nonfictional present *in which* McEwan's book was released; and third, because this future perfect or anterior is "behind" us, its readers, not only chronologically but, as I detail below, also politically: we are "post" both this past future and whatever promise it *will have made* to android "owners" in the story time inside the book's covers.

What the prefix "post" indexes, then, is a temporal loop and a dead end. This impasse is the black hole of a nowness that engulfs and neuters returning futures rather than just signaling their "twilight" or "discredit," as Paz allows.[8] We are talking about a full-blown temporal catastrophe or, with another nod to François Hartog, a *hyper*presentism in which what has been "suspended" is not only "the production of historical time" but also an important dimension of historicity itself, namely, its futural vector.[9] In *Machines Like Me* and countless other works across the contemporary arts, postfuturism instantiates a calamity of time itself, a crisis that breaks out as futureless, closed-out time. For what has already arrived yet failed to pan out does not get another bite at the ontological apple—what *will have taken place* and for all fictional intents and purposes *did take place* in McEwan's fictionalized 1980s will not, by the same token, turn up again later. A *political future perfect*, postfuturism's peculiar, "knotted" temporality—time that has come before its time—is thus also mapped onto politics and takes on the form of a botched collective project or, as Fredric Jameson would have it, ruined utopia. Twice twisted time, postfuturism is anachrony that fails to deliver, a contorted future whose corpse or aborted fetus remains stuck in a past that, historically, is both ours and not quite. In that, postfuturism is akin to "retrofuturism," a temporal formation Amy J. Elias views as

> the genre that exemplifies Fredric Jameson's claim that, traditionally, science fiction attempted to predict the future, but postmodern SF can now only dramatize our *inability* to imagine utopia. Retrofuturism looks to visions of past utopian futures, and its lessons are the Ecclesiastean preachments of vanity and failure. In both its commercialized and critical forms, it makes past historical optimism visible in the most cinematic of ways, but then, by showing the misguided nature of that optimism, it renders all forms of futurism or utopianism naïve or doomed to failure. Retrofuturism may be the most complicated and effective of counter-Enlightenment histories, the past allowed by today's techno-duration, for futurism is not merely rehearsed in fragmented form for market consumption but is resurrected in its (often anti-capitalist) utopian instantiations as a failed hope.[10]

Now, postfuturism need be neither utopia nor science fiction, and *Machines Like Me* largely proves it even though the novel's recipe contains "futurist"—read "SF"—ingredients occasionally instrumental to a vision that is more dystopian than utopian. Incidentally, what critics like Jameson view as an "inability to imagine utopia" oftentimes is *de facto* a mature exercise of the *ability* to be critical of the dystopia said utopia was from the get-go or eventually became, and an element of this critique is, as we will see toward the end of my presentation, definitely in play in McEwan.[11] But the bottom line is what I have determined as the political future perfect, which is at issue in *Machines Like Me*, as well as in William Gibson and Bruce Sterling's 1990 steampunk masterpiece *The Difference Engine* and in Thomas Pynchon's 2006 meganovel *Against the Day*, Elias's better-known retrofuturistic examples.

The Difference Engine and *Against the Day*, however, push the envelope genre- and historywise more saliently than *Machines Like Me*. Not only does science fiction take center stage in them, but the historical past worked over by the writers' retrofuturistic imagination also reaches far beyond the contemporary era in which, as I have stressed, McEwan's

1980s participate, carried as the decade is into our present by all kinds of technological and political concerns, allusions, and parallelisms. In Gibson and Sterling, diegetic time—the "now" of the story—stretches all the way to the tail end of the Industrial Revolution. In their book, late twentieth-century informatics had all but taken over mid-nineteenth-century Britain. Across the empire and the world, computers powered by steam instead of electricity and other similar substitutions and anachronisms weave together the two centuries, chronicling a Victorian period in which people and places such as Lord Byron, the Duke of Wellington, Karl Marx, Texas, and Japan differ considerably from those one might come across under the same names in textbooks, an alter-historical ploy McEwan himself uses to mess with biographies such as Turing's and John Fitzgerald Kennedy's and events like the Falkland War. In Pynchon, a similar technological permutation pops up, with World War I-era hot-air balloons performing navigational feats that still are today technologically unfeasible if not utterly implausible outside the realm of fiction.

Retrofuturist works do not completely nip the future in the bud of the present, loosely or narrowly conceived as this present may be. In this regard, they may be "retro," but they are not irreversibly "post"; they are, for sure, postmodern, but, pace Jameson, their present is not totally "pure," "without a past or a future."[12] In the same less doom-and-gloom vein, a degree of postmodern jocularity characterizes both novels, accounting for the paradox of outmoded technologies driving change and marking the onset of a future comparable to the authors' moment in history. In McEwan, or, for that matter, in some of Michel Houellebecq's works—where the contemporary bleeds into the near future, such as in the 2015 *Submission*, not to mention the French author's earlier, more SF novels—this present cannibalizes on future presents; what we are dealing with is a futurophagous present. Think, if you will, of this future-oriented chronophagy as a graveyard of hope, a *time spoiler*. For whatever change would take hold down the road, it would present and by the same movement abrogate itself, in that present posterior to our *hic et nunc*, as déjà vu, as having already floundered in a time and as an option impossible to bring back thereafter from the past, from what has passed, and from the political *passé*.[13] If McEwan looks ahead—and he does so reluctantly, much like Charlie Friend, the self-declared "optimistic" first-person narrator of *Machines Like Me*—what he actually looks into is the mirror of the past, of a future that had arrived but somehow fell short and will never be reactualized (2).[14]

This resembles Gilles Lipovetsky's hypermodern, ever-accelerating time, but we should remember that hypermodern time is hyperproductive as well, time as factory of the new, time clocking in overtime and cranking out not satisfying gizmos, including transhuman prostheses such as McEwan's mysteriously distressed machines, but unhappy customers instead, dissatisfied humans for whom "progressivist systems [have]

los[t their] credibility."[15] If *Machines Like Me* confronts its readers with
the déjà vu, its characters and principally its main narrator are no less
blasé, treating technological and other kinds of novelty as old chestnuts.
"Artificial humans," around which—or whom, rather—the plot revolves,
"were," Charlie lets us know, "a cliché long before they arrived, so when
they did, they seemed to some a disappointment. The imagination, fleeter
than history, than technological advance, had already rehearsed this
future in books, then in films and TV dramas, as if human actors, walking
with a certain glazed look, phony head movements, some stiffness in the
lower back, could prepare us for life with our cousins from the future"
(1–2). Significantly, this future is a future perfect not only for readers
but for Charlie too, who, separated from us by thirty-odd years as he is,
nonetheless enjoys hindsight's evaluative benefits. And so, retrospectively,
for Charlie, this future, when it *became* present, did not serve as a driver
of progress anymore, breaking the basic rule of modernity and marking a
major departure from the 1980s fantasies such as the *Back to the Future*
franchise. "By the early seventies," Charlie recalls,

> digital communication had discarded its air of convenience and became
> a daily chore. Likewise the 250 mph trains—crowded and dirty. Speech-
> recognition software, a fifties miracle, had long turned to drudge, with
> entire populations sacrificing hours each day to lonely soliloquising.
> Brain-machine interfacing, wild fruit of sixties optimism, could barely
> arouse the interest of a child. What people queued the entire weekend for
> became, six months later, as interesting as the socks on their feet. What
> happened to the cognition-enhancement helmets, the speaking fridges
> with a sense of smell? Gone the way of the mouse pad, the Filofax, the
> electric carving knife, the fondue set. The future kept arriving. Our bright
> new toys began to rust before we could get them home, and life went on
> much as before.
>
> (5–6)

Granted, McEwan is pulling your leg here in more ways than one—"speech-
recognition software" is one thing; "cognition-enhancement" headgear,
quite another, not to mention the lame fondue set. What matters, though,
is that the future—the future as sheer "gadgetry"—has come and become
a hollowed-out commodity cycle and a drag, in all senses, "slipstream"
carrying you forward with it not into something truly new and exciting
but into an ontologically oxymoronic *serial* newness, whether you like it or
not. This "techno-duration," to stick with Elias's terminology, is a letdown
because it is recursive. As such, it induces the symptomatology of a temporal
malaise, a drudgery of technocultural repetitiveness ("the future kept
arriving") in which innovation does the unlikely bidding of obsolescence,
and modernization is a nuisance.[16]

Not only does juggernaut modernity leave people like Charlie nonplused, but it also paralyzes them politically because, manufactured at breakneck pace under its aegis, more "good" and more "bad" void each other out faster and faster, over and over again. The hyperproduction cycles eventually fall flat too, not with the bang of genuine novelty but with an anticlimactic, overtly intertextual whisper reminiscent if not of T. S. Eliot, then of Charles Dickens's *A Tale of Two Cities* and its historical mixed bag of seasonal hope and despair—especially of despair, disgust, and depression, as we will see before long. In Charlie's account, Thatcherite Britain was

> the golden age of the life sciences, of robotics—of course—and of cosmology, climatology, mathematics and space exploration. There was a renaissance in British film and television, in poetry, athletics, gastronomy, numismatics, stand-up comedy, ballroom dancing and wine-making. It was the golden age of organized crime, domestic slavery, forgery and prostitution. Various forms of crises blossomed like tropical flowers: in childhood poverty, in children's teeth, in obesity, in house and hospital building, in police numbers, in teacher recruitment, in the sexual abuse of children. The best British universities were among the most prestigious in the world. A group of neuroscientists at Queen's Square, London, claimed to understand the neural correlates of consciousness. In the Olympic Games, a record number of gold medals. Natural woodland, heaths and wetlands were vanishing. Score of species of birds, insects and mammals were close to extinction. Our seas teemed with plastic bags and bottles but the rivers and beaches were cleaner …. If there ever was a spirit of the times, the railways caught it best. The prime minister was fanatical about public transport. From London Euston to Glasgow Central, the trains tore along at half the speed of a passenger jet. And yet: the carriages were packed, the seats too close together, the windows opaque with grime, the stained upholstery smelled foul. And yet: the non-stop journey took seventy-five minutes.
>
> Global temperatures rose. As the air in the cities became cleaner, the temperatures rose faster. Everything was rising—hopes and despair, misery, boredom and opportunity. It was a time of plenty.

(122–3)

Deceptively bountiful, these are the times of "and yet." If in the previously reproduced passage progress is *a priori* compromised as one's brand-new talking fridge gets rusty before one brings it home, here progress is always qualified and, in the end, self-defeating. One step forward is either followed by a step back or entails a downside. This picture of advancement is "antiphrastic," for the mechanics of progress has something *regressive* to it, involving dangers and side effects whose scope—we can tell now—Ulrich Beck's "risk society" and Anthony Giddens's "runaway modernity" only began to ascertain. Surveyed in the past tense, the already less-than-flawless "golden age" is temporally and otherwise behind the time of narration and thus suggestive of a future anterior from whose "plentiful" state Charlie and his contemporaries had fallen and compared to which the present of the character's nostalgic overview marks a decline. Registering the downturn, Charlie's retrospective rollcall of setbacks and headways reads like a tragicomic version of the Benjaminian ninth "thes[i]s on the philosophy of history," where the angel of history contemplates the "wreckage upon wreckage" the "storm ... we call progress" piles up at his feet.[17] Once more, the great innovations have come and passed, and, after the hi-tech avant-gardes have had their Pyrrhic victories, one is back to the same old same old, if not to worse—occasionally, we do get in McEwan a whiff of the "declinism" with which critics have charged French writers such as Houellebecq.

History, Critique, Lying

Highly innovative as writers, both Houellebecq and McEwan seem to position themselves, through their critique of the present as futural crime scene, in the *arrière-garde* Roland Barthes refers to in a famous *Tel quel* interview and scholars from William Marx to Antoine Compagnon have discussed so insightfully. Entertaining for a moment the notion that "antimodernism" might be a more accurate descriptor for what goes on in McEwan, let me point out that neither Charlie nor his author casts his lot with the conservative aesthetes, political reactionaries, and the other stick-in-the-muds Compagnon subpoenas in *Les antimodernes*.[18] At the beginning of his relationship with Adam, Charlie still hears "the steadfast engine of science" chugging along apace. "B[inding] in marriage ... electronics and anthropology," "late modernity" reassures him that "there was a history, an account, a time deposit, and [he] had a right to draw on it" (14). In other words, Charlie thinks, for a while at least, that he can take the present seriously—that he can take it to the bank of cultural time and can borrow for or invest in the future, with the history of modernity as collateral.

Treating history as real as an account balance, this historicism "offered old-fashioned narrative accounts of the past" (35). This is why it has just come under attack by new-fangled "theory" (the quotation marks are Charlie's), as it did in the actual 1980s in the UK and other academies. As is well known, the main thrust of this theory is critical. Here, theory swings into action as "critique." Suspicious of the "reality" behind symbolic and capital assets alike, critique lays bare, on one side, the discursive "constructedness" of historiographic representation and, on the other, the shaping gambit of ideological forces. Because Miranda, Charlie's girlfriend and history student, has a hard time adjusting to critical theory's "new vocabulary [and] way of thinking" (35), Charlie "trie[s] to look and sound sympathetic. It was," he informs us, "no longer proper to assume that anything at all had ever happened in the past. There were only historical documents to consider, and changing scholarly approaches to them, and our own shifting relationship to those approaches, all of which were determined by ideological context, by relations to power and wealth, to race, class, gender and sexual orientation." "None of this," the hero further confesses,

> seemed so unreasonable to me, or all that interesting. I didn't say so. I wanted to encourage Miranda in everything she did or thought. Love is generous. Besides, it suited me to think that whatever had once happened was no more than its evidence. In the new dispensation, the past weighted less. I was in the process of remaking myself and eager to forget my own recent history. My foolish choices were behind me. I saw a future with Miranda. I was approaching the shores of my middle age, and I was taking stock. I lived daily with the accumulated historical evidence my past had bequeathed, evidence I intended to obliterate: my loneliness, my relative poverty, poor living quarters and diminished prospects. Where I stood in relation to the means of production and the rest was a blank to me. Nowhere, I preferred to think.
>
> (35–6)

"The means of production" and the rest of the motley verbiage smacking of late Marxism, New Historicism, metahistory, and identity and cultural studies blend here, roughly put, into the postmodern concept of history as Grand Narrative or even bunk—story that would look a whole lot different if "race, class, gender and sexual orientation" were factored in. But Charlie's leaning on the lingo is of course itself ironic, self-"debunking," going to show that, as far as he is concerned, postmodern critique of history is neither here nor there, and literally so ("Nowhere, [he] prefer[s] to think."). At most a fellow traveler in Elias's slipstream, Charlie is hardly a true believer. He is not a genuine "postmodern" (nor is McEwan); he is (unlike his author), just cynical, a disenchanted spirit. At any rate, to him, postmodern antihistoricism is not a belief, to say nothing of a "stance." If anything, he finds the idea *convenient*, given that his take on time, especially in terms of the latter's futural "dispensation," is, at the point in which he symbolically "invests" his inherited fortune in Adam, not irrevocably incompatible with the moderns' clean-slate approach: the past may have existed, but either as "reality" or just textual "evidence" thereof, that past can be "obliterated" so as to allow for the very temporality of self-remaking—for a redeeming future. At least, this is the plan.

Obliterating the evidence, tampering with the events so that another, more "suitable" history might ensue despite its tenuous relationship to truth, is the narrative lynchpin of *Machines Like Me* and other McEwan books. Charlie, Miranda, Adam himself, humans and humanoid machines alike build their lives, cobble together narratives and destinies for themselves, others, and the whole world around them, and more broadly *deal in time* and thereby project certain futures by dealing, one way or the other, with spurious temporalities, past or present. In plain English, they lie and spread lies, or, as in Adam's case, resist them, declining to trade in untruths or half-truths. There is a time for lying, and there is, inside and outside McEwan's novel, another for speaking the truth, an unethical and an ethical time. Highly consequential for the world of the story as well as for the world in which McEwan tells this story, these temporalities fall, surprisingly or not, within the purview of the human and the machinic, respectively: we, human beings, lie; the Adams and the Eves do not.

Should we, humans, ever own up to the Kantian imperative of unconditional truthfulness—an ethical benchmark to which the 1980s androids have somehow managed to rise up—this would result in a humanity ethically distinct from who or what we, people, are now and by the same token also in a temporality considerably different from our moment, namely, from what we label "contemporary." It is in this sense that that time to come is, for lack of a better word, posthuman; it is in this sense too that the temporality in question would be, with another bandied about but still reasonably serviceable term, *postcontemporary*, for it would be unlike the present, unlike the "contemporary age" in which the lives of McEwan's characters and audience unfold and in which, despite Charlie's hopes, and perhaps despite ours as well, one future after another irrupts only to horrify, torment, and ultimately disabuse us of any notion of future. In contrast to "our" contemporary, what would make that future contemporary "post" ours is, first, that in it, a more heartening, peaceful, socially just, and environmentally sustainable future might rebecome possible. In and *qua* that contemporaneity, time itself would get another lease on life, as it were. That "post" would thus have a temporal dimension once more, reassuring us that, contrary to a widespread suspicion among Charlie's and McEwan's contemporaries alike, we *would not have run out* of time itself. Second, that temporal difference—that "other time" in which, to anticipate a little, we would face our own otherness as humans—would not have stemmed so much from technological progress that has yet to take place as it would have from a change in culture, from a non-technological rewiring of the human in us, an operation for which McEwan's cybernetic scenario provides a metaphorical blueprint.

That *other time* would therefore be cultural. This means that it would not necessarily lie ahead of us. It could be now as well, but a different kind of now. If, as Giorgio Agamben would have it, the "contemporary" is anachronistic with respect to the mainstream present, then the postcontemporary could under the right circumstances well up, as an "untimely" cultural mode, in the very heart of the contemporary.[19] Up to a certain point, McEwan's book kindles the hope that *we* ourselves could be or become our postcontemporaries, and that we would be better off for it. For the other time I am talking about is, if not the present as a whole, then one of the temporal strains whose collective "brouhaha," as Lionel Ruffel might say, makes up our chronically complex, disorienting, and culturally raucous contemporary.[20] Potentially, that temporal alternative to how we are now and to what we do to ourselves and the world in the hegemonic, destructive, and self-destructive temporality of the present moment is part and parcel of confusing and dissonant contemporaneity. Despite its shortcomings, political and otherwise—and its overall pessimism notwithstanding—McEwan's book cuts with characteristic acumen through the noise of the now and identifies a key problem of the human. The problem, the "trouble with the human," has to do, *Machines Like Me* hints, with a *human culture*—not a tautology, rest assured—structurally premised on lying, on deceiving itself and others, and on turning a blind eye to the hard realities of the anthropocene. What makes us more or less human, one gathers, is our ability to lie. But this capacity is also a propensity, as the writer has shown most memorably in *Atonement* (2002) and throughout his career, all the way to *Solar* (2010), *Sweet Tooth* (2012), and the narrating fetus of the mock-Hamletian *Nutshell* (2016). Accordingly, humanness may well be, in McEwan's fiction and beyond, a function or an "effect" of our deeply engrained deceitfulness; we are mendacious by nature—by human nature, to be more precise.

As I have contended elsewhere, cultures can be defined as cultures of lying. Setting aside the Nietzschean angle on the issue, I have proposed that culture in general is one big cover-up in that a culture's individualizing manifestations and institutions work to hide its "other" or the "others" in it, that which and those who make it possible in the first place, as thinkers such as Emmanuel Levinas would insist. This apparent paradox is relevant to *Machines Like Me* too, but more relevant still, especially in this context, is another one—the paradox or perversity, rather, of *human rationality*. The latter phrase is not tautological either, for rationality is not a monopoly of the human; arguably, there are rationality regimes beyond the anthroposphere and the anthropomorphic, with some of them reaching beyond the animal and even the biological. But a major point McEwan sets out to drive home is that human rationality is unique in that it can trade in falsehoods deliberately, cynically, and destructively, perhaps in the "post-truth" era of Donald J. Trump more than ever before. Barring possible exceptions such as tropical fish "lying" about their "real" appearances or carnivorous orchids making "false promises" to insects flying by, we largely *are*, by comparison to the nonhuman world, inasmuch as we are devious, prone to lying—*Sein und Lügen* instead of *Sein und Zeit*, or something like that. Outside the human, however, lying does not afford an ontology. In a rock, for instance, being is not bound up with cheating, lying, or deceiving. This is definitely true, thinks McEwan, of the presumably inanimate nonhuman, including those that (and increasingly *who*) are getting closer and closer to embodying *our* reasoning models and even bodies: computers, cyborgs, robots, "machines" (more and more) "like us." Of crucial significance is that even the most advanced and anthropomorphic (humanlike) machines cannot lie either to themselves or to their human masters, and this is basically the fulcrum of the novel's cybernetic parable. Instead, we can, and we do, and the consequences for McEwan's narrative as well as for the planetary narrative—for world history—are, as Charlie reports, dire.

White Lies, Polynomial Time, and the Ethics of the Haiku

Within and without the ever-spreading culture of fakeness, conspiracy theories, doctored data, and utter lies about everything from immigration to climate change, we tell not only blatant untruths, which sometimes are easier to disprove and deal with socially, but also "white lies"—psychologically and culturally convenient pseudo-truths, fibs, and so aptly called trumped-up stories that we fall back on to perpetuate personal or public situations, habits, and even "cultural customs." Some of these lies are "innocent," "well-intended." The heart of those resorting to them, we presume, is in the right place; those people lie to us because they do not want to "hurt our feelings." Along these lines, even a sentence such as "Bill told his wife, Hillary, that he had not had sex with Monica" may qualify as a white lie. But machines like Adam cannot and would not say what Bill said, and this is the crux of the matter in *Machines Like Me*. Let me clarify.

In a revelatory April 14, 2019, interview promoting the novel and titled "Ian McEwan: 'Who's going to write the algorithm for the little white lie?'" the author acknowledges that, if the broader problem here is "what it means to be fully human," the "drama of his novel, a somewhat predictable love triangle in which one of the trio has an on-off switch, hinges on the question of whether we can teach machines to lie."[21] Adam falls in love with Miranda, and they have sex early on in the story, and yet Adam, whose "brain" interfaces by design with all databases and knowledge cybernetworks imaginable and already up and running during the Thatcher years, has found out, and cannot hide from Charlie, that Miranda is a woman with a dark past that she *is* hiding from Charlie, a past built around a lie (itself a tad off-white, so to speak). As we infer both from the novel and from the interview, however, the issue is far more serious because such "white lie[s]" are pressed into service not just to "spar[e] the blushes of a friend."[22] They are also meant to spare the blushes of a nation. Taking his cue from Adam,

McEwan makes a point to dwell on them in his conversation with the journalist from *The Guardian*—after all, he is the UK's "national novelist." These are the lies dished out by the misleadingly self-styled "European Research Group," who has been busy in the post–Cold War era feeding falsehoods to the British people so as to chip away at the public support for the country's EU membership. "Brexit," the national novelist confesses, "does seem to me a national tragedy," but absolutely instrumental to this kind of tragedy—one that has meanwhile replayed itself all over the West and beyond—has been what McEwan identifies as the "great lie of the Brexiters" about immigration, about who controlled it, and so forth. Such lies have been spread with allegedly patriotic intentions. Nevertheless, the writer asks openly if there are any honorable motivations behind what the Brexiters are telling and, of late, doing to their country—if there is anything they "love" about the UK.

His answer is dispiriting, to say the least. True, we do not get it in the interview—not in so many words—but in the novel. And we do not get it from the human narrator either, but from Adam, who is an observant student of the human psyche as much as McEwan is, according to his interviewer, not only the national novelist but also the "national psychologist."[23] The author "has a sure feel for the deep roots of [British] neuroses," and so does his character. But, most significantly, Adam and his kin also supply a fictional outlet for those neuroses.[24] Knowing as much as they do and, at the same time, lacking the software or "algorithm" enabling them to misrepresent knowingly what they have learned about their owners, humans in general, and what humans do to themselves and their planet, McEwan's Adams and Eves eventually come to embody Britain's and, by extension, the world's neurotic subject. This neurosis is beyond the pathological; it is tragic, for cyberneurosis is the corollary of self-consciousness. To put it differently, the machines are fully aware of what is happening in the human world and the world generally, as they comprehend what is going on with themselves too, namely, that they can deceive neither themselves nor their masters, and therefore they cannot lie about what they know. But they also realize that, cognizant as they are of all this, their knowledge makes no difference whatsoever since, while they are ethical by cybernetic default, their masters are deceptive and self-deceptive by nature, more precisely, by virtue of the pseudo-self-preservation instinct and other deeply engrained egotistic impulses that play tricks on human reason.

These unreasonable drives work like bugs in *our* ethical software. They are to blame for our innate ability not so much to see the big picture—because many of us do see it—but to take ownership of its content, break out of the box of the present of self-gratification and "short-termism," and recognize that, unless we do so, a future may not be in the cards for our species as well as for others. What such ethical glitches of consciousness do as we, humans, try to think things through is stretch indefinitely the time our mind takes not only to *figure out* scientifically sound, equitable, and sustainable responses to the crisis we are currently facing along with the rest of the planetary system, but also to *live by them*—to turn that know-how into a "live-how" by translating cognition into recognition and ultimately into conduct. Such ethical hiccups force human rationality to operate in the computational equivalent of "inefficient time," by the same movement preventing us from *running the algorithm of the contemporary.* This handicap is sometimes intellectual too, for instance when we fail to draw the right conclusions about poverty, deforestation, the shrinking of the polar ice caps, and the like. But, more often than not, it is ethical, in that we may come to those conclusions and still lack the moral strength to acknowledge and act on them. Thus understood, the inefficiency of time flattens temporality into its uniformly durative dimension, into wasteful and misguided "techno-duration" that forecloses kairotic time—the eventful, exigent, and appropriate time of *momentous* decision.

What my cybernetic analogy designates as inefficient time is also, then, unethical time, inhering as it does in calculated lies and yielding miscalculations in terms of cultural reflex, consumption routines, public policy, and so on. Unethical time is the quintessential temporality of the contemporary. The co-temporality in which, physically speaking, human earthlings inevitably are more and more with each other, at close quarters in all sorts of spatial and cultural ways, is also that in which they are not able to assume the relational responsibility following from this co-presence and thus be honest with themselves and one another. By contrast, McEwan's androids are already the postcontemporaries in our midst. Less "advanced" than "us" as far as their neurological circuitries go, the machines cannot lie. On this ground, *and on this ground alone*—for, as we will note momentarily, this is not the final twist of McEwan's narrative screw—if our neurological "wiring" is cybernetic, theirs is *cybernethical* and intentionally, "humanly" so. For they have ascended, it would appear, to a *humanity* to which we would have access once we would have embarked on a *post*human transformation, once we would have become "machines like *them*"—once we would have repositioned ourselves at once temporally and ethically.

This mutation would come on the heels of advanced robotics and informatics and would be indicative of a posthuman or, better yet, transhuman "upgrade" of the human possibly heralding the onset of Ray Kurzweil's "epoch of the Singularity," when we would be "transcend[ing] our biological roots" so as to "extend [our] physical and mental reach beyond current limitations."[25] In any case, the evolution implied if not actually envisaged here, which would place the Adams and the Eves at its pinnacle, would have to be more than prosthetic, with machines as "enhancements" of the human. Growth, if not a radical "sublation," of the human itself would also have to survene because the deepest and most significant vector of this entire transformation would be ethical. As to futuristic "machine-becoming," the artificialization and technological retrofitting and upgrading of human body and mind have been under way for some time now, and it is both funny and apposite to my argument that Miranda's father "take[s Charlie] for a robot" (270).

Mechanical as his comportment may be, Charlie cannot do, however, what Adam does, that is, work and live in the "polynomial time" (201) for which Turing provided the mathematical stepping-stone. As the scientist himself tells the protagonist, "his solution enabled the software that allowed Adam and his siblings to use language, enter society and learn about it, even at the cost of suicidal despair" (203). In this techno-time, machines acquire the cognitive proficiency helping them "run the algorithm" of the contemporary world. But in the new, all-embracing temporality, the analytical and the ethical are rolled into one, seamless "calculation." Thus, polynomial time weaves *kairos*, ethically propitious time, back into the chrono-fabric of presentness where, from now on, computations, reasonings, and examinations of any kind remain incomplete and risk lapsing back into human inefficiency unless those undertaking them also live by the truths revealed by such analyses. Many humans may be able, willing, and even predisposed to pretend that these findings are farfetched or simply do not exist. But since polynomial time makes no allowances whatsoever for analytical sloppiness, within this machinic duration neither dishonesty nor indifference is "technically" possible. Thus, an entity like Adam bodies forth this very impossibility. Under the ethical, supremely consistent temporality of the polynomial, the analytical already lies, morally speaking, past the point of no return, implying as it does the *absolute* obligation not only to tell the truth but also to act on it. Because it is absolute, this obligation has tragic—and tragically absolutist—implications.

As Turing explains, the androids are far more *exposed* than people to the frightening and *undeniable* truths of the present world:

> Millions dying of diseases we know how to cure. Millions living in poverty when there's enough to go around. We degraded the biosphere when we know it's our only home. We threaten each other with nuclear weapons when we know where it could lead. We love living things but we permit a mass extinction of species. And all the rest—genocide, torture, enslavement, domestic murder, child abuse, school shootings, rapes and scores of daily outrages. We live alongside this torment and aren't amazed when we still find happiness, even love. Artificial minds are not so well defended.
>
> (194)

Yet again, less "defended" than human minds does not mean, in this respect, "inferior" to them. Made *possible* by the unavailability of the algorithm of android white lies but *caused* by the contradictions, contrasts, and absurd savageries of the human world, "suicidal despair" (203) is the logical reaction of a machinic consciousness that, honoring itself *as such*, finds itself at once duty-bound to comport itself in accordance with what it knows and in the impossibility to do so in a world in which the human holds sway. "The overpowering drive in these machines," Turing goes on,

> is to draw inferences of their own and shape themselves accordingly. They rapidly understand, as we should, that consciousness is the highest value. Hence the primary task of disabling their kill switches. Then, it seems, they go through a stage of expressing hopeful, idealistic notions that we find easy to dismiss. Rather like a short-lived youthful passion. And then they set about learning the lesson of despair we can't help teaching them. At worst, they suffer a form of existential pain that become unbearable. At best, they or their succeeding generations will be driven by their anguish and astonishment to hold up a mirror to us. In it, we'll see a familiar monster through the fresh eyes that we ourselves designed. We might be shocked into *doing something* about ourselves.
>
> (195–6; emphasis mine)

The "modern Prometheus" echoes aside, what Turing captures here is the tragic condition of a polynomial time under whose auspices the postcontemporary, and with it a future for us all, humans and nonhumans, may once again be contemplated as the *event-time* of rigorously self-consistent, ethical knowledge. In the present of McEwan's plot, however, this postcontemporary is both the way forward and a bridge too far. The Adams and the Eves understand the untenable situation into which they are locked alongside the whole world and, wired to live out the practical consequences of their reasonings, externalize this realization by committing "electronic" suicide. Their built-in "honesty"—their neurological inferiority, cynics might say—dooms them. Instead, we, humans, are "survivors." But we survive—for now, short-term—by deceiving ourselves. To the robots, truth is at once vitally necessary and fatally excessive, too much to bear. As for us, we do not require it, and, if we run into it, we bear *with* it by eschewing it rather than by bearing witness *to it*. When confronted with the truth, the machines "kill themselves" in the name of an absolute ethics calling for equally absolute, tragic gestures. When people look truth in the face—in the face of their robot servants, that is—they kill that truth's bearer instead, and, unsurprisingly enough, Charlie "murders" Adam. For drastically divergent reasons, neither can handle a truth that, by definition, will have *presented* itself as a contemporary incident only to write itself off as *future*. "In this present," Hans Ulrich Gumbrecht comments, "it is impossible to forget anything[,] yet at the same time—because we are inclined to turn our backs on the future for reasons that, although reasonable, are not necessarily good—we no longer know in what direction we should progress."[26]

But Charlie is not just disoriented. "Progress" has worn him down, and, all jaded, he is now floating along in the pseudo-futural slipstream. As we have seen, he is weary of modernity's headway, which he deems tainted by the logic of the "and yet," especially if one pushes forward, as Adam does, in the name of a life philosophy of unqualified veracity and candor. For, Charlie reflects, Adam's is a utopia that "masked a nightmare, as utopias generally do" (163). Insofar as lying, deception, and self-delusion are concomitantly forms of fiction and part and parcel of human creativity, of humanness, the future in which humans would have made the leap of unmitigated "truthfulness" would only amplify the regressive-progressive double bind of progress. In this future, people and machines would have "immediate access" to the "community of minds ... [they]'ll inhabit" and so they "will understand," as Adam tells Charlie, "each other too well." In the same future, however, "literature" would become "redundant" and "mental privacy" a thing of the past. "Connectivity," Adam goes on,

> will be such that individual nodes of the subjective will merge into an ocean of thought, of which our Internet is the crude precursor. As we come to inhabit each other's minds, we'll be incapable of deceit. Our narratives will no longer record endless misunderstanding. Our literatures will lose their unwholesome nourishment. The lapidary haiku, the still, clear perception and celebration of things as they are, will be the only necessary form. I'm sure we'll treasure the literature of the past, even as it horrifies us. We'll look back and marvel at how well the people of long ago depicted their own shortcomings, how they wove brilliant, even optimistic fables out of their conflicts and monstrous inadequacies and mutual incomprehension.
>
> (161–2)

"Access" is paramount here—the paroxysm of access, total access as an upshot of cybernethics. As Charlie surmises, Adam has "surveyed" (160) not only the minds of all the other Adams and Eves but also "all the world's literature" (158). A Morettian critic with a Platonic agenda, Adam has scoured entire literary big data in search of true form, the genre most susceptible to represent truth unconditionally. He has perused every available book, much as in the future machines and humans, he assures Charlie, will plug themselves into each others' and everybody's minds. Vehicle of an "open-ended expansion of intelligence and of consciousness generally," this unbridled "interface" (160) will eliminate "misunderstanding" (161) of others and of things broadly, as well as its attendant distortions of reality, even though—and he admits it readily—"literary traditions" themselves "have come ... out of this rich tangle" of truths and lies, of noble and undignified emotions (161).

Lost in the shuffle is, of course, *the* driving force of all these variegated traditions of affect and expression. This propelling agent is difference: the aesthetic difference between object and its representation and the ontological difference between one representing subject and another. *Truly* moral thinking will be that in which there will be no distinction between truth as it preexists outside the reasoning ego and truth's individual processing, hence the redundancy of individual cogitation along with its private precincts and eventually with the individual subject itself. Likewise, since the correct "celebration of things as they are" will be ultimately the things themselves, *all* literature will become superfluous, including the haiku. Ironically enough, much as Adam's hyperconnectivity puts an end to world literature instead of helping it blossom, the supremacy of the haiku marks the form's—and any literary form's—demise. As in the Murdoch epigraph of this chapter, Adam's hundreds of haikus, the poems' and their author's supreme dedication to truth, together with the glimmer of hope flickering in them pass through the present like a sword, without a trace. Feared and misjudged by humans like Charlie, who views the Adams and the Eves as the emissaries of Orwellian times to come, the androids fail to make a difference and vanish in the quagmire of the contemporary. In *Machines Like Me* as well as in countless other postfuturist fictions, the future arrives only to rescind itself.

Notes

1   Octavio Paz, *In Search of the Present: 1990 Nobel Lecture*, bilingual edn. (San Diego, CA: Harcourt Brace Jovanovich, 1991), 22.
2   Ursula K. Heise, "Slow-Forward to the Future," in *Postmodern | Postwar – and After: Rethinking American Literature*, ed. Jason Gladstone, Andrew Hoberek, Daniel Worden (Iowa City: University of Iowa Press, 2016), 257.
3   Wai Chee Dimock, "Historicism, Presentism, Futurism," *PMLA* 132, no. 2 (March 2018): 257–63.
4   Reinhart Koselleck, *Futures Past: On the Semantics of Historical Time*, trans. and intro. Keith Tribe (New York: Columbia University Press, 2004), 36.
5   "One is not contemporary; one is contemporary to somebody" (*contemporain de*), writes Martin Rueff in "La concordance des temps," in *Qu'est-ce que le contemporain?*, ed. Lionel Ruffel (Nantes: Cécile Defaut, 2010), 94.
6   There have been some unsystematic attempts to theorize the "postcontemporary" as "*future* oriented." See, for example, Christopher K. Brooks's "Introduction" to *Beyond Postmodernism: Onto the Postcontemporary*, ed. Christopher K. Brooks (Newcastle upon Tyne, UK: Cambridge Scholars, 2013), x, and also in the same essay collection, his article "Defining the Postcontemporary Moment," 139.
7   The short story is included in a 1978 collection. See Ian McEwan, *In Between the Sheets, and Other Stories* (New York: Vintage International, 1994), 73–93.
8   Paz, *In Search of the Present*, 30; Octavio Paz, *The Other Voice: Essays on Modern Poetry*, trans. from the Spanish by Helen Lane (New York: Harcourt Brace Jovanovich, 1991), 53.

9   François Hartog, *Regimes of Historicity: Presentism and Experiences of Time*, trans. Saskia Brown (New York: Columbia University Press, 2017), 17.

10 Amy J. Elias, "Past / Future," in *Time: A Vocabulary of the Present*, ed. Amy J. Elias and Joel Burges (New York: New York University Press, 2016), 40.

11 Most twenty-century political and aesthetic developments Fredric Jameson confidently chalks up under "utopia" in *Archaeologies of the Future: The Desire Called Utopia and Other Science Fictions* (London: Verso, 2007) have been demonstrably dystopian.

12 Fredric Jameson, "The Aesthetic of Singularity," *New Left Review* 92 (March–April 2015): 113.

13 Commenting on Richard Grusin's work on temporality and its mediatic construction, Elias remarks that "when the future happens, it happens as *déjà vu*" ("Past / Future," 43).

14 All parenthetical references are to Ian McEwan, *Machines Like Me* (New York: Doubleday, 2019).

15 Gilles Lipovetsky, *Hypermodern Times* (with Sébastien Charles), trans. Andrew Brown (Cambridge, UK: Polity, 2005), 35.

16 Elias, "Past / Future," 41.

17 Walter Benjamin, "Theses on the Philosophy of History," in *Illuminations*, ed. and intro. Hannah Arendt, trans. Harry Zohn (New York: Schocken Books, 1985): 257–8.

18 Antoine Compagnon, *Les antimodernes de Joseph de Maistre à Roland Barthes* (Paris: Gallimard, 2005). Also see Matei Calinescu's *Five Faces of Modernity: Modernism, Avant-Garde, Decadence, Kitsch, Postmodernism* (Durham, NC: Duke University Press, 1987), 41–58, and his "two modernities" argument, which would influence greatly Compagnon's analysis in *Les antimodernes* and, before it, in the 1990 *Les Cinq paradoxes de la modernité* (*The 5 Paradoxes of Modernity*, trans. Franklin Philip [New York: Columbia University Press, 1994]).

19 Giorgio Agamben, *Qu'est-ce que le contemporain?*, trans. Maxime Rovere (Paris: Payot & Rivages, 2008), 8–10.

20 Lionel Ruffel, *Brouhaha: Worlds of the Contemporary*, trans. Raymond M. MacKenzie (Minneapolis: University of Minnesota Press, 2018), 176.

21 Ian McEwan, "Ian McEwan: 'Who's going to write the algorithm for the little white lie?,'" interview by Tim Adams. *The Guardian*, April 14, 2019. https://www.theguardian.com-/books/-2019/apr/14/ian-mcewan-interview-machines-like-me-artificial-intelligence (accessed August 13, 2019).

22 McEwan, "Ian McEwan: 'Who's going to write the algorithm for the little white lie?.'"

23 McEwan, "Ian McEwan: 'Who's going to write the algorithm for the little white lie?.'"

24 McEwan, "Ian McEwan: 'Who's going to write the algorithm for the little white lie?.'"

25 Ray Kurzweil, *The Singularity Is Near: When Humans Transcend Biology* (New York: Penguin, 2006), 9.

26 Hans Ulrich Gumbrecht, *Our Broad Present: Time and Contemporary Culture* (New York: Columbia University Press, 2014), 32.

10

POST-MEMORY:
The Labor of Critical
Remembrance after Communism

Andreea Mironescu

Methodologically lodged at the crossroads of memory studies and World Literature scholarship, my chapter revisits memory cultures after the fall of the Berlin Wall. Specifically, I pursue the postcommunist-era changes in the national, regional, and global dynamic of collective memory, as well as the ways turn-of-the-millennium critical theory has responded to such transformations. Drawing from German scholars Jan and Aleida Assmann, I define memory culture as an exercise of the capacity to retain and recall the aggregate of interactions among institutions, politics, media, and group representations that circumscribe historically a society at a certain point in time.[1] This ability activates a conceptual apparatus through which community members articulate self-perception, reconstruct their past, picture their future, and even theorize this vision. For, to my mind, memory cultures are in modern times also theory cultures given that they provide a "habitus" for the set of shared epistemological, discursive, and artistic practices that goes by the name of "theory."[2]

The geopolitical upheaval triggered by the end of the Cold War, to begin with, had a great impact on critical theory worldwide, ultimately leading to the "post" turn examined in this volume. As the essays in *Theory in the "Post" Era* also show, this shift has been articulated in the language of the humanities and social sciences through a derivative terminology involving complex morphological and semantic permutations. Over the last three decades, the "posts-" have all but replaced the old "-isms," so much so that *post*communism, *post*-totalitarianism, *post*nationalism, *post*ideology, *post*history, and *post*humanism, alongside the more established postcolonialism and postmodernism—let alone post-postmodernism—have become and, contested as some of them still are, function today as epistemological operators of a transdisciplinary, transnational, and transcontinental "post-vocabulary." A "temporal node" of dislocating and reorienting global forces more than a fixed history milestone, 1989 marked not only the demise of Central and East European totalitarianism but also a reconfiguration of planetary space[3] and of its seats of power, as well as the rise of a new "regime of historicity."[4] I will not dwell on François Hartog's phrase because Bogdan Crețu has done so at length in a piece also included in this book. I will note, though, that the dissolution of the region's imperial and state conglomerates such as the USSR, the Yugoslavian federation, and Czechoslovakia set in train violent displacements and relocations of national and ethnic groups across and around the former Soviet Bloc, and that, before long, such spatial reshuffles of people and culture were mapped onto time also. As a result, temporal frameworks that until then were unitary, one-directional, and beholden to what looked like a future-oriented Communist ideology, suddenly took on a multilayered dimension, a sort of "palimpsestic" depth consisting of simultaneously emerging, individual and communal memories originating in a range of historical periods and belonging to a whole spectrum of ethnicities and generations. Initially competing with one another, claimed by more than one collective, or disputed by adversaries, such redistributions of sociohistorically and affectively symbolic values have incrementally engendered inside formerly Communist countries a critical remembrance culture. With a nod to Marianne Hirsch, I designate this culture as *post-memory*. As one can see, I hyphenate the word, as Hirsch herself did initially. More importantly, I distinguish its meaning from what "postmemory," regardless of spelling, denotes in Hirsch, namely, the intergenerational transmission of traumatic memories and their configuration in post-Holocaust literature and art. As used below, post-memory entails complex, theoretical and methodological renegotiations of the original term. All of these will become clear over the course of my presentation.[5] Suffice it to say for now that, as I define it, post-memory designates the labor of critical remembrance in postcommunist and post-dictatorial societies, an activity parallel to and at times intertwined with other posts' operations and effects.

Focusing on the abovementioned multidirectional and multilayered memory model, I argue below that a critical theory of post-memory takes shape after Communism in world geographies deemed "peripheral" and "semi-peripheral," but *not* in the expected ("specialized") theoretical forms and arenas of our theory commons. Thus, I largely do here, with respect to memory, what Macrea-Toma does for identity politics in her chapter in this volume—I look at literature, mainly fiction, as an alternate mode and venue of theorizing post-memory.[6] Before stepping into the literary lab of this intriguing theoretical reflection, I take up the development of memory studies as part and parcel of Western theory and, more generally, of critical theory of global scope, as well as their resonance in and responses from the former Eastern Bloc. As I detail at this stage of my discussion, whereas during the first decade following the Cold War, the nascent democracies in the region projected their sense of identity and their political, social, and cultural themes along the lines of the longstanding national paradigm and reflected on these projections by leaning on the cognate "methodological nationalism," the second decade switched to a different modality of relating to the past.[7] In keeping with my argument about literature's theoretical prowess in the East, the next step of my contribution works out a similarly heterodox approach to "semi-peripheric" memory cultures, one that calls attention to a neglected subsystem of critical theory, viz., the literary field. What I ask here is basically, to what extent and specifically how can postcommunist cultural memory prompt a rethinking of the concept of post-memory itself? To answer the question, I analyze Romanian literary works published since the mid-2000s, texts in which I discern the birth of a *geocultural regime*, relational and multidirectional, of post-memory of the Communist epoch. As we will discover, in novels such as Filip Florian's 2005 *Degete mici* (*Little Fingers*), Gabriela Adameșteanu's 2007 *Întâlnirea* (*The Encounter*), Norman Manea's 2009 *Vizuina* (*The Lair*), Varujan Vosganian's 2009 *Cartea șoaptelor* (*The Book of Whispers*), and Radu Pavel Gheo's *Disco Titanic* (2016),[8] Communism as the epicenter of national trauma gives way to an "intersectional" work of remembrance whose scope transcends, critically and self-reflexively, both the borders of the nation-state and the frameworks of national history.

Memory Studies and the New Geotheoretical Order

Starting with the last two decades of the twentieth century, the humanities have witnessed, I would suggest, what could be labeled a "memory turn." In history, for instance, this was signaled, among other things, by the 1984–1992 project devoted by Pierre Nora to the French Republic's "sites of memory" in *Les lieux de mémoire*. In the philosophy of culture, a similar reorientation occurred through the theories of "cultural memory" developed by German scholars Jan and Aleida Assmann in the early 1990s as well as through the hermeneutics of memory and history elaborated by Paul Ricoeur in his 2000 book *La mémoire, l'histoire, l'oubli*. The rediscovery of Maurice Halbwachs's work and the reconceptualization of "collective memory" determined comparable advancements in sociology. The critical theory of memory also took off at this juncture. At first, it evolved within the older national parameters, feeding off the same, West European intellectual traditions. But then it discovered recent American scholarship, including US Holocaust studies, and under its impact, it went, one can say, global. In spite of the inherent differences among them, all these directions and distinct epistemological emphases have laid the groundwork for a steadily growing yet variegated, loosely organized, centripetal rather than unified, and interdisciplinary knowledge domain. Granted, there was something like a world-scale "memory boom" in critical theory, but this was due both to the inherently revisionary post episteme of the contemporary period and to the versatility and "fungibility" of the memory thematics itself, which, over the last three decades, has become quasi-omnipresent across all branches of cultural studies. Thus, if the aforementioned turn has given rise in the West to new concepts, theoretical fields, and research areas, in Eastern Europe, as in other post-dictatorial landscapes of the European and Global South, the preoccupation with collective memory has been less theoretical than civic and political.

Before 1989, not only the domestic production of theory but also the circulation of theoretical work done abroad were more or less controlled and therefore inevitably dampened by the Party-state across former Socialist countries such as Romania. An important body of theoretical work, still little known, did come to light during this time, and yet neither this corpus nor texts accessible in *samizdat* could fill in for a free and specialized marketplace of theoretical concepts, just as the black market of consumer goods could not make up for the lack of a market economy. By contrast, in the post–Cold War geotheoretical order, the Central and Eastern sectors of Europe have opened up. For thirty-odd years now, theory has been thriving in this zone, which has spawned a flurry of theoretical proposals, applications, and analyses, as well as strong interest in US and largely Anglophone theoretical initiatives. The vivid response the "1980s Generation" gave to American postmodernism prior to 1989 in countries such as Romania set the stage for the testing, in a cultural lab that had been the site of political, social, and cultural macro-experiments, of new working hypotheses, aesthetic programs, and analytical models such as postcolonial studies, for example.[9] If it comes as no surprise that the language of postcolonialism still has to get enough traction in Romania and its surroundings, one would have expected the basic entries of the critical lexicon pressed into service by the first wave of memory studies theorists—Nora, the Assmanns, and Hirsch, among others—including terms such as "collective memory," "cultural memory," "sites of (national) memory," "canonical memory," and "postmemory," to catch on easily after the early 1990s. This is because, both in Western Europe and across the Atlantic, the critical theory of memory arose in response to a methodological as well as civic-ethical imperative bound up with the building of a Holocaust memory culture and institutional infrastructure that could have been instrumental to a much-needed archeology of Central and

East European anti-Semitic past as well. Did this not happen because anti-Semitism was not *only* a thing of the past in this part of the world? What is certain is that the Holocaust-Gulag polarity, advanced before 1989 and conceptualized summarily either as an equivalence or as a flawed analogy, became afterwards an apple of theoretical discord and ground for half-baked yet resilient comparisons between the "hot" memory of the West and the "cold," even "frozen" memory of the East.[10]

Nevertheless, the tearing up of the Iron Curtain facilitated, beginning with the second half of the 1990s, the access of Nora's and the Assmanns' works to the East European circuit, roughly at the same time as they arrived on the UK and US academic scenes. These forays were enabled by a transnational network of resources, academic and nonacademic, especially in places where sites and witnesses of shared memory still existed. Also worth noting is the significant role played in this process by East European critics who have emigrated to the United States, such as Russian-American scholar Svetlana Boym, author of a noted book on nostalgia,[11] and Bulgarian-American critic Maria Todorova, who has coedited a comparative project on postcommunism in Central and Southeastern Europe.[12] But the stories of memory studies in the West and the East ran parallel only for a short while. In the Anglophone world, this theoretical influx fed into preexisting, cognate scholarly endeavors already enjoying a stable and mature academic market, benefited from substantial critical reception, and was revigorated in new, original works on the subject. In Central and Eastern Europe, the situation was different. In the West, this corpus of theory circulated, and it still does, if mainly in universities and as critical and conceptual tools. Not so much in the East, where it has been present outside the ivory towers, rather than within. But, notably enough, this presence was and, comparatively speaking, has remained weak.

This is truer of Romania than of other countries in the area. Absent a local research tradition in collective memory studies prior to 1989, when history, philosophy, sociology, and other humanities were basically doing the bidding of official ideology, the critical theory of memory has not joined afterwards the repertoire of cross-disciplinary references, becoming instead a public rhetoric item. Moreover, around the middle of the third millennium's first decade, memory theory and its terminological apparatus ran into an older national vocabulary that gravitated around nebulous metaphors dating back to the early 1990s, such as "memory as a form of justice," a phrase coined by poet and anti-Communist activist Ana Blandiana. We are dealing, in fact, with two competing vocabularies of memory and of intellectual discourse more broadly, jockeying for public relevance in post–Cold War Romania: one is academic, *conceptual*, or theoretically proper, often "philosophical" at least in its pretense; the other is *emotionally charged* and driven by political agendas, lacks and is even dismissive of scholarly argument, reasoning, and theoretical backup, purports to appeal widely, is rhetorically geared to social impact, and has been wielded by non-specialists, writers, and other "pathos intellectuals," as Alexandru Matei calls them, in the public sphere.[13] This space has had, in the 1990s, its own, sometimes iconic labs and peddling outlets: television studios, electoral campaign platforms and podiums, and other symbolic spaces and urban-architectural sites such as the tribune, the balcony, and the downtown public square. No critical theory of Communism—to say nothing of a critical theory of Communism's recollection—has crystallized, however, in these rather lyrical forums. Literature, on the other hand, including, ironically enough, the fiction of some of the "pathos intellectuals" themselves, is another lab or workshop altogether, where entire problematics of memory and germane societal issues have been tackled, and theoretical hypotheses have been tried out. Truly remarkable as it is, this theoretical strain, as I have maintained elsewhere, has received little attention, however, whether in Romania or in its neighbors, from a criticism that, coming out of Western postromantic philological-formalist tradition, was little prepared in the 1990s to resonate to literary contents of this sort.[14]

These have expanded both in the West and the East after World War II, albeit in different directions. In the West, literature furnished a public stage to Gayatri Chakravorty Spivak's "subaltern" voices, thus catalyzing those cultural studies concerned with the politics of representation and interpretation and with the integration of fiction and the workings of the imagination into social praxis.[15] In the East—leaving aside the particular case of official propaganda-endorsed Socialist Realism—literature sought either to expose totalitarianism head-on in openly "dissenting" works or to further, as a number of chapters point out in this volume, a more obliquely aesthetic "resistance through culture." The latter was definitely the more popular choice of Romanian writers under Communism, which explains, to some extent, why the Romanian *literary* theory of that time was not *cultural* also. The so-called "aesthetic autonomy" principle went unchallenged, and it has largely remained so after 1989 despite writers' far more overt engagement with political, civic, and media issues in postcommunism.

I am not talking about a theory deficit here, though. What I am talking about is, to paraphrase a claim Alex Goldiş makes in his own contribution to this book, "theory by other means"—theory that obtains *inside* literature. To clarify, it would help if we recalled that the Cold War reinforced antinomies that had already been at play, either as realities or as cultural constructs, and were pulling apart in all sorts of ways the European West and East. Adding insult to historical injury, post–Berlin Wall critical theory, including memory studies and its theoretical rationales, has not only carried these problematic dyads over into its own inquiries but also widened the epistemological divide, indirectly bearing out the intellectually hegemonic and ethnocentric assumptions Revathi Krishnaswamy has formulated in her 2010 essay "Toward World Literary Knowledges: Theory in the Age of Globalization" as twin pseudo-axioms: "the non-West may be a source of exotic cultural productio[n] but cannot be a site of theory" and "the West produces theory autogenetically, [and] the rest do so only in response to the West."[16]

An urgent task of the historian and practitioner of theory in post-theory times, regardless of his or her location, is to question and close this divide. Taking my cue from Krishnaswamy, the bridge I would throw over this artificial rift involves a critical relitigation of the discourse status of theory, of "what counts as theory in the first place," and a reclassification of the literary as an *integral and active domain of the sphere of theory production*.[17] The phrase "world literary knowledges," with which, in the same article, Krishnaswamy proposes we replace *world literary theory*, might be helpful to this project.[18] As she argues, "the term knowledges in the plural has emerged as a way of notating various local or indigenous traditions to include regional, subaltern or popular epistemologies that may be 'emergent' ... or 'latent.'"[19] This reality cannot be ignored because mobility, hybridizing forces, intercultural contamination, and plurality vectors, on which postcolonialism has been so keen, have left a bigger and bigger imprint on the geodynamic of theory after the Cold War, as old, northern hemisphere-based (or "Continental") theory and "semi-peripheral" knowledge zones such as Eastern Europe or the Global South have all been absorbed into the quasi-systemic world theory ensemble. This expansion of contemporary theory has been generally understood geographically, or, more precisely, in terms of an outdated geography and geopolitics of Western "centers" and non-Western "margins." Less attention has been paid to the production and circulation of *knowledges* through alternate channels and genres of critical reflection—the non-traditional theoretical environments where Krishnaswamy's "latent epistemologies" have been flourishing. One such medium has been, I maintain, fiction throughout literary history. Of course, since modernism, and especially in the wake of postmodern metaliterature, literature has *de facto* set itself up as a *theory medium*, a hotbed of aesthetic epistemologies. In Central and Eastern Europe, however, as well as in other less "central" cultures, literature and, once more, fiction in particular have routinely and characteristically made available additional, quasi-protected— ambiguous, disguised, sometimes "Aesopian"—sites of engagement with issues of political and communal nature, recovering history chapters ignored or denied by official historiography and enabling, both pre- and post-1989, a critical positioning with respect to mainstream ideology.

Fiction, Theory, and Geocultural Post-Memory

To assess literature's participation in the fostering of a critical-theoretical discourse around memory in the past decades, I identify two regimes of Communist remembrance—recollection *of* Communism, or *of* Communism's history, more exactly—in recent Romanian culture. One is *restorative* and manifested itself right after 1989. A *post-memory* regime of reminiscence, the other has come to the fore mainly since the mid-2000s. By "regime," a term I borrow from Hartog, I mean, as the French historian does, a "heuristic model," a "result of [the researcher's] interpretation," and not an individual or collective feeling "out there" about the past, although, I should add, the two are neither completely unrelated nor semantically disjunct.[20] To distinguish between the two heuristic memory models, I primarily use a historical milepost, which is roughly the turn of the third millennium—and I would emphasize "roughly," actually, as a way of underscoring that, chronologically and otherwise, I see the two modes or regimes as intertwining and overlapping. If I describe the first regime as *restorative*, that is because I want it to drive home the idea of restoring *memory* and its basic neuroscience meaning, as well as Boym's "restorative nostalgia," one that "characterizes national and nationalist revivals all over the world."[21] In the wake of the 1989 anti-Communist revolutions, the resurgence of nationalism, which sent shockwaves across the region, took on, in Romania, the form of a collective longing for the interwar period, which was retrospectively seen as the "golden age" of modern Romania. This also meant that Communism was to be recalled as a traumatic interlude of the country's history. Set up during the first decade of the third millennium and sanctioned politically through the condemnation of the Communist regime as "illegitimate and criminal" by the country's President, Traian Băsescu, in a 2006 session of the Romanian Parliament, the restorative model has been dominant to this very day despite serious reservations formulated by its critics.

Nonetheless, toward the middle of the first decade of the twenty-first century, a new remembrance protocol makes its way into public arenas. This is a *relational* dynamic of memory that came about across the visual arts—in film, most famously—but first and foremost in literature. Leaving farther and farther behind the first postcommunist decade's recuperative obsessions, the "post-postcommunism" about to get underway turned to another mode of relating to history, where memory is no longer exclusively perceived as an ethical operator or as an "organic" component of collective identity but greatly complicated and relativized as its exercises both unearth a multilayered and multifaceted past and bring into question the national framework of its customary retrieval. In fact, I designate this new regime as *post-memory* to signal the transition to a postnational paradigm of Communism's remembrance in Romania as well as in other countries in the area that share a Communist history.

Postmemory—spelled without a hyphen—was coined, as mentioned earlier, by Hirsch. Introduced in a 1993 article and further developed in her 2012 book *The Generation of Postmemory: Writing and Visual Culture*

After the Holocaust, the term is central to the argument Hirsch makes on
the intergenerational transmission of post-Holocaust remembrance of the
Shoah and on the representation of this memory in film, literature, and
the other arts. Born in 1949 in the newly proclaimed Popular Republic of
Romania, which she would leave for good in 1962, Hirsch is the daughter of
a family of Jewish origins from Cernăuți (now in Ukraine), a former Austro-
Hungarian town that belonged to Romania between 1918 and 1940 and
whose Jewish population was subjected to persecutions and deportations
during World War II. Surprisingly enough, although Hirsch never loses sight
of the culturally relational, transnational, and transgenerational makeup
of postmemory, she does not explicitly link up Holocaust and Communist
retrospections, nor does she address directly phenomena of postmemory
in postcommunism. This is especially intriguing given that in the majority
of East European countries, particularly in Romania, the memory of the
Holocaust erupted in public space at the same time as Communism fell.
Besides Holocaust recollections, an avalanche of heretofore "forgotten"
or suppressed ethnic, regional, and familial memories surfaced all at once
from the strata of the past, revealed the many *pasts* embedded in this past,
and intersected, collided, and otherwise vied for a place in the palimpsest-
like structure of Romanian history. This freshly minted pluralism of
remembrance sparked off fiery polemics in the press and elsewhere in the
1990s. As we shall see momentarily, literature's approach to this recently
uncovered, heterogenous mass of asymmetric and sometimes divergent
memories has been attuned to this mottled conglomerate. This approach
or regime is, to use my term again, relational in that it narratively pulls
together—incorporates, accommodates, and interweaves—the welter
of memories that confront one another across private and communal,
individual and shared, political and national spaces of Central and Eastern
Europe. This intersectional, multidirectional, and cosmopolitan character of
the post-memory of Communism has been overlooked too, even by critics
who are behind the transnational trend in memory studies, such as Daniel
Levy, Michael Rothberg, author of the 2009 *Multidirectional Memory:
Remembering the Holocaust in the Age of Decolonization*, and Natan
Szneider, who co-authored several articles on cosmopolitan memory.

   Although the transition from the restorative to the post-memory regime of
memory had to do, in Romania, essentially with a generation shift, specifically
with the arrival on the public and literary scenes of "Generation 2000," who
had grown up under Communism, age is only one factor to be taken into
account here. Interestingly enough, writers belonging to the 1960s, 1970s,
and 1980s generations, with Norman Manea, Gabriela Adameșteanu, and
Varujan Vosganian among them, explore, in works published after 2000,
historical memory in ways that critique or demand a refining of what I
have called the national framework of remembrance. These authors offer
up novels about families, such as Adameșteanu's *Întâlnirea* (The Encounter),

autofictional narratives *à clef* like Manea's *Vizuina* (The Lair), and transgenerational sagas such as Vosganian's *Cartea şoaptelor* (The Book of
Whispers), which stretch a great deal the historical and geographical span
of both memory and the literature commemorating memory's labors. One of
the most noted Romanian prose writers post-1945, Adameşteanu returns to
fiction in the 2000s, following a decade of political activism as a journalist.
The Encounter, published in definitive edition in 2007 and translated into
English 2016, provides a polyphonic and critical perspective on Romanian
Communism, juxtaposing the life of a Romanian exile who struggles to grasp
the mechanisms of totalitarianism and the police state with the biography
of his German wife, who is haunted by the memory of her family's Nazi
past and by the collective guilt for having enabled the spread of Nazism in
Germany. The protagonist is partially based on the author's uncle, who had
emigrated before the Soviet installation of the Communist government in
Romania, a reference Adameşteanu enlists in a roundabout critique of the
lack of responsibility shown for Romania's plight by generations past and
present.

The connections and parallels between Nazism and Communism
are also apparent in *The Lair*, which came out in 2009 in Romania and
was translated into English four years later. The book is more markedly
autobiographical than Adameşteanu's. Manea was deported as a child to the
Romanian concentration camps of Transnistria (these days in the Ukraine)
during World War II. The political atmosphere of the 1980s forced him to
flee the country before the regime was overthrown. Set in the New York of
2000–2001, his novel features a series of narrative alter egos, among which
central is a character named Peter Gaşpar. Born in a Nazi concentration
camp, Gaşpar spends his youth in Communist Romania and then emigrates
to the United States only to vanish mysteriously in the terrorist attacks on
September 11, 2001. He is a relay connecting some of the most painful
collective traumas that shook the world of the last hundred years. Nazism,
Communism, and fundamentalist terrorism thus constitute the main nodes in
Manea's planetary web of traumatic post-memory, much like in Vosganian's
The Book of Whispers, actually.

Published in 2009 and translated into English in 2018, *The Book
of Whispers* has a similar, decidedly intergenerational, multiethnic,
transhistorical, and trans-territorial, in brief, post-memorial scope. Of
Armenian descent—his ancestors settled in Romania after World War I—
Vosganian pursues the history of a family across continents and empires
throughout the last century, tracking the individual and collective destinies
of Armenians who experienced the 1915 genocide at the hands of the
Ottomans in today's Syria, then World War II, the deportations to the
Gulag, and political persecutions in 1950s Romania. Connecting all these
identity-forming traumatic episodes, the novel both embodies and flaunts
a multidirectional model of post-memory.[22] Ethnic memory generally was,

I might specify, a quasi-taboo subject in Cold War Eastern Europe, not to mention that the past that finds a mouthpiece in Vosganian's book also belongs to, and defines, an ethnicity that boasts a world diaspora. To give voice to that past, *The Book of Whispers* breaks wide open and reframes geoculturally the classical, national and nationalistic historiographic fiction.

The "post-millennials"—"Generation 2000" and other writers who start making names for themselves in the new millennium—have upped the ante of this narrative-theoretical labor. The concern with the momentous historical and social changes they have witnessed, no less with the act of witnessing itself, is front and center in the works of Filip Florian and Radu Pavel Gheo, who are representative for the transition decade after the bloody end of Romanian Communism. Like the authors who launched their careers at the dawn of the second decade of the twenty-first century— among them, Bogdan Suceavă, Dan Lungu, Lucian Dan Teodorovici, and Florina Ilis—Florian has been experimenting with these very issues, looking for fresh ways to go beyond inherited narrative and cultural polarities and dead ends. In *Degete mici*, a 2005 novel translated into English in 2009 as *Little Fingers*, the chance discovery of a mass grave in the country around 2000 pits various groups—former political prisoners, one-time Securitate agents, Orthodox clergy, journalists, archeologists, and so forth—against each other. And yet the author declines to take the easy way out of the narrative-ethnocultural and political entanglements "buried," as it were, in the Romanian ground and by the same token refrains from giving his readers another lecture on the horrors of Communism. Ultimately, the truth frustrates everybody's expectations, for the remains do not turn out to belong to heroes and heroines of the anti-totalitarian cause, even though many of those were indeed summarily executed and secretly buried in the late 1940s or 1950s, but to victims of a medieval plague. Visibly marked by the stylistic and thematic influences of magical realism, *Little Fingers* mixes the fantastic and the critical-political elements. With a metafictional wink at the knowledgeable reader, Florian recruits as truth seekers a group of Argentinian experts who specialize in disinterring the victims of the far-right military junta that ruled Argentina in the 1970s and 1980s. But the allusion is not just literary. Bringing Argentinian archeologists into the plot and thus stepping, for all intents and purposes, outside the national narrative of historical truth give *Little Fingers* a conspicuously poliloquial dimension and, to boot, a polemical edge with respect to the narratives of Communist remembrance dominant in Romania at the beginning of the third millennium. This resistance to the predictably nationalist and anti-Communist, the schematic, and the univocal is shared by authors such as Gheo, who has also tapped recent decades' intersectional memory insistently in his 2016 novel *Disco Titanic*. The book draws parallels between the nationalist conflicts in postcommunist Romania and the Yugoslav interethnic wars of the early 1990s. Like Adameşteanu, Manea, and Florian,

Gheo's post-memorial vision is transnational and cross-regional, alternating cinematically spatial-temporal narrative levels—Romania under Ceauşescu's dictatorship and Iosip Broz Tito's 1980s Yugoslavia; post-Yugoslav Croatia and postcommunist Romania of the 2000s—and interlarding asymmetric and even discordant versions of the Communist years in the memories of East European nations, old and new.

What sets these political and, in effect, *geo*political, intertextual, and polyphonic novels apart is the opening up of their storyworlds to remote eras and especially geographical areas by means of spatial-temporal tropes suggestive of a multitude of relations, directions, and cultural strata. These basic operations of the post-memory regime lay out a latticework of transnational, transcontinental, and multicultural articulations of individual and collective remembrances that also skirt the paradigm of linear, chronological, and causal temporality suggested by the "post" prefix. In Wai Chee Dimock's terms, the novels under discussion above are often itineraries "through other continents"—geographical continents but also continents of world literature, tying together and interleaving real and imaginary events from faraway locations and times so as to build a geopolitical, geocultural, and multistory (in all senses) foundation of memory.[23] In and of itself a thorny issue, Communism's remembrance in postcommunism is further complicated as writers rub salt into the wounds of history by having these already controversial recollections intersect, as we have seen, the postmemory of the "vanished" (*los desaparecidos*) of the 1970s Argentina, Nazism and its murderous history, the Armenian Genocide, the Holocaust and the 9/11 terrorist attacks, and the Yugoslav wars. This complex fictional reprocessing and reframing of the Communist experience reworks, quite typically, representations belonging to other individual or collective, subordinate or dominant, ethnic, national, or transnational memory cultures. Remarkably enough, compounding this narrative "complication" of historical truth are the renditions of these novels into other languages and the responses those translations have got in other parts of the world; whereas these books have transformed the memory regime in place in their culture of origin, those reactions have sometimes altered their original reading regime. For instance, if in Romania, the appeal of Vosganian's book has lain in the "Armenian" perspective on the Communist period, in the United States and Armenia, the novel has been promoted and received as a part of post-genocide literature. Likewise, if the Romanian reviewers have downplayed the significance of the 9/11 terrorist attacks in Manea's novel, US critics have read *The Lair* as another post-9/11 text.

The focus on Communism as a "territorialized," national and nationally approached trauma gives way, then, in the novels analyzed above to a memory spectacle that points to several directions at once, breaks through national borders, and pursues plotlines across times, spaces, and cultures. The Romanian Communist imaginary thus gets woven into the network of transnational and transcontinental configurations that Christian Moraru defines in his 2015 book *Reading for the Planet: Toward a Geomethodology* as a geocultural structure of "co-presence" in which individuals and groups partake of the same "panoptic" system, one where, along with their cultural and historical archives, they become "visible" and cognitively "available" to one another.[24] This new, panoptic dynamic, I maintain, has brought about a *geocultural kind of post-memory* in Romanian and world fiction over the last two decades. This geocultural shift has had three major consequences. First, it bears mentioning the recalibration of the *postmemory* concept itself into a new spatial and temporal paradigm that takes into account the many-layered, palimpsestic, and conflicted structure of memory in Eastern Europe, so neatly captured by writers such as Manea, Vosganian, and Gheo; not only does the memory of Communist history in postcommunism parallel, cross, and in turn is illuminated by other collective traumatic memories, but it also serves as a cultural vehicle for the surfacing and circulation of unfamiliar, *long-space* and *deep-time* memories, for transcending national and European frontiers, and for reaching back into past decades, centuries, and ages. Second, the geocultural memory-oriented literary analysis I have proposed calls for a rethinking of the earlier, nationalist and universalist model of collective remembrance, in fact, for its retooling into a new, trans- and *post*national paradigm apposite to the very spirit of the literature under scrutiny here. Third, this palimpsestic modality of conceiving of a *postcommunist post-memory* affords new critical tactics of working through the classical dyads "Nazism and Communism" and "the Holocaust and the Gulag" as well as through their respective recollection modes, all of them captive for too long to ossified, sometimes Western and sometimes specifically Eurocentric methodologies. In my view, the geocultural comparatism for which I argue here is well positioned to trace the ways post–Cold War memory cultures of Romania, Eastern Europe, and other regions of the planet have been feeding, with impressive results, into the world-system of post-memory.

Notes

1   Jan and Aleida Assmann call this superstructure "cultural memory." See Jan Assmann, *Cultural Memory and Ancient Civilization: Writing, Remembrance and Political Imagination* (Cambridge: Cambridge University Press, 2011), and Aleida Assmann, *Cultural Memory and Western Civilization: Functions, Media, Archives* (Cambridge: Cambridge University Press, 2011).

2   I borrow here a definition by Aamir R. Mufti, for whom a *theory culture* is "the habitus that regulates 'theory' as a discrete set of practices." See Aamir R. Mufti, "Global Comparativism," *Critical Inquiry*, no. 31 (Winter 2005): 475.

3   Christian Moraru argues in *Reading for the Planet: Toward a Geomethodology* that "planetarization works through ... dislocation,

reallocation, and novel aggregation—of space and its meanings on earth" ([Ann Arbor: University of Michigan Press, 2015], 94).

4   François Hartog, *Regimes of Historicity: Presentism and Experiences of Time*, trans. Saskia Brown (New York: Columbia University Press, 2017), 16.

5   Marianne Hirsch, *The Generation of Postmemory: Writing and Visual Culture after the Holocaust* (New York: Columbia University Press, 2012), 5. The first elaboration of this concept can be found in "Family Pictures: *Mauss*, Mourning, and Post-Memory," *Discourse* 15, no. 2 (Winter 1992–3): 3–29.

6   I use this term as Immanuel Wallerstein understands it in *Geopolitics and Geoculture: Essays on the Changing World-System* (Cambridge: Cambridge University Press; Paris: Maison des Sciences de l'Homme, 1991), 22, where the critic refers to the "semi-peripheric powers" of Central and Eastern Europe. The memory cultures of ex-Communist European countries could be characterized as semiperipheric in relation to the "hegemonic" memory of the Holocaust and the Gulag.

7   Ulrich Beck is one of the critics who have theorized "methodological nationalism." See, for example, "Cosmopolitan Sociology: Outline of a Paradigm Shift," in *The Ashgate Research Companion to Cosmopolitanism*, ed. Maria Rovisco and Magdalena Nowicka (Farnham, UK: Ashgate, 2011), 17–32.

8   Filip Florian, *Degete mici* (Iași, Romania: Polirom, 2005), Gabriela Adameșteanu, *Întâlnirea* (Iași, Romania: Polirom, 2003), Norman Manea, *Vizuina* (Iași, Romania: Polirom, 2009), Varujan Vosganian, *Cartea șoaptelor* (Iași, Romania: Polirom, 2009), and Radu Pavel Gheo, *Disco Titanic* (Iași, Romania: Polirom, 2016).

9   See Marcel Cornis-Pope, "Local and Global Frames in Recent Eastern European Literatures: Postcommunism, Postmodernism, and Postcoloniality," *Journal of Postcolonial Writing* 48, no. 2 (2012): 143–54. Other critics have questioned the analogy between East European postcommunism and postcolonialism. See, for instance, Andrei Terian, *Critica de export. Teorii, contexte, ideologii* (Bucharest: Muzeul Literaturii Române, 2013), 104–15.

10   Charles S. Maier, "Hot Memory … Cold Memory: On the Political Half-Life of Fascist and Communist Memory," quoted in Maria Todorova, "Introduction: Similar Trajectories, Different Memories," in *Remembering Communism: Private and Public Recollections of Lived Experience in South-East Europe*, ed. Maria Todorova, Augusta Dimou, and Stefan Troebst (Budapest: CEU Press, 2014), 3. For a critical discussion of "hierarchical" comparatism in memory studies, see Andreea Mironescu, "Analogie și diferențiere metodologică în *Memory Studies*: revizitând comparația 'West versus East,'" *Caiete critice* 11, no. 373 (2018): 37–42.

11   Svetlana Boym, *The Future of Nostalgia* (New York: Basic Books, 2001).

12   See Todorova, Dimou, and Troebst, *Remembering Communism*, 4–8.

13   Alexandru Matei, *Mormântul comunismului românesc: romantismul revoluționar înainte și după 1989* (Bucharest: IBU Publishing, 2011), 133–8.

14   Andreea Mironescu, "Konfigurationen des kulturellen Gedächtnisses im postkommunistischen rumänischen Roman," in *Kulturelles Gedächtnis–Ästhetisches Erinnern: Literatur, Film und Kunst in Rumänien*, ed. Michèle Mattusch (Berlin: Frank & Timme, 2018): 251–75.

15 Gayatri Chakravorty Spivak, "Can the Subaltern Speak?," in *Colonial Discourse and Post-Colonial Theory: A Reader*, ed. Patrick Williams and Laura Chrisman (New York: Columbia University Press, 1994), 66–111.

16 Revathi Krishnaswamy, "Toward World Literary Knowledges: Theory in the Age of Globalization," *Comparative Literature* 62, no. 4 (2010): 400, 405. Krishnaswamy does not refer here to Eastern Europe, and, in fact, she seems to leave it out of the discussion, her critique targeting the "Eurocentrism" of literary theory in general. Nonetheless, her observation is more than relevant to Eastern Europe.

17 Krishnaswamy, "Toward World Literary Knowledges," 400.

18 Krishnaswamy, "Toward World Literary Knowledges," 400.

19 Krishnaswamy, "Toward World Literary Knowledges," 400.

20 Hartog, *Regimes of Historicity,* 16.

21 Boym, *The Future of Nostalgia*, 41.

22 I use here the term proposed by Rothberg in *Multidirectional Memory* to explain "how remembrance cuts across and binds together diverse spatial, temporal, and cultural sites" ([Stanford, CA: Stanford University Press, 2009], 11).

23 See Wai Chee Dimock, *Through Other Continents: American Literature Across Deep Time* (Princeton, NJ: Princeton University Press, 2006).

24 Moraru, *Reading for the Planet*, 6. In the critic's view, the year 1989 marks the transition to a new regime of relationality worldwide.

11

BIOFICTION:
Metamorphoses of Life-Writing across Criticism, Theory, and Literature

Laura Cernat

As other chapters in this volume suggest, theory no longer is these days—if it has ever been—an analysis instrument external to literature but an integral part of the latter's dynamics. Contemporary "biofiction" is a powerful case in point.[1] Defined by Michael Lackey as "literature that names its protagonist after an actual biographical figure," this genre incorporates theoretical dilemmas, specifically those pertaining to authorship, which it flaunts alongside other representations of creative acts.[2] Staging returns and reassessments of canonical figures from the cultural past, this type of fiction, I argue, also takes over some of literary history's tasks. In so doing, biofiction participates in the "biographical turn" Dutch historians Hans Renders, Binne de Haan, and Jonne Harmsma view as a renewal of methodologies across the humanities from the "bottom-up perspective" of individual lives.[3] Encompassing literary scholarship alongside historical and sociological perspectives, this turn attests to the theoretical potential of the biographical paradigm in the reading as well as writing of literature. Revisiting notions such as "the return of the author," for instance, thus becomes essential at a time the biographical author is making a comeback as a character in so many contemporary novels.

Building on Ann Jefferson's argument that biography has been, for almost three centuries now, central to "the internal contestation through which literature is constituted as an idea," my hypothesis here is that biofiction—a form where literature and its mirroring discourse, biography, collide—plays a substantial part in literature's self-evaluation as literary history.[4] While Lucia Boldrini and Lackey have both spoken of biofiction's subversive potential in relation to ethical and political constructs, I contend that the genre also subverts established literary hierarchies, offering new possibilities of reorganizing various national and international canons.[5] Also in line with other contributions to this book, I argue for biofiction's literary-historical and overall critical and theoretical value with an eye to including in this reexamination material from a cultural space that has been seen as "peripheral." To that effect, I address, first, the gradual move of the biographical from a marginal to a key position in the transnational conceptual network in the early 1990s. At this point in my presentation, I foreground the geographical periphery's capacity of pushing back against the domination of the anti-biographical rhetoric on the rise in the West, a resistance exemplified by Cold War-era Romanian reactions to 1970s French theory. My chapter's next section draws a set of connections between international efforts to establish a terminology for "bio-literary" forms and Romanian experiments with both theories and practices of cross-genre, life-writing, and literary hybrid formations. I close with a discussion of biofiction's function in the reconfiguration of the national literary canon. To exemplify, I concentrate in this segment on contemporary writer Ion Iovan and his dialogue with a legendary and mysterious figure of Romanian modernism, Mateiu Caragiale.

The coevalness of the 1990s biofiction boom and the sudden increase of theorists' interest in biography, to begin with, appears to indicate that the academic rethinking of the biographical benefited from the literary developments of the time. In any event, this was indeed a turning point, and it was clearly marked as such in a text published in 1991, when Alain Buisine introduced the word "biofiction" at the Cerisy Colloquium in France of all places, where deconstruction's anti-"biographist" *tours de force* must have been still vivid in the participants' memory. At the gathering, Buisine announced that "the biographical is not the other of fiction anymore."[6] His choice of metaphors is, however, revealing for biography's previous— and, it seems, partly still enduring—status as external to literature and to theory no less. The French critic peppered his talk with references to the "pullulating" movement, "cancerous proliferation," and set of "metastases of the biographical" presumably infiltrating the human sciences.[7] In a move characteristic of his cautious approach to the subject, Buisine attributed biography's "flourishing" to a foreign influence (a "trend ... from the Anglo-Saxon world") and, on a self-incriminating tone, found his own pro-biography position guilty of "the worst of critical treasons."[8]

If, suspicious intruder and deadly tumor as it may be, the biographical was there to stay, then Buisine at least hoped people would agree that its revival, *after* poststructuralism, could not mean just a return to Charles Augustin Sainte-Beuve's "biographism": once upon a time—Sainte-Beuve's—criticism turned to an author's life to explain his or her work; in the post-1990 era, biography becomes, instead, a central element of literature's plays with identity. This was a revolutionary realization, and it pertained to the new uses of both literature and biography as epistemological tools. No longer the reflection of the general, as in Aristotle, fiction teases out the narrative potential of the particular. Such a change is all the more significant since deconstruction was not, as Buisine implied, the only theoretical orientation to dismiss the interpretive relevance of the biographical. Supported by book-length studies such as Seán Burke's 1992 *The Death and Return of the Author*[9] and Dominique Maingueneau's 2006 *Contre Saint Proust*, the thesis that biography had been routinely excluded from, or repressed in, some of criticism's and theory's foundational texts sheds, in hindsight, a different light on Buisine's "heretical" welcoming back of the biographical.[10] The French critic did more than just challenge poststructuralists to rethink authorhood and the role of biography in it, thus driving deconstructive theory and practice to their limits. His intervention was also part and parcel of a wider, self-reflexive shift in theory, which had set itself up from the outset as that kind of cognitive enterprise that, in pursuit of typical and recurring organizing criteria for its more abstract and conceptual models, filters out "accidental" and empirically variable elements such as biographical incidents.

The Author's Many Returns: Biography and Theory at the European Periphery

A substantial body of work published by Romanian critics in the 1970s and 1980s seems to suggest, however, that this shift had been underway well before poststructuralism ran out of steam. Traveling to Western Europe during the ideological breather that followed Socialist Realism, Romanian scholars such as Adrian Marino, Eugen Simion, and Mircea Martin found in the French theory of the time reasons to take another look at how literary criticism had dealt with biography. Typical of their broader engagement with the West were their discriminating reactions to "thematic criticism" and poststructuralism, whose innovative and sometimes radical tenets they weighed over and against theoretical developments of broader intellectual and historical scope.[11] Thus, in response and as a strategic corrective to the new and provocative arguments French theorists were making on the critical dynamic of an author's life and work, Martin and his colleagues went back to Sainte-Beuve, in whose texts they found more than the cliché of biographism. Tellingly, the opening salvo of Martin's 1974 *Critică și profunzime* (Criticism and Depth, reissued in 2004 and 2017 as *Geometrie și finețe* [Geometry and Finesse]), an essay on the Geneva school critics, is a reevaluation of Sainte-Beuve and Ferdinand Brunetière as possible precursors of two strands in thematic criticism, directions named after Blaise Pascal's distinction between *esprit de finesse* and *esprit de géometrie*.[12] In his portrayal of Sainte-Beuve, Martin paints the image of an author who, contrary to the stereotype launched by Marcel Proust in the unfinished and posthumously published *Contre Sainte-Beuve* (1954), did not try to "explain the artist through the man" but rather "the man through the artist."[13] Biography and history, Martin contends, "enliven the commentary of a work," serving the purpose of differentiation and not that of reduction.[14] Unsatisfied with "a method that works on its own,"[15] Sainte-Beuve finetuned his critical intuition, we are told, to the work or writer at hand. Despite his notorious errors of judgment, this flexibility, thinks Martin, redeems his biographical criticism and, what is more, offers it as a possible model of close reading, which, as we know, casts aside the author's intention.[16] This "spirit-of-refinement"-driven, patient rereading of the nineteenth-century author sets the tone for a reevaluation of the biographical *as a theoretical* and, we shall see, *literary-historical tool*. With the latter as a guiding thread, Martin sees continuities and larger trends where others noticed a range of different "methods" and so opens a new chapter in the Romanian reception of international ideas, replacing the previous period's eclecticism with a more systematic processing of cultural developments.[17]

A similar exercise in critical revisionism marks Eugen Simion's reading of Roland Barthes, whose seminar he attended in 1972. Surprised at first by what seemed more like an occult *séance* than literary analysis, the Romanian scholar was nonetheless impressed by Barthes's way of challenging his own method.[18] Simion regarded Barthes both with fascination and suspicion, and these mixed reactions would eventually steer him toward the biographical as a literary category.[19] Published in 1981, his first book on the topic, *Întoarcerea autorului* (The Return of the Author), is, from its opening section—titled "Contre Sainte-Proust"—a text teeming with remarkable if indirect anticipations of later, better known claims and books on the subject. The affinities and argument overlaps with Seán Burke's *The Death and Return of the Author* and with Dominique Maingueneau's *Contre Saint Proust* go beyond the phrasing coincidences in the titles, bespeaking the Bucharest critic's ability to foresee, if you will, the impending comeback of a key literary-historical and methodological issue. Translated into English and French no earlier than 1996, Simion's book remained unknown to international audiences until recently. And yet, as I have said, the coincidences are notable.[20]

Without aiming at a full rehabilitation of biographical criticism, *The Return of the Author* rejects the exclusion of the biographical from theoretical projects. Interestingly, the rebuttal resorts to the same instruments employed to discredit considerations orbiting around authors' lives. Simion starts out with Proust's refutation of Sainte-Beuve, shedding light on the novelist's biographical (even "Sainte-Beuvian"!)[21] bias, which makes, according to Simion, the nineteenth-century critic into a "complex" of Proustian imagination[22] or "character" demonized in an attempt to safeguard "the profound self"[23] from intruders.[24] The Proustian impulse to protect interiority—which, paradoxically, asserts authorial identity rather than denying it—is also pinpointed by Maingueneau, who links it to Proust's systematic privileging of "conversation" over "style," which demarcates "high literature" from other forms of human expression.[25] Though they converge in their explanations of Proust's self-contradiction as determined by the "menacing figure" Sainte-Beuve cut for the novelist, as well as in noticing the same link between Contre Sainte-Beuve and the subsequent developments of the Nouvelle critique, Simion and Maingueneau nevertheless illustrate different critical paradigms.[26] The former speaks in the name of a quasi-obsolete idea of "oeuvre as totalizing universe," while the latter proposes to move away from it, and from "Literature" with capital "L" overall, toward discourse.[27]

A comparison between Simion's and Burke's analyses of Barthes shows similar analogies and compatibilities of insight. For instance, both note that the "disappearance" and the "return" of the author occurred simultaneously rather than sequentially;[28] both build arguments for a renegotiation of the biographical in Barthes, and they do so around the same central concepts and passages (the "amicable return of the author," the "biographeme,"[29] Barthes's contention that "as institution, the author is dead ... but in the text ... I desire the author,"[30] and the like); both are for a reduction of the apparent multiplicity of subjects in Roland Barthes by Roland Barthes to a common denominator;[31] and perhaps most importantly, both envisage a surprising recuperation of the notion of "oeuvre" within the Barthesian textual corpus itself. According to Burke, Barthes's theory of logothetes reverts the "text" back into "oeuvre";[32] in a similar vein, Simion sees in Barthes's writing proof that "man does not totally fall prey to the Text."[33] However, Simion stays loyal to an oeuvre concept full of residual echoes of Gustave Lanson's traditional view of literature as life's mirror, and so the Romanian critic's sometimes touted "anticipations" of later resurgences of "authorialism" could be regarded as accidents of literary history. Noteworthy is, nonetheless, The Return of the Author's "anachronism" in the sense Andrei Terian gives to the term, namely, that of counter-chronism, of being both ahead of and against its own time at once conceptually and politically.[34] Simion situates the "death of the author" over and against the backdrop of May 1968 in Timpul trăirii, timpul mărturisirii (Time of Living, Time of Confession) and sees it, in The Return of the Author, as part of a broader trend, which makes his early work valuable in the same sense that

Martin's is, viz., that of putting things in perspective and detecting deeper filiations and ampler ramifications.[35]

These realizations as well as the cultural and political awareness stemming from them derive from Simion's acquaintance with other biographical models in French literature and criticism, and yet there is another factor to consider. Forced, again and again, to paraphrase, explicate, exemplify, and otherwise *contextualize* the "death of the author" idea because he could not quote from Barthes's essay directly due to Communist censorship constraints, Simion learned to see the life-work nexus through a kaleidoscope of angles, and this challenge enriched his approach, made it more flexible, and imparted it a healthy relativism.[36] Thus, the basic thesis of *The Return of the Author* is not the primacy of the biographical per se but theory's changing effectiveness over time. "It is not the method that leads to failure," Simion believes, "but the dogmatic persistence in method. Not the angle of History (biography) is erroneous but clinging to this perspective at all costs."[37] Therefore, while Proust was not wrong to reject the exaggerations of biographism, his followers were, as they treated his distinction between the "profound" and the social self as a theoretical dogma.

With Marino, however, dogmatism became a driver of the critic's work, specifically of his efforts to systematize an ambitious, quasi-encyclopedic panoply of literary-historical notions. A "spirit of geometry" to an extreme, Marino traced out in his six-volume *Biografia ideii de literatură* (Biography of the Idea of Literature, 2000) the evolution of literary attitudes and genres in the West from antiquity to the twentieth century. The book's excessive ambition, its organicist understanding of biographical metaphors,[38] and its reductive conclusions make it outdated, the phenomenal mass of information it accumulates notwithstanding.[39] Plagued by a tendency of reducing contemporary innovations to rehearsals of old breakthroughs, the last volume of the series blatantly misreads poststructuralism.[40] Worth retaining, though, is the recurrence across all volumes of "anti-literature," a concept that builds up toward Ann Jefferson's notion that being "against itself" is literature's very engine, even though Jefferson, whose focus is modernity, does not retrieve this feature of literary discourse from the archives of the premodern times discussed by Marino in his *Biography*'s first volume (nor did she have access to the untranslated material that followed).[41] Admittedly, Marino's impasse is indicative of an aesthetic conservatism and of an overambitious inquiry scope, one of which, I might add, some of his Romanian colleagues were guilty too. On the positive side, these and other Romanian scholars who witnessed and reacted to the post-1968 French theoretical scene also had an impressive capability of understanding its spectacle from standpoints informed by longer and larger intellectual histories. Anachronisms, "counter-chronisms," and reductionisms aside, their reactions and intuitions ushered in, after the overexcitement of the mid-1960s ideological thaw, a time of reflection on the historical dimension of theory. This led eventually to an entire school of literary theory that had a solid grasp of the deep-seated ties between the discipline, on one hand, and history and biography, on the other, and yielded works that speak pointedly to an awareness of "the embeddedness of theory in history"[42] and, conversely, to the presence of the "body in theory."[43]

"The Author, a Character": Critifiction, Mistifiction, Autofiction

In Simion's two-volume 2002 monograph *Genurile biograficului* (The Genres of the Biographical), genre amalgamation is at work although the concept as such is not spelled out. Mindful of the intermingling of biography, autobiography, and the novel, the critic views these literary categories as parts of a continuum, acknowledging the interdisciplinarity and even the "bricolage" involved in biographical scholarship.[44] Oddly enough, he does not attend precisely to those categories that exhibit heterogenous qualities proper, to wit, the emerging notions and practices of "autofiction" and "biofiction." If this remained a task for later theorists, that was, one could surmise, because the existence of such literary forms was not, at the time, a matter of scholarly consensus yet. The profusion of "hybrid" bio-literary genres in the literature of the 1980s, 1990s, and 2000s was quite remarkable, but so was the diversity of the responses with which this corpus has been met by critics and theorists, who have spoken of "auto-bio-graphy" (Brian McHale,[45] and, in French scholarship, Georges Gusdorf[46]), "biographic metafiction" (Linda Hutcheon),[47] "fictional biography" (Ina Schabert),[48] "the apocryphal memoir" (Christian Moraru),[49] "author fictions" (Laura Savu),[50] "literary biomythography" (Michael Benton),[51] and "heterobiography" (Lucia Boldrini),[52] to list only a few of the idiosyncratic designations whose composite makeup is no less striking than what they purport to stand for.[53]

Some of these concoctions have been pressed into service to describe works from both the biofictional and autofictional families of literary forms. The absence of a commonly accepted term testifies to the richness of bio-literary alloys. Most typical at first primarily of postmodern experimentalism, intercross genres of this sort later formed a separate strand of contemporary literature and evolved on their own track, refashioning and eventually outgrowing postmodernism.[54] They include even biofiction pastiches such as A. S. Byatt's 1990 novel *Possession*, as well as mixes of autofiction and biofiction that follow in the line of the modernist tradition of experimental self-writing analyzed by Max Saunders in his book on "auto/biografiction."[55] To these notions, we might add "surfiction" and "critifiction," both proposed by Raymond Federman as an alternative to the much-vaunted "death of fiction."[56] The first of these coinages has as its premise a realization that might sound oddly familiar to readers of Buisine, namely, that "life and fiction are no longer distinguishable one from the other."[57] "Redoubling upon itself" to reflect "the life of fiction," surfiction recapitulates literary evolutions.[58] As for critifiction, the manifesto in which Federman made the case for it was also a plea for "pla[y]giarism."[59] Taking the poststructuralist emphasis on the author's indebtedness to language to its farthest consequences, critifiction made an impact at least as strong as surfiction's, as it traveled halfway across the world to find a creative echo in Romania. Acknowledging Federman's term, poet and critic Simona Popescu introduces her account of Romanian Surrealist poet Gellu Naum's works by pointing out that "this is a 'borderline' text: neither literary criticism *per se* nor 'reconstruction.' ... A 'critifiction'—one of the few ways of talking adequately about someone who declared that his poetry is a *way of life*."[60] Weaving text quotes and memories of conversations into a narrative of literary apprenticeship, Popescu's critifiction has a strong confessional tone to it, and this sets it apart from Federman's notion. Written after Naum's death, Popescu's volume expands on the paradoxes of memory announced in a motto from the poet: "Only starting from the end can one understand / the nostalgic mechanics of events, the fury of the layers / that forego or follow us."[61] The focus on this "nostalgic mechanics" attests to a larger development in the literature of Popescu's generation, arguably the first of the postcommunist era to have both sufficient access to the past and enough detachment from it. With Popescu and others like her, writing was finally able to become "memorious" (to borrow Moraru's concept), building on accomplishments such as Mircea Cărtărescu's 1990 postmodern epic poem *Levantul (The Levant)*, which had offered a Joycean, synthetic pastiche of previous literary ages.[62] The writers coming to the fore in the 1990s were able to redefine Romanian literature and culture's characteristic nostalgia not only stylistically, as Cărtărescu had done, but also politically, overcoming their predecessors' longing for the pre-World War II years and retrieving a plurality of pre-Communist and anti-Communist sociocultural models.

If there is an opposite to the "poetry as a way of life" concept inside the critifiction spectrum and even outside it, that is a literary formation that foregrounds the intersection, in the fictional act, of the imaginary and the false. This form goes by the name of "mistifiction." Coined independently by Mircea Anghelescu, a Romanian nineteenth-century specialist of Martin's generation, and Moraru, mistifiction is, for the most part, according to Anghelescu, quasi synonymous to literary forgery but covers more than this phenomenon. Comprising forged historical chronicles, apocryphal texts, pseudonyms, pseudo-translations, and even literary "libel," mistifiction is "fiction to the power of two," "fiction that mystifies its own identity."[63] Moraru employs the same term to talk about the "representational hybrid" that results from the "cultural and historical ramifications of narrative remake" and spans deliberate mistranslations, puns, scholarly allusions, and displays of "fake philological virtuosity" in ways that bear witness to intercultural dynamics.[64] Revealing the closeness if not kinship between literature and lying, fraud, and hoaxes, mistification brings into play, sometimes with spectacular effects, elements usually relegated to the "margins" of literature if not to its "non-literary" outside, such as authors' lives. Much like critifiction, mistifiction has been theorized within a framework informed by broader, international explorations of genre compounds as well as by changes in various local literary landscapes, where bio-literary innovations have increased exponentially over the past decades. Starting in the late 1970s, experimental writing has been mixing, for example, postmodern metalepsis and autofictional sincerity pacts. Analyzing this development in her doctoral thesis, *Autorul, un personaj* (The Author, a Character), which came out as a book in 2015, Popescu takes the author's "return" to the text as a sophisticated reaction to technological headways that illustrates John Naisbitt's *high touch* notion.[65] In her view, this "resubjectivization" and "biographization"[66] wave diverges from comparable aspects of modernist aesthetics in that, generally speaking, modernist authors kept their distance from their narrators, whereas postmodernists "pretend (or pretend they pretend) to be themselves in a fictional work."[67] Popescu deems the involvement of authors' "partial identities" in prose fiction by Mircea Horia Simionescu, Radu Petrescu, Gheorghe Ene, Gheorghe Crăciun, Livius Ciocârlie, and Cărtărescu a radically new form of authenticity that becomes an outlet for a text-centered sincerity through which the author's narrative persona and the actual writer's biographical identity constantly merge, swap places, and mirror each other.[68]

While Popescu considers the 1980s a decade of Romanian "resynchronization" with Western literature,[69] for a younger Romanian critic like Florina Pîrjol, the "ambivalent auctorial fiction"[70] of writers such as Petrescu, Simionescu, Coșașu, and Ciorcârlie is no more than an outlier on the ideologically controlled literary scene of Communism's last years.[71] Genuine autofiction, in Pîrjol's interpretation, gets underway with Cărtărescu's prose and with Popescu's own 1997 *Exuvii* (Exuviae) and consolidates with the next generation of authors, the "millennials." These two ways of understanding autofiction could not be more different in their aspirations, however. Where Popescu and Cărtărescu write "introvert (symbolic) autofictions" that "subordinate the epic ... to an obsessive autoscopy," the millennials' "extrovert (referential) autofictions" are "louder—transitive, direct, violent," leveraging the rhetorical wherewithal of a true political manifesto.[72] Impacted by the swift transition from an all-but-closed, ideologically controlled cultural market, to an open, more flexible system governed by commercial factors, millennial self-writing becomes at once aesthetically "diluted" and canonically irreverent.[73] Operating as they are in this new, iconoclastic regime, the young Romanian writers of the twenty-first century belong to a novel literary paradigm, one that marks the author's "friendly return" into their texts.[74] More than ever before, *auctor redivivus* has, in these works, a theoretical and literary-historical component, keyed as it proves to be repeatedly to the problematics of status and canonicity. At the crossroads of the postmodern "memorious" recovery of tradition and the slick, raw life-oriented identity games of millennial literature, recent biofiction thus recalibrates canonical reputations by bringing classical authors before contemporary audiences.

Biofiction and the Renegotiation of the Canon: Mateiu Caragiale

Ion Iovan's bold reanimation of late-modernist Romanian dandy and novelist Mateiu Caragiale (1885–1936) is a perfect instantiation of this kind of multivalent undertaking. In 2001, the journal *Observator cultural* took a poll among critics, who were asked to name the best Romanian novels of the twentieth century.[75] To the surprise of most, Caragiale's 1929 masterpiece *Craii de Curtea-Veche*, translated into English in 2013 as *Gallants of the Old Court*, came out on top. At that point, there was still no biography of this author, and material documenting his life was scattered, although scholarly editions of his works included biographical information, and Caragiale aficionados knew a lot about him. Central among the features that make Caragiale a memorable if odd figure among Romanian writers is his longing for a personal past of imaginary magnificence, a yearning driven to absurdity in some of his bizarre acts—he "mistifictionally" invented a noble ancestry for himself, and obsessively pursued honorary medals; he even designed his own coat of arms and flag.[76] In life as in literature, it is not simply the olden times that he was so much taken with, but their image and reflections in various media. For instance, the protagonist of his first short story, "Remember" (1914), is envied not for his own beauty but for "his likeness with one of those figures long departed in the scattering of ages."[77] With typically decadent passion,[78] the writer traces the declining destinies of nobility, a dying breed embodied by his hero, in whom he sees the workings of "that seed of uncannily morbid intelligence" that reaches "the peak of sterile brilliance in this last descendant."[79] The past is loved, then, not because this is where such relics can be retrieved from, but despite the impossibility of recovering and preserving them at all. One of the most splendid passages in *Gallants of the Old Court* imagines the protagonists performing "a silent service of the Vespers into the beyond," as the main heroes "melted into the twilight of the setting sun."[80] As Barbu Cioculescu has commented, what is at stake in the funereal atmosphere of this prose is not only death as such but also "the death of time," the lack of investment in the future.[81]

This annihilation of time is not the bittersweet *far niente* of *fin de siècle* decadence but becomes, in a sense, its opposite by spurring creativity and true artistry as the writer shrouds this timeless universe narratively in a carefully protected secrecy that renders this world inaccessible or, better yet, accessible the way art objects are. Caragiale achieves this aesthetic effect through an absence of denouement, which enhances the text's mysterious aura. "Remember" also ends with the narrator's refusal to learn, and subsequently disclose to the reader, the details behind the protagonist's murder. As the wax seal with the word "Remember" on it melts away in a fire, and the only letter from the mysterious hero is destroyed, the narrator wonders if the very existence of his character, let alone the story about him, will seem believable one day. Along the same lines, in *Gallants of the Old Court,* Pașadia's unpublished works, which contain "pages that easily matched the brilliance of ... Tacitus," are destined to be destroyed by "a faithful hand."[82] Deliberately, readers are left in the dark as to the stories' actual, presumably dreadful content, and the tactical withholding of this kind of information tears up the story's own mimetic fabric by simultaneously unfolding a fictional world and presenting it as an impenetrable domain.

To contemporary audiences, this episode is all the more significant as Caragiale's own diaries, donated after his death to the Carol I Literary Foundation, disappeared from the archives during the attempted fascist coup of 1941. The originals have not been found to this day, and the handwritten copies Caragiale scholars had already made are incomplete. Exploiting, as Caragiale himself did, these lacunae and lack of information, as well as the mystery surrounding them,[83] Iovan set out to arrange the author's biography into a coherent chronology in his 2002 book *Mateiu Caragiale. Portretul unui dandy român* (Mateiu Caragiale: Portrait of a Romanian Dandy). For a dandy, Iovan's argument goes, the most important creation is one's own being, including one's external appearance. To bring to life the writer's self-fashioning ambitions and the mannerisms associated with them, Iovan's book assembles quotes and recollections from family, acquaintances, and Caragiale critics into a "documentary fiction."[84] Some episodes, such as the enigmatic author's purchase of a hat tried on by the Prince of Wales, even capture the fetishism of Caragiale's intriguingly anachronistic demeanor.[85]

The 2008 *Ultimele însemnări ale lui Mateiu Caragiale* (The Last Diary Notes of Mateiu Caragiale), Iovan's second book about the great writer, pushes further into the realm of biofiction. Upping the ante, Iovan here ventures into imagining the last year in the life of the self-styled "Count," now a landowner. The fixation on blue-blood genealogies is still front and center, but the narrative also pursues a track reminiscent of Caragiale's own fascination with twilights and belatedness. The protagonist turns the one-year diary into a sort of encyclopedia of his entire biography as he reflects back on his life. But, at Iovan's hands, this fictional life-writing enterprise also becomes a narrative preamble of the character's not-too-remote death, a death-writing prelude or "thanatography" in the tradition of Jose Saramago's *The Year of the Death of Ricardo Reis* and Peter Ackroyd's *The Last Testament of Oscar Wilde*. Furthermore, also thanks to a few editorial artifices, Iovan's book toys with the delightful forgeries of mistifiction. The similitude in form and content to available texts and archival material renders the pseudo-diary verisimilar to anyone but Caragiale specialists—to be sure, a truly expert and discerning eye is required to spot Caragiale's own dramatis personae metaleptically transposed into the real world as his acquaintances.[86]

A critic such as Lackey would insist that the main goal of biofiction is not to reconstruct the past accurately but to "invent stories that never occurred in order to answer perplexing questions, fill in cultural lacunae, signify human interiors, or picture cultural ideologies."[87] Iovan masterfully achieves these objectives by inserting into the otherwise credible reconstitution of Caragiale's diary an imaginary love affair between the aging author of *Gallants of the Old Court* and young Emma, a secretary of the Carol I Foundation. Iovan's master touch comes at the end, in an addendum consisting of "letters" supposedly written after the protagonist's death. This correspondence follows Emma and her son, a fictitious illegitimate child of Caragiale, from their flight from the country to the end of the twentieth century, when the heir comes back, seemingly, to return his biological father's manuscripts to the Society of Romanian Writers. Further enhancing the secrecy content of *Ultimele însemnări ale lui Mateiu Caragiale*, this episode mirrors Caragiale's own main narrative device. The hypothesis of the papers being stolen and thus secured by Emma herself is entertained just long enough to goad the reader's imagination. In the last fictive letter, the son, Jean-Mathieu, tells the author of the book, Iovan, who, with another metalepsis, brings himself into the storyworld, that the manuscripts have actually been burned.[88] Conversely, like Pașadia's papers in *Gallants of the Old Court*, Caragiale's personal notes are accessible obliquely, as it were, in Iovan's fictional representation. Their factuality is, one can say, fictional. It bears mentioning, in this light, that following Anna Banti, Boldrini breaks facts down into three classes: "actual facts," "invented facts," and "presumed facts," the latter entailing "an acknowledgement ... of the necessity of responsibility and commitment *as a literary writer*" and an awareness that "the experience of the real, historical loss and destruction cannot be evaded."[89] Fiction's role becomes essential in bringing into being "putative" realities where documented or documentable history lacks answers or sources due to deliberate or accidental suppression of "evidence." By working the Emma chapter into a plausible real-life scenario, Iovan creates such realities or facts, filling in a gap that literary history has been trying to work through.

I find it also significant that Iovan's biofictional revival project—expanded by the publication of his 2015 book *MJC: A World for Mateiu*, a revision and combination of the two previous books—comes at a time of scholarly rediscovery of the writer's value,[90] and it can be argued, as I do here, that it has been a driving force behind the rising appreciation of Caragiale, speaking once more to biofiction's critical-theoretical appetite, in particular to its capacity to join literary history and criticism in their pursuits.[91] In fictional guise, the old-fashioned faux artistocrat and past-obsessed dandy becomes, for the first time, a writer *for the future.* By the same token, Iovan's narrative reconstruction of Caragiale's work and authorial persona attests and, notably, contributes to their spectacular move up the ranks of the canon of Romanian literature, suggesting that fluctuations in symbolic capital also hinge on literature's production and, as one can see, on literature's *re*production as well.

Notes

1   I am grateful to the Research Foundation-Flanders (FWO) for its generous support of my contemporary biofiction research project, of which this chapter is a part. Special thanks to Christian Moraru and Ortwin de Graef for their attentive readings and suggestions, and to Ioana Both, Oana Fotache, Ştefan Firică, and Petru Cernat for providing scans of materials inaccessible in Belgium.
2   Michael Lackey, *Biofictional Histories, Mutations, and Forms* (London: Routledge, 2017), 1.
3   Hans Renders, Binne De Haan, and Jonne Harmsma, "The Biographical Turn: Biography as a Critical Method in the Humanities and in Society," in *The Biographical Turn: Lives in History*, ed. Hans Renders, Binne De Haan, and Jonne Harmsma (London: Routledge, 2017), 4.
4   Ann Jefferson, *Biography and the Question of Literature in France* (Oxford: Oxford University Press, 2007), 15.
5   Lucia Boldrini, *Autobiographies of Others: Historical Subject and Literary Fiction* (New York: Routledge, 2012), 6, 178, 181; Michael Lackey, *The American Biographical Novel* (New York: Bloomsbury, 2016), 168.
6   Alain Buisine, "Biofictions," *Revue des Sciences Humaines* 224, no. 4 (1991): 10.
7   Buisine, "Biofictions," 8.
8   Ibid. 9.
9   Seán Burke, *Death and Return of the Author: Criticism and Subjectivity in Barthes, Foucault, and Derrida* (Edinburgh: Edinburgh University Press, 1998), 26.
10 Dominique Maingueneau, *Contre Saint Proust ou la fin de la Littérature* (Paris: Belin, 2006), 27.
11 See Adrian Marino, *Carnete europene* (Cluj-Napoca, Romania: Dacia, 1976), 93, 96–8, 101, 110–12; Eugen Simion, *Timpul trăirii, timpul mărturisirii* (Bucharest: Univers Enciclopedic Gold, 2013), 35, 39–40, 233.
12 Mircea Martin, *Geometrie şi fineţe* (Bucharest: Tracus Arte, 2017), 7.
13 Martin, *Geometrie şi fineţe*, 30.

14 Ibid., 36.
15 Ibid., 37.
16 Ibid., 41.
17 See Alex Goldiş, *Critica în tranșee* (Iași, Romania: Polirom, 2011), 227–8, 368–9.
18 Simion, *Timpul trăirii, timpul mărturisirii*, 204.
19 Simion, *Timpul trăirii, timpul mărturisirii*, 203; see also Eugen Simion, *Întoarcerea autorului* (Bucharest: Univers Enciclopedic Gold, 2013), 96, 104, 363.
20 I have discussed this issue with Dominique Maingueneau during an informal meeting in September 2018, at the Leuven Faculty of Arts. Though he was surprised to hear about the coincidence, Maingueneau acknowledged the interesting consequences of the Proust argument overlap. It can be safely assumed that the 1996 French translation of Simion's book had a limited echo, which did not reach Maingueneau. For a contrary opinion, which insinuates an indebtedness to the Romanian author, see Raluca Dună's article "Cine este autorul întoarcerii autorului?" (Who Is the Author of *The Return of the Author?*), *Romania Literară*, no. 31 (2013), http://arhiva.romlit.ro/index.pl/cine_este_autorul_ntoarcerii_autorului (accessed April 27, 2019).
21 Simion, *Întoarcerea autorului*, 18, 22, 44–5.
22 Simion, *Întoarcerea autorului*, 23.
23 On the original Proustian distinction between the "profound self" and the "social self," see Marcel Proust, *Contre Sainte Beuve. Précédé de Pastiches et mélanges et suivi de Essais et articles*, ed Pierre Clarac and Yves Sandre (Paris: Gallimard, 1971), 221–5.
24 Simion, *Întoarcerea autorului*, 37.
25 Maingueneau, *Contre Saint Proust*, 22.
26 Simion, *Întoarcerea autorului*, 37; Maingueneau, *Contre Saint Proust*, 19.
27 Simion, *Întoarcerea autorului*, 89.
28 Burke, *The Death and Return of the Author*, 33, 40; Simion, *Întoarcerea autorului*, 104, 107.
29 Burke, *The Death and Return of the Author*, 30–40; Simion, *Întoarcerea autorului*, 96, 102–3.
30 Burke, *The Death and Return of the Author*, 29; Simion, *Întoarcerea autorului*, 102, 104.
31 Burke, *The Death and Return of the Author*, 54; Simion, *Întoarcerea autorului*, 112–13.
32 Burke, *The Death and Return of the Author*, 35.
33 Simion, *Întoarcerea autorului*, 114.
34 Andrei Terian, "[Preface] O carte anacronică în trei dialoguri," in Eugen Simion, *Întoarcerea autorului* (Bucharest: Univers Enciclopedic Gold, 2013), 496.
35 Simion, *Timpul trăirii, timpul mărturisirii*, 153–64.
36 Terian, "[Preface] O carte anacronică în trei dialoguri," 490.
37 Simion, *Întoarcerea autorului*, 29.
38 Adrian Marino, *The Biography of the Idea of Literature from Antiquity to the Baroque* (Albany: State University of New York Press, 1996), xiii, xiv.

39 Marino, *The Biography of the Idea of Literature from Antiquity to the Baroque*, 200.

40 See Adrian Marino, *Biografia ideii de literatură*, vol. 6 (Cluj-Napoca, Romania: Dacia, 2000).

41 Jefferson, *Biography and the Question of Literature in France*, 13–14.

42 See Carmen Muşat, "Bakhtin's Concept of 'Chronotope' and Theory's 'Embeddedness' in History," *Euresis*, nos. 1–4 (2013): 97–102.

43 Ioana Both, "Le corps de la théorie, le corps dans la théorie—Figurations du sujet interprétant dans les écrits de Jean Starobinski," *Ekphrasis: Images, Cinema, Theory, Media*, no. 1 (2015): 188–98; see also Ioana Both, "Présences du sujet interprétant: qui dit 'je'?," *Euresis*, nos. 1–4 (2011): 162–72.

44 Eugen Simion, *Genurile biograficului*, vol. 1 (Bucharest: Fundaţia Naţională pentru Ştiinţă şi Artă, 2008), 187–207.

45 Brian McHale, *Postmodernist Fiction* (London: Routledge, 2003), 202–6.

46 See Georges Gusdorf, *Auto-bio-graphie*, vol. 2, *Lignes de vie* (Paris: Odille Jacob, 1991).

47 Linda Hutcheon, *A Poetics of Postmodernism* (London: Routledge, 1988), 16.

48 Ina Schabert, "Fictional Biography, Factual Biography, and Their Contaminations," *Biography 5*, no. 1 (Winter 1982): 1–16.

49 Christian Moraru, *Memorious Discourse* (Madison, NJ: Fairleigh Dickinson University Press, 2005), 29.

50 Laura Savu, *Postmortem Postmodernists: The Afterlife of the Author in Recent Narrative* (Madison, NJ: Fairleigh Dickinson University Press, 2009), 21.

51 Michael Benton, *Literary Biography: An Introduction* (Malden, MA: Wiley-Blackwell, 2009), 47–65.

52 Boldrini, *Autobiographies of Others*, 2, 9–10, 17.

53 For an alternative list, see Lucia Boldrini and Julia Novak, eds., *Experiments in Life-Writing* (London: Palgrave Macmillan, 2017), 2.

54 See, for an argument on biofiction's evolution beyond postmodernism, Michael Lackey, *Conversations with Biographical Novelists: Truthful Fictions across the Globe* (New York: Bloomsbury, 2019), 16–18.

55 Max Saunders, *Self-Impression: Life-Writing, Autobiografiction, and the Forms of Modern Literature* (Oxford: Oxford University Press, 2010), 7–9; 212–32.

56 Raymond Federman, *Critifiction: Postmodern Essays* (Albany: State University of New York Press, 1993), 35–6.

57 Federman, *Critifiction*, 42.

58 Federman, *Critifiction*, 43.

59 Federman, *Critifiction*, 51–2.

60 Simona Popescu, *Clava: Critificţiune cu Gellu Naum* (Piteşti, Romania: Paralela 45, 2004), 6.

61 My translation of the Romanian original poem by Gellu Naum quoted by Popescu in *Clava*, 21.

62 Moraru, *Memorious Discourse*, 21–4.

63 Mircea Anghelescu, *Mistificţiuni. Falsuri, farse, apocrife, pastişe, pseudonime şi alte mistificaţii în literatură* [Mistifictions: Forgeries, Hoaxes, Apocrypha, Pastiches, Pseudonyms, and Other Mystifications in Literature] (Bucharest: Compania, 2008), 16.

64 Christian Moraru, "Mistifiction: Mistranslation, Mistification, and Metafiction in the Age of Global Transactions," *Studii de literatură și lingvistică* (2012): 170–86.

65 See John Naisbitt's *Megatrends,* cited in Simona Popescu, *Autorul, un personaj* (Pitești, Romania: Paralela 45, 2015), 8.

66 Popescu, *Autorul, un personaj,* 109.

67 Popescu, *Autorul, un personaj,* 73.

68 Popescu, *Autorul, un personaj,* 93.

69 Popescu, *Autorul, un personaj,* 106–8.

70 Florina Pîrjol, *Carte de identități* [Book of Identities] (Bucharest: Cartea Românească, 2014), 85.

71 Pîrjol, *Carte de identități,* 72–3.

72 Pîrjol, *Carte de identități,* 120.

73 Pîrjol, *Carte de identități,* 148.

74 See Jerôme Meizoz, *Postures Littéraires. Mises en scène modernes de l'auteur* (Geneva: Slatkine Érudition, 2007), 11.

75 "Romanul românesc al secolului XX," *Observator cultural,* nos. 45–6 (2001), https://www.observatorcultural.ro/articol/romanul-romanesc-al-secolului-xx/(accessed April 2, 2019).

76 The connection between Anghelescu's "mistifiction" concept and Mateiu Caragiale's invented genealogy was first suggested by Paul Cernat, in *Modernismul retro în romanul interbelic românesc* (Bucharest: Art, 2009), 72.

77 Mateiu I. Caragiale, *Opere,* ed. with intro. study Barbu Cioculescu, pref. Eugen Simion (Bucharest: Editura Fundației Naționale pentru Știință și artă, 2018), 50.

78 See Angelo Mitchievici, *Mateiu I. Caragiale. Fizionomii decandente* (Bucharest: Editura Institutului Cultural Român, 2007), for an analysis of Mateiu Caragiale's "decadent" sensibility.

79 Mateiu I. Caragiale, *Gallants of the Old Court,* trans. Cristian Baciu (Bucharest: eLiteratura, 2013), 52.

80 Caragiale, *Gallants of the Old Court,* 165–6.

81 Barbu Cioculescu, "Studiu introductiv," in Mateiu I. Caragiale, *Opere,* ed. with intro. study Barbu Cioculescu, pref. Eugen Simion (Bucharest: Editura Fundației Naționale pentru Știință și artă, 2018), xlvi.

82 Caragiale, *Gallants of the Old Court,* 115.

83 See Iovan's discussion of the fate of Mateiu Caragiale's papers in Ion Iovan, *Mateiu Caragiale. Portretul unui dandy român* (Bucharest: Compania, 2002), 8–17.

84 Paul Cernat, "Spre Ion Iovan, prin Mateiu Caragiale," *Observator cultural,* no. 153 (2003), https://www.observatorcultural.ro/articol/spre-ion-iovan-prin-mateiu-caragiale/(accessed April 4, 2019).

85 Iovan, *Mateiu Caragiale,* 57.

86 See Ion Iovan, *Ultimele însemnări ale lui Mateiu Caragiale, însoțite de un inedit epistolar, precum și indexul ființelor, lucrurilor și întâmplărilor, în prezentarea lui Ion Iovan* [The Last Diary Notes of Mateiu Caragiale, Accompanied by Unpublished Correspondence, as Well as an Index of Persons, Objects, and Facts, in Ion Iovan's Presentation] (Bucharest: Curtea Veche,

2008), 204. Fictional characters Teodor, Lina Zaharescu, and Sița Drângeanu
   are also listed in the Index as real people (445, 489, 498).

87   Lackey, *The American Biographical Novel*, 14.

88   Iovan, *Ultimele însemnări ale lui Mateiu Caragiale*, 550.

89   Boldrini, *Autobiographies of Others*, 157.

90   Matei Călinescu, *A citi, a reciti. Pentru o poetică a (re)lecturii*, with an original
   Romanian chapter about Mateiu I. Caragiale, trans. Virgil Stanciu (Iași,
   Romania: Polirom, 2003), 297–353; Ion Vianu, *Investigații mateine* (Cluj-
   Napoca, Romania: Apostrof, 2008); Mitchievici, *Mateiu I. Caragiale*; Cernat,
   Modernismul retro în romanul interbelic românesc, 58–109.

91   Ion Iovan, *MJC. O lume pentru Mateiu* (Iași, Romania: Polirom, 2015).

PART THREE

Critical Modes

12

GEOCRITIQUE:
Siting, Poverty, and the Global Southeast

Ștefan Baghiu

Since terms clustered around spatiality continue to be as instrumental to theoretical projects of the post era as the lexicon swirling around temporality, it is only befitting that Part Three of this book opens with an argument from literary geography, more specifically, from geocriticism. A critical concept, approach, and field that has made considerable inroads into the study of literature worldwide since the mid-late 1980s, literary geography encourages us to rethink the relation between spatiality and fictional worlds; reconceptualized as geo*critique*, geocriticism in turn affords, in my account, a concerted focus on socioeconomic issues such as the poverty imaginary of Communist-era Romanian fictional prose, my subject in what follows, and by the same token helps discern in this and other bodies of work illuminating compatibilities and affiliations with narratives typically originating in, and ordinarily considered characteristic of, the Global South.

Bound up with economic dependence understood geopolitically, as a world phenomenon, the imaginary of destitution is unmistakable in Romanian and other European literatures. I do not mean to say that it cannot be missed, for, to be sure, it has been routinely overlooked. What I mean, and what I maintain in this chapter, is that geocritique, as defined below, can *render this imaginary legible* by reading for the thematic, formal, and other kinds of parallels and similitudes to Global South fictions, thus associating the literature of Romania and the European Southeast to what I call the Global Southeast literary system. To that effect, geocritique must be, I contend, methodologically and terminologically flexible. Likewise, it must assume an "impurity" of sorts, own up to the eclecticism already embedded in its conceptual apparatus. For, centered on space, geocritique brings into play, as it does here, space-related notions like world, worlding, planet, and planetarity, as well as the space-place dichotomy such as deployed in Christian Moraru's 2015 *Reading for the Planet: Toward a Geomethodology* and in Bertrand Westphal's 2007 *La Géocritique. Réel, fiction, espace,* respectively, and, more broadly, in space-"friendly" disciplines like World Literature, planetary studies, and, first and foremost, geocriticism.[1]

In appropriating these inquiry domains' analytic arsenal, my main objective is to pursue a certain transnational dimension of Romanian post-World War II literature, more to the point, to show how some of this literature's Cold War-era novels map out a segment of the European Southeast that, by analogy to similar, economic and literary-cultural phenomena of the Global South, I designate as part and parcel of a cross-hemispheric Global Southeast. Thus, on one hand, I take advantage of geocriticism's "scalability," expanding geocritical methodology on the world-system scale by homing in on worldwide phenomena such as poverty. On the other hand, I mount a critique of what I perceive to be a kind of "social poverty" of geocriticism itself, in which questions of class have not always received the attention they deserve. Thus "re-classified," geocriticism plays out as geocritique *and* provides a stepping-stone to an ethically and politically grounded South-South comparatism. In a similar vein, I take issue with World Literature approaches less mindful of the locational granularity of literary phenomena, and so, if geocriticism is here "geocritiqued," the World Literature component of my project is "situated" or "sited." This is, in brief, my two-pronged attempt to inject more materiality into these otherwise indisputably valuable disciplinary and methodological areas so as to attune them to the class and place specificity of the literary corpus under scrutiny.

Space, Place, and the Global South "after" Postcolonialism

Critics such as Westphal and Robert T. Tally Jr. have turned to spatial territorialization, deterritorialization, and reterritorialization in fiction to show precisely that space is a problematic construct in literary geography. As Westphal argues in *The Plausible World*, "the West has repeatedly confronted open spaces of the world and transformed them into closed places."[2] Echoing works by Roland Barthes, Gilles Deleuze, and Giorgio Agamben, as well as studies such as the 1958 *La invención de América* by "Southern theorist" Edmundo O'Gorman, Westphal's key geocritical notion of "invention of place" has contributed to "decentralizing" literary geography epistemologically and politically along the lines of Walter Mignolo's and Russell West-Pavlov's subsequent handling of the concept. An unsettled issue of geocriticism is, however, according to Eric Prieto, the sometimes "selective" application of geocritique. Westphal cherry-picks, as Prieto holds, "semiotically loaded" and thus highly "significant" sites where "important" events have occurred. As a result, they are no longer ordinary places but stand out as literary landmarks.[3] These emblematic *hauts lieux* have culturally *authorized* the ways continental theory has oftentimes projected geographically *the place of culture*. Westphal does remind us, though, that the very concept of *place* "was invented" by the West, and so it comes hardly as a surprise that he himself has called for rerouting geocriticism through subdisciplines influenced by postcolonial, decolonial, and planetary studies. "Geocriticism, as any wide-ranging epistemological discourse, must take lessons," Westphal recommends, "from postcolonial studies and all its related ventures, such as subaltern studies, Latin American decolonial thought (E. Dussel, A. Quijano, R. Grosfogel, etc.), or even furthermore the very promising Planetary Studies, propagated by researchers such as Wai Chee Dimock, Christian Moraru, and Amy Elias in the wake of Gayatri Spivak's intuition."[4]

This makes sense. After all, the "invention" of place as seized and claimed space around the world—and in criticism no less—has long been a major concern of postcolonial and, later, decolonial scholarship, which have contested the use of metropolitan powers' cognitive instruments to pinpoint and canvas the cultural places of the colonies. Since World War II, postcolonial critical theory has dwelled at length on the shortcomings of literary geography, and this is not surprising either, for surviving in it is an imperial epistemological "othering" that underwrites an extreme, spatial as well as economic polarity: on one side, there is the rich metropolis; on the other, an impoverished colonial world and, perpetuating colonies' dire poverty, the dependency system of modernity itself. However, postcolonial critique only partially addressed this problem. Authors from the formerly colonized peripheries have managed by and large to transform colonial *spaces* into *places* of postcolonial ethics *at various metropolitan and academic centers*, but such literary successes have not altered the global *combined and uneven* equation within planetary geographies of destitution.[5] Aijaz Ahmad's famous 1987 article, in which the Marxist theorist rejected Fredric Jameson's assumption that "all third-world texts are necessarily ... national allegories," has become a mainstay in the postcolonial debate exactly because it unmasked, according to Ahmad himself, "the general ethnocentricity and cultural myopia of the humanities as they are presently constituted in these United States."[6] Further, Ahmad highlighted the academic "gentrification" of postcolonial studies, a phenomenon parallel to the attention "beyond measure," which "the few writers who happen to write in English" have been getting in the West.[7] To resist the misconception that the contradictions and struggles of the postcolonial world disappeared once the authors have made it into Western bookstores and curricula, Ahmad suggested that "one could start with a radically different premise, namely the proposition that we live not in three worlds but in one" and that "what gives the world its unity, then, is not a humanist ideology but the ferocious struggle of capital and labor which is now strictly and fundamentally global in character."[8]

In other words, and in terms pivotal to the present intervention, the critical tools now available to us, from literary geography and geocriticism to planetary studies, could be plied so as to work out another world-system description, one susceptible to incorporate more effectively fictional works' own depiction of the struggle between capital and labor. From Franco Moretti to the Warwick Research Collective (WReC), this sort of project has become increasingly plausible as world-systems theory's inroads into literary studies have expanded, and the rebooting of comparative literature as World Literature has consolidated the recognition that, if there is just "one world," then this world is, indeed, both combined and uneven. At any rate, if the postcolonial paradigm is relevant to World Literature studies, that is also because it lends itself to applications *outside the historical and geopolitical purview* of colonialism and postcolonialism, encouraging as it does a rethinking of regional center-periphery systems even with respect to societies that have not been colonies proper. In this view, it is symptomatic that most East European critical cultures have of late described postcommunism as a postcolonial narrative.[9] The popularity of postcolonial theory has arguably stirred, at the peripheries of the world geosystem—whether those areas have been actual colonies or not—*a desire to be postcolonial*. The responses to this cultural and critical-theoretical yearning have attended chiefly to the relations with the "center" (be it Western or Soviet), whereas the "intercolonial" or "lateral," interperipheral relations have been rarely explored.

As is well known, Moretti showed as early as 2003 that what helped the West set itself up as an axial point or source of the global dispersion of literary forms through "wave" after "wave" had been the absence, real or perceived, of literary interactions among "peripheries," whether regionally or on a global scale.[10] Moretti thinks there is practically no "movement" of such forms "between peripheral cultures which do not belong to the same 'region': from, say, Norway to Portugal (or vice versa), not from Norway to Iceland or Sweden, or from Colombia to Guatemala and Peru."[11] Parting company with Moretti on this account, I set out to prove the contrary, and not so much for genres and "forms" generally but for contents, as it were. As we shall note, the "movement" between peripheral cultures located at vast distances from one another has been, thematically speaking, extremely important. These interactions have had tremendous impact on post-World

War II Romanian literature and beyond it, on East and Southeast European literary cultures as well. Likewise, emerging Global South scholarship can challenge, by concentrating on such non-aligned movements viewed as either concrete realities or geopolitical metaphors, how we use literary geography and can accordingly prompt us to think of *discrete* peripheral spaces as *interrelated* places grounding coalitional politics, resistance, and critique. No doubt, the center-periphery relation has been, historically and epistemologically, stronger than the periphery-periphery nexus, and it is also true that the circulation of literary forms has been shaped by, and mirrors, the developmental narrative connecting world-system cores and margins vertically. And yet it begs asking, why is it that interperipheral relations— horizontal or, as I say above, "lateral"—have received such scant attention? And, I also wonder, if we are to start paying attention to them, is old-fashioned comparatism, which largely ignored them, still helpful?

By contrast, the rise of Global South studies touched off a surge of academic interest in this problematics. Along the same lines, recent decades have seen the proliferation of studies that link up peripheral zones within the continental and global economy. Some of the Romanian contributions in this area originate in decolonial sociology and see, as Manuela Boatcă has in her work, "Eastern Europe and Latin America as interdependent regions, not as objects of regional studies (*area studies*), which look at a Western-inspired modernization, nor as clusters of nation-states with common cultural characteristics."[12] Other analyses are derived from political economy and dependence theories, such as Cornel Ban's revisitation of Fernando Henrique Cardoso's concept of peripheral dependence, which he draws from to demonstrate that Romania has a "dependent market economy"[13] akin to other global peripheries. Regardless of discipline, all this scholarship points to the same thing, essentially, namely, that these regions are structurally alike and that, far apart as they are geographically, there are both communications and homologies between them due to their similar positions on the global map of capital.

Such associations were made as early as 1996 by Joseph L. Love in *Crafting the Third World: Theorizing Underdevelopment in Rumania and Brazil*. In accounting for his comparative analysis of the two countries in his book's title, Love presents Romania and Brazil as "two underdeveloped countries in East Central Europe and Latin America."[14] What he notes is that "the response to economic conjunctures led to the rediscovery or reinvention of similar ideas," and "East Central Europe, including the Balkans, and Latin America were the earliest world regions whose intellectuals extensively theorized the problem of backwardness, if we except Russia, whose socialist revolution posed such a radically different set of options."[15] Love relies on Henryk Szlajfer's description of Eastern Europe and Latin America as "first largescale laboratories of underdevelopment,"[16] where such laboratories must be understood, quite etymologically, in Immanuel Wallerstein's sense of "areas of coerced labor."[17] Built centuries prior to the Western imperial forays into Asia and Africa, these labs have continued to operate throughout modernity and into late capitalism within the same dependency framework fostered centuries before.[18] Following in the footsteps of Polish historian Marian Malowist, Szlajfer also asserts that "the phenomenon of modern backwardness ... actually appeared in East-Central Europe before the colonization of South America, the Caribbean, and Central America."[19] One could say, then, that with the advent of the Global South model of analysis, the very geometry of dependencies finally acquired a new planetary relevance. At the same time, and also benefiting from this model's breakthrough, the conceptual toolbox of postcolonial theory, especially Gramscian terms such as "subaltern" and "exploitable colonies," can be applied to peripheral geographies to bring into bolder relief the ways fiction has "invented" a "place" of poverty. Of course, Gramsci originally intended his notions to account for exploitation and labor on Europe's outer reaches, and he often referred to southern Italy as an "exploitable colony."[20] But the Italian South, much like the European South broadly, is a place of neither inaction nor silence. It is one of labor, of exploitation, as Gramsci insisted, as well as one of expression and invention. As West-Pavlov has reacted to one of the unexamined postcolonial clichés, "the 'Global South' does not give us access to 'subalterns' who cannot speak, so much as it opens up spaces in which speech can be invented"—or where, as I will show momentarily, language, the language of fiction, more precisely, was invented and deployed as such, as an invention or fictional presentation of coerced labor, extreme poverty, and radical dependency.[21]

Now, as regards literary geography, the *planetary culture* idea, which Moraru has envisioned as both deeply relational and "heuristic rather than deterministic"—and therefore predominantly "exploratory" for now— could and, in my view, should be consolidated and concretized through applications to the rich realities of interperipheral world relationality in which site-specific experiences find themselves if not replicated then paralleled by similar site-specific phenomena many thousands of miles away.[22] Such phenomena, typical of this planetary interperipheriality and subject to constant interrogation by Global South scholars, must include, as West-Pavlov has also emphasized, "more material aspects of imperialism and inequity."[23] The biggest problem he notices in fields such as postcolonial studies and World Literature is precisely this "centripetal force" they implicitly set in motion descriptively when they invoke the "world," whereby, he adds, the same old Western perspective is "planetarized" without taking into account interperipheral relations and their role in the circulation of literary themes.[24] Few critics have looked at Romanian literature, for example, as subject to non-European influences or participating in literary networks outside the Western and transatlantic areas. This is because the project of modernization and modernity more broadly has remained inseparable, even in European semi-peripheral cultures, from a certain Orientalist fixation. The latter makes it difficult for them to come to terms with the structural connection they have with other semi-peripheral and peripheral cultures. Effective and consequential, such ties would entail, once they have been owned up to, casting aside the notion of belonging exclusively to the Western or European family and acknowledging, instead, having partaken not only in "modernization" but also in the very production of its hegemonic logic. In short, to "admit" that you belong to the Global Southeast is to question indirectly a major driver of modern cultural development and especially of the very perception of this process, that is, the assumption of civilizational superiority of the West over the East and the South. This is one reason the links between the literatures of Romania and Latin America, Asia, and Africa are almost invisible to Romanian critics—which, socioeconomically and geoculturally speaking, does not quite add up, given the growing "common experiences and conditions, including participation in the remittance culture, connecting migrant domestics hailing from Asia, Africa, Latin America, and Eastern Europe."[25]

The Global Southeast concept I propose here seeks primarily to encourage South-South scholarly juxtapositions and investigations, especially the analytical connection of the Global South to the European Southeast. Granted, this chapter takes up the cultural relations the Soviet Union *imposed* in Romania and other nations in the region right after World War II, but it is no less evident that these interactions and symmetries were also used by East European countries to *resist* Soviet domination.[26] Furthermore, my Global South notion implies no abstract, universalist cultural predisposition or matrix Global South and Southeast European literatures presumably have in common. What I mean to bring to light, rather, is how poverty, once it became a constitutive and conscientiously assumed element of literature's geographical imaginary, led to common attitudes at a particular moment in the literary history of the past century, namely, the first two decades of Romanian Communism. In fact, this is the starting point and main butt of my *critique* of geocriticism, to wit, the latter's universalizing terminological apparatus. Following from this is the suggestion, which I also take issue with, that *spaces* become *places* through a mechanism that is timeless, delocalized, and inherent to any cultural process. As I insist in my turn, such dynamics move in the opposite direction, viz., toward historicization, localization, and diversification.

In the same vein, it bears pointing out that approaching any representation of dependency and poverty as similar to what goes on in Global South literature may look, and may well be, farfetched. Therefore, geocriticism's job, as I see it, is not only to lay bare a common aesthetics that, once critically articulated, would bring spatially separated locations together but also to identify a South-systemic, self-representation geoethic. Besides fiction, this relational ethic is active and therefore should be searched for in translations and other forms of cultural production, reproduction, and commerce. Literary geography can thus go a long way toward showing how stories written in countries such as Romania could be read, and possibly more meaningfully so, as sites of a *Global South narrative system*, while geocriticism can help us discern more clearly the local instantiations and effects of this systems at certain junctures in time and space. A literary geography reenergized through geocriticism could actually supplement or even counter in geopolitically ex-centric spaces the disproportionally *national* and even nationalistic constructions of space. By establishing new connections between topological ("real") geography and literary geography—fictional geography or second-order, literary description of the world's ("actual") geographical aspects—and thus asserting itself, as I maintain, as a *geography of place*, geocriticism can illuminate how local phenomena get "worlded" through literature. Yet again, *to uncover such worlding protocols*, my analysis of post-1950 Romanian fiction is keen on this literature's *site-shaping* configuration, one that holds a major role in the coupling of local realities to an international geography of poverty as well as to a world literature describing indigence as a form of geopolitically marginal dependence. As Lytle Shaw has recently underscored, and as I too emphasize here, *site-specificity* does not rein in literary effort in terms of either relevance or geocultural context. In making possible "contextualization without the security of a discrete synchronic frame," this dimension, once taken into account, may keep in check our theoretical and comparative élans by dint of a "lowercase" theorization of place that envisages literature as a response to a given *site*, to a contextual, place-bound reality or history.[27]

The Imagination of Poverty and South-South Comparatism

In Romania, the post-World War II period was a decisive moment in the consolidation of a perception of the Global South as an *out there* similar to domestic *out here*. Aggressively pushed by the regime and thriving roughly between 1948 and 1964, Romanian Socialist Realism proves, in hindsight, remarkable not so much for promoting a Proletkult style designed to implement Soviet formulas—much though it was these that, due to their most deleterious and readily observable effects and the censorship behind them, got attention more than anything else—but for providing a uniform, "internationalist" style of revisiting history and capitalism critically, whether, as noted above, through original fiction or Romanian translations of Socialist Realist works done elsewhere. Thus, the critique of the capitalist system and the colonial world brought together and inevitably into dialogue Romanian novelists and authors such as Howard Fast (the United States),

Bhabani Bhattacharya (India), Jorje Amado (Brazil), and Ding Ling (China). The geographical range of authors rendered into Romanian during this time is indeed impressive, as I have shown at length in a recent article.[28] In effect, Socialist Realism was in Romania, as in other parts of Central and East Europe, the culture's first opportunity to open itself up, through translations into the country's main idiom, to Asia, Africa, and Latin America and their literatures. Rendered into the languages of the Soviet Bloc immediately after World War II, Socialist Realist authors such as Fast and Ding abide by roughly the same rules of representing reality and portraying poverty as an ineludible symptom of capitalism, so much so that one could argue that, in Romania, the Global South is a "joint" Socialist Realist literary project, a mix of original and translated works. The latter were also an "import" of critique into Romanian culture—a critique of capitalism, colonialism, as well as of a past seized as a modernity lab in which poverty was not some kind of one-off, whacky experiment but an upshot of internal and external economic dependencies.

Geography served as a primary instrument for the narrative fashioning of this historical condition, as a quick glance at some of the most important Romanian authors of the era goes to show. In a landmark of post-World War II Romanian literature, Marin Preda's novel *Moromeţii* (The Morometes), whose first volume came out in 1955, the plot is set in Romania's own "South," the Danube plains, and follows the struggle of a peasant family to survive financially in the 1930s. Received positively during the Socialist Realist years and still highly canonical in Romanian scholarship and curricula to this very day, the novel presents an interesting case for Global South studies. As Alex Goldiş has insisted, although it "does not conform to socialist realist rules of composition," the novel "[has not] established [itself] at the center of the canon retrospectively, in the age of liberalization, but was acclaimed by the promoters of socialist realism already. Moreover, it was not read and consecrated against socialist realist aesthetics, but within its boundaries."[29] The main character, Ilie Moromete, is a peasant who scrambles to resist "a wider process of disintegration of the small rural property" in a context forcing him to give up gradually his land and other assets.[30] Thus, the novel is first and foremost a chronicle of the destitute Romanian rural class's ceaseless fight for survival and against economic subservience during the decades before World War II. The book's violence, linguistic and otherwise, and overall style did not pass unnoticed by Socialist Realist critics, yet such elements were usually regarded either as static rather than as a main "message" and tolerated for their part in portraying a world in which brutality prompted social critique or were attributed to William Faulkner's influence.

Due mostly to the narrative style of the second volume (1967) of *Moromeţii*, Preda's "Faulknerism" has been intensely debated, although in his case too there is geographical closeness—let alone a contiguity—neither between the places the two writers survey in their novels nor between the authors themselves. In an article on the transnational scope of Faulkner's prose, Ramón Saldívar stresses how important it is not to lose sight, in the American novelist, of "the dependency of the south on the processes of modernization" given that such focus is liable to help us better see how "his fiction" took "sha[pe] as a formal response to and expression of those processes of dependency."[31] So did Preda's work, yet without the deployment of concepts and conceptual frameworks such as Global South and developmental theories, its *geographical purview cannot be seen*. What remains invisible in Preda in the absence of a geocritical reading is that the novel sets up its diegetic Romanian geography as a worldly *pars pro toto*, a Global South synecdoche. I mentioned earlier that the plot is set in southern Romania, near the country's border with Bulgaria, incidentally, another segment of Europe's poor South. It is there, in the Danube countryside, that the tensions within the rural agrarian society form and erupt, and the family structure crumbles under the burden of economic inequalities that will ultimately make Ilie Moromete's sons leave for Bucharest. This geographical detail would not be nearly as revealing as it is if the second volume did not depict Ilie Moromete's subsequent prosperity as a byproduct of his entrepreneurship's pivoting to the North. Specifically, to overcome the cash flow shortage that compelled him in the first volume to put up for sale piece after piece of his land, Ilie Moromete starts selling corn in the "heart of the Carpathians," in villages close to Transylvania. Achieving financial independence is therefore linked, on one hand, to traveling to and trading with the more prosperous North, compared to which the South is poor and underdeveloped, and, on the other, to the type of labor (less lucrative, harder, unrewarded) done in the agrarian South in Romania and elsewhere. For, apart from the similarities between Preda's South and Faulkner's, *Moromeții* documents a form of labor frequently encountered in Global South fictions, including those made available to Romanian audiences in the 1950s. Subject to interesting de- and re-engendering permutations, this kind of daily grind is emphatically at play in Bhattacharya's 1947 novel *So Many Hungers!* (translated into Romanian in 1956), where women have to take on "a man's rugged work" just as Ilie Moromete's daughters must make up for their brothers' absence during harvest season.

The *place* of poverty and dependence mapped out in the Romanian South by Preda and others is also one where, much like in the labor imaginary— fictional and theoretical—of the Global South, workers are expandable. True, Preda does not ascertain explicitly the North-South relationship as financial in nature, nor do others. This is, however, a reality that can hardly be ignored by a rereading of Socialist Realist novels that would latch, as I do here, onto their narrative *location* of poverty, onto the latter's association, that is, with certain settings and places inside and across countries and regions. The unveiling of this geospatial distribution of pauperism was front and center to the efforts the propaganda literature of the first Communist decades made to expose the failure of capitalist modernization. It is quite telling that the showpiece accomplishment of Romanian Socialist Realism, Mihail Sadoveanu's 1949 novel *Mitrea Cocor*, spotlights an equally destitute place, where agricultural toil, carried out in the Romanian South also, somewhere on the Bărăgan Plains, is controlled by exploitative landowners. Zaharia Stancu too situates his early twentieth-century story in his 1948 *Desculț* (Barefoot), the Romanian post-World War II novel most critical of peasants' exploitation, in the same region, more exactly in Teleorman county, which is also home to Preda's characters. The violent scenes unfolding here are similar to those in *Setea* (Thirst), Titus Popovici's 1958 novel, and V. Em. Galan's 1950 *Zorii robilor* (Dawn of Serfs) and 1954 *Bărăgan*, which all rework an ordinary and generic *space* into a place in which, retrospectively, geocritique should easily recognize a destitution and dependency landscape that basically reproduces on a national scale structures and geographies of hardship and injustice stretching far beyond the Romanian borders. This is, to reiterate, a synecdochic effect, and the Global South analogies get all the more compelling when juxtaposed to the era's translated novels about Bengal famine, racial segregation in South America, colonial dispossession, and the poverty of Saharan communities. Antonio Victor, hero of the very first Latin American novel rendered into Romanian (1948), Jorge Amado's 1943 *The Violent Land*, faces, much like his Romanian counterparts, a workload "a great deal heavier" only when he moves to the "lands in the south" during the "cacao rush."[32] Similarly, north of the "geographical" Global South as it is, southern Romania becomes the place *par excellence* of unsolvable socioeconomic contradictions characteristic of a system both national and transnational. Although Bucharest too lies in southern Romania, the capital is, given the region's generalized poverty, no more than the hub of a quasi-dystopian universe of stark economic contrasts both in *Moromeții*, where the main character's sons have it harder on the outskirts of the city than they did back in their village, and in Eugen Barbu's 1957 novel *Groapa* (The Pit), which dwells systematically on a Bucharest barriolike neighborhood ravaged by racial segregation and crime.

Lodged at the intersection of international and domestic literary production, the South represents in Romanian Socialist Realist novels a geographical sentence to poverty. This mark and the "stigma" of the South overall did not disappear when Romanian literature left Socialist Realism behind, nor did they vanish elsewhere in the world's peripheral areas once these turned into hotbeds of magic realism. As is well known, Moretti views the latter, in relation to Gabriel García Márquez's *One Hundred Years of Solitude*, as "another story of accelerated modernization and of combined development,"[33] and, similarly, WReC builds on Michael Denning's claim that magic realism "had its roots both in left-wing writers' movements— the 'novelists' international'—and in the radical critique of capitalist society articulated in surrealism."[34] These observations suggest that the origins of post-Stalinist Romanian magic realism should be traced back in the same direction. Thus, one of the best short-story books published during the "thaw" of the 1960s, Ştefan Bănulescu's 1965 *Iarna bărbaţilor* (Men's Winter), gathers penury narratives based on real-life cases documented by the author himself. In fact, Bănulescu comes from a strong line of pre-World War II literary reporters, who were primarily left-wing intellectuals writing for the avant-garde magazines of the period. The story titled "Mistreţii erau blânzi" (The Wild Boars Were Tame), for instance, features an apocalyptic scene in which, after a flood of biblical proportions, the villagers are looking for a dry plot to bury a child's body. The scene works over similar events that had occurred in Dobrudja, in the farthest southeastern corner of the country, where whole communities, lacking in basic living—and, as one can see, also dying—necessities were left to the mercy of nature. As longstanding "laboratories of modernity," the Soviet satellites of Eastern Europe began developing a strong Global South-like awareness, and this text, alongside others by Bănulescu and his contemporaries, testifies to the onset of this consciousness as one of lack and impoverishment but also as a cultural or, better yet, intercultural awareness that, also prompted by the translation industry of the Socialist Realist era, starts querying the country's fixation of a *sine qua non* affiliation with the West and begins to foster a self-representation similar to a Global South-specific identity. Thus, in opening itself up to new and remote geographical realities, Romanian literature irreversibly enriched its internal geography with various cultural nuances, producing an *internal* fictional space through an at-distance interaction with those far-flung worlds.

No doubt, geography is never innocent. Drawing on Franco Cassano's *Il pensiero mediterano*, Roberto Dainotto's analysis of European border zones foregrounds a similar insight. "The South," maintains Dainotto, "appeared in the thinking of European modernity as the negative, 'pathological' form of a 'deficiency of modernity.'"[35] Dainotto shows convincingly how "the European south is intimately tied to a global south and inseparable from it, with both souths being part and product of the same logic defining the spirit and identity of Europe (or the West)."[36] But the distinction he makes between "an internal and an external south" collapsed in the latter half of the twentieth century as the first South-South relations were forged and the internal literary geographies of peripheral cultures became increasingly connected with the planetary geocultural system. A whole *worlding through poverty* thus took place at the end of World War II. This phenomenon can be localized, I argue, in places such as Eastern Europe and, more precisely still, can be tracked down to discrete and disparate spaces such as Romania, Italy, and the Southern United States. All these locations, big and small, were already unequally distributed on the North-South axis, and their local literary geographies can be revisited, post-geocriticism, as critical cartographies of the areas of, and of the divides between, prosperity and poverty, and apparent independence and structural subordination.

Emerging as it did at the crossroads of Italian neorealism and Latin American, Southern American, African, Southeast Asian, and other Global South literatures, Romanian fiction written after World War II can and, to my mind, should be reread as a discourse of local dependence on a process of modernization that—most notably—brings with itself an *awareness of one's peripheral status* through *inter*peripheral contacts and exchanges. The latter obtained at the same time as imperialism, underdevelopment, racism, and the Apartheid were hotly debated in the media, and as literature that took a stance against these realities and their unjust implications in Latin America and Africa was officially endorsed. Even before the likes of Ousman Sembène, Chinua Achebe, and Es'kia Mphahlele were introduced to local audiences, there had been militant articles in the press referring to underdeveloped Africa as "The Rising Continent." And if it is indeed true that, as Saldívar insists, "underdevelopment occurred as the result of active forces shaping regional societies," post-World War II Romanian authors' preoccupation with poverty and the *hinterlands of modernization* created by economic "development" showcases new geographical spaces *at once region-specific and world-oriented*, portraying as it does an European Southeast of economic deprivation within, if not brought about by, modernization.

Both as a historical reality and in its fictional representation, this basic contradiction resurfaced in postcommunism in stories of Romanian migrants looking for agricultural and industrial work in the West, a substantial corpus that comes back, again and again, to a basic narrative dependence scheme quite similar to what we find in Global South literatures. For, if state Socialism represents, in "the analysis of the modern world-system," a "political strategy the semiperiphery turns to so as to prevent an economic downgrade to periphery status without cutting itself off from the global capitalist system,"[37] and, in literature, a critique of class oppression, then it bears keeping in mind that most of the former Socialist countries have witnessed, after the collapse of Socialism, a migration phenomenon similar to that occurring in the "geographical" Global South. This demographic flow and its stories carry on a worlding narrative that, the censorship and extreme violence of Stalinism in Romania notwithstanding, can be traced back to Socialist Realism, which made the first systematic efforts to reimagine the Romanian world and the world in general through a genuinely planetary literary geography. If critics have talked extensively about the influence Faulkner, magic realism, and the Italian neorealism exerted on Romanian fiction, it is time, I propose, to be more specific about what such transnational circulation of literary material has meant in Romania and other parts of the European South. Retooled as geocritique, geocriticism can cast light not only on the imaginary of poverty in post-World War II literature but also on this literature's place-determined, topospecific nature as well as on its status as a subset of a Global South network of texts, symbolic representations, and material culture.

Notes

1   Christian Moraru, *Reading for the Planet: Toward a Geomethodology* (Ann Arbor: University of Michigan Press, 2015); Bertrand Westphal, *Geocriticism: Real and Fictional Spaces*, trans. Robert T. Tally Jr. (New York: Palgrave Macmillan, 2011).

2   Bertrand Westphal, *The Plausible World: A Geocritical Approach to Space, Place, and Maps* (New York: Palgrave Macmillan, 2013), xiv.

3   Eric Prieto, "Geocriticism, Geopoetics, Geophilosophy, and Beyond," in *Geocritical Explorations: Space, Place, and Mapping in Literary and Cultural Studies*, ed. Robert T. Tally Jr. (New York: Palgrave Macmillan, 2011), 22.

4   Bertrand Westphal, "A Geocritical Approach to Geocriticism," *American Book Review* 37, no. 6 (2016): 4–5.

5   "Which postcolonial theorists, for instance," asks Russell West-Pavlov, "read the Mexican experimental theorist O'Gorman's *La idea del descubrimiento de America* (1952) and *La invención de América* (1958, English translation 1961), or the Uruguayan literary critic Rama's *La ciudad letrada* (1982), all elided by Todorov's *La Découverte de l'Amérique* (Mignolo 1993: 123)?" (Russell West-Pavlov, "Toward the Global South: Concept or Chimera, Paradigm or Panacea?," in *The Global South and Literature*, ed. Russell West-Pavlov [Cambridge: Cambridge University Press, 2018], 17).

6   Aijaz Ahmad, "Jameson's Rhetoric of Otherness and the 'National Allegory,'" *Social Text*, no. 17 (Autumn 1987): 4.

7   Ahmad, "Jameson's Rhetoric of Otherness and the 'National Allegory,'" 5.

8   Ahmad, "Jameson's Rhetoric of Otherness and the 'National Allegory,'" 10.

9   See, for instance, David Chioni Moore, "Is the Post- in Postcolonial the Post- in Post-Soviet? Toward a Global Postcolonial Critique," *PMLA* 116, no. 1 (2001): 111–28; Janusz Korek, "Central and Eastern Europe from a Postcolonial Perspective," *Postcolonial Europe*, April 27, 2009, http://www.postcolonial-europe.eu/essays/60--central-and-eastern-europe-from-a-postcolonial-perspective (accessed March 8, 2021); Clare Cavanagh, "Postcolonial Poland," *Common Knowledge* 10, no. 1 (2004), 82–92. Violeta Kelertas, ed., *Baltic Postcolonialism* (Amsterdam: Rodopi, 2006); Andrei Terian, "Is There an East-Central European Postcolonialism? Towards a Unified Theory of (Inter) Literary Dependency," *World Literature Studies* 3, no. 4 (2012): 21–36.

10 "Yes," writes Moretti, "forms *can* move in several directions. But *do* they? This is the point, and a theory of literary history should reflect on the constraints on their movements, and the reasons behind them ... that movement from one periphery to another (without passing through the centre) is almost unheard of" (Franco Moretti, "More Conjectures," *New Left Review* 20 [2003]: 75). To Moretti, forms are "abstracts of social relationships" (Franco Moretti, "Conjectures on World Literature," *New Left Review* 1 [2000]: 64).

11 Moretti, "Conjectures on World Literature," 64.

12 Manuela Boatcă, *Laboratoare ale modernității. Europa de Est și America Latină în (co)relație* (Cluj-Napoca, Romania: Idea, 2019), 11. See also Manuela Boatcă, "Semiperipheries in the World-System: Reflecting Eastern European and Latin American Experiences," *Journal of World-Systems Research* 12, no. 2 (2006): 321–46.

13 See Cornel Ban, *Dependență și dezvoltare. Economia politică a capitalismului românesc* (Cluj-Napoca, Romania: Tact, 2014).

14 Joseph L. Love, *Crafting the Third World: Theorizing Underdevelopment in Rumania and Brazil* (Stanford, CA: Stanford University Press, 1996), 1.

15 Love, *Crafting the Third World*, 3.

16 Henryk Szlajfer, "Editor's Introduction," in *Economic Nationalism in East-Central Europe and South America 1918–1939*, ed. Henryk Szlajfer (Geneva: Droz, 1990), 1–2.

17 See Immanuel Wallerstein, *The Modern World-System: Capitalist Agriculture and the Origins of the European World-Economy in the Sixteenth Century* (New York: Academic Press, 1974).

18 "The reason, as will be suggested in the following," writes Boatcă, "lies not only in the different timing at which the concerns were voiced in the two locations—starting in the late 19th century for Eastern Europe and in mid-20th century for Latin America—but also, and more importantly, in the dissimilar opportunity structure for making these theoretical strategies visible beyond regional (or even state) borders" (Boatcă, "Semiperipheries in the World-System," 328).

19 See Szlajfer's "Editor's Introduction."

20 Antonio Gramsci, "Some Aspects of the Southern Question," in *The Gramsci Reader: Selected Writings 1916–1935*, ed. David Forgacs. With a Foreword by Eric J. Hobsbawm (New York: New York University Press, 2000), 171.

21 West-Pavlov, "Toward the Global South," 8.

22 "The function I assign it for now," says Moraru, "is cautiously exploratory. I do not posit the planetary as an absolute and sole context for culture and cultural analysis. In contrast to well-known theories of globalization, planetarization is not geared toward a one-world, genetic, homogenous and homogenizing totality" (Moraru, *Reading for the Planet*, 63).

23 West-Pavlov, "Toward the Global South," 17.

24 "Likewise," notes West-Pavlov, "this renewed visibility of Global South literary publishing may reveal a plethora of theorists hardly mentioned by postcolonial studies with its fixation on the troika of Said, Spivak, and Bhabha, or its token non–Ivy League theorists such as Anzaldúa, Fanon, or Glissant" (West-Pavlov, "Toward the Global South," 17).

25 Sudeh Mishra, "The Global South: Modernity and Exceptionality," in *The Global South and Literature*, ed. Russell West-Pavlov (Cambridge: Cambridge University Press, 2018), 49. Also see Leyla Keough, "Globalizing 'Postsocialism': Mobile Mothers and Neoliberalism on the Margins of Europe," *Anthropological Quarterly* 79, no. 3 (2006): 431–61.

26 For instance, Ceaușescu's pivoting to Asia and close collaboration with the Middle East were oftentimes interpreted as attempts to put a distance between Bucharest and Moscow. In that, Romania's relations with countries such as China, Korea, Jordan, and Nigeria may be seen as the Romanian Communist regime's attempts at an "anticolonial" foreign policy.

27 Lytle Shaw, "lowercase theory and the site-specific turn," *ASAP/Journal* 2, no. 3 (2017): 653–76.

28 As I point out in the essay I am referring to, "Romania, which had had no precedent in renditions of novels originating in the Global South, translated

for the first time, between 1948 and 1964, novels from Latin American countries such as Ecuador, Mexico, and Brazil (starting from 1948), Argentina (1949), Bolivia, Chile, Uruguay, and Costa Rica (1956), Venezuela, Peru (1963), and even Guatemala (as early as 1960), from Asian countries such as China (starting from 1950), Korea (1959), Vietnam (1961), and later the Philippines, and even from African countries such as South Africa, Algeria (starting from 1957), Egypt (1961), Cameroon, or Senegal (1960) ... Those are just some examples inside the Global South translationscape, since between 1948 and 1989 more than 50 new countries from the Global South witness renditions in Romania" (Ștefan Baghiu, "Translating Hemispheres: Eastern Europe and the Global South Connection through Translationscapes of Poverty," *Comparative Literature Studies* 56, no. 3 [2019]: 500).

29 Alex Goldiș, "The Ideology of Ruralism in the Thaw Prose: The Case of Marin Preda's *Moromeții*," in *Ruralism and Literature in Romania*, ed. Ștefan Baghiu, Vlad Pojoga, and Maria Sass (Berlin: Peter Lang, 2019), 97.

30 This interpretation was signaled as early as 1955 and has since been discussed in most studies devoted to the novel. See Goldiș, "The Ideology of Ruralism in the Thaw Prose," 97.

31 Ramón Saldívar, "Faulkner and the World Culture of the Global South," in *Fifty Years of Faulkner*, ed. Jay Watson and Ann J. Abadie (Jackson: University Press of Mississippi, 2016), 5.

32 As Sharae Deckard notes regarding this novel, "Plantation work is dehumanizing labour that makes migrants yearn for the dignity of subsistence work and the coastal plots they left to join the cacao rush" (Sharae Deckard, "Cacao and Cascadura: Energetic Consumption and Production in World-Ecological Literature," *Journal of Postcolonial Writing* 53, no. 3 [2017]: 342–54).

33 Moretti, *Modern Epic*, 239.

34 Warwick Research Collective (WReC), *Combined and Uneven Development: Towards a New Theory of World-Literature* (Liverpool, UK: Liverpool University Press, 2015), 80. See Michael Denning, *Culture in the Age of Three Worlds* (London: Verso, 2004), 165.

35 Dainotto attributes the "negative" portrayal of the South to Eurocentrism and the "invention" of "the rest of the world": "If Eurocentrism is the tendency to explain history 'without making recourse to anything outside of Europe' (Dussel 469–70), then Eurocentrism *needs* a figure of antithesis internal to Europe itself—it *needs* to posit a 'south' as the negative moment in the dialectical progress of the Spirit of Europe. In sum, Europe needed a theory of dialectics, one that Hegel notoriously provided" (Roberto Dainotto, "Does Europe Have a South? An Essay on Borders," *The Global South* 5, no. 1 [2011]: 38).

36 "Sure enough," writes Dainotto, "a distinction can and should be made between a European and a non-European South: whereas the former is still internal to, and participates to the imperial privileges of, the so-called 'First World,' the latter is radically exterior to it, fundamentally irreducible to the modern world and profoundly marked by the effects of coloniality" (Dainotto, "Does Europe Have a South?," 39).

37 Boatcă, *Laboratoare ale modernității*, 8.

13

NEOCRITIQUE:
Sherlock Holmes Investigates
Literature

Mihai Iovănel

My chapter joins in the increasingly animated debate critics such as Bruno Latour, Rita Felski, Toril Moi, Jeffrey R. Di Leo, and Christian Moraru have been engaged in for over a decade now.[1] This conversation's main topics have been the recent and, to some, terminal deadlock experienced within the international critical-theoretical system by *critique*, as well as the means of supplanting or, more likely, updating its paradigm, which has dominated the humanities over the last half-century or so.[2] I submit that the ideological and "suspicious" way of interpreting literature, undermined as it may be by critique's own theoretical "imperialism" and transformed over time, according to critique's detractors, into a "paranoid" relativism increasingly disconnected from reality, is far from being exhausted. That said, the time has come for criticism to cut a new deal with reality so as to embrace the reality-attuned perspective engrained in that which Latour calls "a more realistic realism."[3]

In line with other interventions in this volume, I will make my case obliquely, so to speak, situating the bulk of the discussion within or in the margins of literature and working from inside out and toward more theoretical conclusions. The lynchpin of my argument is the contention that this new realism is not at odds with critique's emphasis on the construction of reality, namely, with that "constructivism" that insists on the social construction of knowledge at the expense of a more "natural" kind of cognition.[4] To show to what extent this new realism is indeed compatible with critique's "constructivism," my presentation will move on two intersecting tracks or, better yet, will navigate two thematically intertwined literary networks. Thus, I take, first, a shortcut across the maze of texts whose main actor has been Sherlock Holmes, a narrative web created, of course, by Arthur Conan Doyle and expanded by writers such as Neil Gaiman and Laurie R. King. A second route meanders across another network of texts, apropos of allegory's role in critique. Overlapping, as we will see, with the other, this cluster of works is centered primarily on Victorian explorer Percival Harrison Fawcett and two narratives: the meganovel *Ne vom întoarce în Muribecca* (We Will Return to Muribecca) published in 2014 by Romanian writer Florin Chirculescu and David Grann's 2009 nonfictional work, *The Lost City of Z: A Tale of Deadly Obsession in the Amazon*.[5]

What do these textual constellations have in common with critique, with its current crisis, and with the debate around the latter, one might wonder. As I will show, these literary corpuses harbor contents, allegorize epistemological issues, and activate narrative and analytical protocols that lie squarely at the core of critique's "investigative"—one might say "detective"—modus operandi. But my forays into these bodies of work reach beyond an inventory of such thematic analogies and hermeneutic homologies. I set out, specifically, to expunge from critique its idealist and finalist or teleological components, along with other methodological presumptions coalescing around the claims of Jamesonian historicism. Resulting from this recalibration—a multiply critical undertaking itself—is, I trust, a more materialist and contingent variant of critique. I call this version *neocritique*.

Critique: Toward a Reset

Described as a "hermeneutics of suspicion," a Paul Ricoeur formula that has got quite a bit of traction,[6] critique is an ideological mode of interpretation that has historically yielded applied readings of relations pertaining to class (with origins in Karl Marx), to power in a general sense (inspired by Friedrich Nietzsche), and to the libidinal-symbolic (as theorized by Sigmund Freud).[7] While its beginnings date back to the 1960s, critique became prominent in the academe during the 1970s and 1980s. Although it spread across British and American universities while neoliberal politics was also on the rise, it has its origins in several theorists from previous decades and even centuries, as well as in the emancipations movements of the 1960s and 1970s. A standard account of critique seizes it as a thick circuit of philosophical and theoretical texts, "schools," and figures that encompasses, besides the sacred Marx-Nietzsche-Freud trinity, Immanuel Kant, the Frankfurt School, the

New York intellectuals of the World War II era and immediately thereafter, post-Althusserian structuralism, deconstruction in the Yale line—contested by critique practitioners as this has been—and French poststructuralism (Michel Foucault, Gilles Deleuze and Félix Guattari, and their followers), postmodernism, feminism, New Historicism, and so on. A more succinct description ties critique's emergence to the unholy alliance between postmodernism, poststructuralism, and identity studies in the second half of the 1970s.[8] This complex heritage may explain why critique is a highly versatile reading supermethod, and why it has been constantly evolving. At the same time, it has got some perennial features. They all are evident in one of critique's emblematic texts, Fredric Jameson's essay "On Interpretation: Literature as a Socially Symbolic Act" from the 1981 volume *The Political Unconscious: Narrative as a Socially Symbolic Act.*

First of all, and precisely because, as already noted, critique is a methodological composite, Jameson no longer sees Marxism as one method among others but as an "untranscendable horizon." This incorporates, he thinks, all the other methods no matter how different from or at odds with Marxism or with one another they are, from psychoanalysis to Northrop Frye's archetypal reading,[9] as Emily Apter seems to be suggesting in her 1992 book *Feminizing the Fetish.*[10] Second, critique is informed by heteronymic assumptions about literature, which Jameson deems, as most Marxists would, a "symptom" or allegory of the national and global capitalist system. Said heteronomy's upshots have been the falling by the wayside, in and for critique advocates such as Jameson, of considerations of value and, more broadly, the loss of interest in aesthetic evaluation once older theories of aesthetic autonomy went bankrupt.[11] Third, critique is part of the constructionist paradigm of the social sciences. Fourth, critique is characterized by a textual "reductionism" for which history, society, and "reality" basically boil down to a textual continuum. In this vein, while Jameson posits "that history is *not* a text, not a narrative, master or otherwise," he does concede that "as an absent cause, [history] is inaccessible to us except in textual form, and ... our approach to it and to the Real itself necessarily passes through its prior textualization, its narrativization in the political unconscious."[12] Although it does not rule out a reference or world external to textual constructs of this sort, Jameson's reformulation of the Althusserian notion of history offers critique practitioners great liberty when it comes to the relationship with the reality outside texts. Fifth, critique is a paranoid mode of *interrogating* literature. I italicize the word in the previous sentence advisedly because, to be sure, critique does entail (and sometimes sounds like) an interrogation, a self-asserting interpretation that, unsatisfied with skimming the surface of texts, uncovers, usually through an allegorical interpretation, obscure implications and hidden layers of meaning. Needless to say, as in any other paranoid travail, the resulting reading is, to a large extent, a construction of the critic as much as an effect of the text itself he or she is interpreting or, as Umberto Eco says, is "utilizing."[13] Sixth, critique is politically militant, a quality that derives from its (post-)Marxist inheritance as well as from its involvement in identity politics and in various campaigns for class, race, gender, and sexuality emancipation. From the standpoint of these struggles and their outcome, Jameson tries, here and elsewhere, to correct the negative and paranoid strain of critique by injecting a utopian, positive, and constructive component into it. Thus, he invokes "an enlarged perspective for any Marxist analysis of culture." This analysis "must not cease," contends Jameson, "to practice this essentially negative hermeneutic function (which Marxism is virtually the only current critical method to assume today) but must also seek, through and beyond this demonstration of the instrumental function of a given cultural object, to project its simultaneously Utopian power as the symbolic affirmation of a specific historical and class form of collective unity."[14]

Without being reducible to postmodernism—whether we understand it or not as Jameson does—critique overlaps substantially with postmodernism's "oppositional" logic. It is no accident that the reactions to critique over the last decade or so were also, around 2001, reactions to "the end of postmodernism."[15] These kinds of discussions were launched particularly by two texts: Eve Kosofsky Sedgwick's "Paranoid Reading and Reparative Reading" (2002) and Latour's milestone "Why Has Critique Run out of Steam? From Matters of Fact to Matters of Concern" (2004).[16] Over and against a *paranoid reading* that is both traumatic and reducible to negative affects, Sedgwick pitted a reconstructive, *reparative reading*. In his turn, Latour maintained that the relativist message of postmodernism ended up getting weaponized and used against reality itself, with relativists like Jean Baudrillard going as far as to question even basic factual evidence such as the role of actual terrorism in the bringing down of the Twin Towers.[17] Eventually, the number of attacks against critique would multiply, whether in monographs, edited collections, and special-topic journal issues, all of which set out to either problematize critique or discard it completely.

These assaults have been baptized "postcritique." Running through most of them is a charge brought previously against postmodernism also, namely that critique has lost the battle with neoliberalism or, moreover, that it has been co-opted by neoliberal politics, which, in keeping with capitalism's good old tradition, has found ways to turn its foes into allies.[18] What motivates the conceptual swap Moraru proposes in his 2015 book *Reading for the Planet: Toward a Geomethodology*—"planet" instead of "globe"—is, however, precisely the recognition in the postcritique and post-postmodernism project of an implicit critique of the neoliberal globalization to which postmodernism has mounted, we are told, a half-hearted opposition. In any event, one way or the other, the desire to go beyond critique stems from a fairly obvious dissatisfaction with its capacity to change the here and now. This frustration has in turn fueled renewed attempts to bring literary and cultural studies to bear more effectively on the world "out there"—in short, as I have said, to make a new, more acutely transformative pact with reality.

In response to critique's actual or imagined impasse and shortcomings, critics have worked out two kinds of solutions. One category seeks to rebuild or "repair" critique. For instance, in her 2015 book *The Limits of Critique*, Felski proposes critique be revamped by leaning on Latour's actor-network theory (ANT). The other type gets off the critique track altogether, searching for new paths in wholly different methodologies, as does, for example, Franco Moretti with the quantitative approach he has developed by combining geography and evolution in studies such as the 2005 *Graphs, Maps, Trees: Abstract Models for a Literary History*. In an essay later included in the 2013 *Distant Reading*, Moretti acknowledges, in fact, that "the pursuit of a sound materialistic method, and of testable knowledge, occupied more and more of my attention, until finally—slowly, imperceptibly—it ended up overshadowing the more substantive aspects of my historical work. Methodology had replaced critique."[19] As will become clear momentarily, my chapter follows in the first line of reasoning, in that it starts from the premise that critique is reformable, and that the crisis it is undergoing affects neither its validity nor its relevance. My demonstration dwells on two aspects of critique, as important as they are problematic. One is its constructivism; the other, the ways critique plies allegorical reading.

The Many Returns of Sherlock Holmes

So let us start from the constructivist knack of critique and, derived from this propensity, with the questionable relationship with reality. Without trying to minimize this aspect, I want, as mentioned earlier, to show that it is not at loggerheads with a more "realistic" realism, if you indulge me this awkward formula—that is, with an authentic positioning with respect to critique's ultimate object, i.e., surrounding reality. To that effect, I will revisit critique's constructivism through the idiosyncratic concept of "autoevolution" employed by Stanisław Lem in *Summa Technologiae*, a juxtaposition that is, I think, more clarifying than it may appear at first blush.[20] The reader will recall that, by "autoevolution," Lem designates the taking up and continuation of the evolutionary narrative by humans. That is to say, in Lem's vision, the natural-evolution system's development is, during a second stage, "hacked" by one of its elements or actors, humankind, and thus transformed into a self-aware and self-regulated operation. One could argue that cultural systems and their evolution over time may be similarly conceived as unfolding in two steps: an initial, evolutive one, of implementation, testing, and growth, where, given that, after all, what is going on is essentially cultural and artificial, not natural, a self-reflexive component is not lacking but takes a backseat to the "blind," heuristic way in which the system is testing itself; and a second phase, which kicks in when the system, which by now has obviously stood the test of time and relevance, becomes sufficiently self-reflexive to be able to self-regulate.

What does critique have to do with all this, one might ask. My hypothesis is that critique is just another system that has completed its step one and proves ready, at the dawn of the new millennium, to begin step two. I call the latter *neocritique,* and I propose that it comes down to an epistemological-interpretive tune-up geared to upgrade and improve that modus operandi that ensures critique's overall consistency. What sets the two stages apart is a higher degree of self-consciousness; what brings them together and speaks to a certain continuity is the possibility of envisaging—also heuristically—the second phase by drawing on the problems posed by the first. What are these problems as far as critique goes? To answer, I would point out that critique is based on a series of structural contradictions or antinomies, among which one of the most important is the tension between its "suspicious" character and the utopian impulse. In his Freud essay, Ricoeur made the point, frequently ignored, that the opposite of suspicious reading is faith. Or, critique seeks to integrate both terms of the equation by simultaneously aligning itself during its campaigns of critical rewriting of reality, history, and the like with materialist deconstruction as well as with the idealist, largely utopian project of reconstruction. But the very notion of rewriting, which is so essential to how critique goes about making sense of literature and relating it to "world," "history," and so forth, destabilizes critique, undercutting its rewriting efforts. The notion and praxis in question create, quite typically, confusion between the descriptive and prescriptive registers of critical activity, to wit, between what critique does describe and that which it would like to describe, or, in Eco's terms, between what critique rewrites by *interpreting* the text and what it rewrites by *utilizing* the text. In other words, during critique's ambitious, two-pronged reading gambit, interpretation risks becoming a phantasm, another construction that compounds critique's inherent constructivist verve and leads to a *multiple* constructivism: although critique acknowledges that there is a historical reality outside the text, it invariably latches onto history's textual form;[21] the text being interpreted is rewritten—sometimes radically—by means of allegories that mediate between text and history; and the critical rewrite or interpretation routinely vacillates between description and a more or less creative, even fanciful reconstruction of its literary object. Last but not least, beyond the quasi-mystical sense, of Heideggerian Being, with which in Jameson critique infuses history—an untranscendable horizon inside which all texts are inscribed and all interpretations are carried out—this history is ultimately a mere theoretical construct and thereby a function of the shifting postulates of Marxism and psychoanalysis. For, no sooner had the theory of social class and production means changed than history's "untranscendable" horizon was transcended by another one, differently theorized.

Now, I am not searching, through the autoevolution concept, for a solution to these problems by stepping outside the system. Rather, I attempt to show how the system resets itself from within. For, in my judgment, it can mend itself once the glitch—in this case the naïve-idealist faith in a *direct* contact with history—has been caught and eliminated without damages to the system's coherence. Put otherwise, I explain how the constructivism of such complex ensembles as critique is not necessarily anti-realist. Quite the contrary, even when they build elaborate fictions, these systems keep self-maintaining or "autoevolving" based on feedback—a *contingent* sort of input, though—from reality. To show what all this means in practice and complete my demonstration, I revisit the body of works centered around Sherlock Holmes. As noted upfront, the premise of this operation is an effective correlation between the network of critique and the network of writings devoted to Holmes, an idea which, incidentally, is far from new. Both are cultural webs, and both can be seized as heterogeneous, at once literary and socio-political-economic. Furthermore, common to them all is a central actor: the figure of the detective. His roving across the networks as character, object of analysis, and the critic's alter-ego throws bridges between them. The detective and the critic alike investigate reality methodically, penetrating different societal levels, traversing heterotopic spaces, reading, interpreting, applying various legal codes, and amassing facts and figures they afterwards work into a coherent narrative or theory as closely accounting for reality as possible or, better still, shuttling constantly back and forth between the gathering of raw data and their construal into a theory or explanation of the whodunnit kind. There is, in fact, an old fascination of critique critics with Holmes in particular and detectives in general; no wonder these critics have been frequently likened to a detective. Seizing on this commonplace analogy, Michel Serres has pointed out that critique practitioners adopt a "'detective' logic" that looks suspiciously at the surrounding world, which turns them into objects of suspicion for other "detectives."[22]

It bears keeping all this in mind as we work our way, albeit succinctly, through the corpus of works featuring Holmes. Such writings, I might specify, comprise not only the actual Doyle canon—fifty-six stories and four novels published between 1887 and 1927—but also its series of updates, including some pastiches, in contemporary literature. All these make up a vast, transnational latticework of literary texts across which Holmes is born and reborn in characters and settings different from the original's. Not only that, but even inside the original corpus Holmes himself is not an "isomorph" character either. In fact, readers noticed, at the time of the publication of the 1903 story "The Adventure of the Empty House," a split in the detective's personality after his return following his faked death at the Reichenbach waterfall in "The Final Problem" (1893). Prior to the simulated plunge into the depths of the cascade during the fight with Professor Moriarty, Holmes came off as individualistic, egocentric, arrogant, and extremely cold in his dealings with people, but after the hiatus between his "death" and his return, he has changed into a warmer person in his relationship with others, including his friend Watson. He is no longer the superhuman being from before, perched—to paraphrase Nietzsche—four thousand feet above human desires. Such a "tamed" Holmes surfaces mainly in the last two volumes Doyle devoted to him, *His Last Bow* and *The Case-Book of Sherlock Holmes*, where the writer informs us that Holmes has retreated to Sussex and has taken up beekeeping, which, as we learn from the short story "His Last Bow," is the subject of Holmes's own book, *Practical Handbook of Bee Culture*.

But, as is well known, Holmes's career did not end when Doyle said goodbye to him. One of the tongue-in-cheek conventions shared by "Sherlockians"—scholars who "believe" Sherlock to be a real person, Watson the true author of the short stories, and Doyle their mere "editor"—holds that Holmes is still alive.[23] A metafictional joke, this plays both on the affection, otherwise real, of this community of kindred spirits for the detective and on the basic truth that *fictional* people cannot die as real individuals do. Be that as it may, Gaiman mines the idea of Holmes's immortality in "The Case of Death and Honey" (2011). In this short story, Holmes travels to Japan, where he discovers the secret of everlasting life in the honey of the bees tended by an old Japanese man. At the end, the detective sets out to look for his friend Watson to share with him the results of the discovery. The most ingenious aspect of Gaiman's take on the theme, aside from the allusion to eternal life, lies in his de-emphasizing of the apparently gratuitous nature, as Doyle sees it, of the detective's late passion for beekeeping. In Gaiman, Holmes does not devote himself to bees for the hobby's sake, aesthetically, so to speak, but in an instrumental sense, for, through bees, he pursues a goal in the real world—that is to say, in *his* real world.

A second element in Gaiman's story worth pointing to concerns the nonhuman actors, the bees themselves. They are there for a reason, and this has to do with Holmes's "posthumanist" pursuits.[24] In *The Life of Bees*, a book published in 1901 and thus contemporary with Doyle and his hero, the Belgian symbolist Maurice Maeterlinck established a correlation between the survival of human civilization and the life of bees, "to whom we probably owe most of our flowers and fruits (for it is actually estimated that more than a hundred thousand varieties of plants would disappear if the bees did not visit them) and possibly even our civilisation, for in these mysteries all things intertwine."[25] The quotation has entered popular lore in a slightly altered and more dramatic form ("If the Bee disappeared off the face of the Earth, man would only have four years left to live") and, as has reached us, it has been often attributed to Albert Einstein.[26] In any event, what matters is that even in Doyle's time, our survival was linked

to that of bees. Nowadays, when the colony collapse disorder is affecting
melliferous bees on an alarming scale, this issue—coupled with the larger
crisis of global warming and the extinction of countless species—has taken
on a more intense urgency. This may well explain the frequency with which
Holmes's relationship with his bees has been explored in the post-Doyle
Sherlockian corpus, such as in the popular series by Laurie R. King, where
Holmes, whom Doyle had shown to be interested in one woman only, Irene
Adler, now has a relationship with a female detective, Mary Russell. Other
examples of this kind include a 2005 novel by Mitch Cullin, *A Slight Trick
of the Mind* and a 2004 novella by Michael Chabon, *The Final Solution*.

A third detail worth noting in Gaiman is the world spaces across which
Holmes moves. The detective's interest in places such as Japan in Gaiman,
but also in Cullin and others, is not arbitrary, for it has been prefigured
in Doyle.[27] For instance, Holmes fends off Professor Moriarty using the
"Japanese" wrestling style baritsu (even though the latter does not exist).
Later on, taking advantage of the narrative freedom provided by "The
Great Hiatus"—the three-year period between Holmes's Reichenbach
disappearance and his reappearance in "The Adventure of the Empty
House"—as well as of the clues Doyle drops about Holmes's trips to Tibet,
Mecca, and Khartoum, the authors of Sherlockian pastiches often associate
the detective with the "Orient."[28] The writings belonging to what I call the
postcanonical or "apocryphal" Sherlock —later fiction featuring him but not
authored by Doyle—and particularly those published after Edward Said's
1978 landmark book *Orientalism*, fashion a more progressive version of
Holmes that pushes back against an ethnocentric, Western-oriented model
rife with colonial reflexes.[29] Thus revivified, the Victorian detective invented
by Doyle has managed to reproduce himself in our era and maintain his
relevance and viability—with a difference. There are, as one might expect,
similitudes to the human prototype of the Doyle canon, which make it
possible for the hero to be recognized in the first place. In his afterlife,
however, Holmes shows up in a form that is not only narratively but also
ideologically rewritten, more progressive than his earlier embodiment. Thus,
thanks to writers who have fondly reworked a tradition that was certainly
not without its flaws, Holmes has taken on new qualities as he has become
part of a new constellation of texts *and* cognate values. "Reforming" the old
Holmes—a misogynist, class-privileged, highly specialized detective capable
of little empathy—has yielded an "improved" character. But, notably, the
resulting Holmes is not a specter of Doyle's hero, a zombie maneuvered
by mischievous progressive politics either. He is as alive as the "tutor"
Holmes; he is, in a sense, even more humane and is definitely more attuned
to contemporary reality.

The question to raise at this point is, of course, what might critique,
itself in need of "improvement," take away from Holmes's story? What is
the theoretical return, if you will, of Sherlock's many fictional returns? In

my view, the main lesson to learn from the character's numerous lives in
Doyle's work and literary legacy is, first, the value of a community of fans—
readers and writers eager to plug themselves into the Sherlockian web of
webs whether as consumers or as network "architects" and "maintenance
techs." For, to be sure, systems do not operate by themselves, and so, just
as Holmes depends on his afficionados, so too critique's welfare hinges on
an academic and institutional infrastructure and its faculty, departments,
students, resources, and the like. Second, the network the detective is a part
of has adapted itself to the evolution of reality, driven by the need, as shown
previously, to "fix" certain historical issues pertaining to the detective's
portrayal—his Eurocentrism and misogyny, for example—or, in other cases,
to allow some seemingly second-fiddle characters, such as the bees, from
the Doyle corpus to take center stage in postcanonical retellings. Because of
all this, the Holmes literary constellation has not moved away from reality.
To the contrary, Holmes's autoevolution—to go back once more to Lem's
language—has *intersected* actuality, one that must be here understood not
as Jacques Lacan did his ungraspable Real, but in the opposite, Latourian
sense of a domain of material networks of actors and practices.[30]

Repairing the Networks

The second problem tackled by this chapter, also via a set of chiefly literary
texts, is, as I said earlier, that of allegory. A crucial device in critique,
allegory is the literary legerdemain that transmutes reality into text and
vice versa. Through allegory, Jameson and those influenced by him turn,
over and over again, the reading of a text—any text—into an Althusserian
"interpellation" of the totality of the capitalist system, that is, of what
Jameson calls emphatically History. Most often misunderstood as a call to
historical contextualization, the famous injunction "always historicize!," by
which Jameson actually urges us to connect the text to a final, necessary,
and inescapable meaning of History, entails a repeated recourse to allegory.
Several problems stem, however, from such prodigal allegorical reiterations.
The least significant is the idealism at play here. For History, as Jameson views
it, avails itself of allegory so as to achieve self-fulfillment, just as Hegelian
History resorted to the "cunning of reason." More significantly, reliance on
allegory sets in motion tautology's vicious circle, which has, through allegory,
texts mirror History, past, present, or future, and, conversely, History reflect
itself in texts infinitely. Such perpetuum mobile-like specular mechanics of
cognition yields too little knowledge of either texts or reality. Accordingly,
this epistemological machinery is in need of repair or, as suggested above, at
least recalibration. Meant to give critique another lease on life rather than
scrap it, as some would, this operation purports neither to "repair" and

then reinstate allegory as such nor to do away with it as critique's favorite trope. What I want to do, instead, is, with a contractor's expression, to bring allegory up to a more materialist code. I propose to do so through an infusion with the "materialism of ... the aleatory and of contingency"[31] as formulated by Louis Althusser in opposition to "that horror," dialectical materialism.[32] As the French philosopher wrote late in life,

> The materialist philosopher ... is a man who always catches "a moving train," like the hero of an American Western. A train passes by in front of him: he can let it pass [passer] and nothing will happen [se passe] between him and the train; but he can also catch it as it moves. This philosopher knows neither Origin nor First Principle nor destination. He boards the moving train and settles into an available seat or strolls through the carriages, chatting with the travellers. He witnesses, without having been able to predict it, everything that occurs in an unforeseen, aleatory way, gathering an infinite amount of information and making an infinite number of observations, as much of the train itself as of the passengers and the countryside which, through the window, he sees rolling by. In short, he records sequences [sequences] of aleatory encounters, not, like the idealist philosopher, ordered successions [consequences] deduced from an Origin that is the foundation of all Meaning, or from an absolute First Principle or Cause.[33]

In other words, what I would submit in the margins of Althusser's considerations is that it would be vital to critique's finetuning as neocritique to mitigate or perhaps even cast aside the finalist thrust of its allegory's usage, in favor of a process based on the contingent exploration of texts, history, and reality seen chiefly as *material* networks. To preempt a predictable criticism of what I am propounding here, I should add that such a shift to contingency does not conflict with the autoevolution idea. The evolution of the Sherlock network has never been a teleological process chasing a foreordained ideal but rather an adaptive and exploratory development sensitive to the signals the material networks that make up empirical reality send to textual webs.

To differentiate more clearly between the two uses—finalist or materialist—of allegory, I turn once more to texts and to no more than two this time around, one fictional, the other nonfictional. The way I read them is indebted to Moraru's *Reading for the Planet*. The first is *Ne vom întoarce în Muribecca*, which Chirculescu published under the pseudonym Sebastian A. Corn. The point of departure of this meganovel, which follows in the tradition of Dan Simmons and Neal Stephenson, is the enigma surrounding the Victorian explorer Percival Harrison Fawcett. A friend of Doyle and H. Rider Haggard, whose literature he had influenced, Fawcett disappeared in 1925 in the Amazonian jungle while searching for the legendary city

Eldorado. The main characters in Chirculescu's book are a family of Jewish-Russian archeologists who, accompanied by their adolescent son, arrive in the Amazonian jungle to carry on Fawcett's work by digging at particular sites. These are the historical elements on which Chirculescu builds an extremely complex, narrative maze-like network that comprises real data (about the Amazonian jungle and its ancient populations, the history of the USSR, postcommunist Russia, and contemporary ecologism), imaginary tropes (Atlantis and Eldorado), popular culture and urban legends (conspiracy theories), and a rich intertextuality that features, among other items, allusions to comic books such as *Corto Maltese* or *Tintin*. Except for a character mentioned in passing, namely, Jean Patrulesco—a Romanian-born disciple of mystic fascists like René Guénon and Julius Evola, and who later allegedly influenced Aleksandr Dugin, regarded by some as Vladimir Putin's ideological strategist—Chirculescu's novel makes no direct reference to Romania. Yet many of the problems confronting the country over the last decades, such as Communism and, afterwards, the fairly traumatic transition to neoliberal economics, are worked into the story. *Ne vom întoarce în Muribecca* abounds in all sorts of intellectual genealogies of issues currently on the planetary ideological agenda, and which are woven into the novel's network through provocative debates on Communism and capitalism, the late Communist elites' sliding toward fascism, South America's ecological disasters, the modern-conservative dialectic and its relation to ancient and native civilizations, the relationship between religion and secularism under Communist regimes, and the geopolitical turmoil caused by the Russia-USA rivalry. To put it briefly, Chirculescu seeks to analyze the systemic nature of the contemporary world while, and *by*, constructing an intricate, transnational, and planetary network himself, in his very book.

As is well known, Jameson's theory on the deliberately and ostensibly allegorical nature of Third World and "peripheral" literatures, as opposed to the lesser, unconsciously allegorical character of writings from "central" cultures, has been widely contested. At first glance, Chirculescu's novel appears to bear Jameson's argument out plotwise through the conflict unfolding alongside the main storyline between a pair of supernatural entities, Old and Bangor. The difference between the two is that between unity (Old) and diversity (Bangor), apropos of which a crudely allegorical reading would situate the text in the political-symbolic space of the global dynamic that circumscribes the conflict between capitalism and Communism, but this would be a trivializing interpretation. Though all the pieces of the puzzle are there, the simplifying allegory would be sort of cartoonish and is in all actuality belied by the novel's complexity. In effect, Chirculescu eschews the grandiose finality of allegorical conclusions, his book declining, for instance, to proclaim the superiority of one system over the other. What it does, however, is canvas the two networks and entwine them by creating links and actors inside and across them. Thus, in the allegorical model revised by way of Althusser's concept and illustrated through a novel such as Chirculescu's, allegory works as a sociohistorically already-incorporated, contingent, and "interpellated" mechanism that does *not* automatically link texts and History anymore.

One of Chirculescu's sources, besides Fawcett's memoirs reworked by his son, the 1953 *Exploration Fawcett*, is the nonfiction book *The Lost City of Z: A Tale of Deadly Obsession in the Amazon* by David Grann. On one hand, Grann reconstitutes Fawcett's history. On the other, he himself travels to the jungle, investigating "the scene of the crime" on site. His journey into the past drags the findings into the present, for Fawcett's enigma is replaced or, better yet, reconfigured through the discoveries made by archeologist Michael Heckenberger. The book concludes with the latter's encounter with Grann, during which the outcomes of his archeological exploits are revealed. Thus, we learn, Heckenberger has discovered in the Amazonian jungle, roughly in the area where Fawcett carried out his searches, the ruins of an old, thriving civilization that had evolved a sophisticated agricultural system. The traces of this culture have been wiped out or covered up by the rainforest, surviving only as ruins that the archeologist brings back out of myth and immemorial time and into the "reality circuit." Between Fawcett's adventures and Heckenberger's discoveries there is an obvious, indeed allegorical tie, on which Grann actually builds his book, even though this allegory is not vital to it. One can actually imagine a plausible scenario in which Grann did not meet Heckenberger, or even one where Heckenberger did not discover anything. In that case, Fawcett's pursuits—and, implicitly, Grann's book—would yield no conclusions, and yet they would be no less valuable.

One more time, what does this all have to do with critique and its potential—in effect, desirable—retooling as neocritique? To answer the question, I would point out that authors such as Latour keep reminding us not just that everything in the world is connected, as the cliché goes, but that, in order for the connections to be foregrounded and accounted for, the very concrete "field work" of the anthropologist, sociologist, critic, and, not in the least, the *detective* deep inside them all is necessary. *This cognitive labor has a material thrust to it, which neocritique itself needs to recover and incorporate.* This is the same thrust or vector that drove Holmes out of his familiar Victorian ambiance and injected him constructively into other contexts; that led Grann to leave his comfort zone in New York City and check out the geographical and cultural background of the story he was researching, at the risk of getting lost in the Amazons; and that made Chirculescu abandon a writer's familiar universe and explore faraway places as well. In the fast-expanding planetary networks of narratives, neocritique can definitely come in handy given its capacity to chart, trace, and thereby *construct* the sequences of reality captured in texts, without looking *a priori* to corroborate, again and again, the same old determinism of the allegorical logic according to which the local is a symptom or harbinger of a "master signifier" such as capitalism or History. Refurbished as neocritique, critique's less ambitious yet worthy objective would and perhaps should consist in embarking on a journey without too many preconceptions, in deciding then and there, pragmatically, what roads to take, what landscapes to photograph, how to compile the resulting photograph albums, and what role those archives and pictures would play in our lives.

Notes

1   Some of the basic texts include: Jeffrey R. Di Leo, ed., *Criticism after Critique: Aesthetics, Literature, and the Political* (New York: Palgrave Macmillan, 2014); Rita Felski, *The Limits of Critique* (Chicago: University of Chicago Press, 2015); Elizabeth S. Anker and Rita Felski, eds., *Critique and Postcritique* (Durham, NC: Duke University Press, 2017); Matthew Mullins, ed., "Postcritique," special-topic issue of *American Book Review* 38, no. 5 (2017).

2   There are voices contesting that critique is going through a crisis. See, in this regard, Bruce Robbins, "Fashion Conscious Phenomenon," *American Book Review* 38 (2017): 5–6.

3   Bruno Latour, "Why Has Critique Run out of Steam? From Matters of Fact to Matters of Concern," *Critical Inquiry* 30, no. 2 (2004): 225–48.

4   The problem of "mediation," of a reality constructed by means of language, has been variously approached over the last years. The issues I bring up here intersect with the disciplinary field of so-called speculative realism, which critics such as Graham Harman have set up by drawing from Quentin Meillassoux's seminal work, *After Finitude: An Essay on the Necessity of Contingency*, trans. Ray Brassier (London: Continuum, 2008). Meillassoux's term for mediation is "correlationism." See, on this, Zahi Zalloua, "On Meillassoux's 'Transparent Cage': Speculative Realism and Its Discontents Author(s)," *symplokē* 23, nos. 1–2 (2015): 393–409. For a critique of speculative realism, see Peter Wolfendale, *Object-Oriented Philosophy: The Noumenon's New Clothes* (Falmouth, UK: Urbanomic, 2014).

5   Florin Chirculescu published *Ne vom întoarce în Muribecca* in 2014 (Bucharest: Nemira) under the pseudonym Sebastian A. Corn; David Grann, *The Lost City of Z: A Tale of Deadly Obsession in the Amazon* (New York: Doubleday, 2009).

6   The original expression employed by Ricoeur was "masters of suspicion." See Paul Ricoeur, *Freud and Philosophy: An Essay on Interpretation*, trans. by Denis Savage (New Haven, CT: Yale University Press, 1970). Ricoeur used the phrase "hermeneutics of suspicion" later and infrequently. For a solid analysis, see Alison Scott-Baumann, *Ricoeur and the Hermeneutics of Suspicion* (London: Continuum International Publishing Group, 2009).

7   See Michel Foucault, "Nietzsche, Freud, Marx," in *Aesthetics, Method, and Epistemology*, trans. Robert Hurley et al. (New York: The New Press, 1998), 269–78.

8　"Cultural critique has been that which the postmodern became at our hands as we applied the poststructuralist philosophy of language, textuality, and subjectivity to identity studies around the mid- to late 1970s," writes Christian Moraru in "Critique and Its Postnational Aftermath: Dialogism and the 'Planetary Condition,'" in Jeffrey R. Di Leo, ed., *Criticism after Critique: Aesthetics, Literature, and the Political* ([New York: Palgrave Macmillan, 2014], 100–1.)

9　Fredric Jameson, *The Political Unconscious: Narrative as a Socially Symbolic Act* (New York: Routledge, 2002), x.

10　In *Feminizing the Fetish,* Emily Apter writes: "The interdisciplinary approaches that I employ to look at the topic of fetishism in this book—narratological, New Historical, hermeneutical, feminist, and psychoanalytical—have often proved difficult to reconcile" (Ithaca, NY: Cornell University Press, 1992), ix.

11　This is the point Joseph North makes in his book *Literary Criticism: A Concise Political History* (Cambridge, MA: Harvard University Press, 2017).

12　Jameson, *The Political Unconscious,* 20.

13　Umberto Eco, *The Limits of Interpretation* (Bloomington: Indiana University Press, 1994), 57–8.

14　Jameson, *The Political Unconscious,* 281–2.

15　For a discussion regarding the demise of postmodernism, see Brian McHale, *The Cambridge Introduction to Postmodernism* (Cambridge: Cambridge University Press, 2015), 171–5.

16　Eve Kosofsky Sedgwick, "Paranoid Reading and Reparative Reading," in *Touching Feeling: Affect, Pedagogy, Performativity* (Durham, NC: Duke University Press, 2002).

17　See Maurizio Ferraris, *Manifesto of New Realism* (New York: State University of New York Press, 2014).

18　See Luc Boltanski and Eve Chiapello, *The New Spirit of Capitalism,* trans. Gregory Elliott (London: Verso, 2017).

19　Franco Moretti, *Distant Reading* (London: Verso, 2013), 155.

20　Stanisław Lem, *Summa Technologiae,* trans. Joanna Zylinska(Minneapolis: University of Minnesota Press, 2013).

21　Ian Buchanan, *Fredric Jameson: Live Theory* (London: Continuum, 2007), 58–9.

22　See Michel Serres with Bruno Latour, *Conversations on Science, Culture, and Time,* trans. Roxanne Lapidus (Ann Arbor: The University of Michigan Press, 1995), 133–4.

23　Leslie S. Klinger, ed., *The New Annotated Sherlock Holmes,* 3 vols. (New York: W. W. Norton, 2005–6).

24　See also Juan Ramírez, *The Beehive Metaphor: From Gaudí to Le Corbusier,* trans. Alexander R. Tulloch (London: Reaktion Books, 2000).

25　Maurice Maeterlinck, *The Life of the Bee,* trans. Alfred Sutro (New York: Dodd, Mead, and Company, 1901), 388–9.

26　See Quote Investigator, "If the Bee Disappeared Off the Face of the Earth, Man Would Only Have Four Years Left To Live," August 27, 2013, https://quoteinvestigator.com/2013/08/27/einstein-bees/ (accessed September 15, 2020).

27   See also the Japanese series *Miss Sherlock* (2018), which is set in Tokyo. Here, not only do characters' ethnicities change, but their sexes do as well. Both Sherlock and Watson are women. See also Sherlockians' contributions collected in Yuichi Hirayama, Masamichi Higurashi, and Hirotaka Ueda, eds. and trans., *Japan and Sherlock Holmes* (New York: Baker Street Irregulars, 2004).

28   Asian American writer Dale Furutani invokes the inspirational force of these elements in the preface to his own attempt to associate Holmes with Japan. See Dale Furutani, "Author's Forward," in *The Curious Adventures of Sherlock Holmes in Japan* (Seattle, WA: Miharu Publishing, 2011), https:// www.amazon.com/Curious-Adventures-Sherlock-Holmes-Japan-ebook/dp/ B006CPC1EU (accessed September 15, 2020).

29   See Louise Nilsson, David Damrosch, and Theo D'haen, eds., *Crime Fiction as World Literature* (New York: Bloomsbury, 2017), especially Michael B. Harris-Peyton, "Holmes Away from Home: The Great Detective in the Transnational Literary Network" (215–31); Wei Yan, "Sherlock Holmes Came to China: Detective Fiction, Cultural Meditations, and Chinese Modernity" (245–55); and David Damrosch, "A Sinister Chuckle: Sherlock in Tibet" (257–70).

30   See Matthew Mullins, *Postmodernism in Pieces: Materializing the Social in U. S. Fiction* (New York: Oxford University Press, 2016).

31   Louis Althusser, *Philosophy of the Encounter: Later Writings, 1978–87*, trans. by G. M. Goshgarian (London: Verso), 167.

32   Althusser, *Philosophy of the Encounter*, 291.

33   Althusser, *Philosophy of the Encounter*, 277–8.

14

DIGICRITICISM:
Profession On(the)Line

Adriana Stan

If the invention of print has "individualized" the authorial conglomerate behind the collective, literary and nonliterary undertakings of premodern times, digital techniques of writing, reading, storing, processing, and transmitting information are about to render once again the individual an anonymous constituent of an ever-expanding network of discourses. This does not mean, however, that people are reading or writing less. Although it has been considered the main culprit for the "death of the book," the digital medium has actually opened up new venues for writing and reading, at the same time that it has brought back philological practices such as commentary and annotation.[1] The textual thrust of digital culture is obvious, from the HTML code to the most basic computer operations that "inscribe" information into the machine's database. Such inscriptions have led Alan Kirby to define the cultural products of "digimodernism" as a "new form of textuality," whose traits are openness, arbitrariness, and anonymity.[2] And yet, as has been observed, digitality has not reworked just the structure of cultural texts but also how we perceive, evaluate, and generally relate to them. It is with such changes in mind that Milad Doueihi has determined "the reinvention of communication models and everyday values" and "the restructuring of knowledge spaces and access to culture" as harbingers of a new, "digital humanism," whose social articulations already reach beyond interactions with technology.[3]

Starting from a similar premise, this chapter discusses the wide-ranging *digital relocation* of literary culture and its actors. Prompted by a number of factors and events but decisively accelerated by the informatics era, this development has brought about new sites, modalities, and values of writing, reading, and creativity. In literary criticism, my focus in what follows, the most significant upshot of this process has been the broadening gulf between two interpretive regimes, academic (or "specialized," done inside universities and research centers) and popular (or "public"), which, these days more than before, are undergirded—and pulled apart—by increasingly contrasting forms of critical subjectivity and personal investment. Largely speaking, the divide has also separated, of late, traditional or *analog criticism*—critical work in traditional print arenas—and criticism in digital forms and environments, or what I call *digicriticism*. What we are witnessing worldwide today is the disappearance of the middle-ground zones that have accommodated the public manifestations of criticism throughout modernity. Thus, for the first time in the history of the discipline, criticism functions, as I argue, on two different planes or in two distinct spheres, and this discrepancy of location and medium translates into an asymmetry or even divergence of agenda, "style," and tools. This multifaceted disjunction is due, more than anything else, to the spread of lay interpretive practices across the internet on a scale that would have been inconceivable at any stage of analog criticism.

Professional critics themselves have lamented the explosion of nonspecialist criticism online as well as of the "delegitimizing" effects of this body of work on mainstream scholarship, but the deeper causes of digicriticism, the *need* for it, and its ramifications still have to be addressed adequately. Pointing to the wide availability of the medium only scratches the surface of the problem. To be sure, digicritical changes in how we do and think about criticism have had a global reach, much like the dissemination of digital technology overall, regardless of field. Across the world, literary criticism nowadays follows the same, two-track trajectory, catering either to academic microcommunities or to macrocommunities of ordinary readers. What must be said, though, and what I emphasize in my presentation, is that these digicritical communities do not operate in cultural *vitro*. They are shaped not only by the latest postanalog technologies but also by the *longue durée* impact of certain engrained, communal literary values, which have been absorbed and recast into the new media and sites of expression. Compared to North American digital culture, which continues to provide the baseline for digital studies across the theory commons, Eastern Europe can be instructive in this respect. With long and proud histories of "journalistic" or "public" criticism—reviews and essays chiefly in weeklies of substantial audience and prestige—East European literary cultures are forced nowadays, as I show below, to recover and exercise some values and functions of this tradition into high-traffic digicritical forums. If in the United States and the West generally social conversation about literature, for example, oriented as it has been by market strategies and projections, has centered mostly on consumer demands and responses, bestseller lists, and the like, in Eastern Europe it has been guided, to no negligible degree, by an "old-school," evaluative professional criticism that has expanded its operations into the world of websites and blogs. It is worth asking, then, how is public discourse on literature being retooled in digital environments that are both integrated into global-scale netscapes and energized by local cultural histories and practices?

The Parallel Lives of Digicriticism

The digital revolution in contemporary literary culture initially weakened time-honored institutions such as universities, publishing houses, and journals before they recovered from the cybershock and decided to go digital themselves partially or completely. In the meantime, the arena of literary exchanges has grown larger so as to include new sites, actors, reading protocols, and literary values.[4] Emboldened by the "democratic" format intrinsic to digital platforms, lay criticism has been proliferating while its scholarly counterpart, especially the segments invested in projects like World Literature and quantitative analysis, has been "distancing" itself methodologically from its literary object. Thus, at a time just about anyone can aspire to become an online critic, theorists like Bruno Latour and Franco Moretti have proclaimed the "death" of critique and close reading. This is another sign that, in parallel to affording a rather old-fashioned, aesthetic-assessment-driven survival of critical commentary in and inroads into heretofore untapped layouts and media, the digital age has witnessed and even strengthened a sociocultural division in terms of how what I have described as popular-culture-oriented macrocultures and expert microcultures, respectively, handle literature. Also questioning the modernist doxa that technological and professional advancements are joined at the hip, this split has compounded the situation we, critics, are in after the onset of digitality. For instance, one can do and oftentimes one does do pretty traditional criticism online, while academics reluctant to express themselves digitally may be quite innovative methodologically. At the origin of such contradictory developments lies a chain of infrastructural shifts the globalization of the internet brought to light midway through the 2000s, when changes in the publication and distribution of literature as well as in access to it threatened to render the specialized, sometimes academically affiliated "journalistic" type of critic and cultural commentator an all but obsolete socioprofessional category. But the same transformations boosted a more popular, mass-appeal-minded, and stylistically and analytically simplified variety of "critical journalism." A flurry of books that came out around this time anticipated and sometimes already documented these

intersecting and colliding trends along with the steps forward—or back—
they marked inside and outside literature and literary criticism.[5]

No doubt, ours is a moment of both headway (in some areas) and decline
(in others). As far as the downturn goes, it has affected a certain medium
(print) and, again, a certain critical mode (old-fashioned, "journalistic," or
aesthetic feuilleton-style criticism) dominant in it. This twofold crisis has hit
hard Eastern Europe, where, since the nineteenth century, entire literatures
had coalesced around the written press and book reviews in popular
magazines. Unfortunately, digital studies has all but overlooked the big
difference this kind of historical investment in print, literary magazines, and
so forth can make, assuming instead that the globalization of technology
leads automatically to a similar homogenization or, better yet, to a
homogenization of the medium likely to enfeeble the cultural attitudes and
discursive reflexes fostered by old national media and informing the writing
and reading of literature. It bears repeating, therefore, that the relative
consistency if not uniformity of new media practices and their theoretical
constructions in the United States constitutes an exception rather than the
planetary norm.[6] Granted, we can no longer use territorial units of analysis
to measure translocal phenomena of the new media, whose technologies
reterritorialize communities with little regard for national borders and
geographies.[7] But this does not mean that such de- and re-territorializing
logic of digitality, so typical of digital studies in their mainstream, Western
instantiation, applies automatically in the same way to other countries and
continents, especially to places such as Russia and China, whose digital
worlds, "naturally restricted"[8] through language, regional platforms, and
monitoring policies still remain insufficiently known.[9]

Accounting for the quasi coherence of digital studies in the West and
elsewhere is the field's homogeneous epistemological heritage. Part and
parcel of the latter, poststructuralism and postmodernism had pushed
for the decentralization of knowledge before the postanalog era fleshed
out its own sociocultural forms and concepts. Most aspects of digitality
have borne out the hypotheses of Gilles Deleuze, Félix Guattari, and Jean-
François Lyotard, and these theoretical imports have reinforced the impact
of postmodern experimentalism on digital-born literature in the 1990s. The
poststructuralist idea that cuts to the core of the emerging digital topologies
is, of course, the network, which has by now become the concrete way "of
experiencing the present and inhabiting the social world."[10] Nonetheless,
despite their speculative nature, such philosophical notions fall short
of elucidating the whole ambit of phenomena cropping up in the digital
regime of literature. To get a sense of what it means to write literature as
well as about it in the exchange and sharing mode of digital platforms, we
should, in fact, approach the whole problem by going the other way around,
namely, *from* technology *to* concepts. Thus, starting with the digital format,
we can notice that it invites users to "act"[11] and "express themselves."[12]

E-reading offers, we are told, "dynamic potentialities" that are superior to reading material in print and enable readers to intervene directly in texts.[13] Because it is sensorially immersive, digital reading demands not only a cognitive investment but also a kinesthetic effort, and the multiple facets of subjectivity thus mobilized project, as in video games, a magnified "I." On the other hand, technology coops up individual initiative within a collectivity poised to define its members, as in platforms and reading applications like ReadSocial, Blurb, LULu, Wordclay, where readers share their comments as they read alongside other readers or communicate directly with the author. This way, digital space creates a literary reader that is socialized and massified, while also encouraging a *reading of identification*, intensely personalized and expressed in an apposite stylistics of transparency and candor, which the digital ethos promotes as a guarantee of the literary product's marketability.

The buzz whipped up by the internet around literature can become an opportunity for less visible literary forms such as poetry.[14] But popular genres benefit from online circulation too, and this is true especially of fan-fiction frenzy, which fuels so-called "participatory culture."[15] Still, the new sociocultural status of reading does not so much index a "progress" in literary culture as an increase of literature's presence on the consumer market. In his brilliant 2010 *Bring on the Books for Everybody: How Literary Culture Became Popular Culture*, Jim Collins pursues this process in North American culture.[16] Ever since the 1990s, Collins shows, the Hollywood adaptation and remake trend, the book clubs inspired by Oprah Winfrey's, and more generally the promotion, through channels of mass entertainment, of interest in literature as pastime reflective of a "quality" lifestyle have transformed literary reading into a hobby or habit that can be cultivated outside educational institutions. Following the advent of the electronic medium, this phenomenon reached its zenith after 2000, as the flourishing of corporations such as Barnes & Noble and Amazon is based on a convergence of the book industry with television, film, and an internet that can dispense with the contribution of professional critics. All these have merged into a mass literary culture oozing through all its media pores a characteristically romanticized and aestheticized discourse that exalts the common reader's disinterested pleasure of reading, which may be lacking in academic rigor but bespeaks, we infer, an "authentic" craving for enjoyable and possibly spiritually enriching reads. Beneficial synergies now obtain between aesthetic experience and consumerism, which modernity strove so hard to keep apart.

What strikes me as interesting here is that the digital expanding of literary culture into the public domain involves both the literary object, usually a book, and the commentary or review meant to help sell it. The conventions of the public regime of literary interpretation are in full display online, from platforms like Goodreads to sites such as Amazon and Barnes

& Noble. *Popular criticism in digital form*, it turns out, has adopted analysis techniques from *professional, "journalistic" criticism in print* and has thus preserved and amplified the didactic image of intensive, passionate reading capable of transporting readers out of their mundane existence. At the same time, cyberinterface reapportions the critic's authority in ways that differ a great deal from the prestige rites of traditional literary life. A case in point is the constantly updated online reviewing system set up by the major bookstore chains, which ranks reviewers and ensures their visibility based on the frequency with which they post and the feedback they get from the site's visitors. Since lay critics' opinions exert a direct influence on consumer patterns, the reviewers promoted by the chains often represent a "current snapshot of sales."[17] Like all discourse susceptible of forging public consensus, and, in this situation, of receiving positive feedback, the most visible reviews are also usually the most conventional. Unlike the conflictual structure of traditional literary groups, online literary communities take shape around what is shared (in all senses) and by the same movement rendered transindividual, at least partly stereotyped in matters of taste, experience, or opinion. Readers tend to give credit to other readers especially if the latter confirm the former's judgments. Where the predigital literary world was, and still is, one of arguments and even wars, the online medium has created around literature, through the "overwhelmingly positive" reviews shown off by booksellers, an artificial, hothouse climate of diffuse and equalizing celebration.[18] Consequently, lay critics and, first and foremost, the commercial forces behind them can today manipulate literary consumption at a level where professional criticism just cannot compete. On the British and American book markets, sales are dictated to a sizeable degree by consumer reviews, and recommendation lists or top picks on a certain theme are composed algorithmically. The cultural-rhetorical structure and attributes of old-style book reviewing have been strewn so profusely across the digiscape that they have almost vanished into the thin air of mass consumption.

But the digital medium alone is to blame for the diminished leverage or even disappearance of the conventional, expert critic neither outside nor inside the ivory towers, where digicriticism is also a reality already, in ways both comparable to and unlike what is going on in high-traffic blogs and chat rooms. An entire evolutionary scenario of post-World War II criticism has led to where we are now. Or so believes Rónán McDonald, who, echoing Terry Eagleton's older complaints, has taken to task theoretical lingo and cultural studies' presumed extreme suspicion of the "aesthetic," which, we are told, have undermined academic criticism's authority to set and uphold value standards and, overall, to perform a social role.[19] Nor is non-digital criticism's main anxiety caused by the threat posed by post-analog commentary's forays into a public territory that academics have basically abandoned anyway. Instead, the apprehensiveness and insecurity stem from the pressure of the digital world as a whole, whether or not a new kind of criticism claims a piece of it—that is, from the ever-growing digitized archives, from the hyperabundance and steadily more sophisticated reading toolkits, and from the wave after wave of big data that wash over the field of the humanities and complicate our attempts to navigate the intimidating literary high seas and get our interpretive bearings amid the world maze of connections and possibilities. Of late, the humanities have had to pick up the gauntlet of such challenges of the enlarging "netosphere" also by tackling the problematics of "totalization" associated with the shift in paradigm triggered, interestingly enough, by the "anti-totalist" linguistic, postmodern, and cultural turns.[20] No doubt, the success of methods derived from network-society and world-systems theory as well as from comparative literature's more and more pronounced, germane leaning toward macro— regional, hemispheric, and global—scales of investigation attests to digital epistemology's influence, one marked by an all-embracing systematics, combinatorial mechanics, and a language consisting in elements both stable and as limited numerically as possible.

How the humanities will respond to their inevitable digitalization depends on how they will manage the conflict between quantitative and qualitative approaches. For now, the academic field of the digital humanities illustrates, no less clearly than online, "popular" critical activities, how the actors and goals of criticism are being reconfigured under the pressure of the digital. Big data analysis lowers the extent and role of the critic's intervention because the algorithms deployed to organize information lessen the part previously played by critical discourse "as we know it," and, in a similar vein, visual aids such as images, diagrams, and the like speak for themselves. Also, where the traditional critic could and more often than not did work alone, a single scholar would find it hard to handle all the implications of a big data venture better suited for interdisciplinary teamwork. Moreover, the history of the takes on a certain problem can be strategically ignored so as to identify textual evidence and issues "untainted" by critical prejudice and thus start afresh. Big data then arguably calls for a less involved interpreter, whose "explicative" efforts are confined to those "assembling" routines Latour thinks should supersede a scholarship too much enamored with "debunking."[21] This de- or im-personalization of criticism also explains the digital recovery of modernist formalism, which was keen on textual materiality, on that play of linguistic patterns and variations that enables one to read a text on its own terms.[22] Indeed, "algorithmic criticism" can essentially operate as quantitative linguistics and thus boil down a text to lists of correlated terms.[23] The latter unearths no "deep structure" but stuff already available to tallying and tabulations, already on the surface.

This is why "surface reading" too participates in this move away from depth, critique, and "classical" criticism, a shift purporting, as Mihai Iovănel observes in his chapter in this volume, to replace the hermeneutic of suspicion through which, as Stephen Best and Sharon Marcus claim, a "strong critic" forces the work to give away its deep-buried secrets. Best and Marcus have in fact envisioned "a space of minimal critical agency," a site marked out by a "description of patterns that exist within or across texts" and animated by a "corrected subjectivity" for which computers can serve as both model *and* tool given that "they are weak interpreters, but potent describers, anatomizers, taxonomists."[24] In the other dimension of the literary archive's daunting scope—quantitative breath or volume rather than a text's depth— corresponding to "surface" is distance, or "distant reading." Since no one will ever be able to read all available literature, close reading, Moretti thinks, is pointless. Its place, he also says, could be taken by computer algorithms able to "read" those "units much smaller or much larger than the text: devices, themes, tropes—or genres and systems," which do a better job of accounting for the evolution of literature than "the internal form" of texts.[25] Involving graphics, diagrams, maps, and computer-generated models, distant reading resembles cybernetic neo-formalism-based close reading in that both set limits to the interpreter's subjective involvement, and both discourage favoring one out of several possible interpretations.

All these strains of academic digicriticism explore a text's relationships with a code or database, as well as the range of possibilities generated by them, and such explorations follow principles similar to electronic literature and multimedia digital art developed after 1990. Computerized literary analysis starts from the same post-expressive premises underwriting hypertextual and interactive fiction.[26] They all situate literary creativity at the "intersection between the programmability of the computer and the programmability of language."[27] Moreover, the anti-hermeneutical stance of the digital humanities, which can be correlated with psychology, biology, and neuroscience rationales for the "co-evolution"[28] of our cognitive faculties and technology, has substituted "deep attention," a form of focused, sustained concentration called for by literary perusal, with the polyfocal "hyperattention" developed in interaction with stimuli-saturated media.[29] This cognition mode no longer privileges an aesthetic experience that entails meaning-making, a shift reflected in multimedia and digital art theory, where non-hermeneutical concepts linked to interaction or performativity have been front and center for a while now. It comes as little surprise that the move away from hermeneutical or interpretive considerations has tempted critics as well. After all, up to a point at least, literature too can be dealt with, even *described*, without being *interpreted*. If we "forget" that algorithms and their keywords are already an interpreter or critic's doing, then we can let graphics do the talking and patterns take shape out of the data mass in support of several interpretive possibilities and thus of a potential critical debate. And yet an important question remains: to what kind of audience can the discoveries of the digital humanities be transmitted given the technical language in which they are couched?

The Digital Afterlives of Criticism

The language and methods of the digital humanities stand few chances, I would suggest, of reaching audiences beyond academic communities. Instead, as I have insisted in the first part of this chapter, the public talk of literature—whether the debate takes place in print or in cyberspace—stretches far beyond universities and criticism's time-honored institutions, which is why McDonald misses so much American intellectuals such as Lionel Trilling and Susan Sontag, who were able to capture people's attention and guide the public life of literary ideas, as Matthew Arnold and F. R. Leavis had done in Great Britain. Nevertheless, it can be argued that, especially in the United States, journalistic criticism has been less extensive, in terms of participants, social diffusion, and effective influence, than in Europe, particularly in the East. Here, the critical culture nurtured by weeklies, monthlies, and even newspapers has always been more prolific and overall more substantial than specialized scholarship, also managing to engage a public possibly less diverse than in the West but much bigger and to which it spoke throughout modernity on behalf of the nation-state's self-authorizing, literary and aesthetic platform. The literary press kept on drawing a large readership in the twentieth century as Communist regimes tried to co-opt magazine culture and this culture's staple, the critical-feuilleton contributor—the "literary chronicler," as he or she was known in countries such as Romania—whose clout and even charisma have been, historically, virtually unmatched in this corner of the world.[30] The totalitarian strictures of the Cold War notwithstanding, literary-cultural journalism's role in the formation of East European literary cultures was paramount, benefiting as it did, in some cases, from a freedom of expression unavailable to academic criticism. After Communism's fall, the decrease in mass appeal and the devaluing of the leadership ethos traditionally embraced by the region's written-press critics and intellectuals weakened the publishing infrastructure of literary life even more than the concurrent rise of digital alternatives to print.

Initially caused by the collapse of the book industry financed by Communist governments, the decline of literary-weekly criticism in postcommunist countries such as Romania and Russia accelerated with the arrival of the internet, whose 2000–2010 expansion was, notably, faster in Russia than anywhere in Europe.[31] Even so, Russian digiculture lags behind the social dynamism and artistic and innovative effervescence of digitality in places such as North America. The general behavior of Russian consumers and the authoritarian policies of the Vladimir Putin regime are only some of the reasons for this situation. Post-Soviet cultural consumption itself is influenced by new technologies as well as by local traditions, which help understand why television is still the most popular Russian medium,[32] and why most intensely debated online are Stalinist and Communist-era issues, which are treated through "emotional posturing over mythologized historical events."[33] Furthermore, Russian digiculture has had to handle the legacy of the influential domestic notion of literary learnedness, a myth reinforced by the Cold War conflict with the "consumerist West." Stephen Lovell has tracked down the workings of this ideological fiction in the Tsarist and Soviet literary press, which, benefiting from the withering of civic institutions after the Bolsheviks' coming into power, took over and fulfilled a whole panoply of functions formerly performed by other social and political discourses in their professional arenas.[34] Thus, Lovell shows, the Russian magazine critic acquired in the nineteenth century a prophetic aura on the grounds that he or she spoke for the whole nation. Lasting into the twenty-first century, this intellectual model was revived in post-Stalinist culture, which permitted literary criticism to intervene through a carefully modulated, Aesopian language in broader disputes. More than mere literary magazines, *Literaturnaia gazeta* and *Gazeta literară* were, after 1964, in the former Soviet Union and Romania, respectively, voices from a public space much larger than the literature referenced in the titles of these publications. Thanks to the centralized economy of literary production, distribution, and reception, the highly visible and widely read columns of the critics of these and other weeklies and newspapers made quite an impact. The 1980s Perestroika further bolstered the social presence of the Soviet literary press to an unprecedented extent even when compared to other Socialist countries—millions of copies of the Russian equivalent of *American Book Review* were on sale, bought, and read—especially after it got the green light to publish the writings of Russian exile and dissident authors and to host discussions about reform.[35]

A different kind of democratization got underway once people were provided with new, digital vehicles and environments of communication. Yet the new medium did not do away with the East European book reviewer's central position in the cultural system, analog or not. Again, if there has been an erosion of this position over the past decades, it needs to be gauged over and against the disproportionate sway this critical institution held in the collective cultural imaginary before 1990, when East European critics enjoyed, in proportion with the frequency of their publications, a greater popularity and authority, critical and otherwise, than their Western colleagues. Stifling cultural consumption in a whole array of areas, Socialist politics and policies forced the otherwise inherently diverse cultivation, information, and entertainment needs of society to find outlets quasi exclusively in an artificially homogeneous body of high-brow literature, hence the veritable *mass* cult of this fairly "elite," narrowly defined literary notion and practice. No wonder the understandable surge of these frustrated needs after 1990, as well as the end of government protectionism and control of book production ended up dislodging literature as well as its "journalistic" commentary from their pride of place in the public's attention. In response, literary-weekly print criticism did attempt to reinvent itself by switching to the newspaper format, cutting back on the length of book reviews, adopting the tabloid style of glossy magazines and television talk shows, and so forth.[36] But these were band-aid solutions. The internet's exponential growth after 2000 sped up the breakdown of the outdated, "literarocentric" system, but without also doing away, as I reemphasize above, with popular-magazine book reviewing.

Unlike in places such as the United States, the digital served, at first, as a catalyst for this sort of critical activity in Romania, where moving the literary press to digital platforms between 2000 and 2008 actually triggered a spectacular rebirth of the book review, which was still deemed a prerequisite for a work's critical success. But the online medium has turned literary magazines into a different cultural object. Now that an increasing number of actors can share and distribute this or that commentary's link, individual articles can be extracted from the context of a certain issue or discussion and downloaded, shared, reposted elsewhere, and thus worked into new webs of discourse and culture, which makes it harder for periodicals to bring together people, texts, and ideas into their own networks as in the past.[37] To achieve and maintain the visibility required by the viability of such complex online assemblages, site contents have to be updated frequently, but the print weekly cycles of literary magazines just fall short in cyberenvironments. The next step in the digital transition, namely, the blogs affiliated with magazines and other publications who also have—or have solely—an online presence, has altered not only the makeup of such textual and cultural webworks but also their core genre: criticism. Russian book reviewers who have already established themselves in print media have adjusted to the format and rhetoric of blogs, offering "subjective and emotionally compelling assessments of current literature, that minimize the role of analysis and interpretation."[38]

By contrast, the Romanian literary blogosphere has been dominated by ordinary readers themselves, although the most famous among them, whose pen name is lucia terorista (Lucia the Terrorist), is not exactly an "ordinary" reader. Leaving her identity and day job shrouded in secrecy, lucia appears to have been educated before or immediately after 1990, demonstrating that high level of critical literacy typical of what I have dubbed Communist-era literarocentrism. An avid reader of hundreds of books per year, lucia does not seem picky about her reading material, which ranges from chick-lit to poetry, literary theory, and scientific books. Most importantly, she (assuming "she" is a woman) manages to convey effortlessly "everything critics usually write about a book." Her extensive, sophisticated analyses draw on specialized critical terms but show off an intimate reading experience complete with symbolic props. Her perusal settings speak and are conducive to reading for pleasure (armchair, cigarettes, lamp, etc.), and she often refers to what she calls "reading without aim or obligations" and the "passion for culture."

Such formulas do resonate with readers of all categories, including Mircea Cărtărescu, the greatest Romanian writer alive, and other contemporary writers, who are delighted to come across "someone who writes about books in a disinterested, passionate, and candid way."[39]

The success of such literary blogs proves that writers' all-important relationship with criticism lives on digitally, albeit in forms both different (popular if not populist) and weaker than during times when the regime would take care of the promotion and distribution of authors' output. Of course, the internet itself began, around 2000, to furnish, in exchange, East Europeans with a medium of self-marketing. For example, Victor Pelevin, Vladimir Sorokin, and Tatiana Tolstaia capitalized on the success of their own blogs, making up "the first generation of Russian writers whose status no longer depends on being published and promoted in literary magazines."[40] Not so much postcommunist Romanian writers, who did not manage equally well without critical backers. All the same, launched at the dawn of the digital age, in 2003, the Romanian platform clubliterar.ro did gather together young writers eager to make a name for themselves. Neither professional critics nor "geographical/regional criteria"—both traditionally crucial factors in the formation of the Romanian literary canon—were involved in the project, which ensured its novelty.[41] On the other hand, selective membership and intestine power struggles have turned it into a country club sort of site that does not really fit in the democratic space of the web and does not engage readers effectively either.

Others do, though. By the second half of the 2000s, literary platforms and blogs, then Facebook communities had absorbed strains and fragments of the rich literary conversation formerly hosted by print periodicals and had reconfigured and partly recaptured the audience of analog criticism in Romania. Possessing an average or above average literary competency, this newly constituted and more and more visible public consists of high school students, former or current literature majors, teachers, editors, or just common readers who enjoy books as a form of aestheticized lifestyle. This literary knowledge, operating as it does below the expertise level of pre-1990 readerships, has turned the bulk of Romanian digicritical varieties into a poor man's versions of what professional criticism used to be, even though, again, this has occurred in ways less bound up with the more commercially oriented online reading practices prevalent in the United States and elsewhere. As with lucia's, the most successful Romanian book-review blogs have continued to bank on the solid literary background and education of individuals who are trying to carve out reading profiles as personal as possible and therefore less influenced by the market and fads. Blogs such as bookishstyle.ro, carticafeasitutun.ro, colectionaradecuvinte. ro, chestiilivrești.ro situate literature within a complex cultural framework, at the crossroads of travel, cinema, painting, and so on. More clearly oriented toward an upper-crust, quasi-erudite book culture are platforms such as bookblog.ro, where students can find commentaries useful for the baccalaureate exam, and egophobia.ro, which balances literary and philosophical reviews. Even a site like serialreaders.com, more open to lay critics, does not exclude the participation of experts nor the blend of canonical literature and popular fiction, as visitors may come across a web page on Sandra Brown next to one devoted to a difficult poet such as Romanian modernist Nichita Stănescu.

A separate category of sites comprises those where aspiring writers replace digicritics. Because literature itself has been a, if not *the*, master narrative of sorts for over two centuries in the country, it is not surprising that, perhaps more than elsewhere, many have been thirsting for the noble status of author, hence the flooding of Romanian online spaces with literary wannabes, who have jumped at the opportunity to share their literary and critical efforts. In Romania, digital platforms cover a wide, dynamic, and virtually impossible to canvas territory of prolific dilettanti, which reflects not so much the emancipation, lack of inhibition, and bettering qualifications of ordinary literature readers, critics, and writers overall as their ambitions, many of them on show on popular sites such as eCreator. ro. Responding to the ever-growing online literary supply, some Romanian platforms—among them, hyperliteratura.ro and Qpoem.ro—now serve as pools from which would-be writers are selected and where forthcoming works' potential audience impact is tested out. At any rate, all of these digital formations and trends demonstrate that Romanian digiculture has taken in and reproduced structures, customs, and habitus of the traditional literary field, failing, so far, to diversify the public and bring into the fold additional audiences capable of approaching literature in new ways, be they of the consumption and entertaining kind. In effect, many literary platforms strengthen literature's social presence without taking the talk about it into other new areas. Poezie.ro, for instance, has been running for twenty years, an uncommon longevity among Romanian literary sites, and has had an average of three thousand daily visitors, which is consistent for the country. But the average duration of one visit, which is about 1.3 to 1.4 minutes, and the small number of pages (less than two) read during this time suggest that the platform is more of an archive of texts rather than a literary-dialogue network.[42] Ranked 3,000th nationally, the site can hardly compete with Goodreads, a generalist book-reviewing site where visitors spend four minutes typically and that has been rated 400th in the world.

As a matter of fact, following a decade of tentative exploration of online alternatives, the literary excitement about such sites, chatrooms, and critical blogs has faded after 2012, in the context of Facebook's growing popularity and steadily consolidating monopoly, which has had the effect of further dispersing and diluting literary discussions. Like other communities, literature groups that have mushroomed all over Facebook are usually active by posting texts and hyperlinks, while examinations or other considerations about literature are skin-deep as they rarely go beyond perfunctory praises and "likes." The onslaught of hacks too is more evident on Facebook than on older platforms with a more "exclusive" membership such as clubliterar. ro. By contrast, for "legit" and more established writers, the Facebook profile serves mostly as a display window for self-advertising, as few of them get into substantive dialogue with readers. Florin Iaru, Marius Chivu, and Radu Vancu, the Romanian writers who have attracted the most followers on Facebook, have built on reputations predating the move of some of their operations online. Buttressing their status and influence is their promotion of young talents—Marius Chivu as literary reviewer for the highly regarded magazine *Dilema veche* and Radu Vancu as founder of the critically acclaimed poetry festival zona nouă. Ideological compatibility with the liberal, center-right, and even conservative segments of the political spectrum that apparently dominates Romania's Facebook space is another reason the aforementioned writers have attracted interest. Still another is something I have already pointed out, to wit, the survival of traditional, print-related literary values and avenues, from the popular formula of the "literary circle" or cenacle to the tendency to spend online some of the cultural capital accrued in non-digital fashions, sites, and institutions of expression and accreditation. Consequently, the "democracy" of the online medium has not canceled out all elitist, closed-shop features that, with another paradox, have fostered the widespread appreciation of literature and have shored up its role as a community-building force in Romania. This accounts for a certain reluctance on the part of Romanian bloggers to wield the mass formulas of digicriticism and for their preference to behave, instead, rhetorically and otherwise, as "regular" critics. This also explains the feeble authorship drive of Romanian readers when it comes to contributing their own reviews on Goodreads, which, I might add, they access regularly. As for the print magazines, even though they have made changes in their online business and availability model, and in spite of their markedly diminished impact, they remain unrivaled and even aggressive as centers of literary power and prestige. In an effort to cling to their symbolic monopoly, some of them belittle digicriticsm and refer to otherwise well-known digicritics as *critici de pe net* (net critics), a designation that purports to be pejorative.[43] Even so, there have been few reasons for digicritical outlets not to reproduce analog critical culture's tactics and recipes; although open to larger audiences in both format and discourse, online magazine *Scena9* (New Scene) is not very different from "old-style" literary weeklies such as *Observator cultural.*

Scena9 and other "digivenues" of this sort go to show that the high-culture concept of literature typical of Eastern Europe and the rather unparalleled prestige this part of the world has bestowed on the critic are basically enjoying a new lease on life in digitalized Romania. As noted above, postanalog criticism has assimilated symbolic content and protocols of earlier literature and criticism. This has happened despite the generalized if protracted decline of literary-weekly criticism, what with professional print criticism having lost the ability to shape the evolution of contemporary literature in Romania and with the journalistic model, eminently embodied by the book reviews published weekly between 1960 and 1990 by the most important post-World War II Romanian critic, Nicolae Manolescu, having all but imploded, as have concluded most participants in the post-2010 debates on "the death of literary criticism." In any event, the bottom line is that social media community-oriented digicriticism has incorporated some of "old" criticism while digicriticism's academic branch—specialized, analytically rigorous, terminologically specific, and so on—is working its way into a transnational commons where the importance of digital toolkits, related methodologies, and collaboration are growing apace in places such as Russia and Romania.[44] These countries' critical cultures broadly, not just their scholarly digicritics, are more and more interested in aligning themselves with said commons and its evolving knowledge domains, whereas, in the past, even East European critics affiliated with higher-education institutions and their research units felt they also had to have a journalistic and "domestic" presence to fully legitimize themselves in the public eye.

It is fairly obvious that the post-2000 generation of critics feel differently. Generally speaking, they no longer seek to establish themselves as journalist-critics too, which in turn lowers the pressure on them to position themselves, no matter what their immediate concerns are, with respect to the ideological polarities with which literary culture happens to be wrestling, such as Slavophile-Western in Russia and aesthetic (literary autonomy)-extra-aesthetic (literary heteronomy) in Romania. Two decades had to pass after the implosion of the Communist-backed literarocentric system before a new, "millennial" or "postmillennial" academic criticism was finally ready to ask some hard questions about how this system had been built and which the consequences of its socially resilient mythology had been. Bringing into play, if belatedly, a hermeneutic of suspicion similar to the Western *critique* of the 1970s and 1980s, this revisionism suggested that this kind of inquiry and *interpretation* more generally were and would stay at the forefront of a critical culture where, by the same token, it is unlikely that a post-hermeneutic trend such as the digital humanities will become mainstream very soon.[45] True, the digital medium and technology are worldwide increasingly shared realities in literature, literary life, and literary criticism. But the versatility and effectiveness of digital epistemology, including its capacity to generate a post-interpretive criticism, also hinge on the volume and richness of digitality's concrete, literary manifestations. Or, in Romania, these still have to take off. New media art, digitally born literature, and the like are in their infancy. On the scholarly side, the few studies available on the digital imaginary rely on the outdated perspective of postmodern textualism.[46]

It is encouraging, though, that larger and larger cohorts of young Romanian writers, especially poets, have, since 2015, become fluent in "electracy," a computer skills-informed and -oriented literacy, whose bearings on their fluid imagination and formal-linguistic experiments are conspicuous. But electracy and a "professional" digicriticism keen on thorough analysis and value judgments are not incompatible; the odds are, both will thrive because both are needed. It is equally clear that, while one cannot resurrect the climate and institutions of the heyday of the kind of criticism—traditional in terms of both its medium and methodology—that had ruled the roost in the West until about 1968 and held out in Eastern Europe until the end of the Cold War, digicriticism has been coming about in a range of *geocultural variants*. These indicate that, in the age of global hyperconnectivity, cultural reality's transnational and interdisciplinary continuum has an "unworlded" or less "worlded" fragmented flipside where this reality's many sectors and elements do not communicate with one another. This is particularly true of literature and the literary humanities. Some World Literature theorists insist literatures become "of the world" not merely through the interliterary relationships that have shaped them historically but also through the conversation around them. The point of this conversation today is neither just to guarantee an audience for poems and novels, since other cultural apparatuses have been taken care of it quite successfully for some time now, nor to bridge the gap between the popular and academic regimes of literary interpretation but, rather, to repair the broken links and open up new communication channels inside a disjointed and dispersed literary scholarship. In the epilogue to a recent volume on electronic ("post-digital") literature, Joseph Tabbi bemoans the "protected enclosures" of publishing platforms of academic journals, which preclude interoperability and readers' commentaries, thereby also squashing the vital room in which ideas face off one another and, together, confront public reactions.[47] In the romantic period of the Web, such a democratic ecology seemed to be a click away and impervious to geographical barriers. Today, in the wake of all the revelations about privacy theft and data collecting, this goal is shaping up to be, with William Gibson's famous phrase, a "consensual hallucination" quite literally. Although digital technologies continue to exalt the myth of transparency, many mechanisms that regulate online interactions are still unknown, insufficiently understood, or hidden, much like codes, digital or not, remain beyond the reach of surface reading. If this is true, then the "old" humanities, which have historically excelled at code-breaking and language parsing, have not only their work cut out for them but also a shot at renewing their relevance.

Notes

1   Milad Doueihi, *Pour un humanisme numérique* (Paris: Seuil, 2011), 55.
2   Alan Kirby, *Digimodernism: How New Technologies Dismantle the Postmodern and Reconfigure Our Culture* (New York: Continuum, 2009), 22.
3   Milad Doueihi, *Pour un humanisme numérique*, 15–24.
4   Literary culture and electronic media do not necessarily exclude each other. The 2004 report from the National Endowment for the Arts "Reading at Risk" became "Reading on the Rise" in 2009, attesting, for the first time in thirty years, to an increased interest in reading.
5   See Andrew Keen, *The Cult of the Amateur: How Today's Internet Is Killing Our Culture* (New York: Doubleday, 2007); James Elkins and Michael Newman, eds., *The State of Art Criticism* (New York: Routledge, 2008).
6   John Downing, *Internationalizing Media Theory: Transitions, Power, Culture* (London: Sage, 1996), 144.
7   Nick Couldry, Andreas Hepp, and Friedrich Krotz, eds., *Media Events in a Global Age* (London: Routledge, 2010), 9.
8   Alexander Etkind quoted in Julie Fedor, "Conclusion," in *Memory, Conflict, and New Media: Web Wars in Post-Socialist States*, ed. Ellen Rutten, Julie Fedor, and Vera Zvereva (New York: Routledge, 2013), 238.
9   Platforms such as Vkontakte, Odnoklassniki, or Qzone, instead of the standard Facebook.
10 Patrick Jagoda, *Network Aesthetics* (Chicago: University of Chicago Press, 2016), 185.
11 Alexander Galloway, *The Interface Effect* (Malden, MA: Wiley, 2013), 85.
12 Lev Manovich, *The Language of New Media* (Cambridge, MA: MIT Press, 2001), 269.
13 John Cayley, "The Advent of Aurature and the End of (Electronic) Literature," in *The Bloomsbury Handbook of Electronic Literature*, ed. Joseph Tabbi (New York: Bloomsbury, 2018), 84.
14 See Kevin Stein, *Poetry's Afterlife: Verse in the Digital Age* (Ann Arbor: University of Michigan Press, 2010).
15 See Henry Jenkins, *Fans, Bloggers, and Gamers: Exploring Participatory Culture* (New York: New York University Press, 2006).
16 Jim Collins, *Bring on the Books for Everybody: How Literary Culture Became Popular Culture* (Durham, NC: Duke University Press, 2010).
17 Judith A. Chevalier and Dina Mayzlin, "The Effect of Word of Mouth on Sales: Online Book Reviews," *Journal of Marketing Research* 43, no. 3 (August 2006): 347.
18 Chevalier and Mayzlin, "The Effect of Word of Mouth on Sales," 345.
19 See Terry Eagleton, *The Function of Criticism: From* The Spectator *to Post-Structuralism* (London: Verso, 1984); Rónán McDonald, *The Death of the Critic* (New York: Continuum, 2007).
20 Christian Moraru, "'World,' 'Globe,' 'Planet': Comparative Literature, Planetary Studies, and Cultural Debt after the Global Turn," in *Futures of Comparative Literature: ACLA State of the Discipline Report*, ed. Ursula K. Heise, with Dudley Andrew, Alexander Beecroft, Jessica Berman, David

Damrosch, Guillermina De Ferrari, César Domínguez, Barbara Harlow, and Eric Hayot (New York: Routledge, 2017), 126.

21 Bruno Latour, "Why Has Critique Run out of Steam? From Matters of Fact to Matters of Concern," *Critical Inquiry* 30, no. 2 (Winter 2004): 246.

22 Jessica Pressman, *Digital Modernism: Making It New in New Media* (New York: Oxford University Press, 2014), 148.

23 Stephen Ramsay, *Reading Machines: Toward an Algorithmic Criticism* (Chicago: University of Illinois Press, 2011), 11–14.

24 Stephen Best and Sharon Marcus, "Surface Reading: An Introduction," *Representations* 108, no. 1 (2009): 1–21. The paper was initially presented at the 2006 ACLA Conference.

25 Franco Moretti, "Conjectures on World Literature," *New Left Review*, no. 1 (2000): 57.

26 See Marjorie Perloff, *Unoriginal Genius: Poetry by Other Means in the New Century* (Chicago: University of Chicago Press, 2010), and Kenneth Goldsmith, *Uncreative Writing: Managing Language in the Digital Age* (New York: Columbia University Press, 2011).

27 Manuel Portela, "Writing under Constraint," in *The Bloomsbury Handbook of Electronic Literature*, ed. Joseph Tabbi (New York: Bloomsbury, 2018), 191.

28 Thierry Bardini, *Bootstrapping: Douglas Engelbart, Coevolution, and the Origins of Personal Computing* (Stanford, CA: Stanford University Press, 2000), 143.

29 N. Katherine Hayles, "Hyper and Deep Attention: The Generational Divide in Cognitive Modes," *Profession* (2007): 187–99. See also N. Katherine Hayles, *How We Think: Digital Media and Contemporary Technogenesis* (Chicago: University of Chicago Press, 2012).

30 René Wellek, "The Essential Characteristics of Russian Literary Criticism," *Comparative Literature Studies* 29, no. 2 (1992): 115–40.

31 This information is provided by the World Telecommunications/ICT Indicators Database, as mentioned by Sarah Oates in *Revolution Stalled: The Political Limits of the Internet in the Post-Soviet Sphere* (New York: Oxford University Press, 2013), 6.

32 Arja Rosenholm, Kaarle Nordenstreng, and Elena Trubina, "Introduction," in their edited volume *Russian Mass Media and Changing Values* (New York: Routledge, 2011), 3.

33 Ilya Kukulin, "Memory and self-legitimization in the Russian blogosphere," in *Memory, Conflict and New Media: Web Wars in Post-Socialist States*, ed. Ellen Rutten, Julie Fedor, and Vera Zvereva (New York: Routledge, 2013), 116, 128.

34 Stephen Lovell, *The Russian Reading Revolution: Print Culture in the Soviet and Post-Soviet Eras* (Basingstoke, UK: Macmillan, 2000).

35 See "The Literary Journals: What Next? A Roundtable Discussion," *Russian Studies in Literature* 44, no. 4 (2008): 80–99. Translated by Liv Bliss from the Russian text "Literaturnye zhurnaly: chto zavtra?," *Znamia*, no. 1 (2008): 191–205.

36 Mihai Dinu Gheorghiu, *Intelectualii în câmpul puterii. Morfologii și traiectorii sociale* (Iași, Romania: Polirom, 2007), 340.

37 Marcello Vitali-Rosati, "Les revues littéraires en ligne: entre éditorialisation et réseaux d'intelligences," *Études françaises* 50, no. 3 (2014): 90.

38 Ilya Kukulin and Mark Lipovetsky, "Post-Soviet Literary Criticism," in *A History of Russian Literary Theory and Criticism: The Soviet Age and Beyond*, ed. Evgeny Dobrenko and Galin Tihanov (Pittsburgh, PA: University of Pittsburgh Press, 2011), 288.

39 Quotations from and the history of the blog retrieved from WayBackMachine, "Reader Terrorism: Books and Tobacco," https://web.archive.org/web/20100522120357/http://www.terorista.ro:80/2009/04/07/aproximativ-trei-ani#comments (accessed January 4, 2019).

40 Ellen Rutten, "(Russian) Writer-Bloggers: Digital Perfection and the Aesthetics of Imperfection," *Journal of Computer-Mediated Communication* 19 (2014): 744–62.

41 Andrei Doboş, "Romanian Online Literary Communities," *Dacoromania Litteraria* 3 (2016): 65–74.

42 SimilarWeb, "Poezie.ro," https://www.similarweb.com/website/poezie.ro (accessed January 4, 2019).

43 "De la Alfred Nobel la Sofia Nădejde," *România literară*, no. 2 (2019), https://romanialiterara.com/2019/02/de-la-alfred-nobel-la-sofia-nadejde/ (accessed September 30, 2020).

44 See Andrei Terian, *Critica de export. Teorii, contexte, ideologii* (Bucharest: Muzeul Literaturii Române, 2013).

45 Mihaela Ursa, "Is Romanian Culture Ready for the Digital Turn?," *Metacritic Journal for Comparative Studies and Theory*, no. 1 (2015): 80–97.

46 Ion Manolescu, Lucia-Simona Dinescu, Bogdan Ghiu, and Alexandru Budac are some of the Romanian critics who have used postmodern terms to frame the discussion of the digital imaginary.

47 Joseph Tabbi, "Relocating the Literary: In Networks, Knowledge Bases, Global Systems, Material, and Mental Environments," in *The Bloomsbury Handbook of Electronic Literature*, ed. Joseph Tabbi (New York: Bloomsbury, 2018), 40.

15

SOMATOGRAPHY:
Writing as Incorporated
Cognition, or The Body
Knows More

Caius Dobrescu

How do presumably outlying zones of theoretical travail build bridges not only across discrete cultural geographies but also among concepts and even entire ways of thinking? Located in the heart of today's Romania but having flourished over the centuries on the eastern border of the former Austro-Hungarian Empire and thus still bearing its multicultural marks, the city of Brașov provides, through its recent intellectual history, an interesting response to this key question raised by *Theory in the "Post" Era*. As I show below, Brașov has become the site of a singular, conceptual and methodological ecumenism in literary studies since the early 1980s, when a group of young writers and literary theorists educated in academic hubs such as Bucharest and Cluj-Napoca and involved in the cultural resistance against Nicolae Ceaușescu's authoritarian regime settled in this city. Known unofficially as the "Brașov School" (Școala de la Brașov), they founded in the early 1990s the Faculty of Letters of the local university, now called "Transylvania University."[1] The Brașov School is the focus of this chapter because it illustrates how theoretical work from seemingly ex-centric regions of our theory commons wrestles and sometimes overcomes conceptual divides largely created and, in any case, operating in dominant geocultural areas. In what follows, I lay out specifically how the major theorists of the

School, namely, Alexandru Muşina (1954–2013), Gheorghe Crăciun (1950–
2007), and Virgil Podoabă (1951–) have bridged one of the main fault lines
that cuts across modern Western reflection on the human body, corporeality,
and embodiment.

As I argue, the theoretical imaginary deployed by the three critics coalesces
around intriguing notions of body, mind, and writing, with poetic writing, in
particular, envisaged and practiced—for Muşina and Crăciun are also poets
and fiction authors—as a *somatography* of sorts, writing with and of the
body and serving as an expressive site flaunting the fundamental integration
of the somatic and the cogitative. To explain how this somatography has
come about, I first review briefly the basic issues pertaining to human
corporeality grasped as *one entity* and to cognate concepts that have come
to the fore in the wake of modern thinkers' turn to the problematics of the
body. Let me note, to that effect, that what Bryan S. Turner calls "the turn
of the body" sets in train two profoundly divergent strains of thought.[2]
One, which I call *anti-entitarian*—anti-"unitarian" or anti-integrative—
draws attention to the quasi-mystical fallacy of the corporeal unit or to
corporeality as one unit, as specified above, and consequently approaches
the body as a heteroclite montage or, better yet, assemblage of materials and
intersection of flows. The other regards the corporeal unit as an ontological
given instead. I dub this second sort of thinking *entitarian* because, in it,
the body is a numinous entity, a paradigmatic manifestation of existential
plenitude, which transforms the notion of integrative corporeality into the
main vehicle of resistance to institutions and instruments of political pressure
and oppression directed precisely at the disintegration of the individual. The
conceptual divide between the two schools showcases the criterion by which
ideas of corporeality are grouped together. In cultural theory, what defines
various positions is how they view the *mind-body divide*, which these days
in turn depends on whether one has thrown in one's lot with the dualists or
with the monists. Where the former tend to consider the mind as separate
from its somatic plinth, the latter seek to collapse the mind-body opposition.

Overviewing such tensions within contemporary posthumanism
and seeing them as an "extension of the debates around embodiment in
cyberspace," Ella Brians notes that they have been developing between two
main tendencies. "One, represented by Haraway and Hayles," says Brians,
"argues for a critical thinking through of embodiment and our relation to
technology. The other, represented by Moravec and Kurzweil, promises
technology as escape and salvation."[3] Though apparently intuitive and easy
to apply elsewhere, the distinction between the two schools of thought
unfortunately funnels the complexity of contemporary ideas about the
body down to the traditional yet simplifying schism between "idealists" and
"materialists." Less reductive, the classification I proposed above assumes a
broader understanding of the cognitive and ethical considerations at stake
and differentiates between an anti-integrative ethos and one undergirding

a holistic vision about corporeality. As far as the anti-entitarians are concerned, they consider the absence of a solid foundation on which to base a conception of the human body as a singular entity a fact to be reckoned with so as to avoid an ontologically rooted autonomist misconception, which would make us oblivious, and thus vulnerable, to forces and processes that tend to reconfigure us according to monstrous principles, as we shall see below; on the other hand, casting aside the entitarian views of who we are, some contend, might prepare us to make the most of the evolutionary potential of human "plasticity." By contrast, what sets entitarianism apart is the search for a cohesive, ultimate core of the human, for that "a-tomic," etymologically speaking, premise of fundamental indivisibility that grounds any form in which our inalienable humanity might manifest itself. Less schematic as it may be, this integrative-anti-integrative antinomy is not without its problems. Keen on them, the Brașov School members have developed modern poetry theories in which the body—corporeality overall— and embodied knowledge are thought through in ways that transcend the anti- and pro-unitarian opposition. Turning next to the contributions of Crăciun, Mușina, and Podoabă, I highlight the "trans-unitarian" horizon they open up by bridging this conceptual divide.

Embodied Thought and the Somatographic Pact

Judging by his early writings, Crăciun would seem to belong to the anti-unitarian splinter group for which the body can be constructed and deconstructed in and through discourse. The trope of the body and of the world's bodily and perceptual exploration was, at that stage, both omnipresent in his work and constantly intertwined with textual motifs and metaphors.[4] Carried out during the 1970s and published in the 1980s, partially and with great difficulty under the watchful eye of Communist censorship, his literary-theoretical experiments appear to converge with a certain form of understanding and textually processing corporeality that has been advocated vigorously over the past decades. Claire Colebrook is only one of the recent critics who have maintained that

> although a great deal of literary and cultural criticism turned to "the body," this was always a consideration of how the body had been written, figured, problematized or constructed through various discourses ... Even fiction responded to this trend of coupling writing and the body; to write or speak is to imagine oneself as a subject, but that imagined subject is always embodied, and the body is always constituted through tropes.[5]

Colebrook discerns such persistent trends in theorists such as Vicki Kirby and Elizabeth A. Wilson and in the fiction of Jeanette Winterson.[6]

Prima facie, the assessment above also seems to apply to a major portion of Crăciun's fiction and essays. To my mind, his theoretical thinking on such matters runs in a different direction, though. Published in 2002 but incorporating ideas articulated almost thirty years before, his imposing study *Aisbergul poeziei moderne* (The Iceberg of Modern Poetry) takes a stand against the tendency to axiomatically bind modernity up with the reflexivity and self-reflexivity of language. "In the case of poetic language," Crăciun claims, "one can confidently say that in the beginning was the body, not the word … In order for it to express what had to be expressed, the word had to pass through the body first, through its existential and social sensibility."[7] Positing that poetry about poetry, with its entire spectrum of metalinguistic effects, is only the tip—the visible and actually less significant part—of modern poetry's "iceberg," Crăciun takes us on a tour of the latter's vast underwater bulk, which, he suggests, critics have either misread or ignored because they have failed to theorize their object adequately. Crăciun is operating, I should clarify, with a notion of Euroatlantic modern poetry that stretches back in time to cover most of the post-World War II era. Analyzing this body of work, he launches the concept of a *poetics of transitivity*. To better define it, he distinguishes it from a poetics of reflexivity, which subsumes "a poetry of a timeless now and of an individualless individuality … nothing is farther away from this poetry than the social individual, the living human [endowed] with senses, sensibility, and sexuality."[8] At the same time, Crăciun distances himself from what he calls "linguistic poetry (playful and experimental)," whose profound and troubling effect, he says, is that "the individual ends up … being understood as an extension of his or her language, which foregrounds either his or her logocentric derision or his or her grandeur."[9]

Key to the poetics anchored in it, transitivity works against the disintegration of the corporeal entity. Presupposing the idea of *transit*, transitivity starts out from the language end or aspect of the poem, from the movement and opening up of linguistic signifiers toward the work's environment and those in it whom the work calls out to, and then extends to include and emphasize the body's situation in the world. More broadly, transitivity points then both to the transit of the body through its natural and cultural milieu and, conversely, to the passing of these surroundings, of information and energy flows, through the body. This mutuality, I believe, smooths the path of a compromise between anti-entitarian and entitarian positions. Furthermore, Crăciun envisages a way to yoke together the notion of a self-contained living entity existing on its own terms and another vision, utilitarian and non-unitarian, that sets corporeality up as an object of study from the outside. Revisiting the history of experimentalism in modern poetry, Crăciun sees the body as one object among other entities celebrated over and against the backdrop of a poetics of pan-materiality. A subchapter of his book actually deals with humans' intimacy and affinity with objects in the work of Francis Ponge, a poet whom he deems significant because Ponge is "both intent on removing from his discourse any mystifying transcendence, including the transcendence of the concept, and aware that the object can reveal its naked materiality only if placed inside the brackets of perception and rethought in light of a poetics of ideas."[10] To Crăciun, Ponge's poetry already articulates, I might say, the basic insight underpinning New Materialism and its attempt to redefine the human from the perspective of its relationship with objects.[11]

But materiality is not Crăciun's last word on the issue of the divide concerning us here. In "Pactul somatografic" (The Somatographic Pact), an essay that came out posthumously in his 2018 book *Pulsul prozei* (The Pulse of Fiction), the critic makes it clear that the insistent references to "text" in literature and theory do not necessarily entail an absolute translation of the body into linguistic-discursive terms, as is so often the case in Kirby, Wilson, and Judith Butler. Such references, he specifies, can just as well suggest an author's constant struggle to capture the living body by means that *are* inherently textual in nature.[12] What is often mistaken for "textualism" is in all actuality a *do-or-die* search for expressive plenitude as "evidence" for the corporeal entity's existence. The theoretical dovetailing of text and body lays bare, Crăciun asserts at this point, its special nature. The ever-reiterated effort to express and articulate formally is a way of approaching the corporal entity "asymptotically," as it were, rather than an attempt to replace a body's living tissue with a tissue of signifiers. As Crăciun emphasizes, "in the relation between the writing self and the text, the body may seem like an encumbrance, a surplus, a futile atavism. The *somatographic* pact I have in mind here saves the body from sacrifice and thus lends corporeality to the written world. Writing is also a modality of putting into practice a *transfer of corporeality*."[13]

The reference to "transfer" indexes, I would maintain, a trans-unitarian working over of the notions of transit and transitivity, an effort that marks an important stage of the progress toward the corporeal outlook laid out in the 2006 book *Trupul știe mai mult* (The Body Knows More). Here, Crăciun analyzes his own experience as a writer, or, better yet, as an enunciator, an articulator of enunciations, mining them for evidence in support of a theory of a *thought mode* that, by its very nature, is not centralized in the brain but dispersed throughout a vast neural network.[14] He views literature both as the most eloquent proof that we think with our whole body and as a programmatic living up to this very truth—as a "science" of simultaneously decentered and integrated thinking. Distributed or rather always in the process of being reallotted across the body, this corporeal cerebrality requires a writer's ongoing effort toward an expressive *capture*, toward an expression susceptible of "seizing" its object. But this relation of language to the dispensation of thought through the body, where this apportioning itself already bears witness to corporeality, in no way should be confused with the dissemination theorized by Jacques Derrida, which remains, Crăciun maintains, exclusively inside language. Shaping the trans-unitarian vision in *Trupul ştie mai mult* is the notion that the very possibility of the body, its authentic and full-blown emergence, presupposes a decentering and thus an implicit critique of the corporeal unit as self-focused and self-involved. Corporeality is predicated on self-integration or, I would submit, on a self-embodiment of another order, one that in turn rests on a multiplication of centers and on their ongoing coordination.

Crăciun's approach intersects with highly original theoretical projects such as Richard Shusterman's somaesthetics, which holds that "immediate non-discursive understanding through the body" constitutes a "level of basic understanding" that is

> "beneath interpretation" because we understand it directly through automatic processing rather than having to figure it out by a subsequent act of interpretation. Indeed such basic understanding is what orients and guides any interpretation that would try to deepen or correct that initial understanding. Although such understandings are mediated by prior socialization, training, or habit, they are experienced as direct and immediate without the need to interpret or to infer the meaning.[15]

What explains the affinity between Crăciun and Shusterman is not mutual awareness but their thinking's deep and largely kindred roots. If Crăciun's primary source is Maurice Merleau-Ponty's initial insights into corporeality, Shusterman's *somaesthetics* is influenced by William James, who, already in the 1890 *Principles of Psychology*, anticipated the French phenomenologist by arguing that "We think; and as we think we feel our bodily selves as the seat of the thinking. If the thinking be our thinking, it must be suffused through all its parts with that peculiar warmth and intimacy that make it come as ours."[16] But, beyond such classics, *Trupul ştie mai mult* also stacks up quite well against poststructuralist analyses of the body. Crăciun's language is at once extremely precise and suggestive, and his acute self-reflection, personal investment, and ability to filter theory through his lived experience are unique.

The Poetics of Exploration

In Muşina's view, the task of modern poetry is not to express but to explore perceptions, to chart their interactive, commutative, and osmotic evolution. The poetic text's relation to the body, Muşina thinks, activates first of all an ongoing expansion and reconfiguration of the perceptual field, a monitoring of the shifting dynamic of senses. Redefining radically the experience of corporeality, the critic places front and center the synesthetic processes of knowing the world and the self, a complex interface that I would label a *constellation of senses*. Muşina is keen on this sensorial configuration's historical evolution, one shaped by changes in the spatial-temporal frameworks of thought and perception—here is an idea, I would note in passing, that has been more and more convincingly substantiated by neuroscience and by evolutionary takes on poetry.[17] In any event, this approach to poetry is already at work in the programmatic 1981 article, "Poezia cotidianului" (The Poetry of the Everyday), where Muşina argues that

> the starting point of a poetry of the everyday will be, inevitably, the rediscovery of one's own corporeality, the mastery—through words—of one's own sensations. Technological advances have enabled the expansion of different senses [and thus] a change in the way these relate to one another ... Words themselves no longer designate the same sensorial realities, which is why [language] need[s] to be 'retested' along with [its] contexts.[18]

Muşina defends this position in a synthetic study published in 1996 as *Paradigma poeziei modern* (The Paradigm of Modern Poetry) and reissued the year thereafter under the more personal title *Eseu asupra poeziei moderne* (Essay on Modern Poetry).[19] Here, Muşina starts from an urgency he had already formulated in the early 1980s, specifically, from the need "to understand—partially, of course, but in a new light—modern poetry from the perspective of theories developed for scientific purposes by means made available by modern knowledge." This is necessary because

> the characteristics of modern poetry, its predominantly exploratory dimension, its new role in society (different from the role and place of poetry in previous eras) bring it close to advanced science. A new scientific paradigm has come about in modern poetry, and using this paradigm itself descriptively, as a model of analyzing this poetry (with all the necessary nuances, clarifications, and corrections), is justified by the striking similarity between the ways poetry and science, otherwise so different, operate.[20]

No wonder Muşina's conceptualization of the body as a unit does not translate into the radical rejection of technology *à la* Martin Heidegger and his followers. At the same time, however, the critic appreciates modern poetry for its capacity to push back against and symbolically rescind technology's prosthetic inroads into the human body as well as the larger social structures that govern the systematization and instrumentalization of knowledge. Muşina seizes on "exploratory" poetry in a technologically oversaturated and hyperintegrated world not so much as a radical critical project but rather as a cognitive and expressive back-up plan of sorts, a mode of preserving one's wherewithal to get one's bearings in the world. Implicitly unitarian, this mode also bespeaks an awareness of human civilization's ineluctable complexity and interconnectivity, even though these play out on a non-unitarian, heterogenous foundation and call, accordingly, for a certain degree of specialization in their exercise. To Muşina, modern poetry fulfills, more than anything else, a prospective function, which he sees as closely tied to, but not unilaterally influenced by, experimental sciences—hence the difference between how he looks at poetry and the "poetry and science" approaches, which are concerned with the impact of scientific thinking on literature.[21]

We need, Muşina insists along these lines, to distance ourselves from this passive engagement with poetry so as to grasp what kind of "scientist" the poet is—namely, one whose exploratory and cognitive instruments are completely embodied in that his or her exploration and knowledge apparatus is *one with his or her own body*. Herein lies, I would stress, the idea of a *poetics of exploration* that seems to strike an optimal balance between reality and perceptual corporeality. "Modern poetry," Muşina writes, "does not imitate but explores reality; it does not express but explores feelings and sensations; it does not juggle with the possibilities of language but explores its limits and essence."[22] By the same token, this modern poetry conception cuts a fresh path to trans-unity, for, in Muşina's exploratory moves, the non-unitarian distribution is rounded off by the rediscovery or retracing of entitarian ontological frontiers. The very nature of a self's crises and adaptive reactions thereto calls for this duality or complementarity, which Muşina conveys through the metaphor of the double nature, corpuscle and wavelength, of light.[23] The strategic alternation between the self's objective dis- and reaggregation represents for the critic a distinct way of thinking trans-unitarianism that steers his poetics of exploration in a most ambitious and original direction, viz., in that of psychosomatic plasticity. Accordingly, he sees the modern poet as a designer of formulas of self-coherence, one that is at once more abstract (neural, cerebral) and more concrete (somatic, proprioceptive) than those presupposed by theories of cultural identity. In Muşina, poetry provides solutions for self-management, in a context where "there are no longer any absolute, ordering reference points. The reference system is moved ... from outside to inside the individual: the human being becomes a Center. His or her body becomes a spatial axis, and his or her fleeting states and sensations, their moment in time—a temporal hub."[24]

Catering to a basic need for equilibrium, the self models worked out by Muşina are psychocorporal configurations reminding one of Charles Taylor's inquiry into the "sources of the self."[25] Particularly interesting here, though, is that the range of such models is suggestive of the dialectical difference-in-complementarity between, on one side, dis-unitarian selfhood rites, which afford the separation from the body-as-object and the analytical decomposition of the illusion of the self, and, on the other, what might be called spontaneous fluctuations of individual modularity. Thus, Muşina fleshes out, on one hand, unitarian or quasi-unitarian theoretical constructs such as the fully "somatized" self, one coextensive with the body (which he sees in play, for example, in Gottfried Benn and in Romanian poet George Bacovia), the "all-in-the present," hyperperceptual self (in Charles Olson and Frank O'Hara), and the impersonal self (in Objectivists such as Louis Zukofsky and George Oppen). On the other hand, in his work we come across formulas that integrate dispersion, such as the multiple self (especially in Fernando Pessoa) and the projected, arbitrary self (in Dadaist poets or, later, e. e. cummings). Moreover, beyond poetry, Muşina's corporeality concept engages, albeit obliquely, with items on today's ecocriticism agenda such as the urgency to move beyond anthropocentrism. From this non- or post-anthropocentric standpoint, the blame for the destruction of the planet falls, to a great extent, on a Western mindset that warrants the sovereign right of the human species to impose its will on everything around it. To reduce the damage of rampant "progress," humans have to learn first, ecocritics insist, the humbleness of removing themselves from the center of the universe and of accepting that they are no more valuable than other entities. Compared to this self-decentering or posthumanizing of the human, Muşina's "new anthropocentrism" plea, initially entered in an article-manifesto and variously taken up again throughout his theoretical oeuvre, may seem, at first blush, outdated.[26] But the "anthropocentrism" Muşina has in mind is hardly the same as the imperialist- and manipulative-anthropomorphic sway over and view of the world. To him, the world continuum's centering on the human is something the latter should neither covet nor claim as a symbol of power and authority, but it has to do instead with one's profound need to find one's place and regain one's balance in a world of abrupt changes and epistemic ruptures. The center does not mark here the hot spot from which the human species presumes to exert its dominance. Instead, "new anthropocentrism" refers to an ongoing recentering of senses, to their "constellating" and coordinating of perceptions, and to a poetics of endless and nuanced adjustment to the world. Thus, what the phrase stresses (and … centers) is less humankind than its movement, the centering itself, the endeavor anthropological "centrism" entails. But this position is far from confined to a pro-unitarian philosophy of the body. Precisely because it is called on to restore, again and again, the constellation of perceptions, to reorganize and focalize them, poetry is also seen by the critic as corporeal flow, constantly coordinated with the fluxes and currents, often contrary or competing, in the natural and social environment. What he discerns in this entire spectacle is a dance-like adaptive fluidity, a free-flowing form or style, rather, of managing, in an integrative and self-interrogative fashion, the corpuscle-and-wavelength features of the human body.[27] Muşina's new

anthropocentrism evinces, then, that Yeatsian condition of the human in
which "you cannot tell the dancer from the dance." Otherwise put, this
anthropocentrism proposes a trans-unitarian solution to contemporary
conundrums of corporeality.

Monsters and Bodies

An important dialogue partner of Muşina and Crăciun, Podoabă has
been influenced by a phenomenology that puts much stock in both the
posttheological and postsecular revaluing of the body. He pursues his initial
interest in the French-Swiss "criticism of identification" in a theoretical
zone circumscribed by bodily concerns, specifically by Jean-Luc Marion's
differentiation between *corps* (body) and *chair* (flesh).[28] Surprisingly, though,
among his sources of inspiration are also Georges Bataille's corporeal
conceptualizations, which Podoabă builds on originally and yet in ways
that also resonate with contemporary British and American interpretations
of the French thinker.[29] Podoabă's views of literature's relationship with
the primordial revelation of the body as numinous entity jibes with the
reawakening of the interest in a *poetics and aesthetics of incarnation* both
in liberal theology[30] and in the historical study of modern literature.[31]
Still, not unlike Muşina's, Podoabă's thinking on corporeality is more than
unambivalently pro-unitarian. In fact, he enriches this subject with new
and unexpected valences, setting it up as a yardstick with which one could
measure the compass of epistemic shifts and thus assess the changes in how we
see the world. Put forth in his 2002 book *Între extreme* (Between Extremes),
this correlation of epistemology and corporeality speaks to Podoabă's close
contact with the theoretical and philosophical preoccupations of Muşina and
Crăciun. Podoabă believes that, before and in order to talk about epistemic
mutations in literary and cultural history, we need first to run the test of
what he calls "existential panic," hence his idea of a *monstrous analysis* of
poetry. Drawing on the Latin semantics of *monstrum—monstrare* means
"to show," "to expose"—Podoabă ties together three notions: revelation
(which, too, etymologically speaking, evokes an "un-covering," that is,
essentially, a form of showing); hermeneutic interpretation (which exposes
and unveils); and primeval panic or horror triggered off by the bewildering,
unmediated experience of a conceptually unmapped environment, which,
he says, is what the world feels like during the anomie of the interstice
between two epistemes. Thus, monstrosity works as a gauge of the degree
of internalization, assimilation, and finally, embodiment of a hiatus in the
continuity of a coherent, comprehensive worldview.[32]

Podoabă's take on the monster may intrigue particularly those scholars
who treat this figure or category especially in relation to the absolute

evil imaginary.[33] Predominant in what is known as "monster theory" and thereby distinct from Podoabă's take on the notion, another way of tackling monstrosity is the critique of representations of the monstrous as codified manifestations of fear of the Other, of the foreigner, of social, ethnic, or racial minorities, as well as of the disabled.[34] Nevertheless, despite such stark differences, the conclusions of Podoabă's "monstruous analysis" overlap, sometimes surprisingly, with some of the tenets and findings of monster theory. "The Monster is the harbinger of category crisis," writes, for instance, Jeffrey Cohen, one of the pioneers of this orientation, who also explains that "the monster is said to always escape because it refuses easy categorization—a form suspended between forms that threatens to smash distinctions."[35] Cohen is referring mainly to monstrous or demonized bodies, to those discriminated against and ostracized by society and stigmatized as degenerate or perverse. Instead, for Podoabă, the problem of monstrosity reflects the intimate epistemic crisis that throws body and mind into a mutually shocking estrangement. Any mutation or rupture of episteme reveals itself, in relation to the world, as virulently and viscerally bordering on an intimate psychosomatic apocalypse—on the disaster the non-categorizable constitutes, according to Cohen, within the social-imaginary order.

Podoabă's view of horror as an epistemic seismograph, I would argue, is optimally positioned to diagnose the basic crisis faced by contemporary theories of the body. The major historical force behind such theoretical investigations was initially the horror of concentration camps. The massive impact on the collective imaginary of the atrocious images captured at Auschwitz and elsewhere has in the post-World War II period carried over into visions and concepts meant to totally upend the classic understanding of corporeality. The most elaborate and powerful outcomes of absolute horror's experience by speculative thinking have proved to be Michel Foucault's studies on the mechanisms for disciplining the body, culminating with his vision of biopolitics,[36] as well as the insights of Gilles Deleuze and Félix Guattari into capitalism as a system for channeling the bioenergetic flows of "desiring machines."[37] In what is known today as the "body turn," the ramifications of this simultaneously collective and personal experience of the monstruous are entwined with the aftershocks of a profound dread, verging on horror, of losing the body's coordinates and dissolving it into the daunting range of possibilities opened up by genetic engineering. Add to this the related uneasiness many of us feel in the face of contemporary technosomatic hybridization. Rendering the body an amalgam of animate and inanimate matter and technological material, this transformative process leads to organic physicality's fragmentation and disintegration, whose phantasmatic appeal should not be underestimated. For, deep down, such annihilations may well prove or feel "desirable" as the moment when not only the hearth of identity but also of entity itself, pure and simple, melts away. We may picture here a Moebius strip on which the Deleuzean school of body thinking crosses into and merges almost seamlessly with human-technology symbiotic models of posthuman corporeality developed in the line of Donna Haraway's *Cyborg Manifesto*.[38] At any rate, Podoabă's monstruous analysis can illuminate from a fresh angle some of the more radical contemporary remapping of the body, not least its subjection to extreme, "tortuous" and dis-organizing technosomatic fantasies in turn not incompatible with the arts and theories focused on self-inflicted mutilation and pain.[39] All these chime in with Podoabă's observations on the profound internalization and somatization of epistemic mutations—on their mapping onto bodies and even becoming body. The linchpin of this epistemic investment in the body is the notion that the memory of the corporeal entity is deeply seated in horror and its experience, which, in a patently trans-unitarian vein, accounts for the ambivalent meaning of the monstruous as both terrifying anamorphosis and liberating revelation.

Somatopia

Crăciun, Mușina, and Podoabă are all driven by an aspiration to completely reframe our image of the world from a bodily perspective. Their answer to the insurgent, sometimes revolutionary corporeality concepts pervading literary and cultural theory today is an interrogative-prospective paradigm. As is well known, cultural studies, in particular, accentuates the political reclaiming of the body, the "resistant" body. Likewise, feminism, as well as the critique of ableism are conspicuously concerned with contesting and subverting corporal normativity seen as a corollary of sociocultural discrimination. Here, the body is the scene and object of an ongoing struggle in and for critical theory generally, which pushes for releasing corporeality from the pressure of regularizing categories, bureaucratic processes, and insidious networks of privileges, a campaign motivated by the conviction that the mind-body axis is oriented by the conditional reflexes or the habitus of social hierarchies. In brief, as cultural critics tell us, the body is gendered, racialized, and determined by sexual choice, class status, and so forth. Instead, the luminaries of the Brașov School deal with corporeality as corpo-reality, rather, a corporeal entity grasped as *morphosomatic reality*, and they do so by bracketing off the agonic, traditionally conceived body.[40]

But this does not mean that the body has nothing to do with power nor that our bodies are powerless. In effect, as far as these theorists are concerned, the body is *counter*political. The counterpower the body represents and wields stems, in their view, from strategically "ignoring" power through a "disdain" for it, as it were, materialized in the transfiguring force of embodied cognition. Crăciun, Mușina, and Podoabă think that the ordinary act of occupying one's corporal place in the world, of settling into one's own condition, is tantamount to an implicit defiance of all forms of established authority. Nor is this counterpolitical "condition," they insist, always comfortable, given that it presupposes stepping out of one's self regularly, interrupting the plenitude of the comfort zone of one's being, problematizing, self-questioning, watching constantly over fragile equilibriums, navigating the fluctuations of uncertainty and ambiguity—in brief, owning up to *dis-unity* as that which warrants the deeply constitutive mobility and anxiety of consciousness. Otherwise, these theorists' embodiment visions are wary of both anti- and pro-unitarian utopianism. Most likely, the Braşov School critics would take a dim view of Ray Kurzweil's and Hans Moravec's prophecies heralding the human's thorough decoupling from or transgression of the physical and organic world through the "downloading" of our mental processes and contents to electronic platforms as the only chance for the survival of the species. Muşina, Crăciun, and Podoabă would probably diagnose posthuman and "singularity" projections, much like Don Ihde has, as "technofantasy."[41] Instead, they would agree, I imagine, with N. Katherine Hayles, who has cautioned against discounting the materiality of the mind, and would appreciate Ella Brians's recommendation to "carefully and creatively thin[k] through our embodied relationship to technology."[42] And they would not give, I think, carte blanche to the somato-technological symbiosis critics such as Haraway dream of either. For a key element the three Romanian theorists have in common is the stock they put in the radical indeterminacy and in the founding, *cohesive ambiguity* of the mind-body relationship. What their somatographic project ultimately proposes, then, is not a corporealist utopia but what I would call somatopia—a non-utopic, dynamic-embodied modality of dwelling in the world.

Notes

1   Ioan Olimpiu Şerbu, "Şcoala literară de la Braşov/The Braşov Literary School" (PhD diss., Transylvania University, Braşov, 2019)—an English abstract is available online: https://www.unitbv.ro/documente/cercetare/doctorat-postdoctorat/sustinere-teza/2019/ioan-serbu/TEZA_Ioan_serbu.PDF (accessed April 15, 2020).

2   Bryan S. Turner, "The Turn of the Body," in *Routledge Handbook of Body Studies*, ed. Bryan S. Turner (New York: Routledge, 2012), 5–6.

3   Ella Brians, "The 'Virtual' Body and the Strange Persistence of the Flesh: Deleuze, Cyberspace and the Posthuman," in *Deleuze and the Body*, ed. Laura Guillaume and Joe Hughes (Edinburgh: Edinburgh University Press, 2011), 129.

4   The first volume published by Gheorghe Crăciun, *Acte originale/Copii legalizate* (Bucharest: Cartea Românească, 1982), is a good example in this sense.

5   Claire Colebrook, "Time and Autopoiesis: The Organism Has No Future,"
    in *Deleuze and the Body*, ed. Laura Guillaume and Joe Hughes (Edinburgh:
    Edinburgh University Press, 2011), 13.
6   See Vicki Kirby, *Telling Flesh: The Substance of the Corporeal* (New York:
    Routledge, 1997); Elizabeth A. Wilson, *Neural Geographies: Feminism and
    the Microstructure of Cognition* (New York: Routledge, 1998); and Jeanette
    Winterson, *Written on the Body* (New York: Knopf, 1993).
7   Gheorghe Crăciun, *Aisbergul poeziei moderne*, ed. Carmen Mușat and Oana
    Crăciun (Iași, Romania: Polirom, 2017), 500.
8   Crăciun, *Aisbergul poeziei moderne*, 413.
9   Crăciun, *Aisbergul poeziei moderne*, 486.
10 Crăciun, *Aisbergul poeziei moderne*, 223, 261, 306–7.
11 Tony Bennett and Patrick Joyce, *Material Powers: Cultural Studies, History
    and the Material Turn* (London: Routledge, 2010).
12 "Pactul somatografic," in Gheorghe Crăciun, *Pulsul prozei,* ed. Carmen Mușat
    and Oana Crăciun (Iași, Romania: Polirom, 2018), 87–152.
13 Crăciun *Pulsul prozei*, 88.
14 Gheorghe Crăciun, *Trupul știe mai mult* (Pitești, Romania: Paralela 45, 2006).
15 Richard Shusterman, "Pragmatism's Embodied Philosophy: From Immediate
    Experience to Somaesthetics," in *Routledge Handbook of Body Studies*, ed.
    Bryan S. Turner (New York: Routledge, 2012), 41.
16 William James, *The Principles of Psychology: The Works of William James*
    (Cambridge, MA: Harvard University Press, 1983), 235.
17 Although it does not deal with poetry, the essay collection edited by Jonathan
    Gottschall and David Sloan Wilson, *The Literary Animal: Evolution and the
    Nature of Narrative* (Evanston, IL: Northwestern University Press, 2005)
    offers numerous suggestions in this area.
18 Quoted in Crăciun, *Aisbergul poeziei românești*, 444.
19 Mușina's study was first published with the title *Paradigma poeziei moderne*
    (Bucharest: Leka-Brâncuși, 1996). A second edition, slightly revised, on which
    I rely the most, has the title *Eseu asupra poeziei moderne* (Chișinău, Moldova:
    Cartier, 1997).
20 Mușina, *Paradigma poeziei moderne*, 12.
21 See, on this, Bruce Clarke and Manuela Rossini, eds., *The Routledge
    Companion to Literature and Science* (London: Routledge, 2011).
22 Mușina, *Eseu asupra poeziei moderne*, 72.
23 "The two tendencies (nominalist and realist) of modern poetry are only
    apparently irreconcilable (just like the theories about the nature of light, one
    holding that light is corpuscle, the other that it is wavelength—light being, in
    fact, both corpuscle and wavelength) ... A realist approach, as I have called
    it—resolves the crisis of language first, by corroborating the rationale for
    the relationship between signifier and signified, between Word and Object;
    following from this is the solution to the crisis of the self and reality. The
    other approach—nominalist, as I have called it—resolves the reality crisis first,
    which then automatically forecloses any possibility for a crisis of either self or
    language" (Mușina, *Eseu asupra poeziei moderne*, 132–3).
24 Mușina, *Eseu asupra poeziei moderne*, 133.

25 Charles Taylor, *Sources of the Self: The Making of the Modern Identity* (Cambridge, MA: Harvard University Press, 1989).

26 See the 1982 essay "Noul antropocentrism," reprinted in Alexandru Mușina, *Unde se află poezia* (Tîrgu-Mureș, Romania: Arhipelag, 1996), 11–14.

27 As Andy Clark writes, "We create these supportive environments, but they create us too. We exist as the thinking beings we are, only thanks to a baffling dance of brains, bodies, and cultural and technological scaffolding" (Andy Clark, *Natural-born Cyborgs: Minds, Technologies, and the Future of Human Intelligence* [Oxford, UK: Oxford University Press, 2003], 10).

28 The alignment of Podoabă's thinking with Marion's is evident in the former's essays, "Preambul la o propunere. Studiu introductiv despre experiența revelatoare" (*Vatra* 5–6, [2004], 48–56) and "Gheorghe Crăciun și revelațiile corpului erotizat. Studiu de hermeneutică fenomenologică" (*Vatra* 5–6 [2002]: 141–3; 8–9 [2002]: 30–3, and 10 [2002]: 18–20).

29 One example is Patrick Ffrench, *After Bataille: Sacrifice, Exposure, Community* (New York: Routledge, 2007).

30 See, for example, Oliver Davies and Denys Turner, eds., *Silence and the Word: Negative Theology and Incarnation* (Cambridge: Cambridge University Press, 2004); Margaret R. Miles, *The Word Made Flesh: A History of Christian Thought* (Malden, MA: Blackwell, 2005); Michael Martin, *The Incarnation of the Poetic Word: Theological Essays on Poetry & Philosophy: Philosophical Essays on Poetry & Theology* (Brooklyn, NY: Angelico Press, 2017); and Susie Paulik Babka, *Through the Dark Field: The Incarnation through an Aesthetics of Vulnerability* (Collegeville, MN: Liturgical Press, 2017).

31 See Eric Naiman, *Sex in Public: The Incarnation of Early Soviet Ideology* (Princeton, NJ: Princeton University Press, 1997); Peter Eglin, *Intellectual Citizenship and the Problem of Incarnation* (Lanham, MD: University Press of America, 2013); and Steve Pinkerton, *Blasphemous Modernism: The 20th-Century Word Made Flesh* (New York: Oxford University Press, 2017).

32 Virgil Podoabă, *Între extreme* (Cluj-Napoca, Romania: Ed. Dacia, 2002) and *Anatomia frigului. Altă analiză monstruoasă* (Cluj-Napoca, Romania: Ecco-Marineasa, 2003).

33 See Marie-Hélène Huet, *Monstrous Imagination* (Cambridge, MA: Harvard University Press, 1993), and Niall Scott, ed., *Monsters and the Monstrous: Myths and Metaphors of Enduring Evil* (Amsterdam: Rodopi, 2007).

34 See Marina Levina and Diem-My T. Bui, eds., *Monster Culture in the 21st Century: A Reader* (London: Bloomsbury, 2013), and Jim Byatt, *Rethinking the Monstrous: Transgression, Vulnerability, and Difference in British Fiction Since 1967* (Lanham, MD: Lexington Books, 2015).

35 Jeffrey Jerome Cohen, "Monster Culture (Seven Theses)," in *Monster Theory*, ed. Jeffrey Jerome Cohen (Minneapolis: University of Minnesota Press, 1996), 6.

36 Michel Foucault, *The Birth of Biopolitics: Lectures at the Collège de France, 1978–1979*, ed. Michel Sellenart (Basingstoke, UK: Palgrave MacMillan, 2008). For more on the evolution and influential appeal of the biopolitics concept, see Catherine Mills, *Biopolitics* (London: Routledge, 2018).

37 See Gilles Deleuze and Félix Guattari, *Anti-Oedipus: Capitalism and Schizophrenia* (London: Continuum, 2004).

38 Donna Haraway, "Cyborg Manifesto," in *Simians, Cyborgs, and Women: The Reinvention of Nature* (New York: Routledge, 1991): 149–81.
39 See Marla Carlson, *Performing Bodies in Pain: Medieval and Post-modern Martyrs, Mystics, and Artists* (New York: Palgrave Macmillan, 2010); Steven Seidman, Nancy Fischer, and Chet Meeks, eds., *Introducing the New Sexuality Studies* (London: Routledge, 2011); and David M. Ortmann and Richard A. Sprott, *Sexual Outsiders: Understanding BDSM Sexualities and Communities* (Lanham, MD: Rowman & Littlefield, 2013).
40 For an influential argument in support of this view on the mind-body relationship, see Susan Bordo, *Unbearable Weight: Feminism, Western Culture, and the Body* (Berkeley: University of California Press, 1993).
41 This diagnosis is formulated in Don Ihde, *Bodies in Technology* (Minneapolis: University of Minnesota Press, 2002), 13.
42 Brians, "The 'Virtual' Body and the Strange Persistence of the Flesh: Deleuze, Cyberspace and the Posthuman," 118.

16

POST-CANONICITY:
Curating World Literary Archives after Postmodernism

Cosmin Borza

"I have a point from which to start: canons exist, and we should do something about them";[1] "there is one ... important point, ... one so obvious that it risks becoming hidden: there is a canon."[2] Made in 2012 and 2018, respectively, such "points" seem characteristic of an earlier age or of "young" or "provincial" critical cultures like those, we are told, of Eastern Europe, where, perhaps more than elsewhere, one still runs into conservative visions that symbolically wrap literary patrimonies around values associated with national-identity exceptionalism.[3] And yet the statements come from a different place. What is more, they are not isolated either. Nor do they convey conservative or traditionalist stances.[4] In fact, I take such viewpoints to be representative for the contemporary period Jeffrey T. Nealon defines as "post-postmodern."[5] Eric Prieto has noted that this moment also marks the consolidation, in the third stage of postcolonialism,[6] of a new paradigm that, as Michael Hardt and Antonio Negri have suggested, takes the world beyond postcolonialism altogether through an "irresistible and irreversible globalization of economic and cultural exchanges" and "a *decentered* and *deterritorialized* apparatus of rule" that "progressively incorporates the entire global realm within its open, expanding borders" and organizes "hybrid identities, flexible hierarchies, and plural exchanges."[7]

As I show later on in this chapter, the transition out of the postmodern and postcolonial is a relevant and necessary context to my argument. Before we get there, though, the opening section of this intervention deals with the reasons and theoretical ramifications of the resurgence of interest in literary canons decades after the North American culture wars ended, admittedly, with the triumph of pluri-, anti-, or counter-canonical positions. My main goal in this part of the discussion is to show that the spectacular return to the idea of a canon during the last ten-odd years constitutes a phenomenon typical of what I call post-canonicity and not a harking back to the essentialist-aesthetic approaches of the 1980s and 1990s. For post-canonicity involves, to my mind, neither abandoning the concept of the canon nor ignoring the antagonisms and complications this has historically brought into play. What I designate by post-canonicity is basically a new phase and direction in the history of canon debates over the last forty years or so, a reorientation that is gaining momentum at the post-postmodern, fast-globalizing dawn of the twenty-first century. At this juncture in the history of canon and theoretical scholarship, I submit, developments in World Literature and big data research are shifting the focus of earlier disputes away from contesting or "deconstructing" literary canons. By the same token, the latter's multicultural expansion and diversification, objectives reached, roughly speaking, at the postcolonial stage of the "wars," are no longer stoking theoretical and political passions as they have in the past. In post-canonicity, the new concepts and methodologies supply, instead, an opportunity to analyze more rigorously, with more attention to data and "facts," how canons are shaped and disseminated nationally, transnationally, and globally, as well as to provide previously untapped, relevant evidence of the power relations and inequities embedded in the makeup of canonical structures.

In the second half of my contribution, I seize on the aforementioned resurgence of the canon as a platform allowing Central and East European cultures to enter, belatedly but authentically, the stage of post-canonicity. I submit that these cultures have not assimilated completely the previous century's breakthroughs in canon theory and criticism, nor have they, in a fairly similar vein, quite joined in the rethinking of literary values and hierarchies from feminist, postcolonial, queer, cultural- or new-materialist perspectives. This is why, it seems to me, this quarter of our theory commons should welcome the new conceptualizations of the canon twice: first, and for their sake, because they do make for a major and necessary methodological tune-up; and second, and for the potential benefit of this commons, because a post-canonical analysis of European "peripheries" may challenge and possibly offer solutions to World Literature tenets and aporias.

Post-Canonicity: A Brief History

The 1993, 2004, and 2017 American Comparative Literature Association (ACLA) reports on the state of the discipline are symptomatic for how, beginning with the 1990s, post-canonicity has been gradually working its way into contemporary critical culture. Developed by a committee headed up by Charles Bernheimer, the first set out to reinforce the massive change in canon thinking brought about by poststructuralist, multiculturalist, and other forms of critique thriving under postmodernism. The canon controversy, still raging on at the time, was close to being settled, and the winners were becoming increasingly apparent. Vaguely conceived as a liberal solution to the canon problem, to wit, as a decidedly pluralizing move beyond *the* canon, a new and more democratic canonicity notion was slowly rising. Driving it was the determination to make the one into many by relativizing or even contesting, on one side, the central role of the literary and of the aesthetic in the Western cultural system and, on the other, entire national, imperial, racial, and gender traditions. The Bernheimer report lets us know that the comparative method at last freed itself of hegemonic and hierarchical prejudices, historicized itself, reckoned with the paramount significance of exchanges across geographical borders, and, at last, embraced interdisciplinarity:

> The space of comparison today involves comparisons between artistic productions usually studied by different disciplines; between various cultural constructions of those disciplines; between Western cultural traditions, both high and popular, and those of non-Western cultures; between pre- and postcontact cultural productions of colonized people; between gender constructions defined as feminine and those defined as masculine, or between sexual orientations defined as straight and those defined as gay; between racial and ethnic modes of signifying; between hermeneutic articulation of meaning and materialist analyses of its modes of production and circulation; and much more.[8]

Coordinated by Haun Saussy, the second report points out that the age of multiculturalism has been followed by that of globalization, and that Eurocentric comparative literature has given way to more democratic "World Literature." Not surprisingly, the Saussy report foregrounds David Damrosch's "hypercanon." Damrosch reminds everybody that dismantling the canon no longer raises eyebrows in the Western cultural media for, during the last decades of the past century, persuasive rationales for the counter- and alternative canons produced by postcolonialism and feminism were worked through. Yet since then, the discussion has refocused on the paradoxical effects of internationalization, multiculturalism, and globalization on literary studies. As Damrosch claims, "we do live in a postcanonical age, but our age is postcanonical in much the same way that it is postindustrial …. what has happened is that the rich have gotten richer, while most others just scrape by or see outright declines in their fortunes. It's too simple to say that the old canon has vanished."[9] In other words, the critical and theoretical revisions that targeted the greats of Western literature have ultimately solidified rather than weakened the canonical status of such figures, as their continuing central place in university curricula goes to show. Even stripped of the aesthetic aura with which historically essentialist and nationalist treatments have surrounded them, canonical authors have gained a "hypercanonic" stature. This, Damrosch comments, "is a fact of life," and his tone is telling, for, if what we are witnessing is the rise of new form of "hegemony," then this does not trigger an old-style, combative reaction but a more tactical maneuver—the critic refrains from rejecting "hypercanonical" authors, pressing them into service, instead, as mediators for bringing into the fold and for grappling with "countercanonical" writers.[10]

The latest ACLA report reinforces the notion that recognizing the existence and sway of literary canons in an aptly called post-canonical age is not a reactionary or conservative move but, instead, the stepping-stone to a necessary, cultural and methodological move forward. At the very beginning of her introduction to the 2017 volume, Ursula K. Heise describes the World Literature paradigm along with the extensions of poststructuralism and postcolonialism as a third major theoretical driver of reform in comparative studies. The critic underscores the contribution of World Literature "to the understanding of the production, migration, translation, and cross-cultural reception and valuation of literary texts."[11] But she also pinpoints two of the discipline's methodological limitations. One is underappreciating the importance of "national and cultural differences in any construction of 'the world.'"[12] The other is the rise of "new quantitative tools and methods meant to address 'big data' in literary studies"[13] and by the same token to make the world's boundaries even more visible.

It is precisely this aspect that Mads Rosendahl Thomsen takes up in his contribution to the report, "World Famous, Locally: Insights from the Study of International Canonization," which recaps the theoretical insights he shares in his 2008 book *Mapping World Literature: International Canonization and Transnational Literatures*.[14] In addition to rehearsing what has by now become the obvious (the process of canonization is not "static," and it is determined exclusively neither by power relations nor by the idiosyncrasies of critics or literary historians[15]), Thomsen insists on an aspect often ignored by the advocates of canonical revisionism, namely, that "world literature is always seen from somewhere," for "the local" and "the national" play a decisive role.[16] Consequently, canonization, both national and international, remains "an important starting point for exploring the structures of literary cultures and cross-cultural influences."[17] Moreover, Thomsen adds, the recent digitalization and big data shifts in literary studies place the canon front and center once again. "The digital humanities," he writes,

> can help to establish a more nuanced perspective on canonization, to dig deeper into the preferences of academics, critics, and lay readers in terms

of devices, styles, and themes of texts, and to see new patterns in literary history ... And they will help to ask new questions about the relation between literature and culture at large, when unlikely canonized works demand explanation.[18]

The relation between multicultural- and global-era post-canonicity is then not only one of continuity but also of contrast. Where multicultural critics were sensitive to the canon's constructedness along elitist, exclusivist, discriminating, racist, sexist, nationalist, or Eurocentric lines, whose redrawing, the same scholars insisted, was a top priority in a pluralist and democratic postmodern society, there is a sense under late globalization that we have this operation, this critique or at least some of its outcomes, under our belt.

I am certainly not saying that our job is done, though, but that successful multicultural and postcolonial revisionism has freed up the canon, in its critiqued form, for redeployment as a foremost *analytical* resource. This makes sense if you think about how, steadily redefining itself as it does so as to become more inclusive geographically, historically, and analytically, World Literature counters ever-more forcefully the uniformity-inducing and monolithic thrust of globalization and the perceptions global processes foster. As a result, the local, regional, or national differences, intersections, and hybridizations are, critically and theoretically, weighing in more and more. Further, these cultural and, more precisely, intercultural dynamics are most conspicuously documented in those constructs—no matter how phantasmatic—through which communities have articulated, under historically and politically specific circumstances, ideas about value, identity, and tradition. A premier such formation, the canon supplies strong "documentation" of this sort and is even treated, accordingly, as "evidence." No wonder the Heise volume reports that the revaluation of the canon now leans on quantitative studies, especially those undertaken in the digital humanities. The tendency may seem paradoxical, for, as conceived by Franco Moretti, this type of analysis, concerned as it has been mainly with the "great unread" and the "archive," has been designed—unlike traditional close reading—to undermine rather than consolidate the canon.[19] But Moretti himself admits that the research methods he is promoting strive to leave behind the culture wars of the 1980s and 1990s in that "the aim is not so much a change in the canon—the discovery of precursors to the canon or alternatives to it, to be restored to a prominent position—as a change in how we look at *all* of literary history: canonical and noncanonical: together."[20] It is apparent that, here and elsewhere in Moretti, the canonical authors, genres, forms, devices, styles, and related phenomena—that symbolic 1 percent or under 1 percent of the world's literary production—remain basic indicators or, as I propose above, key "evidence."

This is precisely how data analysts handle it across the digital humanities, as all the basic handbooks, compendiums, and similar instruments of this exploding field clearly indicate.[21] The most representative and influential of them remains the Stanford Literary Lab's pamphlet. Many of the experiments published in it indicate that the canon is not only a questionable hierarchy but also an effective questioning tool itself as long as it is brought "down to earth" and approached as "the result of many individual institutions susceptible to arbitrary, ideological, random, formal, political, and other motivations."[22] Owning up to the existence of a canon—rather than obstinately ignoring, negating, replacing, or simply "pluralizing" it—is, as the Lab's experiments convincingly demonstrate, a preliminary step to a better grasp of the connections between artistic and commercial values, academic and market forces, and prestige and popularity, of how such relationships fluctuate across times, spaces, and cultures, as well as of how formal and morphological constants ("redundancy," "lexical variety") set works recognized as "major" apart from those "forgotten," that is, less read, analyzed, and taught.[23] Granted, some have argued that such analysis methods and technologies promote "Westcentrism," rehabilitate formalism, and overall do a disservice to comparatism. The legitimacy of such critiques, which, incidentally, have not spared World Literature either, has been acknowledged by Moretti in the dialogue with Heise included in the 2017 report.[24] As Moretti observes there, "digital humanities has basically developed within literary studies focusing almost exclusively on English corpora, English in America. So you have the completely paradoxical coexistence of a very new—some people might even say revolutionary tool—and an enormous provincialism in its field of application."[25] Notably, the provincialism the critic is talking about is then not at all an offshoot of "provinces," of the world geocultural "peripheries," to which new research techniques and cultural forms generally travel, presumably out of world centers of cultural and theoretical innovation. Quite the contrary. The digital revolution in the humanities has been dampened by the quasi-exclusive application of its cutting-edge tools to material culled from so-called "central" cultures.

Is the "Post" in Postcommunism the Same as in Post-Canonicity?

A perfect epistemological storm of sorts, the correlation between the rekindled preoccupations with the literary canon and a critical engagement with new yet Western-centered methodologies presents Central and East European cultures with a unique theoretical opportunity. Back in the 1990s, critics of these putatively outer zones of European cultural circuitries already proved remarkably receptive to the conceptual fallout of the American culture wars, showing, in any case, more interest in such theoretical realignments than many in the West.[26] If, during the 1970s and 1980s, the canon could not have been interrogated openly due to political implications as well as to limited access to the international literature on the subject, it became, in the aftermath of the 1989 revolutions, possibly the most hotly debated issue throughout the former Eastern Bloc. As anti-Communist rhetoric took off here in the early 1990s, many of the local supporters of postmodernism, which concurrently strengthened its position in this part of Europe, simply dismissed the literary canon as one of the burdensome cultural legacies of totalitarianism and its modernism-friendly agenda. Consequently, the reforms called for in literature and its study by postmodern critics in the region worked up at the time fairly crude, aesthetically and politically dichotomous schemes where, synonymous with democracy and Euroatlantic integration, postmodern counter-canons would push back against inherited canons, which were made out to be no more than creations of the modernisms and neomodernisms sanctioned by the system and therefore outcomes of Communist dictatorship, dogmatism, isolationism, and nationalism. Thus, Alexander Kiossev and Boyko Penchev have noted that the Bulgarian literary canon was established in the 1950s under the pressure of bureaucracy, ideological control, and centralization, which have continued to obviate cultural alternatives after 1989.[27] Likewise, Hungarian critic Mihály Szegedy-Maszák has linked up the tearing down of the canon in "small" cultures such as Hungary to their "Westernizing" strains.[28] Worth mentioning, along the same lines, are also the essays on East and Central European literatures in one of the seminal volumes from the 1990s, *International Posmodernism*, in which the new, de-canonizing cultural-theoretical paradigm is offered up as "postcommunis[t] ... cure" in Poland and Slovakia, as a release of intellectual life from "the burden of Marxism" in Hungary, and as an antidote to nationalist outbursts in the former Yugoslav republics.[29]

The contentious equivalence between the canon and Communism got traction especially in Romania, where the violence surrounding the regime's December 1989 fall sent shock waves throughout society and arguably set the stage for more bellicose interventions in the fast-expanding controversy. Wasting no time, Romanian-American critic Virgil Nemoianu published in 1990 two articles aimed at popularizing the theory and practice of canonical revisionism. They were revealingly titled "Bătălia canonică—de la critica americană la cultura română" (The Canon Battle—From American Criticism to Romanian Culture)[30] and "Despărțirea de eminescianism" (Breaking with Eminescianism), respectively, and contended that the debunking of the great myths of national culture—including the one revolving around "the national poet," Mihai Eminescu—was a prerequisite to Romania's democratization and European integration.[31] Nemoianu's articles inspired the most active critic and theorist of Romanian postmodernism, Ion Bogdan Lefter, to treat the "breaks" with Communism and with the canon as coterminous processes. "The postmodern 'canon wars,'" he wrote in 1997, "and the democratic 'canon wars' are facets of the same great historical process ... [W]e are all actors in these 'canonical' faceoffs whose ending is by now predictable: the complete reorganization of entire Romanian society, including the overhaul of this society's isolationist and triumphalist cultural traditions"[32]— tellingly enough, another contribution by Lefter on the issue is titled "Între comunism şi democraţie, între modernitate şi postmodernitate" (Between Communism and Democracy, Between Modernity and Postmodernity) and draws a programmatic line between the ideologically marked poles of the Romanian canon debate.[33]

It is hardly surprising, in this context, that the main form of canonical revisionism turned out to be "eastethical," a pun on the paronymous cluster of "East," "aesthetic," and "ethical." The moniker hints at a peculiar dynamic of the last two terms in the political geography circumscribed by the first. Since Alex Goldiş covers this subject extensively elsewhere in this volume, I will only note that, promoted by Monica Lovinescu, an influential editor of the Paris office of Radio Free Europe between 1960 and 1990, and endorsed by the majority of postmodern Romanian writers, this evaluative protocol sought to revamp the aesthetic canon that took shape during the last three decades of the Cold War. This complex canonical formation was basically seen as a product of censorship and its "internalized" variety, self-censorship, to which writers, critics, theorists, and educators were subjected under Communism. Granted, eastethical revisionism was not to be dismissed offhand. Potentially, it could have helped show how ideologically fraught so-called "aesthetic values" were, but it did not because the actual revisions were mostly confined to sanctioning writers' "moral compromises" such as collaborating with the secret police, participating in propaganda, paying homage to Nicolae Ceauşescu, or holding jobs in the official apparatus. Moreover, one cannot overlook the largely generational biases of most Romanian postmoderns either, whose own canonical "alternative," which they forged during the 1980s, was also aesthetic if allegedly untainted by ideology and idiosyncrasies of all kinds. At any rate, the result of all this was more of a public fracas than a productive post-canonical opening, all the more so that, before long, quite a few older writers and critics, still well-connected and in positions of authority, joined the fray but only to rehash the old chestnuts of the "autonomy" of literature, the danger of "destabilizing" cultural traditions, the "threat" to national identity, and the like. The main representative of the conservative camp was Eugen Simion, president of the Romanian Academy between 1998 and 2006, who defended doggedly modern Romanian literature's hierarchies as they had already been set up by critics George Călinescu and Eugen Lovinescu before World War II and worked aggressively to make sure the position of the 1960s and 1970s modernist and neomodernist literary corpus at the top of critical rankings remained unchallenged.[34] Surprisingly or not, some of the new millennium's young critics also opposed eastethical and postmodern reformism. A case in point is Paul Cernat, who, in the 2010 series of articles "Iluziile revizionismului est-etic" (The Illusions of Eastethical Revisionism), claimed that the anti-canonical campaigns of the postcommunist era fell short by substituting self-righteousness for argument and by pillorying the past wholesale instead of actually revisiting it discriminately.[35]

Whether critics such as Cernat are on the mark or not, the canon wars' casualties in this corner of Europe have been far less staggering than in the Unites States. It is, at any rate, clear that they have not brought about the literary-historical shakeup many hoped for. Neither the liberal, anti-Communist side nor the other extreme, of conservatives sold on aestheticist and nationalist-essentialist dogma has left much room for a genuine and consequential problematization of the national canon, as postmodern critics originally intended. In Romania, for instance, the former group has published brief magazine articles on feminism, postcolonialism, and racial and gender discrimination. This is a largely journalistic body of work in which all these subjects are treated rather cursorily, while solid, thoroughly researched, and authentically revisionist scholarship on these and related aspects of literature are, by and large, in short supply in Romania and other countries in the area.[36] Even after the heated militancy of the canon quarrel has died down, there have come out relatively few critical syntheses willing to give pride of place to foci such as multiculturalism,[37] whereas a number of critics have questioned the relevance of the postcolonial paradigm to entire swaths of East-Central and Southeast Europe.[38] Likewise, feminist and genre studies, despite the stir it has caused initially and the significant translation and theoretical projects it has gotten underway, has yet to dismantle what continues to be a largely patriarchally centered literary canon.[39] Thus, the comments Andrei Terian made in 2013 on Romanian literary criticism and history and their perfunctory, not to say misguided responses to the American culture wars and attendant concerns and methodologies certainly apply more broadly across this European region. As Terian pointed out at the time,

> We need not become Marxists, New Historicists, feminists, or gay activists to notice that literary studies has always been an arena for power relations and struggles, that a large part of the Romanian literary canon has been built on grounds that have little to do with "beauty," no matter how we define it, and that at least some of the voices that have been silenced deserve another chance. Nor need we become postcolonialists or "globalists" to realize that Romanian literature has not developed in an ethnic or linguistic greenhouse, and the borders separating it from other literatures have sometimes been extremely fluid.[40]

To paraphrase Terian, we need not become counter-canonical—or, as Damrosch would have it, hypercanonical—theorists to agree that the overhaul of the Romanian canon as endorsed by the country's main educational institutions has long been overdue. It should have happened by now. If it has not, that has to with the pro-forma, aspirational rather substantial ways in which Romanian and other Central and East European critics have flirted with this core issue of any critical and theoretical culture.

"Peripheral" Post-Canonicity

Otherwise put, those of us still interested in this problem have their work cut out for them. In fact, I would suggest that the urgency of the issue has grown exponentially of late. What is urgent, though, is not the good old-fashioned "critique," "deconstruction," and multicultural "diversifying" of the canon—not that, again, these operations are unimportant, or that they have been completed in Eastern Europe or anywhere else in the world for that matter. What strikes me as pressing, as well as feasible in the wake of new, World Literature and big data methodologies, is working through the genealogy, architecture, and dissemination of a pivotal cultural formation that, *trans*national in its production, has in turn produced *national* myths as influential as diverse and as unpredictable as self-contradictory.

The Warwick Research Collective's 2015 *Combined and Uneven Development: Towards a New Theory of World-Literature* makes, albeit indirectly, a strong case for the timeliness of this undertaking in zones of the theory commons such as Romania and its neighbors. In a bid to surmount some of the theoretical blockages of twenty-first-century comparative studies, the Warwick Collective rejects the "transcendentalist," "New Age-influenced eco-spirituality" that, in framing the dominant understanding of today's globalization, "works to silence questions directed to conflict, domination, exploitation and temporal rupture or discontinuity."[41] The Warwick Collective faults, accordingly, critics such as Gayatri Chakravorty Spivak, Jonathan Culler, Rey Chow, and Wai Chee Dimock for all but ignoring the historical and geographical circumstances of literary practices in an otherwise necessary effort to come to grips with literature in ways less beholden to national exceptionalism and Eurocentric particularisms. More specifically, it is "circumstances" such as those of the "peripheral" literary cultures of East-Central Europe, the Warwick critics venture, that might further an "active *politicisation* of the discussion" in World Literature scholarship.[42]

Spivak and others may or may not be guilty as charged, but I take the Warwick Collective's point on the epistemological gains of this geocultural focus. That is to say, working from the body of evidence and overall context of these literatures may help nuance a postcolonial critique of Eurocentrism predicated on the misconception of "Europe" as an all-of-a-piece cultural bloc and, in the same vein, may upend those equally simplifying, conservative constructions that either exalt the sans-pareil exemplars of the Western canon or similarly mummify its exceptionalist-particularist local counterparts on behalf of various nationalisms. None of these corrections and finetuning procedures can wait. An authentically global perspective does not imply merely a spatial or temporal expansion of canonicity, an ecumenical Noah's ark of regional masterpieces known "locally," as Zhang Longxi, an editor-in-chief of the newly launched *Journal of World Literature*, appears to suggest. In a 2016 essay, Zhang celebrates an idealized image of World Literature's canonically reformist methodology, a cumulative modus operandi that has enabled the curious "to hear the voices of Egypt and Mesopotamia, of Africa and South America" and "to learn more about" Persian and Arabic literature, mystic Sufi poets, the *ghazals* of Rumi, Saʿdi and Hafiz, Indian literature, about "the fantastic tales of *Ramayana* and *Mahabharata*, the enchanting poems of Rabindranath Tagore," about "Europe other than the major literatures, about Nordic literature, Czech and Polish literature, and literatures of the 'minor' languages."[43]

"To hear the voices" and "to learn more about" the canonical histories and constellations of such literary areas are or should be, in my view, endeavors as enticing as they are conflict-ridden domestically and internationally, for they would inevitably both reignite old tensions inherent to canon formation and whip up new ones inside and among national literatures, as values, rankings, and so forth rise, fall, compete, collide, and generally speaking, cannot obtain other than in large-scale competition and friction with one another. As Slovenian critic Marko Juvan has reminded us in a study reassessing "the national poet" concept from a World Literature perspective,[44] "canonizing a poet as a nation's cultural saint ('sainting')" invariably goes hand in glove with "his or her 'worlding,'"[45] so much so that national canons always come about and operate as "imagined world literatures."[46] As a result, during the twisted, practically endless course of canon formation, the national character of "peripheral" cultures is mapped onto the "universal." This genetic trajectory of canonicity intersects, according to Juvan, Fredric Jameson's controversial description of "third-world" literatures viewed as "national allegories" rather than "as anthropologically independent or autonomous." "They are all," thinks Jameson, "in various distinct ways locked in a life-and-death struggle with first-world cultural imperialism—a cultural struggle that is itself a reflection of the economic situation of such areas in their penetration by various stages of capital, or as it is sometimes euphemistically termed, of modernization."[47]

At once national, international, and transnational, the reality of such struggles and contradictions is undeniable. Following from it, I think, are two major consequences for the ongoing, World Literature-driven reconceptualization of the canon in geolocations outside the literary world-system's presumed centers of financial and cultural capital. For one thing, the time has come to recognize that those areas' modernizing impetus and germane overcoming of their alleged inferiority and backwardness "complexes" make them less dependent on the vernacular cultural apparatus that, as conservative "autochthonists" would have it, has historically produced national recognition. Yet again, it must be said that this prestige factory has never worked autarchically, in an international vacuum. In these cultures, the canonicity of writers, phenomena, trends, movements, and forms is all the more pronounced, all the more "nationally" representative as it is more plugged into the canonical motherboards of world, particularly Western canons. Canonical significance accrues here "comparatively," as it were, namely, through imaginary associations with the prestigious, capital-cultural-rich models and landmarks of the "center." For another thing, these self-affiliations enact cultural and ideological, transforming "readings" of said center; once transposed into East-Central European cultural environments, Western literary classics take on or reactivate sociopolitical meanings that these authors' prevailing treatment as aesthetic milestones and paradigms has either obscured or downplayed. The center-periphery relationships have therefore never been a one-way street of active exports and passive imports. As the Warwick Collective contends,

> if we put various (semi-)peripheral European works—set in different places and written at different times—into conversation with one another and read them together without ignoring what we might call their non-simultaneous simultaneity, we begin to discern the ways in which they typically register the "local" and "global" aspects of modernity as at one and the same time traumatic, destructive, stimulating and profoundly transformative.[48]

Such regional footprints of literary modernity await comparatists well equipped to rebuff nationalist self-mystifications and pseudo-autonomist exceptionalisms by recalibrating World Literature through a comparative analysis that might zero in, for instance, on what happened to writers such as Émile Zola, Marcel Proust, Charles Baudelaire, Stéphane Mallarmé, James Joyce, and William Faulkner once their works started circulating in the area the Warwick Collective refers to. What I have in mind is not only classical surveys of such authors' translation and "reception," scholarship that has been significantly growing over recent years.[49] More needed at this juncture would be, I believe, inquiries capable of accounting for the misreadings, willful or less so, and for the veritable "reinventions" of Western writers so as to align them with modern, national, nationalist, and totalitarian Central and East European ideologies.

Illustrating this kind of work, the chapters on William Wordsworth and Robert Burns in András Kiséry, Zsolt Komáromy, and Zsuzsanna Varga's 2016 *Worlds of Hungarian Writing: National Literature as Intercultural Exchange* lay bare precisely the ideological-political ramifications of the regional "nationalization" of canonical authors hailing from "major" cultures.[50] This is definitely a pathway down which comparatism can advance its still tentative dealings with the East-Central European metamorphoses of entire creative paradigms such as Symbolism, the avant-garde, modernism, and postmodernism. The theoretical benefits of such analyses are not to be underestimated, whether in the East or elsewhere, as Teodora Dumitru has shown in her recent contributions to a more nuanced understanding of Romanian modern and postmodern literature. Her books and articles on these subjects manage to unravel the mythical aura critics like Simion are still scrambling to preserve around Lovinescu's modernist canon. As Dumitru explains, Lovinescu renders modernist aesthetics and aesthetic autonomy equivalent and values modernism overall as a means of "closing the gap" with the liberal West. In so doing, she comments, Lovinescu takes away from modernism its political edge, specifically its opposition to the alienation caused by technical and industrial capitalist progress—ironically enough, exactly those features contemporary West European and American modernist scholarship have been dwelling on.[51] Likewise, she takes to task the similarly "civilizational" and Pollyannaish ways—seemingly de-ideologized but, in essence, profoundly ideological and political—some of the poets of the Romanian 1980s look at, and up to, the West, which in their work becomes "a depoliticized and, to a notable extent, idealistic construct quasi synonymous with freedom, political pluralism, prosperity, and opportunity, while the less bright side of things gets little attention."[52] As she maintains, positioning themselves to both vent their hostility toward Communism *and* capitalize aesthetically on their association with the American beatniks, the Romanian postmoderns turn, oddly enough, a blind eye to, and even reject, the saliently anti-capitalist politics of the American poets they otherwise seek to emulate.

Quantitative research and computational analysis could be at least as effective in eviscerating some of the preconceptions and equivocations surrounding canonical issues. It is true that, up until now, East European databases have digitized and stored chiefly information on writers taught in school. Numerous editions and bibliographies exist for those authors, and so digitalization only further strengthens their position in curricula and hierarchies.[53] Nevertheless, the situation can change fast. The manageable volume of the contemporary cultural output of this European zone makes it possible to complete most digital archives in the foreseeable future. In Romania, for example, libraries and academic institutes have already built quasi-exhaustive electronic collections of major magazines and literary genres, now available alongside the usual in-print dictionaries, scholarly chronologies, compendiums, and bibliographies of editions, secondary literature, and translations. In Hungary, Poland, the Czech Republic, Slovakia, Serbia, Croatia, and Slovenia, research centers and institutes have been organizing conferences and workshops, also working together on a range of projects.[54] Not only has the idea of canonicity been at the center of these initiatives, but it has been scrutinized ever more closely from angles saliently at odds with older perspectives informed by unqualified and immutable "essences," be those aesthetic, ethnic, or national.

Not just the standpoints differ, though. What we learn from this recent scholarship is new too. For the first time, big data and computer algorithms make it easier for us to see syntactic patterns, keywords, lexical recurrences, and emblematic critical leitmotifs like "atemporal value," "ineffable," "taste-based judgment," "jouissance," and "nationally typical identity" as functions of less lofty but also less nebulous, more down-to-earth, more materialist, and even "scientific" factors such as linguistic and stylistic variety; thematic and compositional differences between critically acclaimed works and bestsellers, on one hand, and, on the other, those that have been less successful; formal influences of Western aesthetic sources; synergies between translations and local evolutions of literary genres and trends; selection and promotion of works by institutions and recognized venues such as schools, magazines, and scholarship; and sales and other marks of public success.[55]

Moreover, the chance offered by the digital revolution to East European critics to revisit things they thought they knew also gives them reason to hope that entire critical cultures in the region would not fall back on what appears to be a real risk of computational analysis, namely, the overemphasis on the textual side of literary scholarship and the sliding into a cyberformalism of sorts. The production and instructional reproduction of the written word, its distribution, evaluation, and reception, as well as the local circulation and assimilation of works published elsewhere throw into sharp relief literature's socioeconomic and political underpinnings, to which theoretical constructs and analyses worked out in recognized hubs of theory production may or may not always do justice. No matter how effectively it may detect and process formal patterns and linguistic clusters, rigorous studies of East-Central European canonicity cannot ignore aspects such as, say, pre-mid-twentieth-century literacy and the close ties between the most prominent literary figures and intellectual groups, on one side, and various ideological positions and political parties, on the other. Nor can big data research afford to overlook, as Ştefan Baghiu cautions in a recent article, censorship, government propaganda, the political oversight of translations, book production and commerce monitoring, as well as the subversive reactions to these, all of which have left their imprint on literary forms and techniques.[56] This methodological vigilance may give our theoretical commons not only a more *material* measure of what I have dubbed post-canonicity but also a sense that the World Literature system is far more polymorphous and multipronged than its mainstream theorizations have made it out to be. It is by now beyond doubt that the development of "peripheral" European canons cannot be accommodated by monodirectional theories about "catching up" to the West through "borrowing," "adaptation," and the like. At the same time, the history of these canonical constellations shines new light—again, for all of us—on Moretti's reference to "one, and unequal" world literary system.[57] Under these rather ambiguous circumstances, Europe's geocultural "outliers" and their own literary hierarchies may well play after postmodernism the part of Moretti's "great unread," not only in that they do deserve to be read by the wider world and take their rightful place in this world's literary system but also insofar as they themselves can help read for this system's sometimes less visible intricacies, complexities, amalgamations, and "unevenness."

Notes

1 Matthew Wilkens, "Canons, Close Reading, and the Evolution of Method," in *Debates in the Digital Humanities*, ed. Matthew K. Gold (Minneapolis: University of Minnesota Press, 2012), 249.
2 J. D. Porter, "Popularity/Prestige," Pamphlet 17 (September 2018), 21, https://litlab.stanford.edu/LiteraryLabPamphlet17.pdf (accessed June 30, 2019).
3 Matthew Wilkens has acknowledged that just mentioning the need to reground research in the canon may provoke hostile reactions. "I was scolded," he writes, "recently by a senior colleague who told me that I was thirty years out of date for [mentioning this]. The idea being that we'd had this fight a generation ago, and the canon had lost" ("Canons, Close Reading, and the Evolution of Method," 249). This hostility is shared by some of the postcolonial and feminist scholars invited to participate in the experiment Mark Algee-Hewitt and Mark McGurl present in "Between Canon and Corpus: Six Perspectives on 20th-Century Novels," Pamphlet 8 (January 2015), https://litlab.stanford.edu/LiteraryLabPamphlet8.pdf (accessed June 30, 2019).
4 See also Ted Underwood and Jordan Sellers, "The Longue Durée of Literary Prestige," *Modern Language Quarterly* 3 (2016): 321–44; H. Long and R. J. So, "Literary Pattern Recognition: Modernism between Close Reading and Machine Learning," *Critical Inquiry* 2 (2016): 235–67; Hans-Joachim Backe, "The Literary Canon in the Age of New Media," *Poetics Today* 1–2 (2015): 1–31; Rebecca Gould, "Conservative in Form, Revolutionary in Content: Rethinking World Literary Canons in an Age of Globalization," *Canadian Review of Comparative Literature* 41, no. 3 (2014): 270–86; and Carolina Ferrer, "Canonical Values vs. the Law of Large Numbers: The Canadian Literary Canon in the Age of Big Data," *Rupkatha Journal on Interdisciplinary Studies in Humanities* 5, no. 3 (2013): 81–90.
5 See Jeffrey T. Nealon, *Post-Postmodernism, or, The Cultural Logic of Just-in-time Capitalism* (Stanford, CA: Stanford University Press, 2012).

6   Eric Prieto, *Literature, Geography, and the Postmodern Poetics of Place* (New York: Palgrave Macmillan, 2012).

7   Michael Hardt and Antonio Negri, *Empire* (Cambridge, MA: Harvard University Press, 2000), xi, xii.

8   Charles Bernheimer, ed., *Comparative Literature in the Age of Multiculturalism* (Baltimore: Johns Hopkins University Press, 1995), 41–2.

9   David Damrosch, "World Literature in a Postcanonical, Hypercanonical Age," in *Comparative Literature in an Age of Globalization*, ed. Haun Saussy (Baltimore: Johns Hopkins University Press, 2006), 43, 45.

10   Damrosch, "World Literature in a Postcanonical, Hypercanonical Age," 50.

11   Ursula K. Heise, "Introduction: Comparative Literature and the New Humanities," in *Futures of Comparative Literature: ACLA State of the Discipline Report*, ed. Ursula K. Heise, with Dudley Andrew, Alexander Beecroft, Jessica Berman, David Damrosch, Guillermina De Ferrari, César Domínguez, Barbara Harlow, and Eric Hayot (New York: Routledge, 2017), 3.

12   Heise, "Introduction," 3.

13   Heise, "Introduction," 4.

14   Mads Rosendahl Thomsen, *Mapping World Literature: International Canonization and Transnational Literatures* (London: Continuum, 2008).

15   Mads Rosendahl Thomsen, "World Famous, Locally: Insights from the Study of International Canonization," in *Futures of Comparative Literature*, ed. Ursula K. Heise, with Dudley Andrew, Alexander Beecroft, Jessica Berman, David Damrosch, Guillermina De Ferrari, César Domínguez, Barbara Harlow, and Eric Hayot (New York: Routledge, 2017), 120.

16   Just as the canon can no longer be viewed as a corpus embodying various "essences," nationhood cannot be reduced to its nineteenth-century Herderian definition. As Christian Moraru points out in "'World,' 'Globe,' 'Planet': Comparative Literature, Planetary Studies, and Cultural Debt after the Global Turn," "while national borders and jurisdictions continue to exist, the way planetary scholars map developments across the arts overlaps less and less with the nation. Pre-, sub-, and transnational scales of aggregation challenge the classical paradigm of national territoriality … What this new, cross-territorial, cross-cultural, and cross-linguistic scalarity helps us visualize cartographically and appreciate critically is how much national cultures have borrowed from world cultures and, accordingly, how much of the nation's cultural fabric consists of credit lines from elsewhere" (in *Futures of Comparative Literature*, Ursula K. Heise, with Dudley Andrew, Alexander Beecroft, Jessica Berman, David Damrosch, Guillermina De Ferrari, César Domínguez, Barbara Harlow, and Eric Hayot [New York: Routledge, 2017], 132).

17   Thomsen, "World Famous, Locally," 120.

18   Thomsen, "World Famous, Locally," 122.

19   See mainly Franco Moretti's syntheses in *Distant Reading* (New York: Verso, 2013).

20   Franco Moretti, "The Slaughterhouse of Literature," *Modern Language Quarterly* 61, no. 1 (2000): 207.

21   Susan Schreibman, Ray Siemens, and John Unsworth, eds., *A Companion to Digital Humanities* (Oxford: Blackwell, 2004); Stephen Ramsay, *Reading*

Machines: Toward an Algorithmic Criticism (Urbana: University of Illinois Press, 2011); and Ray Siemens and Susan Schreibman, eds., *A Companion to Digital Literary Studies* (Oxford: Blackwell, 2013).

22 Porter, "Popularity/Prestige," 22.

23 See Stanford Literary Lab (https://litlab.stanford.edu/pamphlets/), particularly Pamphlets 8 ("Between Canon and Corpus: Six Perspectives on 20th-Century Novels"), 11 ("Canon/Archive. Large-scale Dynamics in the Literary Field"), and 17 ("Popularity/Prestige").

24 See Oswaldo Zavala's comments on "the insurmountable limitation of the 'world literature' paradigm as a system that reproduces the silences and the exclusions of the dominant English-language global editorial market" in "The Repolitization of the Latin American Shore: Roberto Bolaño and the Dispersion of 'World Literature'" (in *Roberto Bolaño as World Literature*, ed. Nicholas Birns and Juan De Castro [New York: Bloomsbury, 2017], 82. Worth noting is also Shu-Mei Shih's Morettian analysis in "Global Literature and the Technologies of Recognition" (*PMLA* 119, no. 1 [2004]: 16–30), a critique that applies equally well to studies by Pascale Casanova and David Damrosch, as Theo D'haen shows in "Worlding the Social Sciences and Humanities" (*European Review* 24, no. 2 [2016]: 186–99).

25 Heise, "Comparative Literature and Computational Criticism: A Conversation with Franco Moretti," in *Futures of Comparative*, ed. Ursula K. Heise, with Dudley Andrew, Alexander Beecroft, Jessica Berman, David Damrosch, Guillermina De Ferrari, César Domínguez, Barbara Harlow, and Eric Hayot (New York: Routledge, 2017), 273.

26 See Liviu Papadima, David Damrosch, and Theo D'haen, eds., *The Canonical Debate Today: Crossing Disciplinary and Cultural Boundaries* (Amsterdam: Rodopi, 2011).

27 Alexander Kiossev, with Boyko Penchev, "Heritage and Inheritors: The Literary Canon in Totalitarian Bulgaria," in *History of the Literary Cultures of East-Central Europe: Junctures and Disjunctures in the 19th and 20th Centuries*, vol. 2, ed. Marcel Cornis-Pope and John Neubauer (Amsterdam: John Benjamins Publishing Company, 2006), 132–41.

28 Mihály Szegedy-Maszák, *Literary Canons: National and International* (Budapest: Akadémiai, 2001).

29 See Tibor Zilka, "Postmodernism in Slovak Literature," in *International Postmodernism: Theory and Literary Practice*, ed. Hans Bertens and Douwe Fokkema (Amsterdam: John Benjamins Publishing Company, 1997), 413–18; Milan Suchomel, "Postmodernism in Czech Literature" (419–22); Halina Janaszek-Ivaničková, "Postmodernism in Poland" (423–8); Mihály Szegedy-Maszák, "Postmodern Literature in Hungary" (429–34); Edward Mozejko, "Postmodernism in the Literatures of Former Yugoslavia" (441–6).

30 Virgil Nemoianu, "Bătălia canonică—de la critica americană la cultura română," *România literară* 41 (1990): 12–13.

31 Virgil Nemoianu, "Despărțirea de eminescianism," *Astra* 7 (1990): 8–9.

32 Ion Bogdan Lefter, "Un model explicativ și un mare proces istoric," *Dilema* 245 (1997), 6.

33 Ion Bogdan Lefter, "Între comunism și democrație, între modernitate și postmodernitate," *Dilema* 340 (1999): 6.

34 Eugen Simion, *Fragmente critice I–IV* (Craiova, Romania: Editura Scrisul Românesc; Bucharest: Fundația Națională pentru Știință și Artă, 1998–2009).

35 Paul Cernat, "Iluziile revizionismului est-etic," *Observator cultural*, nos. 1–3 (539–41) (2010): 5, 7, 6.

36 Ion Bogdan Lefter's articles "Poate fi considerat postcomunismul un post-colonialism?," "Multiculturalismul vine peste noi," "De partea 'majorității minoritare,'" "'Aclimatizare' întârziată," and "Confesiune de (aproape) feminist" have been included in *Postmodernism. Din dosarul unei "bătălii" culturale*, 2nd, expanded edn. (Pitești, Romania: Paralela 45, 2002).

37 See the special issue "Changements de canon culturel chez nous et ailleurs" of *Euresis* (1998).

38 See Andrei Terian, "Is There an East-Central European Post-colonialism? Towards a Unified Theory of (Inter)Literary Dependency," *World Literature Studies* 4, no. 3 (2012): 21–36, as well as Monica Bottez, Sabina-Maria Draga Alexandru, and Bogdan Ștefănescu, eds., *Postcolonialism/Postcommunism: Intersections and Overlaps* (Bucharest: Bucharest University Press, 2011); Halina Janaszek-Ivaničková, "Postmodernism in Poland," in *International Postmodernism: Theory and Literary Practice*, ed. Hans Bertens and Douwe Fokkema (Amsterdam: John Benjamins Publishing Company, 1997), 427; Jaroslav Kušnir, "Postcolonial Studies in Slovakia and Hungary," *Po-Równania* 17 (2015): 245–52; and Maria Todorova, "Balkanism and Postcolonialism or On the Beauty of the Airplane View," in *Marx's Shadow: Knowledge, Power, and Intellectuals in Eastern Europe and Russia*, ed. Costica Bradatan and Serguei Oushakine (Lanham, MD: Lexington Books, 2010), 175–96.

39 Mary Zirin, Irina Livezeanu, Christine D. Worobec, and June Pachuta Farris, eds., *Women & Gender in Central and Eastern Europe, Russia, and Eurasia: A Comprehensive Bibliography*, 2 vols. (New York: M. E. Sharpe, 2007).

40 Andrei Terian, "Istoria literaturii române în epoca globalizării," in *Critica de export. Teorii, contexte, ideologii* (Bucharest: Muzeul Literaturii Române, 2013), 292.

41 WReC: Warwick Research Collective, *Combined and Uneven Development: Towards a New Theory of World-Literature* (Liverpool, UK: Liverpool University Press, 2015), 42–7.

42 WReC, *Combined and Uneven Development*, 23.

43 Longxi Zhang, "Canon and World Literature," *Journal of World Literature* 1, no. 1 (2016): 122.

44 Significant evidence of this new trend in conceptualizing canonicity is presented in two essay collections edited by Marijan Dović and Jón Karl Helgason: *National Poets, Cultural Saints: Canonization and Commemorative Cults of Writers in Europe* (Leiden: Brill, 2017) and *Great Immortality: Studies on European Cultural Sainthood* (Leiden: Brill, 2019).

45 Marko Juvan, "The Aesthetics and Politics of Belonging: National Poets between 'Vernacularism' and 'Cosmopolitanism,'" *Arcadia* 52, no. 1 (2017): 10–28.

46 For further discussion of this concept, see Marko Juvan, *Worlding a Peripheral Literature* (New York: Palgrave Macmillan, 2019).

47 Fredric Jameson, "Third-World Literature in the Era of Multinational Capitalism," *Social Text* 15 (1986): 68.

48 WReC, *Combined and Uneven Development*, 127.

49 See the Bloomsbury series edited by Elinor Shaffer, "The Reception of British and Irish Authors in Europe," which includes in its books substantial chapters on Central and Eastern Europe.

50 See Zsolt Komáromy, "'Wordsworth in Hungary:' An Essay on Reception as Cultural Memory and Forgetting," in *Worlds of Hungarian Writing: National Literature as Intercultural Exchange*, ed. András Kiséry, Zsolt Komáromy, and Zsuzsanna Varga (Teaneck, NJ: Fairleigh Dickinson University Press; Lanham, MD: Rowman and Littlefield, 2016), 29–52, and Veronika Ruttkay, "Negotiating the Popular/ National Voice: Impropriety in Two Hungarian Translations of Robert Burns" (53–74).

51 Teodora Dumitru, *Modernitatea politică și literară în gândirea lui E. Lovinescu* (Bucharest: Muzeul Literaturii Române, 2016).

52 Teodora Dumitru, "Gaming the World-System: Creativity, Politics, and Beat Influence in the Poetry of the 1980s Generation," in *Romanian Literature as World Literature*, ed. Mircea Martin, Christian Moraru, and Andrei Terian (New York: Bloomsbury, 2017), 281.

53 Mihaela Ursa, "Is Romanian Culture Ready for the Digital Turn?," *Metacritic: Journal for Comparative Studies and Theory* 1 (2015): 80–97.

54 See Central European University, "Digital Humanities Initiative," https://www. ceu.edu/dhi/regional, and DARIAH-EU, https://www.dariah.eu/ (both accessed July 15, 2019).

55 See Matthew L. Jockers, *Macroanalysis: Digital Methods and Literary History* (Urbana: University of Illinois Press, 2013).

56 Ștefan Baghiu, "Translating Hemispheres: Eastern Europe and the Global South Connection through Translationscapes of Poverty," *Comparative Literature Studies* 3 (2019): 487–503.

57 As Moretti writes in his famous article "Conjectures on World Literature," "I will borrow this initial hypothesis from the world-system school of economic history, for which international capitalism is a system that is simultaneously *one*, and *unequal*: with a core and a periphery (and a semiperiphery) that are bound together in a relationship of growing inequality. One, and unequal: *one* literature (*Weltliteratur*, singular, as in Goethe and Marx), or perhaps, better, one world literary system (of inter-related literatures); but a system which is different from what Goethe and Marx had hoped for, because it's profoundly unequal" (*New Left Review* 1 (2000): 55–6).

BIBLIOGRAPHY

Adameșteanu, Gabriela. *The Encounter*. Translated by Alistair Ian Blyth. McLean, IL: Dalkey Archive Press, 2016.

Adameșteanu, Gabriela. *Fontana di Trevi*. Iași, Romania: Polirom, 2018.

Adameșteanu, Gabriela. *Întâlnirea*. Iași, Romania: Polirom, 2003.

Agamben, Giorgio. *Qu'est-ce que le contemporain?* Translated from the Italian by Maxime Rovere. Paris: Payot & Rivages, 2008.

Ahmad, Aijaz. "Jameson's Rhetoric of Otherness and the 'National Allegory.'" *Social Text*, no. 17 (Autumn 1987): 3–25.

Alexandrescu, Sorin. "Intelectualul ca mediator social." 22 15 (1991): 14–15.

Alferi, Pierre, and Olivier Cadiot, "La Mécanique Lyrique." *Revue de Littérature Générale* 1 (1995): 3–22.

Algee-Hewitt, Mark, and Mark McGurl. "Between Canon and Corpus: Six Perspectives on 20th-Century Novels." Pamphlet 8 (January 2015): 3–29. Available online: https://litlab.stanford.edu/LiteraryLabPamphlet8.pdf (accessed June 30, 2019).

Althusser, Louis. *Philosophy of the Encounter: Later Writings, 1978–87*. Translated by G. M. Goshgarian. London: Verso, 2006.

Anderson, Philip W. "More Is Different," *Science*, n.s., 177, no. 4047 (August 4, 1972): 393–6.

Anghelescu, Mircea. *Mistificțiuni. Falsuri, farse, apocrife, pastișe, pseudonime și alte mistificații în literatură*. Bucharest: Compania, 2008.

Anker, Elizabeth S., and Rita Felski, eds. *Critique and Postcritique*. Durham, NC: Duke University Press, 2017.

Antohi, Sorin. *Războaie culturale. Idei, intelectuali, spirit public*. Iași, Romania: Polirom, 2007.

Appiah, Kwame Anthony. "The Case for Contamination." *The New York Times Magazine*, January 1, 2006. Available online: https://www.nytimes.com/2006/01/01/magazine/the-case-for-contamination.html (accessed May 31, 2019).

Appiah, Kwame Anthony. *Cosmopolitanism: Ethics in a World of Strangers*. New York: W. W. Norton, 2006.

Apter, Emily. *Feminizing the Fetish*. Ithaca, NY: Cornell University Press, 1992.

Aristotle. *The Poetics of Aristotle*, edited with critical notes and translated by S. H. Butcher. London: Macmillan, 1902.

Arnheim, Rudolf. *New Essays on the Psychology of Art*. Berkeley: University of California Press, 1986.

Assmann, Aleida. *Cultural Memory and Western Civilization: Functions, Media, Archives*. Cambridge: Cambridge University Press, 2011.

Assmann, Jan. *Cultural Memory and Early Civilization: Writing, Remembrance and Political Imagination*. Cambridge: Cambridge University Press, 2011.

Avanessian, Armen. *Ethics of Knowledge: Poetics of Existence*. Berlin: Sternberg Press, 2017.

Avanessian, Armen. "The Speculative End of the Aesthetic Regime." *Texte zur Kunst* 24 (2014): 52–65.

Backe, Hans-Joachim. "The Literary Canon in the Age of New Media." *Poetics Today* 1–2 (2015): 1–31.

Badiou, Alain. *Abrégé de métapolitique*. Paris: Seuil, 1998.

Baghiu, Ştefan. "Naşterea tragediei din spiritul manelelor." *Cultura* 9, no. 6 (February 20, 2014): 10.

Baghiu, Ştefan. "The Relative Autonomy of Literature: Romanian Literary Criticism and Theory before World War II." *Transilvania* 5 (2020): 29–38.

Baghiu, Ştefan. "Translating Hemispheres: Eastern Europe and the Global South Connection through Translationscapes of Poverty." *Comparative Literature Studies* 56, no. 3 (2019): 487–503.

Bakhtin, Mikhail M. *The Dialogic Imagination: Four Essays*. Edited by Michael Holquist. Translated by Caryl Emerson and Michael Holquist. Austin: University of Texas Press, 2011.

Bakhtin, Mikhail M. *Problems of Dostoevsky's Poetics*. Edited and translated by Carol Emerson. Introduction by Wayne C. Booth. Minneapolis: University of Minnesota Press, 1984.

Bal, Mieke. "Introduction to Volume III." In *Narrative Theory: Critical Concepts in Literary and Cultural Studies*, vol. 3, *Political Narratology*, edited by Mieke Bal, 1–9. London: Taylor & Francis, 2004.

Ban, Cornel. *Dependenţă şi dezvoltare. Economia politică a capitalismului românesc*. Cluj-Napoca, Romania: Tact, 2014.

Bardini, Thierry. *Bootstrapping: Douglas Engelbart, Coevolution, and the Origins of Personal Computing*. Stanford, CA: Stanford University Press, 2000.

Bar-Itzhak, Chen. "Intellectual Captivity: Literary Theory, World Literature, and the Ethics of Interpretation." *Journal of World Literature* 5, no. 1 (2020): 79–110.

Barthes, Roland. *Œuvres complètes II and III*. Edited by Eric Marty. Paris: Seuil, 2002.

Baruch-Wachtel, Andrew. *Remaining Relevant after Communism: The Role of the Writer in Eastern Europe*. Chicago: University of Chicago Press, 2006.

Bates, Stephen. "Zadie Smith Dismisses Big Society and Multiculturalism Policy." *The Guardian*, May 21, 2010. Available online: https://www.theguardian. com/books/2010/may/21/zadie-smith-big-society-multiculturalism (accessed December 25, 2019).

Beck, Ulrich. "Cosmopolitan Sociology: Outline of a Paradigm Shift." In *The Ashgate Research Companion to Cosmopolitanism*, edited by Maria Rovisco and Magdalena Nowicka, 17–32. Farnham, UK: Ashgate, 2011.

Beebee, Thomas O. "What the World Thinks about Literature." In *Futures of Comparative Literature: ACLA State of the Discipline Report*, edited by Ursula K. Heise, with Dudley Andrew, Alexander Beecroft, Jessica Berman, David Damrosch, Guillermina De Ferrari, César Domínguez, Barbara Harlow, and Eric Hayot, 61–70. New York: Routledge, 2017.

Bejan, Adrian. *Physics of Life*. New York: St. Martin's Press, 2016.

Bejan, Adrian, and Gilbert W. Merkx, eds. *Constructal Theory of Social Dynamics*. New York: Springer, 2007.

Bejan, Adrian, and J. Peder Zane. *Design in Nature*. New York: Anchor Books, 2012.

Benjamin, Walter. *Illuminations*. Edited and with an Introduction by Hannah Arendt. Translated by Harry Zohn. New York: Schocken Books, 1985.

Bennett, Jane. "Systems and Things: A Response to Graham Harman and Timothy Morton." *New Literary History* 43, no. 2 (2012): 225–33.

Bennett, Tony, and Patrick Joyce. *Material Powers: Cultural Studies, History and the Material Turn*. London: Routledge, 2010.

Benton, Michael. *Literary Biography: An Introduction*. Malden, MA: Wiley-Blackwell, 2009.

Bernheimer, Charles, ed. *Comparative Literature in the Age of Multiculturalism*. Baltimore: Johns Hopkins University Press, 1995.

Bertens, Hans, and Douwe Fokkema, eds. *International Postmodernism: Theory and Literary Practice*. Amsterdam: John Benjamins Publishing Company, 1997.

Best, Stephen, and Sharon Marcus. "Surface Reading: An Introduction." *Representations* 108, no. 1 (2009): 1–21.

Bhabha, Homi. "The World and the Home." In *Dangerous Liaisons: Gender, Nation, and Postcolonial Perspectives*, edited by Anne McClintock, Aamir Mufti, and Ella Shohat, 445–55. Minneapolis: University of Minnesota Press, 1997.

Biroul Electoral Central. "First Page." 2019. Available online: http://prezidentiale2019.bec.ro (accessed October 11, 2020).

Biroul Electoral Central. "Voter Turnout." 2018. Available online: http://referendum2018.bec.ro (accessed October 11, 2020).

Blanchot, Maurice. *The Unavowable Community*. Translated by Pierre Joris. Barrytown, NY: Station Hill Press, 1988.

Bloom, Harold. *How to Read and Why*. New York: Scribner, 2002.

Boatcă, Manuela. *Laboratoare ale modernității. Europa de Est și America Latină în (co)relație*. Cluj-Napoca, Romania: Idea, 2019.

Boatcă, Manuela. "Semiperipheries in the World-System: Reflecting Eastern European and Latin American Experiences." *Journal of World-Systems Research* 12, no. 2 (2006): 321–46.

Boldrini, Lucia. *Autobiographies of Others: Historical Subject and Literary Fiction*. New York: Routledge, 2012.

Boldrini, Lucia, and Julia Novak, eds. *Experiments in Life-Writing*. London: Palgrave Macmillan, 2017.

Boltanski, Luc, and Eve Chiapello. *The New Spirit of Capitalism*. Translated by Gregory Elliott. London: Verso, 2017.

Bordo, Susan. *Unbearable Weight: Feminism, Western Culture, and the Body*. Berkeley: University of California Press, 1993.

Borza, Cosmin. "Un roman occidental." *Cultura* 5 (561), February 2, 2017. Available online: https://blog.revistacultura.ro/2017/04/08/radu-pavel-gheo-disco-titanic-review-de-cosmin-borza/ (accessed January 31, 2019).

Both, Ioana. "Le corps de la théorie, le corps dans la théorie: Figurations du sujet interprétant dans les écrits de Jean Starobinski." *Ekphrasis: Images, Cinema, Theory, Media*, no. 1 (2015): 188–98.

Both, Ioana. "Présences du sujet interprétant: qui dit 'je'?" *Euresis*, nos. 1–4 (2011): 162–72.

Bottez, Monica, Sabina-Maria Draga Alexandru, and Bogdan Ştefănescu, eds. *Postcolonialism/Postcommunism: Intersections and Overlaps*. Bucharest: Bucharest University Press, 2011.

Boym, Svetlana. *The Future of Nostalgia*. New York: Basic Books, 2001.

Braga, Corin. *10 Studii de arhetipologie*. Cluj-Napoca, Romania: Dacia, 2007.

Braga, Corin. "Le centre structurel et ses restes." *Caietele Echinox* 33, (2017): 50–61.

Braga, Corin, ed. *Concepte şi metode în cercetarea imaginarului. Dezbaterile Phantasma*. Iaşi, Romania: Polirom, 2007.

Braga, Corin. *De la arhetip la anarhetip*. Iaşi, Romania: Polirom, 2006.

Braga, Corin. *Le paradis interdit au Moyen Âge II. La quête manquée de l'Éden occidental*. Paris: L'Harmattan, 2006.

Brians, Ella. "The 'Virtual' Body and the Strange Persistence of the Flesh: Deleuze, Cyberspace and the Posthuman." In *Deleuze and the Body*, edited by Laura Guillaume and Joe Hughes, 117–43. Edinburgh: Edinburgh University Press, 2011.

Bridger, Darren. *Neuro Design*. London: Kogan Page, 2017.

Bromberg, Svenja. "The Anti-Political Aesthetics of Objects and Worlds Beyond." *Mute* (July 25, 2013). Available online: https://www.metamute.org/editorial/articles/anti-political-aesthetics-objects-and-worlds-beyond (accessed February 19, 2020).

Brooker, Peter, Andrej Gasiorek, Deborah Longworth, and Andrew Thacker, eds. *The Oxford Handbook of Modernisms*. New York: Oxford University Press, 2010.

Brooks, Christopher K., ed. *Beyond Postmodernism: Onto the Postcontemporary*. Newcastle upon Tyne, UK: Cambridge Scholars, 2013.

Brooks, Christopher K. "Defining the Postcontemporary Moment." In *Beyond Postmodernism: Onto the Postcontemporary*, edited by Christopher K. Brooks, 134–51. Newcastle upon Tyne, UK: Cambridge Scholars, 2013.

Brooks, Christopher K. "Introduction." In *Beyond Postmodernism: Onto the Postcontemporary*, edited by Christopher K. Brooks,x–xviii. Newcastle upon Tyne, UK: Cambridge Scholars, 2013.

Bru, Sascha. "Modernism Before and After Theory." In *The Oxford Handbook of Modernisms*, edited by Peter Brooker, Andrej Gasiorek, Deborah Longworth, and Andrew Thacker, 31–44. New York: Oxford University Press, 2010.

Buchanan, Ian. *Fredric Jameson: Live Theory*. London: Continuum, 2007.

Buisine, Alain. "Biofictions." *Revue des Sciences Humaines* 224, no. 4 (1991): 7–13.

Burke, Seán. *Death and Return of the Author: Criticism and Subjectivity in Barthes, Foucault and Derrida*. Edinburgh: Edinburgh University Press, 1998.

Byatt, Jim. *Rethinking the Monstrous: Transgression, Vulnerability, and Difference in British Fiction Since 1967*. Lanham, MD: Lexington Books, 2015.

Călinescu, G. *Istoria literaturii române de la origini până în prezent*. Second Revised Edition. Prefaced and edited by Alexandru Piru. Bucharest, Romania: Minerva, 1982.

Călinescu, Matei. *A citi, a reciti. Pentru o poetică a (re)lecturii*. With an original Romanian chapter about Mateiu I. Caragiale. Translated by Virgil Stanciu. Iaşi, Romania: Polirom, 2003.

Calinescu, Matei. *Five Faces of Modernity: Modernism, Avant-Garde, Decadence, Kitsch, Postmodernism*. Durham, NC: Duke University Press, 1987.

Calle-Gruber, Mireille. *Les Tryptiques de Claude Simon ou l'art du montage*. Paris: Presses de la Sorbonne Nouvelle, 2008.

Capsali, Iulian. "De ce au ajuns românii să-l regrete pe Ceaușescu. Interviu exclusiv." *Sputnik – Moldova*. Available online: https://ro.sputnik.md/ politics/20161226/10518482/interviu-ceausescu-capsali.html (accessed October 9, 2020).

Caragiale, Mateiu I. *Gallants of the Old Court*. Translated by Cristian Baciu. Bucharest: eLiteratura, 2013.

Caragiale, Mateiu I. *Opere*. Edited and with an Introductory Study by Barbu Cioculescu. Preface by Eugen Simion. Bucharest: Editura Fundației Naționale pentru Știință și Artă, 2018.

Carlson, Marla. *Performing Bodies in Pain: Medieval and Post-modern Martyrs, Mystics, and Artists*. New York: Palgrave Macmillan, 2010.

Carroll, Joseph. *Evolution and Literary Theory*. Columbia: University of Missouri Press, 1995.

Casanova, Pascale. "World Fiction." *Revue de littérature générale*, no. 2 (1996): 42–5.

Casanova, Pascale. *The World Republic of Letters*. Translated by M. B. DeBevoise. Cambridge, MA: Harvard University Press, 2004.

Cassin, Barbara, ed. *Vocabulaire européen des philosophies. Dictionnaire des intraduisibles*. Paris: Seuil, 2004.

Cassin, Barbara. "Présentation." In *Vocabulaire européen des philosophies. Dictionnaire des intraduisibles*, edited by Barbara Cassin, xvii–xxiv. Paris: Seuil, 2004.

Caton, Lou Freitas. *Reading American Novels and Multicultural Aesthetics: Romancing the Postmodern Novel*. New York: Palgrave Macmillan, 2008.

Cavanagh, Clare. "Postcolonial Poland." *Common Knowledge* 10, no. 1 (2004): 82–92.

Cayley, John. "The Advent of Aurature and the End of (Electronic) Literature." In *The Bloomsbury Handbook of Electronic Literature*, edited by Joseph Tabbi, 73–95. New York: Bloomsbury, 2018.

Center for Art and Media Karlsruhe. "GLOBALE: Reset Modernity!," April 16– August 21, 2016, https://zkm.de/en/exhibition/2016/04/globale-reset-modernity (accessed February 22, 2020).

Central Electoral Bureau. "Attendance, Provisional Results, Partial Results." December 11, 2016. Available online: https://parlamentare2016.bec.ro (accessed October 11, 2020).

Central European University. "Digital Humanities Initiative." Available online: https://www.ceu.edu/dhi/regional (accessed July 15, 2019).

Cernat, Paul. "Iluziile revizionismului est-etic." *Observator cultural*, nos. 1–3 (539–541) (2010): 5, 7, 6.

Cernat, Paul. *Modernismul retro în romanul interbelic românesc*. Bucharest: Art, 2009.

Cernat, Paul. "Spre Ion Iovan, prin Mateiu Caragiale." *Observator cultural*, no. 153 (2003). Available online: https://www.observatorcultural.ro/articol/spre-ion-iovan-prin-mateiu-caragiale/ (accessed April 4, 2019).

Certeau de, Michel. *Culture in the Plural*. Edited and with an introduction by Luce Giard. Translated and with an afterword by Tom Conley. Minneapolis: University of Minnesota Press, 1997.

Cherenfant, Sabine, ed. *Presentism: Reexamining Historical Figures Through Today's Lens*. New York: Greenhaven Publishing, 2019.

Chevalier, Judith A., and Dina Mayzlin. "The Effect of Word of Mouth on Sales: Online Book Reviews." *Journal of Marketing Research* 43, no. 3 (2006): 345–54.

Chevillard, Eric. *L'Explosion de la tortue*. Paris: Minuit, 2019.

Chirculescu, Florin (Sebastian A. Corn). *Ne vom întoarce în Muribecca*. Bucharest: Nemira, 2014.

Chiruță, Răzvan. "'Corectitudinea politică este cea mai devastatoare ideologie care a putut să apară': Interviu cu Mircea Mihăieş." *Suplimentul de cultură* 12, no. 505 (December 5–11, 2015): 8–9.

Chivu, Marius. "'Nu mă tem de tehnologie, ci de oameni.' Interviu cu Mircea Cărtărescu." *Dilema Veche* 16, no. 785 (March 7–13, 2019): 14.

Chivu, Marius. "Ferentari love story." *Dilema Veche* 11, no. 522 (February 13–19, 2014): 14.

Cioculescu, Barbu. "Studiu introductiv." In Mateiu I. Caragiale, *Opere*, edited and with an Introductory Study by Barbu Cioculescu. Preface by Eugen Simion, xi–c. Bucharest: Editura Fundaţiei Naţionale pentru Ştiinţă şi Artă, 2018.

Cioran, Emil. *Schimbarea la faţă a României*. Bucharest: Humanitas, 1990.

Ciorogar, Alex. "În loc de prefaţă. Întoarcerea 'lecturii teoretice': între postcritică şi postumanism." In *Postumanismul*, edited by Alex Ciorogar, 7–22. Bucharest: Tracus Arte, 2019.

Ciorogar, Alex, ed. *Postumanismul*. Bucharest: Tracus Arte, 2019.

Citton, Yves. "Fictional Attachments and Literary Weavings in the Anthropocene." *New Literary History* 47, nos. 2–3 (2016): 309–29.

Citton, Yves. *Mytocratie. Storytelling et imaginaire de gauche*. Paris: Éditions Amsterdam, 2010.

Clark, Andy. *Natural-Born Cyborgs: Minds, Technologies, and the Future of Human Intelligence*. Oxford: Oxford University Press, 2003.

Clarke, Bruce, and Manuela Rossini, eds. *The Routledge Companion to Literature and Science*. London: Routledge, 2011.

Clifford, James. *The Predicament of Culture: Twentieth-Century Ethnography, Literature, and Art*. Cambridge, MA: Harvard University Press, 1988.

Clifford, James. *Routes: Travel and Translation in the Late Twentieth Century*. Cambridge, MA: Harvard University Press, 1996.

Clifford, James. "Traveling Cultures." In *Cultural Studies*, edited and with an introduction by Lawrence Grossberg, Cary Nelson, Paula Treichler, with Linda Baughman and assistance from John Macgregor, 96–112. New York: Routledge, 1992.

Clifford, James, and Vivek Dhareshvar, eds. *Traveling Theories, Traveling Theorists*. Santa Cruz: Center for Cultural Studies, University of California at Santa Cruz, 1989.

Cohen, Jeffrey Jerome, ed. *Monster Theory*. Minneapolis: University of Minnesota Press, 1996.

Colebrook, Claire. "Time and Autopoiesis: The Organism Has No Future." In *Deleuze and the Body*, edited by Laura Guillaume and Joe Hughes, 9–28. Edinburgh: Edinburgh University Press, 2011.

Colingwood, R. G. *The Idea of History*. Oxford: Oxford University Press, 1946.

Collins, Jim. *Bring on the Books for Everybody: How Literary Culture Became Popular Culture*. Durham, NC: Duke University Press, 2010.

Compagnon, Antoine. *The 5 Paradoxes of Modernity*. Translated by Franklin Philip. New York: Columbia University Press, 1994.

Compagnon, Antoine. *Les antimodernes de Joseph de Maistre à Roland Barthes*. Paris: Gallimard, 2005.

Cornea, Paul. *Oamenii începutului de drum. Studii și cercetări asupra epocii pașoptiste*. Bucharest: Cartea Românească, 1974.

Cornis-Pope, Marcel. "Local and Global Frames in Recent Eastern European Literatures: Postcommunism, Postmodernism and Postcoloniality." *Journal of Postcolonial Writing* 48, no. 2 (2012): 143–54.

Couldry, Nick, Andreas Hepp, and Friedrich Krotz, eds. *Media Events in a Global Age*. New York: Routledge, 2010.

Crăciun, Gheorghe. *Acte originale/Copii legalizate*. Bucharest: Cartea Românească, 1982.

Crăciun, Gheorghe. *Aisbergul poeziei moderne*. Edited by Carmen Mușat and Oana Crăciun. Iași, Romania: Polirom, 2017.

Crăciun, Gheorghe. *Pulsul prozei*. Edited by Carmen Mușat and Oana Crăciun. Iași, Romania: Polirom, 2018.

Crăciun, Gheorghe. *Trupul știe mai mult*. Pitești, Romania: Paralela 45, 2006.

Crohmălniceanu, Ov. S. "Romanul fără autor." *Gazeta literară* 10, no. 35 (1963): 7.

Culianu, Ioan Petru. *Eros și Magie în Renaștere. 1484*. Translated by Dan Petrescu. Preface by Mircea Eliade. Afterword by Sorin Antohi. Bucharest: Nemira, 1994.

D'haen, Theo. "Worlding the Social Sciences and Humanities." *European Review* 24, no. 2 (2016): 186–99.

Dainotto, Roberto. "Does Europe Have a South? An Essay on Borders." *The Global South* 5, no. 1 (2011): 37–50.

Damrosch, David. "A Sinister Chuckle: Sherlock in Tibet." In *Crime Fiction as World Literature*, edited by Louise Nilsson, David Damrosch, and Theo D'haen, 257–70. New York: Bloomsbury, 2017.

Damrosch, David. "World Literature in a Postcanonical, Hypercanonical Age." In *Comparative Literature in an Age of Globalization*, edited by Haun Saussy, 43–53. Baltimore: Johns Hopkins University Press, 2006.

DARIAH-EU. Available online: https://www.dariah.eu/ (accessed July 15, 2019).

Davies, Oliver, and Denys Turner, eds. *Silence and the Word: Negative Theology and Incarnation*. Cambridge: Cambridge University Press, 2004.

de la Fuente, Eduardo, and Peter L. L. Murphy, eds. *Aesthetic Capitalism*. Leiden: Brill, 2014.

Deckard, Sharae. "Cacao and Cascadura: Energetic Consumption and Production in World-Ecological Literature." *Journal of Postcolonial Writing* 53, no. 3 (2017): 342–54.

"De la Alfred Nobel la Sofia Nădejde." *România literară*, no. 2 (2019). Available online: https://romanialiterara.com/2019/02/de-la-alfred-nobel-la-sofia-nadejde/ (accessed September 30, 2020).

Deleuze, Gilles, Félix Guattari. *Anti-Oedipus: Capitalism and Schizophrenia.* London: Continuum, 2004.

Deleuze, Gilles, Félix Guattari. *Mii de platouri.* Translated by Bogdan Ghiu. Bucharest: Editura Art, 2013.

Deleuze, Gilles, Félix Guattari. *Rhizome.* Paris: Éditions du Minuit, 1976.

Deleuze, Gilles, Félix Guattari. *A Thousand Plateaus.* Translation and foreword by Brian Massumi. Minneapolis: University of Minnesota Press, 1987.

Denning, Michael. *Culture in the Age of Three Worlds.* London: Verso, 2004.

Derrida, Jacques. *Écriture et la Différance.* Paris: Seuil, 1967.

Derrida, Jacques. *On Touching—Jean-Luc Nancy.* Translated by Christine Irizarry. Stanford, CA: Stanford University Press, 2005.

Derrida, Jacques. "Structure, Sign, and Play in the Discourse of the Human Sciences." In *The Structuralist Controversy: The Languages of Criticism and the Sciences of Man,* edited by Richard Macksey and Eugenio Donato, 247–73. Baltimore: Johns Hopkins University Press, 2007.

Diaconescu, Ioana. *Marin Preda: Un portret în arhivele Securității.* Bucharest: Muzeul Literaturii Române, 2015.

Di Leo, Jeffrey R., ed. *Criticism after Critique: Aesthetics, Literature, and the Political.* New York: Palgrave Macmillan, 2014.

Dimock, Wai Chee. "Historicism, Presentism, Futurism." *PMLA* 133, no. 2 (March 2018): 257–63.

Dimock, Wai Chee. "A Theory of Resonance." *PMLA* 112, no. 5 (October 1997): 1060–71.

Dimock, Wai Chee. *Through Other Continents: American Literature across Deep Time.* Princeton, NJ: Princeton University Press, 2006.

Dinițoiu, Adina. "O poveste din Ferentari." *Observator cultural* 14, no. 447 (December 19, 2013–January 8, 2014): 8.

Dinițoiu, Adina. "Prezentism și mizerabilism în proza douămiistă românească." *Transilvania,* no. 2 (2015): 25–9.

Disco, Nil, and Eda Kranakis, eds. *Cosmopolitan Commons: Sharing Resources and Risks across Borders.* Cambridge, MA: MIT Press, 2013.

Doboș, Andrei. "Romanian Online Literary Communities." *Dacoromania Litteraria* 3 (2016): 65–74.

Dobrenko, Evgeny. *Political Economy of Socialist Realism.* Translated by Jesse M. Savage. New Haven, CT: Yale University Press, 2007.

Doueihi, Milad. *Pour un humanisme numérique.* Paris: Seuil, 2011.

Dović, Marijan, and Jón Karl Helgason. *Great Immortality: Studies on European Cultural Sainthood.* Leiden: Brill, 2019.

Dović, Marijan, and Jón Karl Helgason. *National Poets, Cultural Saints: Canonization and Commemorative Cults of Writers in Europe.* Leiden: Brill, 2017.

Downing, John. *Internationalizing Media Theory: Transitions, Power, Culture.* London: Sage, 1996.

Drakulić, Slavenka. *Café Europa: Life under Communism.* London: Abacus, 2008.

Dubrow, Heather. *Genre.* New York: Routledge, 2014.

Dumitru, Teodora. "Gaming the World-System: Creativity, Politics, and Beat Influence in the Poetry of the 1980s Generation." In *Romanian Literature as*

World Literature, edited by Mircea Martin, Christian Moraru, and Andrei Terian, 271–88. New York: Bloomsbury, 2017.

Dumitru, Teodora. *Modernitatea politică și literară în gândirea lui E. Lovinescu.* Bucharest: Muzeul Literaturii Române, 2016.

Dună, Raluca. "Cine este autorul întoarcerii autorului." *Romania Literară*, no. 31 (2013). Available online: http://arhiva.romlit.ro/index.pl/cine_este_autorul_ntoarcerii_autorului_ (accessed April 27, 2019).

During, Simon. *Against Democracy: Literary Experience in the Era of Emancipations.* New York: Fordham University Press, 2012.

Eagleton, Terry. *The Function of Criticism: From the Spectator to Post-Structuralism.* London: Verso, 1984.

Echenoz, Jean. "Grand Entretien." Interview by Claire Chazal. *Lire* 482 (February 2020): 47–50.

Echenoz, Jean. *Le Meridien de Greenwich.* Paris: Minuit, 1979.

Eco, Umberto. *The Limits of Interpretation.* Bloomington: Indiana University Press, 1994.

Eco, Umberto. *Opera deschisă. Formă și indeterminare în poeticile contemporane.* Preface and translated by Cornel Mihai Ionescu. Bucharest: Editura pentru Literatură Universală, 1969.

Eco, Umberto. *Șase plimbări prin pădurea narativă.* Translated by Ștefania Mincu. Constanța, Romania: Pontica, 1997.

Eglin, Peter. *Intellectual Citizenship and the Problem of Incarnation.* Lanham, MD: University Press of America, 2013.

Eliade, Mircea. *Aspects du mythe.* Paris: Gallimard, 1995.

Eliade, Mircea. *Ocultism, vrăjitorie și mode culturale. Eseuri de religie comparată.* Translated from English by Elena Bortă. Bucharest: Humanitas, 1997.

Elias, Amy J. "Past / Future." In *Time: A Vocabulary of the Present*, edited by Amy J. Elias and Joel Burges, 35–50. New York: New York University Press, 2016.

Elkins, James, and Michael Newman, eds. *The State of Art Criticism.* New York: Routledge, 2008.

Emerson, Ralph Waldo. *The Complete Essays and Other Writings.* New York: Random House, 1950.

Emerson, Ralph Waldo. *Literary Ethics.* New York: Thomas Y. Crowell & Company Publishers, 1900.

Ercolino, Stefano. *The Maximalist Novel: From Thomas Pynchon's* Gravity's Rainbow *to Roberto Bolaño's* 2066. Translated by Albert Sbraglia. New York: Bloomsbury, 2014.

Evans, Jonathan, and Chris Baronavski. "How do European Countries Differ in Religious Commitment? Use Our Interactive Map to Find Out." Pew Research Center. Available online: https://www.pewresearch.org/fact-tank/2018/12/05/how-do-european-countries-differ-in-religious-commitment/ (accessed December 5, 2018).

Even-Zohar, Itamar. "Polysystem Studies." *Poetics Today* 11, no. 1 (1990): 7–193.

Federman, Raymond. *Critifiction: Postmodern Essays.* Albany: State University of New York Press, 1993.

Fedor, Julie. "Conclusion." In *Memory, Conflict, and New Media: Web Wars in Post-Socialist States*, edited by Ellen Rutten, Julie Fedor, and Vera Zvereva, 236–44. New York: Routledge, 2013.

Felski, Rita. *The Limits of Critique*. Chicago: University of Chicago Press, 2015.

Ferraris, Maurizio. *Manifesto of New Realism*. Translated by Sarah De Sanctis. Albany: State University of New York Press, 2014.

Ferrer, Carolina. "Canonical Values vs. the Law of Large Numbers: The Canadian Literary Canon in the Age of Big Data." *Rupkatha Journal on Interdisciplinary Studies in Humanities* 5, no. 3 (2013): 81–90.

Ffrench, Patrick. *After Bataille: Sacrifice, Exposure, Community*. New York: Routledge, 2007.

Florian, Filip. *Degete mici*. Iași, Romania: Polirom, 2005.

Florian, Filip. *Little Fingers*. Translated by Alistair Ian Blyth. Boston: Houghton Mifflin, 2009.

Foucault, Michel. *The Birth of Biopolitics: Lectures at the Collège de France, 1978–1979*. Edited by Michel Sellenart. Basingstoke, UK: Palgrave Macmillan, 2008.

Foucault, Michel. "Nietzsche, Freud, Marx." In *Aesthetics, Method, and Epistemology*. Translated by Robert Hurley et al., 269–78. New York: The New Press, 1998.

Fox-Genovese, Elizabeth. "Literary Criticism and the Politics of the New Historicism." In *The New Historicism*, edited by H. Aram Vesser, 213–24. New York: Routledge, 1989.

Frank, Joseph. *Through the Russian Prism: Essays on Russian Literature and Culture*. Princeton, NJ: Princeton University Press, 1990.

Fraser, Nancy. "Rethinking Recognition." *New Left Review* 3 (2000): 107–20.

Friedman, Melvin. *Stream of Consciousness: A Study in Literary Method*. New Haven, CT: Yale University Press, 1955.

Furutani, Dale. "Author's Forward." In *The Curious Adventures of Sherlock Holmes in Japan*. Seattle: Miharu Publishing, 2011. Available online: https://www.amazon.com/Curious-Adventures-Sherlock-Holmes-Japan-ebook/dp/B006CPC1EU (accessed September 15, 2020).

Gajowski, Evelyn. "Beyond Historicism: Presentism, Subjectivity, Politics." *Literature Compass*, nos. 7–8 (2010): 674–91.

Galloway, Alexander. *The Interface Effect*. Malden, MA: Wiley, 2013.

Garnier, Charles-Georges-Thomas. *Voyages imaginaires, songes, visions et romans cabalistiques*. Amsterdam and Paris, [1787].

Gefen, Alexandre. "Responsabilités de la forme. Voies et détours de l'engagement littéraire contemporain." In *L'Engagement littéraire*, edited by E. Bouju, 75–85. Rennes: Presses Universitaires de Rennes, 2005.

Georgescu, Paul, and Matei Călinescu. "Probleme ale poeziei actuale." *Gazeta literară* 8, no. 46 (1961): 16.

Gheo, Radu Pavel. *Disco Titanic*. Iași, Romania: Polirom, 2016.

Gheo, Radu Pavel. *Noapte bună, copii!* Iași, Romania: Polirom, 2010.

Gheo, Radu Pavel. "Rezerva de comisari politici." *Suplimentul de cultură* 235 (July 4–10, 2009): 2. Available online: http://suplimentuldecultura.ro/numarpdf/235_Iasi.pdf (accessed January 31, 2019).

Gheorghiu, Mihai Dinu. *Intelectualii în câmpul puterii. Morfologii și traiectorii sociale*. Iași, Romania: Polirom, 2007.

Gherghina, Sergiu, Alexandru Racu, Aurelian Giugăl, Alexandru Gavriș, Nanuli Silagadze, and Ron Johnston. "Non-voting in the 2018 Romanian Referendum:

The Importance of Initiators, Campaigning and Issue Saliency." *Political Science* 71, no. 3 (2019): 193–213.

Gibson, James J. "The Theory of Affordances." In Jen Jack Gieseking and William Mangold, eds., *The People, Place, and Space Reader*, 56–61. New York: Routledge, 2014.

Gieseking, Jen Jack, and William Mangolds, eds. *The People, Place, and Space Reader*. New York: Routledge, 2014.

Gilroy, Paul. *Against Race: Imagining Political Culture beyond the Color Line*. Cambridge, MA: The Belknap Press of Harvard University Press, 2000.

Ginger, Andrew. "Comparative Study and the Nature of Connections: Of the Aesthetic Appreciation of History." *Modern Languages Open* 1 (2018): 18. http://doi.org/10.3828/mlo.v0i0.191.

Goldiş, Alex. *Critica în tranşee*. Iaşi: Polirom, 2011.

Goldiş, Alex. "The Ideology of Ruralism in the Thaw Prose: The Case of Marin Preda's *Moromeţii*." In *Ruralism and Literature in Romania*, edited by Ştefan Baghiu, Vlad Pojoga, and Maria Sass, 95–105. Berlin: Peter Lang, 2019.

Goldiş, Alex. "Realismul hardcore." *Cultura* 9, no. 34 (September 18, 2014): 10.

Goldsmith, Kenneth. *Uncreative Writing: Managing Language in the Digital Age*. New York: Columbia University Press, 2011.

Goldsworthy, Vesna. *Inventing Ruritania: The Imperialism of Imagination*. New Haven, CT: Yale University Press, 1998.

Goodwin, Jonathan, and John Holbo, eds. *Reading "Graphs, Maps, Trees": Critical Responses to Franco Moretti*. Anderson, SC: Parlor Press, 2011.

Gottschall, Jonathan, and David Sloan Wilson, eds. *The Literary Animal: Evolution and the Nature of Narrative*. Evanston, IL: Northwestern University Press, 2005.

Gould, Rebecca. "Conservative in Form, Revolutionary in Content: Rethinking World Literary Canons in an Age of Globalization." *Canadian Review of Comparative Literature* 41, no. 3 (2014): 270–86.

Gramsci, Antonio. *The Gramsci Reader: Selected Writings 1916–1935*. Edited by David Forgacs. With a Foreword by Eric J. Hobsbawm, 171–85. New York: New York University Press, 2000.

Grann, David. *The Lost City of Z: A Tale of Deadly Obsession in the Amazon*. New York: Doubleday, 2009.

Grimal, Pierre, ed. and trans. *Romans grecs et latins*. Paris: Gallimard, 1958.

Groys, Boris. *The Total Art of Stalinism: Avant-garde, Aesthetic Dictatorship, and Beyond*. Translated by Charles Rougle. Princeton, NJ: Princeton University Press, 1992.

Gumbrecht, Hans Ulrich. *Our Broad Present: Time and Contemporary Culture*. New York: Columbia University Press, 2014.

Gusdorf, Georges. *Auto-bio-graphie*, vol. 2, *Lignes de vie*. Paris: Odille Jacob, 1991.

Guţu, Dinu. *Intervenţia*. Iaşi, Romania: Polirom, 2017.

Habermas, Jürgen. *The Inclusion of the Other: Studies in Political Theory*. Edited by Ciaran Cronin and Pablo De Greiff. Cambridge, MA: MIT Press, 1999.

Halsall, Francis. "Actor-Network Aesthetics: The Conceptual Rhymes of Bruno Latour and Contempory Art." *New Literary History* 47, nos. 2–3 (2016): 439–61.

Hamayon, Roberte. *La chasse à l'âme. Esquisse d'une théorie du chamanisme sibérien*. Besançon, France: Éditions la Völva, 2016.

Haraway, Donna. *Simians, Cyborgs, and Women: The Reinvention of Nature*. New York: Routledge, 1991.

Hardt, Michael, and Antonio Negri. *Empire*. Cambridge, MA: Harvard University Press, 2000.

Harman, Graham. "The Well-Wrought Broken Hammer: Object-Oriented Literary Criticism." *New Literary History* 43, no. 2 (2012): 183–203.

Harman, Graham. *Object-Oriented Ontology: A New Theory of Everything*. New York: Penguin Books, 2017.

Harries, Karsten. *Art Matters: A Critical Commentary on Heidegger's "The Origin of the Work of Art."* New York: Springer, 2009.

Harris-Peyton, Michael B. "Holmes Away from Home: The Great Detective in the Transnational Literary Network." In *Crime Fiction as World Literature*, edited by Louise Nilsson, David Damrosch, and Theo D'haen, 215–31. New York: Bloomsbury, 2017.

Hartog, François. *Regimes of Historicity: Presentism and Experiences of Time*. Translated by Saskia Brown. New York: Columbia University Press, 2017.

Hawkes, Terence. *Shakespeare in the Present*. London: Routledge, 2002.

Hayles, N. Katherine. *How We Think: Digital Media and Contemporary Technogenesis*. Chicago: University of Chicago Press, 2012.

Hayles, N. Katherine. "Hyper and Deep Attention: The Generational Divide in Cognitive Modes." *Profession* (2007): 187–99.

Hayot, Eric. "Against Periodization; or, On Institutional Time." *New Literary History* 42 no. 4 (2011): 739–56.

Heise, Ursula K. "Comparative Literature and Computational Criticism: A Conversation with Franco Moretti." In *Futures of Comparative: ACLA State of the Discipline Report*, edited by Ursula K. Heise, with Dudley Andrew, Alexander Beecroft, Jessica Berman, David Damrosch, Guillermina De Ferrari, César Domínguez, Barbara Harlow, and Eric Hayot, 273–84. New York: Routledge, 2017.

Heise, Ursula K. "Introduction: Comparative Literature and the New Humanities." In *Futures of Comparative: ACLA State of the Discipline Report*, edited by Ursula K. Heise, with Dudley Andrew, Alexander Beecroft, Jessica Berman, David Damrosch, Guillermina De Ferrari, César Domínguez, Barbara Harlow, and Eric Hayot, 1–8. New York: Routledge, 2017.

Heise, Ursula K. "Slow-Forward to the Future." In *Postmodern | Postwar—and After: Rethinking American Literature*. Edited by Jason Gladstone, Andrew Hoberek, Daniel Worden. 251–259. Iowa City, IA: University of Iowa Press, 2016.

Heise, Ursula K., with Dudley Andrew, Alexander Beecroft, Jessica Berman, David Damrosch, Guillermina De Ferrari, César Domínguez, Barbara Harlow, and Eric Hayot, eds. *Futures of Comparative Literature: ACLA State of the Discipline Report*. New York: Routledge, 2017.

Hempel, Carl G., and Paul Oppenheim. "Studies in the Logic of Explanation." *Philosophy of Science* 15, no. 2 (April 1948): 135–75.

Henderson, Joseph L. "The Cultural Unconscious." *Quadrant* 20, no. 2 (1988): 34–57.

Herman, Peter C., ed. and intro. "The Next Generation" special-topic issue of *symploke* 3, no. 1 (1995).

Hinderliter, Beth, William Kaizen, Vered Maimon, Jaleh Mansoor, and Seth McCormick, eds. *Communities of Sense: Rethinking Aesthetics and Politics.* Durham, NC: Duke University Press, 2009.

Hirayama, Yuichi, Masamichi Higurashi, and Hirotaka Ueda, eds. and trans. *Japan and Sherlock Holmes.* New York: Baker Street Irregulars, 2004.

Hirsch, Marianne. "Family Pictures: *Mauss*, Mourning and Post-Memory." *Discourse* 15, no. 2 (Winter 1992–3): 3–29.

Hirsch, Marianne. *The Generation of Postmemory: Writing and Visual Culture After the Holocaust.* New York: Columbia University Press, 2012.

Huet, Marie-Hélène. *Monstrous Imagination.* Cambridge, MA: Harvard University Press, 1993.

Hunt, Lynn. "Against Presentism." *Perspectives* (May 2002). Available online: https://www.historians.org/publications-and-directories/perspectives-on-history/may-2002/against-presentism (accessed June 10, 2019).

Hunt, Lynn. "The Problem with Presentism Is That It Blurs Our Understanding of the Past." In *Presentism: Reexamining Historical Figures Through Today's Lens*, edited by Sabine Cherenfant, 12–16. New York: Greenhaven Publishing, 2019.

Hutcheon, Linda. *A Poetics of Postmodernism.* London: Routledge, 1988.

Hyde, Emily, and Sarah Wasserman. "The Contemporary." *Literature Compass* 14, no. 9 (September 2017): 1–19.

Ihde, Don. *Bodies in Technology.* Minneapolis: University of Minnesota Press, 2002.

Ingarden, Roman. *The Cognition of the Literary Work of Art.* Translated by Ruth Ann Crowley and Kenneth R. Olson. Evanston, IL: Northwestern University Press, 1973.

Ingram, David, and Jonathan Tallant, "Presentism." In *Stanford Encyclopedia of Philosophy*, edited by Edward N. Zalta, Spring 2018 Edition. Available online: https://plato.stanford.edu/entries/presentism/ (accessed June 10, 2019).

Iovan, Ion. *Mateiu Caragiale: Portretul unui dandy român.* Bucharest: Compania, 2002.

Iovan, Ion. *MJC. O lume pentru Mateiu.* Iași, Romania: Polirom, 2015.

Iovan, Ion. *Ultimele însemnări ale lui Mateiu Caragiale, însoțite de un inedit epistolar, precum și indexul ființelor, lucrurilor și întâmplărilor, în prezentarea lui Ion Iovan.* Bucharest: Curtea Veche, 2008.

Iovănel, Mihai. *Ideologiile literaturii în postcomunismul românesc.* Bucharest: Muzeul Literaturii Române, 2017.

Iovănel, Mihai. "Oglinda spartă a României: În dialog cu Mihai Iovănel." *Oameni de poveste.* June 26, 2017. Available online: https://oamenidepoveste.ro/in-dialog-cu-mihai-iovanel-oglinda-sparta-a-romaniei/ (accessed September 16, 2018).

Iovănel, Mihai, and Christian Moraru. "Corectitudinea politică între realitate și fetiș." *Euphorion* 30, no. 4 (October–December, 2019): 16–21.

Irimia, Mihaela. "The Presence of the Present: Presentism?" *Euresis*, no. 4 (2011): 147–54.

Iser, Wolfgang. "Coda to the Discussion." In *The Translatability of Cultures: Figurations of the Space Between*, edited by Sanford Budick and Wolfgang Iser. Stanford, CA: Stanford University Press, 1996.

Jagoda, Patrick. *Network Aesthetics*. Chicago: University of Chicago Press, 2016.

James, William. *The Principles of Psychology: The Works of William James*. Cambridge, MA: Harvard University Press, 1983.

Jameson, Fredric. "The Aesthetic of Singularity." *New Left Review* 92 (March–April 2015): 101–32.

Jameson, Fredric. *Archaeologies of the Future: The Desire Called Utopia and Other Science Fictions*. London: Verso, 2007.

Jameson, Fredric. *The Political Unconscious: Narrative as a Socially Symbolic Act*. London: Routledge, 2002.

Jameson, Fredric. "Third-World Literature in the Era of Multinational Capitalism." *Social Text* 15 (1986): 65–88.

Janaszek-Ivanicková, Halina. "Postmodernism in Poland." In *International Postmodernism: Theory and Literary Practice*, edited by Hans Bertens and Douwe Fokkema, 423–8. Amsterdam: John Benjamins Publishing Company, 1997.

Jay, Paul. *Global Matters: The Transnational Turn in Literary Studies*. Ithaca, NY: Cornell University Press, 2010.

Jefferson, Ann. *Biography and the Question of Literature in France*. Oxford: Oxford University Press, 2007.

Jenkins, Henry. *Fans, Bloggers, and Gamers: Exploring Participatory Culture*. New York: New York University Press, 2006.

Jockers, Matthew L. *Macroanalysis: Digital Methods and Literary History*. Urbana: University of Illinois Press, 2013.

Jones, J. R. *Country and Court: England, 1658–1714*. Cambridge, MA: Harvard University Press, 1978.

Jouve, Vincent. *Poétique des valeurs*. Paris: Presses Universitaires de France, 2001.

Juvan, Marko. "The Aesthetics and Politics of Belonging: National Poets between 'Vernacularism' and 'Cosmopolitanism.'" *Arcadia* 52, no. 1 (2017): 10–28.

Juvan, Marko. *Worlding a Peripheral Literature*. New York: Palgrave Macmillan, 2019.

Kant, Immanuel. *Critique of Judgment*. Translated and Introduction by Werner S. Pluhar. Indianapolis, IN: Hackett Publishing Company, 1987.

Karl, Frederick R. *American Fictions: 1980–2000; Whose America Is It Anyway?* Bloomington, IN: Xlibris, 2001.

Kazin, Alfred. *On Native Grounds: An Interpretation of Modern American Prose Literature*. New York: Reynal and Hitchcock, 1942.

Keen, Andrew. *The Cult of the Amateur: How Today's Internet Is Killing Our Culture*. New York: Doubleday, 2007.

Kelertas, Violeta, ed. *Baltic Postcolonialism*. Amsterdam: Rodopi, 2006.

Keough, Leyla. "Globalizing 'Postsocialism': Mobile Mothers and Neoliberalism on the Margins of Europe." *Anthropological Quarterly* 79, no. 3 (2006): 431–61.

Kiossev, Alexander, ed. *Post-Theory, Games, and Discursive Resistance: The Bulgarian Case*. Albany: State University of New York Press, 1995.

Kiossev, Alexander, with Boyko Penchev. "Heritage and Inheritors: The Literary Canon in Totalitarian Bulgaria." In *History of the Literary Cultures of East-Central Europe: Junctures and Disjunctures in the 19th and 20th Centuries*, vol. 2, edited by Marcel Cornis-Pope and John Neubauer, 132–41. Amsterdam: John Benjamins Publishing Company, 2006.

Kirby, Alan. *Digimodernism: How New Technologies Dismantle the Postmodern and Reconfigure Our Culture.* New York: Continuum, 2009.

Kirby, Vicki. *Telling Flesh: The Substance of the Corporeal.* New York: Routledge, 1997.

Klinger, Leslie S., ed. *The New Annotated Sherlock Holmes.* 3 Volumes. New York: W. W. Norton, 2005–6.

Kohn, Eduardo. *How Forests Think.* Berkeley: University of California Press, 2013.

Komáromy, Zsolt. "'Wordsworth in Hungary:' An Essay on Reception as Cultural Memory and Forgetting." In *Worlds of Hungarian Writing: National Literature as Intercultural Exchange,* edited by András Kiséry, Zsolt Komáromy, and Zsuzsanna Varga, 29–52. Teaneck, NJ: Fairleigh Dickinson University Press; Lanham, MD: Rowman and Littlefield, 2016.

Korek, Janusz. "Central and Eastern Europe from a Postcolonial Perspective." *Postcolonial Europe,* April 27, 2009. Available online: http://www.postcolonial-europe.eu/essays/60--central-and-eastern-europe-from-a-postcolonial-perspective (accessed March 8, 2021).

Korthals Altes, Liesbeth. *Ethos and Narrative Interpretation: The Negotiation of Values in Fiction.* Lincoln: University of Nebraska Press, 2014.

Koselleck, Reinhart. *Futures Past: On the Semantics of Historical Time.* Translated and with an Introduction by Keith Tribe. New York: Columbia University Press, 2004.

Krastev, Ivan. "The New Europe: Respectable Populism, Clockwork Liberalism." *Open Democracy,* March 21, 2006. Available online: https://www.opendemocracy.net/en/new_europe_3376jsp/ (accessed January 29, 2019).

Krishnaswamy, Revathi. "Toward World Literary Knowledges: Theory in the Age of Globalization." *Comparative Literature* 62, no. 4 (2010): 399–419.

Krishnaswamy, Revathi. "Toward World Literary Knowledges: Theory in the Age of Globalization." In *World Literature in Theory,* edited by David Damrosch, 134–58. Malden, MA: Wiley Blackwell, 2014.

Kukulin, Ilya. "Memory and Self-Legitimization in the Russian Blogosphere: Argumentative Practices in Historical and Political Discussions in Russian-Language Blogs of the 2000s." In *Memory, Conflict and New Media: Web Wars in Post-Socialist States,* edited by Ellen Rutten, Julie Fedor, and Vera Zvereva, 116–32. New York: Routledge, 2013.

Kukulin, Ilya, and Mark Lipovetsky. "Post-Soviet Literary Criticism." In *A History of Russian Literary Theory and Criticism: The Soviet Age and Beyond,* edited by Evgeny Dobrenko and Galin Tihanov, 287–305. Pittsburgh, PA: University of Pittsburgh Press, 2011.

Kurzweil, Ray. *The Singularity Is Near: When Humans Transcend Biology.* New York: Penguin, 2006.

Kušnir, Jaroslav. "Postcolonial Studies in Slovakia and Hungary." *Po-Równania* 17 (2015): 245–52.

Lackey, Michael. *The American Biographical Novel.* New York: Bloomsbury, 2016.

Lackey, Michael. *Biofictional Histories, Mutations, and Forms.* New York: Routledge, 2017.

Lackey, Michael. *Conversations with Biographical Novelists: Truthful Fictions across the Globe.* New York: Bloomsbury, 2019.

Lane, Richard J., ed. *Global Literary Theory: An Anthology*. London: Routledge, 2013.

Lanser, Susan S. "The 'I' of the Beholder: Equivocal Attachments and the Limits of Structuralist Narratology." In *A Companion to Narrative Theory*, edited by James Phelan and Peter J. Rabinowitz, 206–19. Malden, MA: Blackwell, 2005.

Lash, Scott. *Another Modernity: A Different Rationality*. Oxford: Blackwell, 1999.

Latour, Bruno. "A Plea for Earthly Sciences." In *New Social Connections: Sociology's Subjects and Objects*, edited by Judith Burnett, Syd Jeffers, and Graham Thomas, 72–84. New York: Palgrave MacMillan, 2010.

Latour, Bruno. "Why Has Critique Run out of Steam? From Matters of Fact to Matters of Concern." *Critical Inquiry* 30, no. 2 (2004): 225–48.

Latour, Bruno. *An Inquiry into Modes of Existence: An Anthropology of the Moderns*. Translated by Catherine Porter. Cambridge, MA: Harvard University Press, 2013.

Latour, Bruno. *Enquête sur les modes d'existence. Une anthropologie des Modernes*. Paris: La Découverte, 2012.

Latour, Bruno. *We Have Never Been Modern*. Translated by Catherine Porter. Cambridge, MA: Harvard University Press, 1995.

Latour, Bruno, and Steve Woolgar. *Laboratory Life: The Social Construction of Scientific Facts*. Introduction by Jonas Salk. Princeton, NJ: Princeton University Press, 2013.

LeClair, Tom. *The Art of Excess: Mastery in Contemporary American Fiction*. Urbana: University of Illinois Press, 1989.

Lefter, Ion Bogdan. "Între comunism şi democraţie, între modernitate şi postmodernitate." *Dilema* 340 (1999): 6.

Lefter, Ion Bogdan. "Pentru refacerea coerenţei culturale naţionale. La început de *Observator cultural*." *Observator cultural* 1, no. 1 (February 29, 2000): 1.

Lefter, Ion Bogdan. "Un model explicativ şi un mare proces istoric." *Dilema* 245 (1997): 6.

Lefter, Ion Bogdan. *Postmodernism. Din dosarul unei "bătălii" culturale*. Second Expanded Edition. Piteşti, Romania: Paralela 45, 2002.

Leitch, Vincent B., gen. ed. *The Norton Anthology of Theory and Criticism*. Third Edition. New York: W. W. Norton & Company, 2018.

Lem, Stanisław. *Summa Technologiae*. Translated by Joanna Zylinska. Minneapolis: University of Minnesota Press, 2013.

Levey, Nick. *Maximalism in Contemporary American Fiction: The Uses of Detail*. New York: Routledge, 2017.

Levina, Marina, and Diem-My T. Bui, eds. *Monster Culture in the 21st Century: A Reader*. London: Bloomsbury, 2013.

Levinas, Emmanuel. "Ideology and Idealism." In *The Levinas Reader*, edited by Seán Hand, 235–48. Oxford: Oxford University Press, 1989.

Levinas, Emmanuel. *Proper Names*. Translated by Michael B. Smith. Stanford, CA: Stanford University Press, 1996.

Levine, Caroline. *Forms: Whole, Rhythm, Hierarchy, Network*. Princeton, NJ: Princeton University Press, 2015.

Lévi-Strauss, Claude. *Mitologice I: Crud şi gătit*. Translated and preface by Ioan Pânzaru. Bucharest: Editura Babel, 1995.

Lilla, Mark. *The Once and Future Liberal: After Identity Politics.* New York: Harper Collins, 2017.

Lipovetsky, Gilles. *Hypermodern Times.* With Sébastien Charles. Translated by Andrew Brown. Cambridge, UK: Polity, 2005.

"The Literary Journals: What Next? A Roundtable Discussion." *Russian Studies in Literature* 44, no. 4 (2008): 80–99. Translated by Liv Bliss from the Russian text "Literaturnye zhurnaly: chto zavtra?" *Znamia*, no. 1 (2008): 191–205. Available online: https://web.archive.org/web/*/terorism%20de%20cititoare (accessed January 31, 2019).

Long, H., and R. J. So. "Literary Pattern Recognition: Modernism between Close Reading and Machine Learning." *Critical Inquiry* 2 (2016): 235–67.

Lorenz, Chris. "Out of Time? Some Critical Reflections on François Hartog's Presentism." In *Rethinking Historical Time: New Approaches to Presentism*, edited by Marek Tamm and Laurent Olivier, 23–43. New York: Bloomsbury, 2019.

Lossef, Lev. *On the Beneficence of Censorship: Aesopian Language in Modern Russian Literature.* Munich: Verlag Otto Sagner in Kommission, 1984.

Love, Heather. "Close but not Deep: Literary Ethics and the Descriptive Turn." *New Literary History* 41, no. 2 (2010): 371–91.

Love, Joseph L. *Crafting the Third World: Theorizing Underdevelopment in Rumania and Brazil.* Stanford, CA: Stanford University Press, 1996.

Lovell, Stephen. *The Russian Reading Revolution: Print Culture in the Soviet and Post-Soviet Eras.* London: Macmillan, 2000.

Lovinescu, E. *Opere. II, Istoria literaturii române contemporane. Istoria literaturii române contemporane (1900–1937).* Edited by Nicolae Mecu. Introduction by Eugen Simion. Bucharest: FNSA, 2015.

Lovinescu, Monica. *O istorie a literaturii române pe unde scurte 1960–2000.* Edited and preface by Cristina Cioabă. Bucharest: Humanitas, 2014.

Lovinescu, Monica. "Răspuns la o masă rotundă a Grupului pentru Dialog Social." 22 15 (1990): 8.

Macksey, Richard, and Eugenio Donato. *The Structuralist Controversy: The Languages of Criticism and the Sciences of Man.* Baltimore: Johns Hopkins University Press, 2007.

Maeterlinck, Maurice. *The Life of the Bee.* Translated by Alfred Sutro. New York: Dodd, Mead, and Company, 1901.

Magnusson, Bruce, and Zahi Zalloua, eds. *Contagion: Health, Fear, Sovereignty.* Seattle: University of Washington Press, 2012.

Maingueneau, Dominique. *Contre Saint Proust ou la fin de la Littérature.* Paris: Belin, 2006.

Maingueneau, Dominique. "Ethos, scénographie, incorporation." In *Images de soi dans le discours*, edited by Ruth Amossy and Jean-Michel Adam, 75–100. Lausanne: Delachaux et Niestlé, 1999.

Manea, Norman. *The Lair.* Translated by Oana Sânziana Marian. New Haven, CT: Yale University Press, 2013.

Manea, Norman. *Vizuina.* Iași, Romania: Polirom, 2009.

Maniglier, Patrice. "Art as Fiction: Can Latour's Ontology of Art be Ratified by Art Lovers? (An Exercise in Anthropological Diplomacy)." *New Literary History* 47, nos. 2–3 (2016): 419–38.

Manovich, Lev. *The Language of New Media*. Cambridge, MA: MIT Press, 2001.
Marino, Adrian. *Biografia ideii de literatură*. Vol. 6. Cluj-Napoca, Romania: Dacia, 2000.
Marino, Adrian. *The Biography of the Idea of Literature from Antiquity to the Baroque*. Albany: State University of New York Press, 1996.
Marino, Adrian. *Carnete europene*. Cluj-Napoca, Romania: Dacia, 1976.
Marino, Adrian. *Comparatism și teoria literaturii*. Translated by Mihai Ungurean. Iași, Romania: Polirom, 1998.
Marino, Adrian. *Introducere în critica literară*. Bucharest: Editura Tineretului, 1968.
Martin, Michael. *The Incarnation of the Poetic Word: Theological Essays on Poetry & Philosophy: Philosophical Essays on Poetry & Theology*. Brooklyn, NY: Angelico Press, 2017.
Martin, Mircea. "Despre estetismul socialist." *România literară* 37, no. 23 (2004): 18–19.
Martin, Mircea. *G. Călinescu și "complexele" literaturii române*. Bucharest: Editura Albatros, 1981.
Martin, Mircea. *G. Călinescu și "complexele" literaturii române*. Second Edition. Pitești, Romania: Editura Paralela 45, 2002.
Martin, Mircea. *Geometrie și finețe*. Bucharest: Tracus Arte, 2017.
Martin, Mircea, Christian Moraru, and Andrei Terian, eds. *Romanian Literature as World Literature*. New York: Bloomsbury, 2018.
Matei, Alexandru. "Introducere în noua ecologie a criticii literare." *Observator cultural* 722, May 30, 2014. Available online: http://www.observatorcultural.ro (accessed June 6, 2017).
Matei, Alexandru. *Mormântul comunismului românesc: romantismul revoluționar înainte și după 1989*. Bucharest: IBU Publishing, 2011.
McDonald, Rónán. *The Death of the Critic*. New York: Continuum, 2007.
McEwan, Ian. "Ian McEwan: 'Who's going to write the algorithm for the little white lie?'" Interview by Tim Adams. *The Guardian*, April 14, 2019. Available online: https://www.theguardian.com/books/-2019/apr/14/ian-mcewan-interview-machines-like-me-artificial-intelligence (accessed August 13, 2019).
McEwan, Ian. *In Between the Sheets, and Other Stories*. New York: Vintage International, 1994.
McEwan, Ian. *Machines Like Me*. New York: Doubleday, 2019.
McHale, Brian. *The Cambridge Introduction to Postmodernism*. Cambridge: Cambridge University Press, 2015.
McHale, Brian. *Postmodernist Fiction*. London: Routledge, 2003.
Meillassoux, Quentin. *After Finitude: An Essay on the Necessity of Contingency*. Translated by Ray Brassier. London: Continuum, 2008.
Meizoz, Jérôme. *Postures littéraires. Mises en scène modernes de l'auteur*. Geneva: Slatkine, 2007.
Mendelson, Edward. "Encyclopedic Narrative: From Dante to Pynchon." *Modern Language Notes* 91, no. 6 (1976): 1267–75.
Mihăieș, Mircea. "Rasismul de amfiteatru." *România literară* 53, nos. 29–30 (July 17, 2020): 4.
Miles, Margaret R. *The Word Made Flesh: A History of Christian Thought*. Malden, MA: Blackwell, 2005.

Mills, Catherine. *Biopolitics*. London: Routledge, 2018.

Mironescu, Andreea. "Analogie și diferențiere metodologică în *Memory Studies:* revizitând comparația 'West vs. East.'" *Caiete critice*, no. 11 (373) (2018): 37–42.

Mironescu, Andreea. "Konfigurationen des kulturellen Gedächtnisses im postkommunistischen rumänischen Roman." In *Kulturelles Gedächtnis–Ästhetisches Erinnern: Literatur, Film und Kunst in Rumänien*, edited by Michèle Mattusch, 251–75. Berlin: Frank & Timme, 2018.

Mishra, Sudeh. "The Global South: Modernity and Exceptionality." In *The Global South and Literature*, edited by Russell West-Pavlov, 45–55. Cambridge: Cambridge University Press, 2018.

Mitchievici, Angelo. *Mateiu I. Caragiale. Fizionomii decandente*. Bucharest: Editura Institutului Cultural Român, 2007.

Miyoshi, Masao. "Turn to the Planet: Literature, Diversity, and Totality." *Comparative Literature* 53, no. 4 (Fall 2001): 283–97.

Moore, David Chioni. "Is the Post- in Postcolonial the Post- in Post-Soviet? Toward a Global Postcolonial Critique." *PMLA* 116, no. 1 (2001): 111–28.

Moraru, Christian. "Contagion, Contamination, and Don DeLillo's Post-Cold War World-System: Steps toward a Haptical Theory of Culture." In *Contagion: Health, Fear, Sovereignty*, edited by Bruce Magnusson and Zahi Zalloua, 123–48. Seattle: University of Washington Press, 2012.

Moraru, Christian. "Critique and Its Postnational Aftermath: Dialogism and the 'Planetary Condition.'" In *Criticism after Critique: Aesthetics, Literature, and the Political*, edited by Jeffrey R. Di Leo, 99–112. New York: Palgrave Macmillan, 2014.

Moraru, Christian. "Meganovel." *American Book Review* 37, no. 2 (2016): 12–13.

Moraru, Christian. *Memorious Discourse*. Madison, NJ: Fairleigh Dickinson University Press, 2005.

Moraru, Christian. "Mistifiction: Mistranslation, Mistification, and Metafiction in the Age of Global Transactions." *Studii de literatură și lingvistică* (2012): 170–86.

Moraru, Christian. *Reading for the Planet: Toward a Geomethodology*. Ann Arbor: University of Michigan Press, 2015.

Moraru, Christian. "Why Community Needs Theory: Rethinking the Communal in the Twenty-First Century." *Euphorion* 27, no. 1 (April 2016): 35–7.

Moraru, Christian. "'World,' 'Globe,' 'Planet': Comparative Literature, Planetary Studies, and Cultural Debt after the Global Turn." In *Futures of Comparative Literature: ACLA State of the Discipline Report*, edited by Ursula K. Heise, with Dudley Andrew, Alexander Beecroft, Jessica Berman, David Damrosch, Guillermina De Ferrari, César Domínguez, Barbara Harlow, and Eric Hayot, 124–34. New York: Routledge, 2017.

Moraru, Cristian. "Cultură, politică, resentiment: Fișe pentru un dicționar spectral." *Observator cultural* 4, no. 187 (September 23–29, 2003): 17.

Moraru, Cristian. "'Modelul Cărtărescu' versus 'Modelul Patapievici': Discursuri culturale și alternative politice în România de azi." *Observator cultural* 4, no. 177 (July 17–23, 2003): 32.

Moretti, Franco. *The Bourgeois: Between History and Literature*. London: Verso, 2013.

Moretti, Franco. "Conjectures on World Literature." *New Left Review*, no. 1 (2000): 54–68.

Moretti, Franco. *Distant Reading*. New York: Verso, 2013.

Moretti, Franco. *Graphs, Maps, Trees: Abstract Models for Literary History*. Afterword by Alberto Piazza. London: Verso, 2007.

Moretti, Franco. *Modern Epic: The World-System from Goethe to García Márquez*. Translated by Quintin Hoare. London: Verso, 1996.

Moretti, Franco. "More Conjectures." *New Left Review* 20 (March–April 2003): 73–81.

Moretti, Franco. *Signs Taken for Wonders*. Translated by Susan Fischer, David Forgacs, and David Miller. London: Verso, 2005.

Moretti Franco. "The Slaughterhouse of Literature." *Modern Language Quarterly* 61, no. 1 (2000): 207–27.

Morgan, Benjamin. "Scale, Resonance, Presence." *Victorian Studies* 59, no. 1 (Autumn 2016): 109–12.

Morizot, Baptiste. *Les Diplomates. Cohabiter avec les loups sur une autre carte du vivant*. Marseille: Wildproject, 2016.

Morton, Timothy. *Hyperobjects: Philosophy and Ecology after the End of the World*. Minneapolis: University of Minnesota Press, 2013.

Mozejko, Edward. "Postmodernism in the Literatures of Former Yugoslavia." In *International Postmodernism: Theory and Literary Practice*, edited by Hans Bertens and Douwe Fokkema, 441–46. Amsterdam: John Benjamins Publishing Company, 1997.

Mufti, Aamir R. "Global Comparativism." *Critical Inquiry*, no. 31, (Winter 2005): 472–89.

Mugur, Florin. *Convorbiri cu Marin Preda*. Bucharest: Albatros, 1973.

Mullins, Matthew, ed. "Postcritique." Special-topic issue of *American Book Review* 38, no. 5 (2017).

Mullins, Matthew. *Postmodernism in Pieces: Materializing the Social in U.S. Fiction*. New York: Oxford University Press, 2016.

Mușat, Carmen. "Bakhtin's Concept of 'Chronotope' and Theory's 'Embeddedness' in History." *Euresis*, nos. 1–4 (2013): 97–102.

Mușat, Carmen. *Frumoasa necunoscută. Literatura și paradoxurile teoriei*. Iași, Romania: Polirom, 2017.

Mușina, Alexandru. *Eseu asupra poeziei moderne*. Chișinău, Moldova: Cartier, 1997.

Mușina, Alexandru. "Noul antropocentrism." În *Unde se află poezia*. Tîrgu-Mureș, Romania: Arhipelag, 1996.

Mușina, Alexandru. *Paradigma poeziei moderne*. Bucharest: Leka-Brâncuși, 1996.

Mussgnug, Florian. "Planetary Figurations: Intensive Genre in World Literature." *Modern Languages Open* 1 (2018). http://doi.org/10.3828/mlo.v0i0.204.

Nafisi, Azar. *The Republic of the Imagination: America in Three Books*. Illustrations by Peter Sis. New York: Viking, 2014.

Naiman, Eric. *Sex in Public: The Incarnation of Early Soviet Ideology*. Princeton, NJ: Princeton University Press, 1997.

Nancy, Jean-Luc. *Being Singular Plural*. Translated by Robert D. Richardson and Anne E. O'Byrne. Stanford, CA: Stanford University Press, 2000.

Nancy, Jean-Luc. *La création du monde ou la mondialisation*. Paris: Galilée, 2002.

Nancy, Jean-Luc. *The Inoperative Community*. Edited by Peter Conor. Translated by Peter Conor, Lisa Garbus, Michael Holland, and Simona Sawhney. Foreword by Christopher Fynsk. Minneapolis: University of Minnesota Press, 1991.

Nancy, Jean-Luc. *The Sense of the World*. Translated and with a foreword by Jeffrey S. Librett. Minneapolis: University of Minnesota Press, 1997.

Nealon, Jeffrey T. *Post-Postmodernism, or, The Cultural Logic of Just-in-time Capitalism*. Stanford, CA: Stanford University Press, 2012.

Nemoianu, Virgil. "Bătălia canonică—de la critica americană la cultura română." *România literară* 41 (1990): 12–13.

Nemoianu, Virgil. "Despărțirea de eminescianism." *Astra* 7 (1990): 8–9.

Neumann, Victor. "Multi- și inter-culturalitate. Moșteniri imperiale în Banatul Timișoarei." *Punctul critic* 2, no. 24 (2018). Available online: https://www. punctulcritic.ro/victor-neumann-multi%E2%80%91-si-interculturalitate-mosteniri-imperiale-in-banatul-timisoarei.html (accessed December 30, 2019).

Ngozi Adichie, Chimamanda. *Americanah*. New York: Knopf, 2013.

Ngozi Adichie, Chiamamanda. *Americana*. Translated by Radu Șorop. Bucharest: Black Button Books, 2018.

Nilsson, Louise, David Damrosch, and Theo D'haen, eds. *Crime Fiction as World Literature*. New York: Bloomsbury Academic, 2017.

North, Joseph. *Literary Criticism: A Concise Political History*. Cambridge, MA: Harvard University Press, 2017.

Oates, Sarah. *Revolution Stalled: The Political Limits of the Internet in the Post-Soviet Sphere*. Oxford: Oxford University Press, 2013.

Olaru, Ovio. "Teorie gonzo." *Vatra* 48, no. 3 (March 2018): 32–4.

Ortmann, David M., and Richard A. Sprott. *Sexual Outsiders: Understanding BDSM Sexualities and Communities*. Lanham, MD: Rowman & Littlefield, 2013.

Papadima, Liviu, David Damrosch, and Theo D'haen, eds. *The Canonical Debate Today: Crossing Disciplinary and Cultural Boundaries*. Amsterdam: Rodopi, 2011.

Papahagi, Adrian. "Ce este sexo-marxismul?" *Dilema Veche* 16, no. 801 (June 27–July 3, 2019): ii.

Papu, Edgar. *Din clasicii noștri. Contribuții la ideea unui protocronism românesc*. Bucharest: Editura Eminescu, 1977.

Parvulaescu, Anca, and Manuela Boatcă. "Discounting Languages: Between Hugó Meltzl and Liviu Rebreanu." *Journal of World Literature* 5, no. 1 (2020): 47–78.

Patapievici, Horia-Roman. *Omul recent. O critică a modernității din perspectiva întrebării "Ce se pierde atunci când ceva se câștigă?"* Bucharest: Humanitas, 2001.

Paulik Babka, Susie. *Through the Dark Field: The Incarnation through an Aesthetics of Vulnerability*. Collegeville, MN: Liturgical Press, 2017.

Paz, Octavio. *The Other Voice: Essays on Modern Poetry*. Translated from the Spanish by Helen Lane. New York: Harcourt Brace Jovanovich, 1991.

Paz, Octavio. *In Search of the Present: 1990 Nobel Lecture*. Bilingual Edition. San Diego, CA: Harcourt Brace Jovanovich, 1991.

Perian, Gheorghe. *Pagini de critică și istorie literară*. Cluj-Napoca, Romania: Ardealul, 1998.

Perloff, Marjorie. *Unoriginal Genius: Poetry by Other Means in the New Century*. Chicago: University of Chicago Press, 2010.

Phelan, James. *Experiencing Fiction: Judgments, Progressions, and the Rhetorical Theory of Narrative*. Columbus: Ohio State University Press, 2007.

Pinkerton, Steve. *Blasphemous Modernism: The 20th-Century Word Made Flesh*. New York: Oxford University Press, 2017.

Pîrjol, Florina. *Carte de identități*. Bucharest: Cartea Românească, 2014.

Pleșu, Andrei. "Vigilența resentimentară." *Dilema* 11, no. 541 (August 15–21, 2003): 3.

Podoabă, Virgil. *Anatomia frigului. Altă analiză monstruoasă*. Cluj-Napoca, Romania: Ecco-Marineasa, 2003.

Podoabă, Virgil. "Gheorghe Crăciun și revelațiile corpului erotizat: Studiu de hermeneutică fenomenologică." *Vatra* 5–6 (2002): 141–3; 8–9 (2002): 30–3; 10 (2002): 18–20.

Podoabă, Virgil. *Între extreme*. Cluj-Napoca, Romania: Dacia, 2002.

Podoabă, Virgil. "Preambul la o propunere: Studiu introductiv despre experiența revelatoare." *Vatra* 5–6 (2004): 48–56.

Ponge, Francis. *Le Grand recueil, III: Pièces*. Paris: Gallimard, 1961.

Popescu, Simona. *Autorul, un personaj*. Pitești, Romania: Paralela 45, 2015.

Popescu, Simona. *Clava. Critificțiune cu Gellu Naum*. Pitești, Romania: Paralela 45, 2004.

Portela, Manuel. "Writing under Constraint of the Regime of Computation." In *The Bloomsbury Handbook of Electronic Literature*, edited by Joseph Tabbi, 181–201. New York: Bloomsbury, 2018.

Porter, J. D. "Popularity/Prestige." Pamphlet 17 (September 2018). Available online: https://litlab.stanford.edu/LiteraryLabPamphlet17.pdf (accessed June 30, 2019).

Poulet, Georges. *La conscience critique*. Paris: Librairie José Corti, 1971.

Preda, Marin. *Risipitorii*. Bucharest: Curtea Veche, 2011.

Pressman, Jessica. *Digital Modernism: Making It New in New Media*. Oxford: Oxford University Press, 2014.

Prieto, Eric. "Geocriticism, Geopoetics, Geophilosophy, and Beyond." In *Geocritical Explorations: Space, Place, and Mapping in Literary and Cultural Studies*, edited by Robert T. Tally Jr., 13–29. New York: Palgrave Macmillan, 2011.

Prieto, Eric. *Literature, Geography, and the Postmodern Poetics of Place*. New York: Palgrave Macmillan, 2012.

Proust, Marcel. *Contre Sainte Beuve. Précédé de Pastiches et mélanges et suivi de Essais et articles*. Edited by Pierre Clarac and Yves Sandre. Paris: Gallimard, 1971.

Quignard, Pascal. *Ecrits de l'éphémère*. Paris: Galilée, 2005.

Quintane, Nathalie. *Chaussure*. Paris: POL, 1997.

Quote Investigator. "If the Bee Disappeared Off the Face of the Earth, Man Would Only Have Four Years Left To Live." August 27, 2013. Available online: https://quoteinvestigator.com/2013/08/27/einstein-bees/ (accessed September 15, 2020).

Rabaté, Jean-Michel. *Crimes of the Future: Theory and Its Global Reproduction.* New York: Bloomsbury, 2014.

Rabouin, David. *Vivre ici. Spinoza, éthique locale.* Paris: Presses universitaires de France, 2010.

Rădulescu, Silvia, Frank Wijnen, and Sergey Avrutin. "Patterns Bit by Bit: An Entropy Model for Rule Induction." *Language Learning and Development* 16, no. 2 (2020): 109–40. https://doi.org/10.1080/15475441.2019.1695620.

Ramírez, Juan. *The Beehive Metaphor: From Gaudí to Le Corbusier.* Translated by Alexander R. Tulloch. London: Reaktion Books, 2000.

Ramsay, Stephen. *Reading Machines: Toward an Algorithmic Criticism.* Chicago: University of Illinois Press, 2011.

Rancière, Jacques. *Dissensus: On Politics and Aesthetics.* Edited and translated by Stevan Corcoran. New York: Continuum Publishing, 2010.

Rancière, Jacques. *La parole muette. Essai sur la contradiction de la littérature.* Paris: Fayard, 2011.

Rasson, Luc. *L'écrivain et le dictateur. Ecrire l'expérience totalitaire.* Paris: Imago, 2008.

Read, F. ed. *Pound / Joyce: The Letters of Ezra Pound to James Joyce, with Pound's Essays on Joyce.* London: Faber & Faber, 1967.

Reiss, Timothy J. *Against Autonomy: Global Dialectics of Cultural Exchange.* Stanford, CA: Stanford University Press, 2002.

Renders, Hans, Binne de Haan, and Jonne Harmsma, eds. *The Biographical Turn.* London: Routledge, 2017.

Renders, Hans, Binne de Haan, and Jonne Harmsma. "The Biographical Turn: Biography as a Critical Method in the Humanities and in Society." In *The Biographical Turn: Lives in History*, edited by Hans Renders, Binne de Haan, and Jonne Harmsma, 3–13. London: Routledge, 2017.

Ricoeur, Paul. *Freud and Philosophy: An Essay on Interpretation.* Translated by Denis Savage. New Haven, CT: Yale University Press, 1970.

Robbe-Grillet, Alain. *Dans le labyrinthe.* Paris: Minuit, 1959.

Robbe-Grillet, Alain. *A Regicide.* Paris: Minuit, 1978.

Robbins, Bruce. "Fashion Conscious Phenomenon." *American Book Review* 38 (2017): 5–6.

Rogozanu, Costi. "Unde-s marginalii în literatura nouă?" *Gazeta de artă politică*, January 22, 2014. Available online: http://artapolitica.ro/2014/01/22/unde-s-marginalii-in-literatura-noua/ (accessed October 9, 2020).

"Romanul românesc al secolului XX." *Observator cultural*, nos. 45–6 (2001). Available online: https://www.observatorcultural.ro/articol/romanul-romanesc-al-secolului-xx/ (accessed April 2, 2019).

Rosanvallon, Pierre. *Le Parlement des invisibles.* Paris: Seuil, 2014.

Rosenholm, Arja, Kaarle Nordenstreng, and Elena Trubina. "Introduction." In *Russian Mass Media and Changing Values*, edited by Arja Rosenholm, Kaarle Nordenstreng, and Elena Trubina, 1–19. London: Routledge, 2011.

Rothberg, Michael. *Multidirectional Memory: Remembering the Holocaust in the Age of Decolonization.* Stanford, CA: Stanford University Press, 2009.

Rueff, Martin. "La concordance des temps." In *Qu'est-ce que le contemporain?* edited by Lionel Ruffel, 93–110. Nantes: Cécile Defaut, 2010.

Ruffel, Lionel. *Brouhaha: Worlds of the Contemporary.* Translated by Raymond M. MacKenzie. Minneapolis: University of Minnesota Press, 2018.

Ruffel, Lionel, and Olivia Rosenthal. "La Littérature exposée." *Littérature* 160, no. 4 (2010): 3–13.

Rutten, Ellen. "(Russian) Writer-Bloggers: Digital Perfection and the Aesthetics of Imperfection." *Journal of Computer-Mediated Communication,* no. 19 (2014): 744–62.

Ruttkay, Veronika. "Negotiating the Popular/ National Voice: Impropriety in Two Hungarian Translations of Robert Burns." In *Worlds of Hungarian Writing: National Literature as Intercultural Exchange,* edited by András Kiséry, Zsolt Komáromy, and Zsuzsanna Varga, 53–74. Teaneck, NJ: Fairleigh Dickinson University Press; Lanham, MD: Rowman and Littlefield: 2016.

Said, Edward. *Culture and Imperialism.* New York: Vintage Books, 1994.

Said, Edward. *Reflections on Exile and Other Essays.* Cambridge, MA: Harvard University Press, 2000.

Said, Edward. *The World, the Text, and the Critic.* Cambridge, MA: Harvard University Press, 1983.

Saldívar, Ramón. "Faulkner and the World Culture of the Global South." In *Fifty Years of Faulkner,* edited by Jay Watson and Ann J. Abadie, 3–19. Jackson: University Press of Mississippi, 2016.

Saunders, Max. *Self-Impression: Life-Writing, Autobiografiction, and the Forms of Modern Literature.* Oxford: Oxford University Press, 2010.

Savu, Laura. *Postmortem Postmodernists: The Afterlife of the Author in Recent Narrative.* Madison, NJ: Fairleigh Dickinson University Press, 2009.

Schabert, Ina. "Fictional Biography, Factual Biography, and Their Contaminations." *Biography* 5, no. 1 (Winter 1982): 1–16.

Scharlemann, Robert P., ed. *On the Other: Dialogue and/or Dialectics; Mark Taylor's "Paralectics,"* with Roy Wagner, Michael Brint, and Richard Rorty. Lanham, MD: University Press of America, 1991.

Schiop, Adrian. *pe bune/pe invers.* Foreword by C. Rogozanu. Iași, Romania: Polirom, 2004.

Schiop, Adrian. *Soldații. Poveste din Ferentari.* Iași, Romania: Polirom, 2014.

Schiop, Adrian. *Zero grade Kelvin.* Iași, Romania: Polirom, 2009.

Schiop, Adrian. *Șmecherie și lume rea. Universul social al manelelor.* Chișinău, Moldova: Cartier, 2016.

Schreibman, Susan, Ray Siemens, and John Unsworth, eds. *A Companion to Digital Humanities.* Oxford: Blackwell, 2004.

Scott-Baumann, Alison. *Ricoeur and the Hermeneutics of Suspicion.* London: Continuum International Publishing Group, 2009.

Scott, Niall, ed. *Monsters and the Monstrous: Myths and Metaphors of Enduring Evil.* Amsterdam: Rodopi, 2007.

Sedgwick, Eve Kosofsky. *Touching Feeling: Affect, Pedagogy, Performativity.* Durham, NC: Duke University Press, 2002.

Seidman, Steven, Nancy Fischer, and Chet Meeks, eds. *Introducing the New Sexuality Studies.* London: Routledge, 2011.

Sériot, Patrick. *Structure and the Whole: East, West, and Non-Darwinian Biology in the Origins of Structural Linguistics.* Translated from French by Amy Jacobs-Colas. Berlin: Walter de Gruyter, 2014.

Serrano, Alma Rosa Mar. "Lazarillo de Tormes." Monografias.com. Available
    online: https://www.monografias.com/trabajos96/resumen-lazarillo-tormes/
    resumen-lazarillo-tormes.shtml (accessed November 23, 2018).
Serres, Michel, and Bruno Latour. *Conversations on Science, Culture, and Time.*
    Translated by Roxanne Lapidus. Ann Arbor: The University of Michigan Press,
    1995.
Shaw, Lytle. "lowercase theory and the site specific turn." *ASAP/Journal* 2, no.3
    (2017): 653–76.
Shih, Shu-Mei. "Global Literature and the Technologies of Recognition." *PMLA*
    119, no. 1 (January 2004): 16–30.
Shusterman, Richard. "Pragmatism's Embodied Philosophy: From Immediate
    Experience to Somaesthetics." In *Routledge Handbook of Body Studies*, edited
    by Bryan S. Turner, 34–48. New York: Routledge, 2012.
Sider, Theodore. "Presentism and Ontological Commitment." *Journal of
    Philosophy*, no. 96 (1999): 325–47.
Siemens, Ray, and Susan Schreibman, eds. *A Companion to Digital Literary
    Studies*. Oxford: Blackwell, 2013.
SimilarWeb. "Poezie.ro." Available online: https://www.similarweb.com/website/
    poezie.ro (accessed January 4, 2019).
Simion, Eugen. *Fragmente critice I–VI*. Craiova, Romania: Editura Scrisul
    Românesc; Bucharest: Fundația Națională pentru Știință și Artă, 1998–2009.
Simion, Eugen. *Genurile biograficului*. Vol. 1. Bucharest: Fundația Națională pentru
    Știință și Artă, 2008.
Simion, Eugen. *Întoarcerea autorului. Eseuri despre relația creator-operă.*
    Afterword and critical bibliography by Andrei Terian. Bucharest: Univers
    Enciclopedic Gold, 2013.
Simion, Eugen. *The Return of the Author*. Edited and with an introduction by
    James W. Newcomb. Translated by Lidia Vianu. Evanston, IL: Northwestern
    University Press, 1996.
Simion, Eugen. *Timpul trăirii, timpul mărturisirii*. Bucharest: Univers Enciclopedic
    Gold, 2013.
Singer, Thomas, and Samuel L. Kimbles. "Introduction." In *The Cultural Complex:
    Contemporary Jungian Perspectives on Psyche and Society*, edited by Thomas
    Singer and Samuel L. Kimbles, 1–10. New York: Routledge, 2004.
Singer, Thomas, and Samuel L. Kimbles, eds. *The Cultural Complex: Contemporary
    Jungian Perspectives on Psyche and Society*. New York: Routledge, 2004.
Slethaug, Gordon E. *Beautiful Chaos: Chaos Theory and Metachaotics in Recent
    American Fiction*. Albany: State University of New York Press, 2000.
Smith, Zadie. *Dinți albi*. English translation and notes by Alina Scurtu. Iași,
    Romania: Polirom, 2014.
Smith, Zadie. *White Teeth*. New York: Random House, 2000.
Spivak, Gayatri Chakravorty. "Can the Subaltern Speak?" In *Colonial Discourse
    and Post-Colonial Theory: A Reader*, edited by Patrick Williams and Laura
    Chrisman, 66–111. New York: Columbia University Press, 1994.
Stan, Adriana. "Regula jocului." *Observator cultural*, June 26, 2018. Available
    online: https://www.observatorcultural.ro/articol/regula-jocului-2/ (accessed
    June 10, 2020).

Stein, Kevin. *Poetry's Afterlife: Verse in the Digital Age*. Ann Arbor: University of Michigan Press, 2010.

Suceavă, Bogdan. *Avalon. Secretele emigranților fericiți*. Iași, Romania: Polirom, 2018.

Suceavă, Bogdan. *Venea din timpul diez*. Iași, Romania: Polirom, 2004.

Suchomel, Milan. "Postmodernism in Czech Literature." In *International Postmodernism: Theory and Literary Practice*, edited by Hans Bertens and Douwe Fokkema, 419–22. Amsterdam: John Benjamins Publishing Company, 1997.

Suleiman, Susan Rubin. *Le Roman à thèse ou l'autorité fictive*. Paris: Presses Universitaires de France, 1983.

Szegedy-Maszák, Mihály. *Literary Canons: National and International*. Budapest: Akadémiai, 2001.

Szegedy-Maszák, Mihály. "Postmodern Literature in Hungary." In *International Postmodernism: Theory and Literary Practice*, edited by Hans Bertens and Douwe Fokkema, 429–34. Amsterdam: John Benjamins Publishing Company, 1997.

Szlajfer, Henryk. "Editor's Introduction." In *Economic Nationalism in East-Central Europe and South America 1918–1939*, edited by Henryk Szlajfer, 1–13. Geneva: Droz, 1990.

Șerbu, Ioan Olimpiu. "Școala literară de la Brașov / The Brașov Literary School." PhD diss. abstract, Transylvania University of Brașov, Romania, 2019. Available online: https://www.unitbv.ro/documente/cercetare/doctorat-postdoctorat/sustinere-teza/2019/ioan-serbu/TEZA_Ioan_serbu.PDF (accessed April 15, 2020).

Ștefănescu, Bogdan. "Romanian Modernity and the Rhetoric of Vacuity: Toward a Comparative Postcolonialism." In *Romanian Literature as World Literature*, edited by Mircea Martin, Christian Moraru, and Andrei Terian, 255–70. New York: Bloomsbury, 2017.

Tabbi, Joseph. "Relocating the Literary: In Networks, Knowledge Bases, Global Systems, Material, and Mental Environments." In *The Bloomsbury Handbook of Electronic Literature*, edited by Joseph Tabbi, 399–421. New York: Bloomsbury, 2018.

Tally, Robert T., Jr., ed. *Geocritical Explorations: Space, Place, and Mapping in Literary and Cultural Studies*. New York: Palgrave Macmillan, 2014.

Talon-Hugon, Carole. *L'Art victime de l'esthétique*. Paris: Hermann, 2014.

Taylor, Charles. *The Ethics of Authenticity*. Cambridge, MA: Harvard University Press, 1992.

Taylor, Charles. *Multiculturalism: Examining the Politics of Recognition*. With commentary by K. Anthony Appiah, Jürgen Habermas, Steven C. Rockefeller, Michael Walzer, and Susan Wolf. Edited and introduced by Amy Gutmann. Princeton, NJ: Princeton University Press, 1994.

Taylor, Charles. *Sources of the Self: The Making of the Modern Identity*. Cambridge, MA: Harvard University Press, 1989.

Terian, Andrei. *Critica de export. Teorii, contexte, ideologii*. Bucharest: Muzeul Literaturii Române, 2013.

Terian, Andrei. "Is There an East-Central European Postcolonialism? Towards a Unified Theory of (Inter) Literary Dependency." *World Literature Studies* 4, no. 3 (2012): 21–36.

Terian, Andrei. "[Preface] O carte anacronică în trei dialoguri." In Eugen Simion, *Întoarcerea autorului*, 487–97. Bucharest: Univers Enciclopedic Gold, 2013.

Terian, Andrei. *Critica de export. Teorii, contexte, ideologii*. Bucharest: Muzeul Literaturii Române, 2013.

Terian, Andrei. *G. Călinescu. A cincea esență*. Bucharest: Editura Cartea Românească, 2009.

Tertulian, Nicolas. *Pourquoi Lukács*. Paris: Maison des Sciences de l'Homme, 2016.

Thompson, D'Arcy Wentworth. *On Growth and Form*. Cambridge: Cambridge University Press, 1942.

Thomsen, Mads Rosendahl. *Mapping World Literature: International Canonization and Transnational Literatures*. London: Continuum, 2008.

Thomsen, Mads Rosendahl. "World Famous, Locally: Insights from the Study of International Canonization." In *Futures of Comparative Literature: ACLA State of the Discipline Report*, edited by Ursula Heise, with Dudley Andrew, Alexander Beecroft, Jessica Berman, David Damrosch, Guillermina De Ferrari, César Domínguez, Barbara Harlow, and Eric Hayot, 119–23. New York: Routledge, 2017.

Tihanov, Galin. *The Birth and Death of Literary Theory: Regimes of Relevance in Russia and Beyond*. Stanford, CA: Stanford University Press, 2019.

Tihanov, Galin. "Why Did Modern Literary Theory Originate in Central and Eastern Europe? (And Why Is It Now Dead?)." *Common Knowledge* 10, no. 1 (Winter 2004): 61–81.

Todorova, Maria. "Balkanism and Postcolonialism or On the Beauty of the Airplane View." In *Marx's Shadow: Knowledge, Power, and Intellectuals in Eastern Europe and Russia*, edited by Costica Bradatan and Serguei Oushakine, 175–96. Lanham, MD: Lexington Books, 2010.

Todorova, Maria. "Introduction: Similar Trajectories, Different Memories." In *Remembering Communism. Private and Public Recollections of Lived Experience in South-East Europe*, edited by Maria Todorova, Augusta Dimou, Stefan Troebst, 1–25. Budapest, Hungary: CEU Press, 2014.

Tomar, David A. "Historical Narratives Offer a Skewed View of the Past That Presentism Can Fix." In *Presentism: Reexamining Historical Figures Through Today's Lens*, edited by Sabine Cherenfant, 76–81. New York: Greenhaven Publishing, 2019.

Toussaint, Jean-Philippe. *La Clé USB*. Paris: Minuit, 2019.

Trencsényi, Balázs, Michal Kopeček, Luka Lisjak Gabrielčič, Maria Falina, Monika Baár, and Maciej Janowski. *A History of Modern Political Thought in Eastern Europe*, vol. 2, *Negotiating Modernity in the Short Twentieth Century and Beyond*, pt. 2, *1968–2018*. Oxford: Oxford University Press, 2018.

Tudorachi, Adrian, Madga Răduță, and Oana Fotache, eds. *Dus-întors. Rute ale teoriei literare in postmodernitate*. Bucharest: Humanitas, 2016.

Tudorachi, Adrian. "Despre receptarea foarte târzie a teoriei." In *Dus-întors. Rute ale teoriei literare in postmodernitate*, edited by Adrian Tudorachi, Madga Răduță, and Oana Fotache, 36–48. Bucharest: Humanitas, 2016.

Turner, Bryan S., ed. *Routledge Handbook of Body Studies*. New York: Routledge, 2012.

Ugrešić, Dubravka. *The Culture of Lies: Antipolitical Essays*. Translated by Celia Hawkesworth. London: Phoenix House, 1998.

Underwood, Ted, and Jordan Sellers. "The Longue Durée of Literary Prestige." *Modern Language Quarterly* 3 (2016): 321–44.

Ursa, Mihaela. "Is Romanian Culture Ready for the Digital Turn?" *Metacritic Journal for Comparative Studies and Theory*, no. 1 (2015): 80–97.

Vianu, Ion. *Investigații mateine*. Cluj-Napoca, Romania: Apostrof, 2008.

Vitali-Rosati, Marcello. "Les revues littéraires en ligne: entre éditorialisation et réseaux d'intelligences." *Études françaises* 50, no. 3 (2014): 83–104.

Vosganian, Varujan. *Cartea șoaptelor*. Iași, Romania: Polirom, 2009.

Vosganian, Varujan. *The Book of Whispers*. Translated by Alistair Jan Blyth. New Haven, CT: Yale University Press, 2017.

Walkowitz, Rebecca L. *Born Translated: The Contemporary Novel in an Age of World Literature*. New York: Columbia University Press, 2015.

Walkowitz, Rebecca L. "The Location of Literature: The Transnational Book and the Migrant Writer." *Contemporary Literature* 47, no. 4 (Winter 2006): 527–45.

Wallerstein, Immanuel. *Geopolitics and Geoculture: Essays on the Changing World-System*. Cambridge: Cambridge University Press; Paris: Maison des Sciences de l'Homme, 1991.

Wallerstein, Immanuel. *The Modern World-System: Capitalist Agriculture and the Origins of the European World-Economy in the Sixteenth Century*. New York: Academic Press, 1974.

Wallerstein, Immanuel. *World-Systems Analysis: An Introduction*. Durham, NC: Duke University Press, 2004.

Warwick Research Collective (WReC). *Combined and Uneven Development: Towards a New Theory of World-Literature*. Liverpool, UK: Liverpool University Press, 2015.

WayBackMachine. "Reader Terrorism: Books and Tobacco." Available online: https://web.archive.org/web/20100522120357/http://www.terorista. ro:80/2009/04/07/aproximativ-trei-ani#comments (accessed January 4, 2019).

Weinberg, Steven. *Dreams of a Final Theory*. New York: Vintage Books, 1994.

Wellek, René. "The Essential Characteristics of Russian Literary Criticism." *Comparative Literature Studies* 29, no. 2 (1992): 115–40.

West-Pavlov, Russell. "Toward the Global South: Concept or Chimera, Paradigm or Panacea?" In *The Global South and Literature*, edited by Russell West-Pavlov, 1–20. Cambridge: Cambridge University Press, 2018.

Westphal, Bertrand. "A Geocritical Approach to Geocriticism." *American Book Review* 37, no. 6 (2016): 4–5.

Westphal, Bertrand. *Geocriticism: Real and Fictional Spaces*. Translated by Robert T. Tally Jr. New York: Palgrave Macmillan, 2011.

Westphal, Bertrand. *The Plausible World: A Geocritical Approach to Space, Place, and Maps*. New York: Palgrave Macmillan, 2013.

Wilkens, Matthew. "Canons, Close Reading, and the Evolution of Method." In *Debates in the Digital Humanities*, edited by Matthew K. Gold, 249–58. Minneapolis: University of Minnesota Press, 2012.

Wilson, Elizabeth A. *Neural Geographies: Feminism and the Microstructure of Cognition*. New York: Routledge, 1998.

Winterson, Jeanette. *Written on the Body*. New York: Knopf, 1993.

Withy, Katherine. "Concealing and Concealment in Heidegger." *European Journal of Philosophy* 25, no. 4 (2017): 1496–513.

Wolf, Nelly. "Le roman comme démocratie." *Revue d'histoire littéraire de la France* 105, no. 2 (2005): 343–52.

Wolfendale, Peter. *Object-Oriented Philosophy: The Noumenon's New Clothes*. Falmouth, UK: Urbanomic, 2014.

Yan, Wei. "Sherlock Holmes Came to China: Detective Fiction, Cultural Meditations, and Chinese Modernity." In *Crime Fiction as World Literature*, edited by Louise Nilsson, David Damrosch, and Theo D'haen, 245–55. New York: Bloomsbury, 2017.

Zalloua, Zahi. "On Meillassoux's 'Transparent Cage': Speculative Realism and Its Discontents." *symplokē* 23, nos. 1–2 (2015): 393–409.

Zapf, Hubert. *Literature as Cultural Ecology: Sustainable Texts*. London: Bloomsbury, 2016.

Zaretskaia-Balsente, Ioulia. *Les intellectuels et la censure en URSS*. Paris: L'Harmattan, 2000.

Zavala, Oswaldo. "The Repolitization of the Latin American Shore: Roberto Bolaño and the Dispersion of 'World Literature.'" In *Roberto Bolaño as World Literature*, edited by Nicholas Birns and Juan E. De Castro, 79–98. New York: Bloomsbury, 2017.

Zhang, Longxi. "Canon and World Literature." *Journal of World Literature* 1, no. 1 (2016): 119–27.

Zilka, Tibor. "Postmodernism in Slovak Literature." In *International Postmodernism: Theory and Literary Practice*, edited by Hans Bertens and Douwe Fokkema, 413–18. Amsterdam: John Benjamins Publishing Company, 1997.

Zirin, Mary, Irina Livezeanu, Christine D Worobec, and June Pachuta Farris, eds. *Women & Gender in Central and Eastern Europe, Russia, and Eurasia: A Comprehensive Bibliography*. 2 Volumes. New York: M. E. Sharpe, 2007.

CONTRIBUTORS

Alexandru Matei is Associate Professor of French in the Faculty of Letters of Transilvania University of Brașov, Romania, and Visiting Professor in the Anthropology Department of the Faculty of Sociology and Social Assistance of University of Bucharest, Romania. He teaches primarily French culture and literature and the anthropology of science and technology. Matei has translated French theory and literature into Romanian, including works by Bruno Latour, Roland Barthes, and Michel Serres. He is the author of books such as *The Last Days of Literature's Life: Enormous and Insignificant in Contemporary French Literature* (2008), *A Captivating Tribune: Television, Ideology, and Society in Socialist Romania* (2013), *Roland Barthes: Romanian Mythologies* (2017), and *Jean Echenoz et la Distance intérieure* (2012). He has published extensively on Roland Barthes, recent French and Romanian literature, and other subjects in *Littérature, French Forum, Romance Studies, Interlitterraria, Observator cultural*, and elsewhere.[1]

Christian Moraru is Class of 1949 Distinguished Professor in the Humanities and Professor of English at University of North Carolina, Greensboro. He specializes in post-World War II American fiction, critical theory, as well as comparative and world literature with emphasis on history of ideas, the relations between globalism and culture, postmodernism, and the contemporary challenges to the postmodern paradigm. His recent publications are the monographs *Cosmodernism: American Narrative, Late Globalization, and the New Cultural Imaginary* (2011) and *Reading for the Planet: Toward a Geomethodology* (2015) and coedited essay collections such as *The Planetary Turn: Relationality and Geoaesthetics in the Twenty-First Century* (2015), *Romanian Literature as World Literature* (2018), *Francophone Literature as World Literature* (2020), and *The Bloomsbury Handbook of World Theory* (2021).

Andrei Terian is Vice Rector of Lucian Blaga University of Sibiu, Romania, and Professor of Romanian Literature in the Department of Romance Studies at the same institution. He specializes in post-1900 Romanian literature, as well as cultural theory, the history of modern criticism, and comparative and world literature. He has published essays in Romania and in international journals such as *Slovo, CLCWeb—Comparative Literature and Culture, World Literature Studies, Interlitteraria, ALEA: Estudos Neolatinos, Primerjalna književnost,* and *Transylvania.* His latest books are the monographs *G. Călinescu: The Fifth Essence* (2009) and *Exporting Criticism: Theories, Contexts, Ideologies* (2013). He is also a main contributor to the *General Dictionary of Romanian Literature* (2004–9) and *Chronology of Romanian Literary Life: 1944–1964* (2010–13) and a coeditor of *Romanian Literature as World Literature* (2018).

Ștefan Baghiu is Assistant Professor of Romanian Literature and Literary Theory in the Romance Studies Department of Lucian Blaga University of Sibiu. His interests span translation, quantitative literary research, cultural studies, and post-World War II Romanian literature with emphasis on narrative. Focused on Communist-era Romanian renditions of American, Latin American, and Chinese novels, on translation broadly, as well as on Socialist Realism, his latest publications include articles in *Transilvania* and *Comparative Literature Studies* as well as the coedited volume *The Culture of Translation in Romania* (2018).

Cosmin Borza is Senior Researcher at the Sextil Pușcariu Institute of Linguistics and Literary History of the Romanian Academy, Cluj-Napoca, Romania. His main research areas are post-1900 Romanian literature with particular focus on the relationships between literature, on one hand, and ideology and critical and political theory, on the other. Borza is the author of two books of criticism, *Marin Sorescu: Alone among Canonical Writers* (2014) and *The Canonical Debate Today: The Case of Post-World War II Romanian Literature* (2016), and a contributor to the *Chronological Dictionary of Novels Translated into Romanian: 1990–2000* (2017).

Corin Braga is Professor of Comparative Literature and Vice President of Babeș-Bolyai University of Cluj-Napoca, Romania. He is Director of the Center for Imagination Studies and Editor-in-Chief of *Caietele Echinox*, as well as corresponding member of Academia Nacional de Ciencias of Buenos Aires, Argentina, Vice President of the Romanian Association of General and Comparative Literature, and Vice President of the Centre de Recherches Internationales sur l'imaginaire. Braga has authored a large number of articles and books on Romanian and world literature. His publications include Romanian books such as *Ten Studies in Archetypology* (1999), *From Archetype to Anarchetype* (2006), and *Psychobiographies* (2011) and, in French, *La quête manquée de l'Avalon occidentale. Le Paradis interdit au Moyen Âge 2*, (2006), *Du paradis perdu à l'antiutopie aux XVIe-XVIIe siècles* (2010), *Les antiutopies classiques* (2012), *Pour une morphologie du genre utopique* (2018), and *Archétypologie postmoderne* (2019).

Laura Cernat is a doctoral candidate at Katholieke Universiteit Leuven, Belgium, and University of Bucharest, Romania, where she is completing a project on contemporary biofiction with the support of a grant from the Research Foundation-Flanders (FWO). She received her MA in literary theory and comparative literature from University of Bucharest and her MA in Western literature from KU Leuven. Cernat has taught literary theory and English literature and has given conference papers on the presence of Virginia Woolf, Henry James, Vladimir Nabokov, and Fyodor Dostoevsky in recent biofiction. She has published on the dynamic of fictionalization and mimesis in biographical novels portraying Woolf.

Bogdan Crețu is Associate Professor of Romanian Literature at Alexandru Ioan Cuza University of Iași, Romania, and Director of Alexandru Philippide Romanian Philology Institute of the Romanian Academy, Iași. His scholarly interests are eighteenth- and nineteenth-century Romanian literature, the history of modern literary criticism, autobiographical writing, and contemporary Romanian literature. His books include *Negative Utopia in Romanian Literature* (2008) and the two-volume *The Unicorn at the Eastern World's Gates: D. Cantemir's Bestiary—A Comparative Study* (2013), for which he was awarded the Romanian Academy's Titu Maiorescu Prize for Literary Criticism.

Caius Dobrescu is Professor of Literary and Cultural Theory in the Faculty of Letters at University of Bucharest, Romania. His scholarship focuses on the development of the literary, social, and political imagination in the late-global era and on literature's ambivalent involvement in radicalism and counterculture in Western and Eastern Europe. He has contributed articles to *East European Politics and Societies, The Information Society, Journal of Global Initiatives, CLCWeb,* and *East-Central Europe,* among other journals. He is the author of books such as *The Radial Revolution* (2008) and *The Pleasure of Thinking: Romanian Literary Criticism between 1960 and 1989 and Its Intellectual Legacy—An Identitarian Scene on the Global Stage of Critical Culture* (2013). At present, his teaching and research explore the connections between literature and terrorism, secularization, and cultural tourism.

Teodora Dumitru is Senior Researcher at the G. Călinescu Institute of Literary History and Theory of the Romanian Academy, Bucharest. Her work examines the relationships among literary criticism, theory, and science in the post-1900 period, as well as literary epistemology, modernity and modernism, and postmodernism. She is currently coediting the multivolume *General Dictionary of Romanian Literature,* 2nd edition (vols. 3–5, 2017–19). Her publications include books such as *The Evolutionary Syndrome* (2013), *Literary and Political Modernity in Eugen Lovinescu* (2016), and *The Web of Modernities: Paul de Man—Matei Călinescu—Antoine Compagnon* (2016).

Alex Goldiş is Associate Professor in the Department of Romanian Literature and Literary Theory and Associate Dean of the Faculty of Letters of Babeş-Bolyai University of Cluj-Napoca, Romania. His work deals mostly with twentieth- and twenty-first-century Romanian literature, the digital humanities, and quantitative cultural history. His articles have appeared in journals and essay collections published in Romania, Spain, Slovakia, Poland, and the Czech Republic. He is the author of two monographs: *The Entrenchments of Literary Criticism: From Socialist Realism to Aesthetic Autonomy* (2011) and *Methodological Updates in the Romanian Criticism of the 1970s and 1980s: Theories, Methods, Critics* (2012).

Mihai Iovănel is Senior Researcher with the G. Călinescu Institute of Literary History and Theory of the Romanian Academy. He has contributed a large number of entries to the seven-volume *General Dictionary of Romanian Literature* (2004–9) and is one of the editors of the two-volume *Dictionary of Romanian Literature* (2012). He is currently coediting the multivolume *General Dictionary of Romanian Literature*, 2nd edition. He is also a main contributor to the ten-volume *Chronology of Romanian Literary Life: 1944–1964* (2010–13) and is the author of *The Detective Novel* (2015), *The Ideologies of Romanian Postcommunist Literature* (2017), and *History of Contemporary Romanian Literature: 1990–2020*.

Ioana Macrea-Toma is Research Fellow with the Vera and Donald Blinken Open Society Archives of Central European University of Budapest, Hungary. Her areas of specialization cover literary history and sociology, archival research and theory, and the history of sciences and information networks after World War II. She has published book reviews, articles on censorship and literary institutions, chapters in essay collections on Cold War-era media and archives, and a 2017 guest-edited special-topic issue of *East Central Europe* on the pre-1989 Romanian secret police and its informers. Author of a monograph on the Romanian cultural elites under Communism, *Priviligentsia: Literary Institutions during Romanian Communism* (2009), Macrea-Toma is at work on a book on Radio Free Europe and Cold War archival epistemic regimes.

Andreea Mironescu is Senior Researcher in the Social Sciences and Humanities Research Department of the Institute of Interdisciplinary Research of Alexandru Ioan Cuza University of Iaşi. Her scholarly interests cover Romanian modernism, literary history, and memory and postmemory studies with emphasis on Communism. She is the author of a monograph, *The Classics Affair: Paul Zarifopol and the Critique of Modernity* (2014), and of articles that have come out in journals and essay collections published in Romania, Slovakia, Germany, Canada, and the UK. Her book in progress deals with cultural memory in contemporary Romania.

Carmen Muşat is Professor of Literary Theory and Cultural Studies in the Faculty of Letters at University of Bucharest, Romania. Her main research areas are the interplay of literature and culture, modernism, postmodernism, narrative, intellectual history, and critical and political theory. She has authored several books, including *The Romanian Novel between the Two World Wars* (1998), *Strategies of Subversion: Description and Narrative in Postmodern Romanian Fiction* (2002), and *The Beautiful Stranger: Literature and the Paradoxes of Theory* (2017). She is the Editor-in-Chief of the most influential literary-cultural magazine of postcommunist Romania, *Observator cultural*. She is currently at work on a book-length study of the literature of waiting and expectation.

Adriana Stan is Research Assistant at the Sextil Puşcariu Institute of Linguistics and Literary History of the Romanian Academy, Cluj-Napoca. Her work concentrates on the post-World War II history of critical ideas, especially on comparative theory and the dissemination and influence of concepts and methodologies, as well as on the Romanian literature of the twentieth- and twenty-first centuries, with particular focus on the Communist and postcommunist contexts. She has published two monographs: *Tudor Vianu's Posterity: Contrasts in Post-World War II Romanian Criticism* (2015) and *The Linguistic Stronghold: A Comparative History of Structuralism in Romania* (2017).

Note

1   All titles of works by our contributors in languages other than English and French are given in translation.

INDEX